Modern Persian
Spoken and Written

Volume One

Don Stilo, Max Planck Institute
Kamran Talattof, University of Arizona
Jerome Clinton, Princeton University

Yale University Press
New Haven and London

Copyright © 2005 by Yale University.

All rights reserved. This book may not be reproduced, in whole or in part, including illustrations, in any form (beyond that copying permitted by Sections 107 and 108 of the U.S. Copyright Law and except by reviewers for the public press), without written permission from the publishers.

Publisher: Mary Jane Peluso
Production Controller: Maureen Noonan
Editorial Assistant: Brie Kluytenaar
Manuscript Editor: Margaret Otzel
Marketing Manager: Tim Shea

Printed in the United States of America.

ISBN: 978-0-300-10051-8 (cloth: alk. paper)

Library of Congress Control Number: 2004115007

A catalogue record for this book is available from the British Library.

The paper in this book meets the guidelines for permanence and durability of the Committee on Production Guidelines for Book Longevity of the Council on Library Resources.

10 9 8 7 6 5 4 3 2

To the Memory of Jerome Clinton

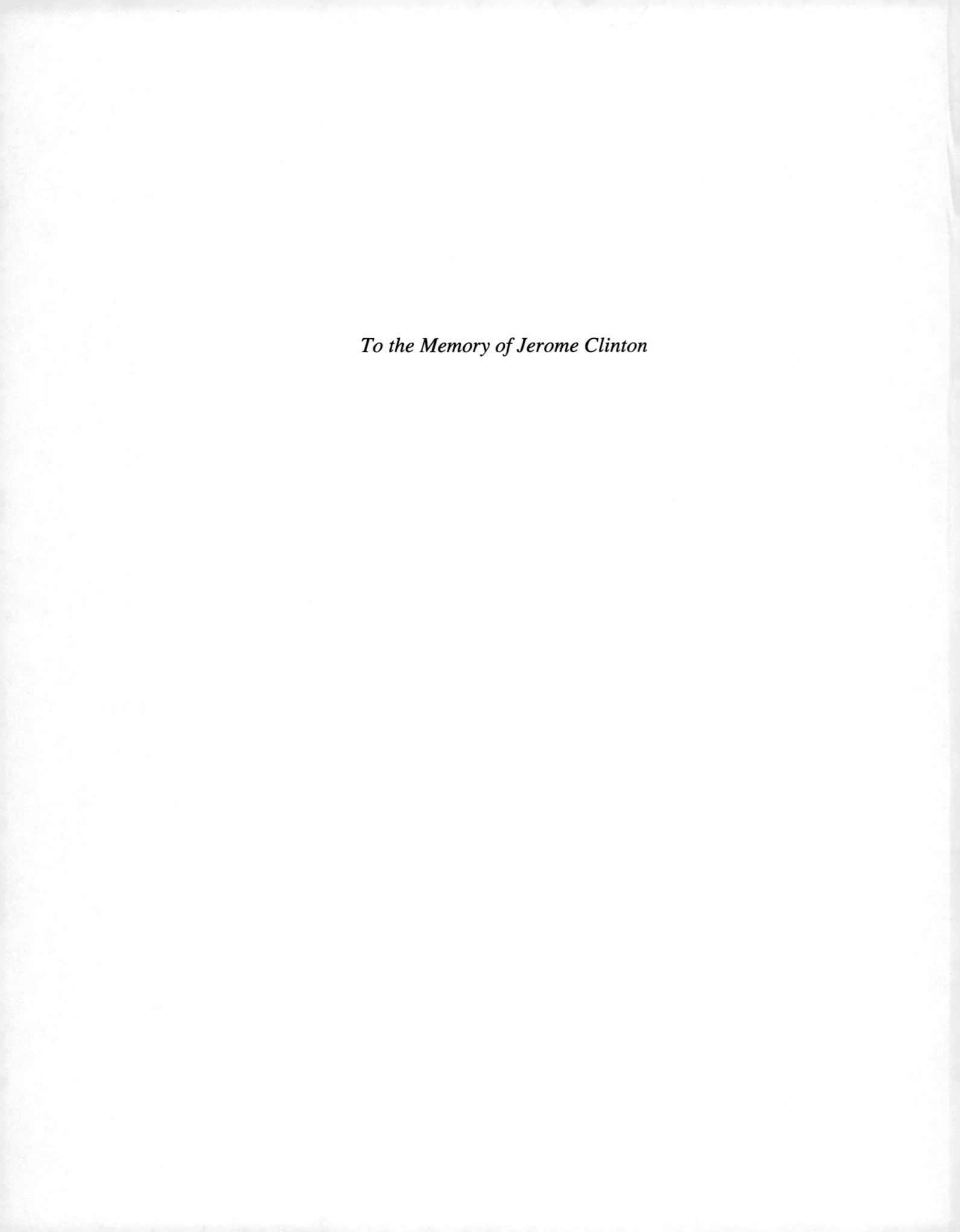

Acknowledgments

We would like to thank University of Arizona students Rebecca Stengel, Arjang Talattof, and Sina Mossayeb for their technical expertise and vital assistance in the production of this book. Thanks also go to Haleh Esfandiary for her useful comments and to Margaret Otzel of Yale University Press and Azar Akhtari of the University of Arizona for their help with the editorial process and the preparation of the final version of the book. We would also like to thank Don and Manijeh Emery for financial support. The students' work was supported by grants from the United States Department of Education Resource Development, the Princeton Language Consortium, the Alavi Foundation, and the University of Arizona.

The authors also thank Ahmad Karimi-Hakkak of the University of Maryland, Mehdi Khorrami of New York University, and Firoozeh Khazrai of Princeton University for reviewing the manuscript.

A great number of the photographs in this book come from *Chereh-i-Iran: Rahnama-ye Siyahati va Mosafarati (Face of Iran: Tourist Guide)*. We are grateful to Gitashenasi Geographical and Cartographic Institute for granting us the permission to reprint these photos. We are also grateful to Majid Behtashi for his generosity in providing us with valuable photos.

Contents

Introduction			xvi
LESSON ONE			1
1.1		Phonology: Contrast of /æ/ and /a/	2
1.2		Glides	4
1.3		Greetings and Cultural Expressions	8
	1.3.1	Cultural Materials: Greetings	8
	1.3.2	Classroom Expressions	10
	1.3.3	Sample Greetings	11
	1.3.4	Exercises	12
🔊 1.4		Dialogue 1	12
	1.4.1	Intonation	12
	1.4.2	Vocabulary List 1	13
1.5		Question Intonation	15
1.6		Substitution Drills	17
1.7		Question and Answer Drills	20
1.8		Situational and Practical Drills	21
1.9		Reading Persian	23
	1.9.1	Reading Persian: The Alphabet	23
	1.9.2	Connecting and Nonconnecting Letters ژ ز ذ	24
	1.9.3	Duplicate Letters	25
	1.9.4	Shape and Position	26
	1.9.5	Digraph	27
	1.9.6	Dots	28
🔊 1.10		Numerals	33
1.11		Grammar Discussion: The Persian Verb and Basic Sentence Word Order	33

Contents

	1.15	Vowel Reduction in English	34
LESSON TWO			37
	2.1	Phonology: /kh/ sometimes as /x/	39
	2.1.1	Phonology: /t/ and /d/	39
	2.2	Vocabulary	40
	2.3	Cultural Materials: Greetings	43
	2.3.1	Variations on Greetings	43
	2.3.2	Good-bye	44
🔊	2.4	Dialogue 2	44
	2.5	Phonology: /r/	45
	2.6	Drills, Part I	46
	2.8	Situational and Practical Drills	48
	2.9	Reading Persian: The Alphabet ج چ ح خ	49
	2.9.1	Reading Exercise 1	50
	2.9.2	Silent و	50
	2.9.3	Syllabification	51
	2.10	Drills, Part II	53
	2.11	Grammar Discussion: Verbs	56
🔊	2.15	Phonology Review	65
LESSON THREE			66
	3.1	Phonology Preface: Phonemic vs. Phonetic	68
	3.1.1	Phonology: Variants of /k/ and /g/	70
	3.1.2	Cultural Materials and Phonology: Forms of Address and Intonation Used When Addressing People	71
	3.2	Vocabulary	73
🔊	3.4	Dialogue 3	79
	3.5	Phonology: /q/	80

Contents

3.6		Drills, Part I	83
3.7		Review	88
3.8		Situational and Practical Drills	89
3.9		Reading Persian: The Alphabet	90
	3.9.1	ک /kaf/, گ /gaf/, ل /lam/	90
	3.9.2	ق /qaf/ and ف /fe/	91
	3.9.3	Glottal Stop ع (glottal stop) and ه /he/	92
3.10		Drills, Part II	94
3.11		Grammar Discussion	99
	3.11.1	Word and Sentence Stress	99
	3.11.2	The Pronouns of Persian	104
	3.11.3	Past Roots of Verbs	107
	3.11.4	The Negative	108
3.12		The Persian Language	109
3.13		Narrative Passage	112
LESSON FOUR			**113**
4.1		Phonology	116
	4.1.1	Syllable-Final /h/	116
	4.1.2	*ya* "or" — Intonation and Usage	117
4.2		Vocabulary	119
4.3		Cultural Material and Classroom Expressions	123
4.4		Dialogue 4	124
4.5		Vocabulary Building	127
	4.5.1	Introduction	127
	4.5.2	Words of Western Origin in Persian	127
4.6		Using Past Stems as Verb Cues	132
4.8		Situational and Practical Drills: Classroom Expressions	137

Contents

4.9		Reading and Writing	139
	4.9.1	Diacritics	139
	4.9.2	تَشدید (ّ)	140
	4.9.3	Vocabulary Review, Spell and Read Aloud	141
	4.9.4	Representing the Unwritten Vowels	141
	4.9.5	Transcribing Foreign Words	144
	4.9.6	Writing Practice	144
4.10		Drills, Part II	144
4.11		Grammar Discussion	148
	4.11.1	Parts of Speech and the Elements of a Sentence	148
	4.11.2	Word Order	150
	4.11.3	Question Order: Persian vs. English	153
	4.11.4	Prepositions and Pronouns	155
	4.11.5	The Ending Pronoun, -esh, "his, her, its"	156
4.12		Meals and Food: Part I	156
LESSON FIVE			161
5.1		Phonology	164
	5.1.1	The Glottal Stop and Lengthened Vowels	164
5.2		Vocabulary	165
	5.2.1	Classroom Expressions and Cultural Materials	172
	5.2.2	Two Persian Compliments	174
5.4		Dialogue 5	175
5.5		Vocabulary Building: Verbalizers	177
5.6		Drills, Part I	179
5.8		Situational and Practical Exercises	182
5.9		Reading and Writing	185
	5.9.1	Consonantal و and ی	185

Contents

	5.9.2	Duplicate Letters	187
	5.9.3	Alphabetization	194
5.10		Drills, Part II	197
5.11		Grammar Discussion	204
	5.11.1	The Noun Phrase: The *Ezafe* Construction	204
	5.11.2	Extended Noun Phrases	208
	5.11.3	The Noun Phrase: Counting Nouns	210
	5.11.4	The Verb Phrase	212
	5.11.5	The Infinitive	212
	5.11.6	Verbs with Obligatory Objects	213
	5.11.7	*to* The Second Person Familiar	214
	5.11.8	Personal Endings	215
5.12		Meals and Food, Part II: Kabab, Khoresh, Polow	219
5.15		Phonology: The Vanishing /h/	225
5.16		Translation Practice	226

LESSON SIX 227

6.1		Phonology: Gemination (تَشدید)	229
6.2		Vocabulary	230
6.3		Classroom Expressions	239
	6.3.1	Additional Possible Classroom answers	239
	6.3.2	A Polite Expression	240
6.4		Dialogue 6	240
6.5		Vocabulary Building: Nationalities and Place Names	242
6.6		Drills, Part I	249
6.9		Reading and Writing Persian: Colloquial/FWP Transformations, Part 1	256
	6.9.1	/-mb-/ ـنب	261

	6.9.2	-e/-æd ~ -æst ‎است‎ ‎ـَـد‎/‎ـه‎	262
	6.9.3	-id/-in ‎این‎/‎اید‎	263
6.10		Drills, Part II	263
6.11		Grammar Discussion	270
	6.11.1	Noun Phrase	270
	6.11.2	Verb Phrase	272
	6.11.3	Grammar and Usage of the Verbs "To Be" in Colloquial Persian	274
6.12		Cultural Materials: Iranian Money ‎پول ایرانی‎ /pul-e irani/	277
	6.12.1	Drill	279
	6.12.2	Drill	279
	6.12.3	Drill	279
	6.12.4	Drill: Review of Numbers	280
	6.12.5	An Expression	280
	6.12.6	Yellow Pages Entries	280
6.13		Long Dialogue (Part I)	283
6.14		Writing Persian	284
	6.14.1	Spoken/Written Transformations: Exercises	284
	6.14.2	soálo jævab	285
6.15		Phonology: Final Consonant Clusters	286
LESSON SEVEN			288
7.1		Phonology: /'/ and /h/ (continued)	291
7.2		Vocabulary	293
7.3		Classroom Expressions	300
	7.3.1	Classroom Expressions	300
	7.3.2	Classroom Drill	301
7.4		Dialogue 7	302

	7.6	Drills, Part I	304
	7.8	Greetings and Telling Time	307
	7.9	Reading and Writing Persian: Colloquial/FWP Transformations, Part II, Rules Affecting Phonology	310
	7.9.1	Vanishing /h/ ح ه	310
	7.9.2	Lengthened Verb Stems	311
	7.9.3	Destinations and Verbs of Motion	313
	7.10	Drills, Part II	314
	7.11	Grammar Discussion	318
	7.11.1	The Colloquial and FWP Forms of "To Be": /-Ø-/ and /hæst-/	318
	7.11.2	Destinations and Verbs of Motion	320
	7.12	Cultural Materials: An Introduction to Iranian Names	321
	7.13	Long Dialogue	328
	7.13.1	خواندن و نوشتن	330
	7.13.2	پرسش	331
	7.15	Writing Persian	331
	7.15.1	Spoken/Written Transformations: Exercises	331
	7.16	Composition	332
LESSON EIGHT			**336**
	8.1	Phonology: (:) and (h) (concluded)	337
	8.2	Vocabulary	339
	8.3	Poetry and Proverbs	347
	8.4	Dialogue 8	347
	8.5	Word-Building: Professions and Professionals	349
	8.6	Drills, Part I	352
	8.8	Situational and Practical Drills	356

Contents

8.9		Reading and Writing Persian: Colloquial/FWP Transformations, Part III	357
	8.9.1	/i/ = <u>e</u>	357
	8.9.2	/o/ = <u>ow</u>	358
	8.9.3	Individual Changes/Isolated Cases	358
	8.9.4	Counting People and Objects	359
	8.9.5	Third Person Singular Pronouns	360
	8.9.6	A Colloquial Ending	360
8.10		Drills, Part II	361
8.11		Grammar Discussion	363
	8.11.1	Endings in Combination with Roots and Ending in Vowels (Colloquial Persian)	363
	8.11.2	Formation of Noun Plurals	368
8.12		Shi'ite Islam	373
8.15		Colloquial to FWP Transformations: Exercises	380
	8.15.1	Spoken/Written Transformations: Exercises	380
	8.15.2	Questions and Answers	380

GLOSSARY: ENGLISH TO PERSIAN G2

APPENDIX A: VERBS IN THE FIRST PERSON G63

GLOSSARY: PERSIAN TO ENGLISH G67

xv

Introduction

The language presented in *Modern Persian: Spoken and Written, Volumes I and II*, is that of contemporary Iran, particularly as it is spoken by educated inhabitants of the capital city, Tehran. The text is designed to provide beginning students with a mastery of modern Persian sufficient to meet most everyday needs. Once students have finished these books, they should be able to understand colloquial Persian spoken at normal speed; to speak it fluently and idiomatically, although with a limited vocabulary and grammatical range; to read elementary but unsimplified texts; and to write legibly. They should also be able to continue learning with a minimum of formal guidance, particularly in a Persian-speaking context. In other words, they should have active mastery of modern Persian, and be able to move easily between its spoken and written forms.

Modern Persian is a living language and in this text is taught as such. It may seem unnecessary to assert the vitality of a language spoken by well over 60 million people, but Persian has traditionally been taught in North American and European universities as virtually a dead language. Only its written form is presented, with classical language given preference over the contemporary. Moreover, this approach relies heavily on memorizing the rules of Persian grammar and applying them to the task of translation. In our experience, even the best students emerge from such instruction with an extensive but largely passive knowledge of the written language. They acquire virtually no ability to speak or understand it. While such students—with heavy reliance on dictionaries—can translate difficult passages of Persian into acceptable English, they usually pronounce it badly and are unable to carry on the simplest conversation.

For us, the most persuasive argument against beginning with an emphasis on passive mastery is that it can prove a serious barrier to gaining active mastery later on. Those with advanced reading knowledge are reluctant to start all over again at the elementary level in speaking. They wish, not unreasonably, to express ideas as complicated as those they can read, forming each sentence in English and then laboriously translating it into Persian, with results

Introduction

frequently either painful or amusing. Those knowing only the written form of the language also often disdain the colloquial, viewing it as an inferior form. They prefer to speak in a bookish and unidiomatic way, because that is the language that seems "right" to them. In doing so, however, they give an impression of stodgy foreignness far from what they intend. Finally, although it is hard to learn the correct sounds and colloquial forms, it is harder still to unlearn frequently rehearsed errors. To speak the language, one should learn to do so sooner rather than later.

Finally, even if students have no immediate need to speak the language, it has been proven repeatedly that students learn all aspects of a language with greater speed, assurance, and permanence when they obtain active mastery in a meaningful context rather than by learning a series of exercises. In practical terms, this means that students learning to speak and understand easily now will spend less time with the dictionary or grammar book once they begin to read in earnest. Gaining control of the spoken language will not only yield quicker access and keener proficiency but will provide students with the spoken form of a living language and all the practical advantages that come with it.

Spoken and Written Persian

Modern Persian in its spoken form is the basis of this text, so we emphasize learning by ear from the very first lesson. Grammar, phonology, and vocabulary will be introduced and drilled orally and explained in writing only once active mastery is achieved. As a result, students will progress more rapidly in speaking and understanding Persian than in reading and writing. As the course progresses, the written language will receive more emphasis, but the spoken language will remain the basis for instruction.

The spoken and written forms of Persian differ in a number of essential ways, and students will, in effect, be learning two separate but overlapping dialects. Mastery will mean, among other things, facility in moving between these two dialects. Drills are included to promote this facility. Students will find that we place far more emphasis on alternating from

Introduction

spoken to written Persian than the reverse, replicating the way Iranians themselves learn the language—first spoken, then written. Our principal reason for stressing the transformation of spoken to written over that of written to spoken is that when learners write they have more time to think ahead to what transformations are needed in writing.

Levels of Usage

A language in its spoken and written forms has a wide range of usage—indeed the whole scope of the language. Neither form is unitary. For example, we do not speak to friends in the same way we do to an employer. Likewise, there are differences among the kinds of written language used for personal letters, formal essays, poetry, and so forth. These varieties of discourse within each category are what we mean by "levels of usage." No single version of either written or spoken language would be appropriate to all these contexts.

Persian is a language that distinguishes many levels of usage in formally marked ways—using different pronouns, deferential word forms, and honorific forms of address. A simple inquiry such as "How are you?" can be expressed at a half-dozen levels of formality in both spoken and written discourse.

It would be self-defeating to attempt to teach comprehension of all possible levels of usage in an elementary language class. The classroom does not provide the appropriate context for using extremes of either informality or formality. Yet students must be prepared to deal with this aspect of modern Persian. Our solution is to choose two levels of usage within the larger categories of spoken/informal and written/formal Persian appropriate both to the classroom and to the socio-economic level of university students. These forms are the basis for most of our instruction and will serve most purposes. Once mastered, they should provide a convenient starting point for acquiring others. More formal and informal levels are also illustrated at appropriate points throughout the text.

In practice, learning to move easily among these various linguistic levels is not as difficult as it may at first appear, and students will probably acquire the skill naturally as new

Introduction

situations present themselves. We mention the issue here principally to prepare you for the efforts of well-meaning friends and relatives to "correct" your Persian by teaching you more or less formal versions of what you have already learned in class. One productive way of dealing with such assistance is to ask what the appropriate context might be for using what they wish to teach you. Is it something that they would say to a teacher, or only to friends? It may turn out that what they want you to know is a textbook version of the language that they would never actually use. In the same way, even educated speakers of American English commonly say "gonna" but would teach a new learner of English to say "going to" because it seems more "correct."

Language and Grammar

Unquestionably, it is impossible to master a foreign language without learning its grammar. To say otherwise would be tantamount to asserting that one could learn it without acquiring vocabulary or phonology. We are as concerned about teaching modern Persian grammar as are the authors of more traditional textbooks. However, our approach to teaching grammar differs from theirs in several ways.

Traditional grammars consist of rules (by which we mean descriptive statements about the language), illustrative examples, and drills. Students memorize the rules, study the examples, and use them to do the drills. The proportion of rules to examples and drills may not be high. Our text contains the same elements, but the proportions differ sharply—there are far more drills and examples than rules, and they are studied in that order. Students first memorize or simply listen to the examples and then do the oral drills based on them, and the study of the grammatical rules is left for study at home when students feel the need for them. This order seems to put the grammar last, but in fact it is first. Our text also contains the same elements and is basically a grammar-based text in underlying organization. A crucial factor in this course, however, is that this organization according to grammatical patterns is "behind the scenes," and the in-class teaching methods do not concentrate on grammar. Since the drills

Introduction

have been carefully arranged in a progression that presents the grammar systematically and cumulatively, as they practice them they are already studying and acquiring the grammar in the most active and practical way possible. Our grammar discussions are intended to be a summary of what students have already internalized in the drills or, occasionally, to serve as further clarification of confusing points of grammar. Because the forms and structures of Persian are relatively easy, we feel that students can read and absorb most grammar explanations on their own, leaving valuable class time for learning activities that require assistance.

As they begin a new set of drills, students may find themselves formulating a "rule" to describe the point of the drill. With increased skill mastery, use of that rule, that grammatical pattern, will become automatic and eventually second nature. As for written grammar explanations, however, we have found that even when patterns are completely self-evident from drills, most of our students feel more comfortable when the rule describing these patterns is made explicit. Some students prefer to preview that grammar before beginning the appropriate lesson or section, while others wait and refer to the written explanations only after they have begun to internalize the patterns through drills and conversation in class. They might even use the grammar as a type of review after they have finished the lesson. Different students have different needs and learning styles. However they approach it, the grammar is written out for their convenience to read whenever they like and as many times as they need. Above all, we think that drills and exercises offer the best aids to help students learn grammatical patterns. Using these patterns in conversation, then, leads to their full absorption to the point that they no longer have to think about them.

In preparing these sections, we have found it necessary to use a certain amount of linguistic terminology to describe Persian grammar. Where special grammatical terms are needed—and sometimes there really are no simple equivalents—we have defined them before putting them to use. To clarify our descriptions and analyses of the patterns of Persian grammar, we have included contrastive analyses of parallel phenomena in English.

The grammar sections can be read independently outside of class but may certainly be

discussed briefly in class once the relevant lesson or lessons have been completed and questions still remain. However, we think that drills and exercises offer the best aids to understanding. Our explanations are not meant to be exhaustive but are tailored to the needs of the text. We have tried to present only what is required to understand the patterns of a lesson, and perhaps a little more. Where there are several stages to a particular grammatical pattern, for example in the usage of definite/indefinite nouns, we have explained each stage as the students' expressive abilities become more sophisticated. We find that students often begin to ask questions about grammar or ways of saying things right before beginning the very lesson that introduces those points. This anticipation of what is to come reinforces the idea that learners need only as much grammar as they are ready to internalize for the purposes of expression and that they will actually learn new grammar points when they are ready to absorb them.

Cumulative Development

By cumulative development, we mean that each lesson grows out of the preceding ones, moving from simple to complex. Drills and exercises are repeated periodically throughout the books to enable students to keep earlier lessons current and active. Of course, the heavy reliance on conversation, both structured and informal, in class is the best way to keep vocabulary and patterns from previous lessons fresh in one's mind. We have endeavored not to oblige students to learn patterns out of the established sequence or to learn vocabulary useful only for the lesson in which it appears.

Lesson Structure

The textbook consists of two volumes and 16 lessons. The first volume includes lessons 1-8 and the second volume includes lessons 9-16. We have grouped the contents of lessons under a number of self-explanatory headings and spread them among sixteen numbered sections. Rarely will any one lesson contain a full complement of sixteen sections. The

Introduction

contents of particular sections may also alter as the lessons progress. Sections 1 and 15 contain phonology drills, but from Lesson 9 on, section 15 is devoted to various writing drills and conversation tasks.

Particularly in Volume I, section 4 in each lesson will emphasize memorization of a brief conversation or dialogue, introducing elements of phonology and grammar that will provide the starting point for drills in sections 6 and 10. The presented phonology is keyed to vocabulary in the dialogue. The grammar presented in section 11 will expand on and explain what has been taught in the dialogue and drills. Sections 3 (classroom expressions), 5 (word building), 8 (situational and practical drills), and 12 (cultural materials) are supplementary and provide a richer and more varied linguistic, cultural, and social context in which to comprehend the language. Section 9 (reading Persian) constitutes a separate set of lessons until the writing system has been fully taught (Lessons 1 through 5). Beginning with Lesson 6, section 9 presents the rules for converting colloquial speech to Formal Written Persian (Lessons 6 through 12), and section 14 presents reading material.

Workbook material accompanying section 9 reading lessons are for learning to handwrite Persian. Our goal in these lessons is to teach adult handwriting. Through years of teaching the script, we have found that adult learners do not go through the same stages as children do when learning to read and write. In our experience, the first rules learners acquire and the first letter shapes they practice form the basis of their future handwriting. We have therefore chosen to skip the formative stages through which children develop mature handwriting and use an already developed handwriting as our model. We often encounter people who learned Persian as a foreign language and have been speaking, reading, and writing it for years, but who feel that their Persian handwriting is still like that of an Iranian second-grader. When seeing our students' handwriting, however, they often say they wish they had been taught a correct adult handwriting from the beginning.

Other sections not previously mentioned include the following: section 2 (vocabulary lists for each lesson), section 7 (review material), section 13 (longer narratives, dialogues, and

Introduction

listening comprehension exercises), and section 16 (compositions). Keys are provided at the end of the text for the drills of section 9.

An ideal lesson consists of the sections listed below. The sections marked by bold letters are those we recommend doing in class. Other sections are more effectively covered at home or in the language lab:

Section	**1**	**Phonology drills**
Section	2	Vocabulary lists for each lesson
Section	3	Classroom expressions
Section	**4**	**Dialogue**
Section	5	Word building
Section	**6**	**Drills**
Section	**7**	**Review material**
Section	**8**	**Situational and practical drills**
Section	9	Reading Persian—The alphabet (Lessons 1 through 6)
		Rules for converting colloquial speech to formal written Persian (Lessons 6 through 12)
Section	**10**	**Drills**
Section	11	Grammar
Section	12	Cultural materials
Section	13	Longer narratives and dialogues
Section	**14**	**Readings** (both at home and in class)
Section	**15**	**Phonology drills** (Lesson 1 through 8)
		Various writing drills and **conversational tasks** (after Lesson 8)
Section	16	Compositions, Translation

Introduction

Although we have numbered the sections within each lesson and arranged them in sequence, there is no set order in which they must be presented to be effective. We think that the lessons work better when dialogue comes before drills, and when drills are interspersed with work on other sections. Grammar need not be covered in class. Students may feel they want to read it before performing the drills, but it can also be effectively studied after the drills. The only inescapable requirement is that each lesson be studied thoroughly before the next is begun.

Language and Expression

Persian is the easiest major language of the Near East for English speakers to learn. Like English, it belongs to the Indo-European family of languages, while Arabic and Hebrew belong to the Semitic and Turkish to the Turkic. This family connection means that Persian, English, and other Western European languages have similarities in matters of grammar, syntax, and word formation. The sound system of Persian also makes few unreasonable demands on American palates, and Persian, like English, is unencumbered with case or gender.

Persian grammatical structure is relatively easy to master. There are essentially three aspects of the language that Americans find difficult to learn: the two sounds represented herein as /q/ and /kh/ (sometimes transcribed as gh and x), which have no equivalents in English; the writing system, a modified form of the Arabic alphabet; and the unfamiliar vocabulary. A substantial portion of modern Persian vocabulary is borrowed from Arabic and is altogether unfamiliar to Americans and Europeans. Arabic loan words in Persian play a role very like that of Latin and French loan words in English. The few cognates existing between Persian and the languages of Europe delight only the hearts of philologists—*madær* ="mother," *pedær* = "father," *bænd* ="bind," and so on. There is nothing like the free gift of hundreds of bonus words received by English speakers studying French or Spanish. As partial consolation, in recent years Persian has borrowed the terms for many objects and concepts from European languages along with the objects and concepts themselves (see Lesson 4, Section 4.5).

Introduction

Beyond that, Persian belongs to a very different world. It is a truism among language teachers that teaching a language is teaching a culture. In this case, that culture has little shared history or experience with American and European cultures. Its central religion is neither Christianity nor Judaism, and never has been. The historical categories Medieval, Renaissance, and Modern have no meaning in Persian history, and Iran had no European neighbors until Russia invaded the Caucasus and Central Asia in the nineteenth century. The absence of cognates between English and Persian is surface witness to deeper distinctions between the two cultures using these languages. Although Persian is in simple, mechanical terms an "easy" language, it expresses itself in ways that do not translate readily into English. One is often at a loss to find even a rough equivalent in one language for terms and expressions absolutely characteristic of the other.

Another truism of language learning is that the more familiar you sound to the person whose language you are learning, the stranger you may sound to yourself. This truism works for the language's cultural levels, as well. In order to become really comfortable with Persian, you must accept concepts and modes of expression that will initially seem strange to you but that are normal and familiar to Iranians.

Vocabulary

We have sought to provide a useful vocabulary for the context in which students are learning Persian. It would be pointless to emphasize cultural situations encountered only when living in Iran and impossible to recreate in the classroom. For example, this text avoids instructing students on matters of daily life in Iran, such as how to hail a taxi or what to say to the greengrocer. We have chosen vocabulary suitable for the average student studying Persian in North America, in the context of an American university campus, interacting with classmates or Iranians resident in the United States. In some cases, we have asked students to imagine a dialogue taking place in Iran, but we have done so without requiring a stretch of the imagination or reliance on unfamiliar cultural material.

Introduction

We have organized the progression of the materials in each lesson, especially the vocabulary, to enable students to talk first about the most basic topics of learning a new language in a new classroom situation. Gradually we have them fan out from these first, most immediate needs to topics of ever-widening circles of interest. We begin by introducing basic greetings and politeness issues, and we give the students the tools to talk first about the classroom and immediate language learning needs, family background and simple personal information, daily activities, and the languages they have studied. From there students will progress to more complex information about personal issues, likes and dislikes, daily activities, family and friends, skills and fields of study, occupations, the wider university environment, places and nationalities, and they eventually will learn to start expressing opinions. They soon begin to talk about qualities, emotions, and physical states, express more complex opinions and learn how to agree/disagree in conversation, use humor, give advice, and work on problem solving. Throughout the course as a whole, we also teach students increasingly more sophisticated ways to ask and talk about their own language learning needs and problems, and we give them ways to explain and define words in Persian, gradually providing tools to help them advance their own learning skills. In this manner, we feel students can learn comfortably and confidently to begin to "own" their own language learning and identify with the language they are learning.

Students in Persian classes in the United States cover a wide range. Some students wish only to read medieval historical texts, for example, and possibly do no more than translate them to extricate information needed for their research. Others are Americans married to Iranians who desire to speak only the most colloquial Persian at home with their spouses or in-laws as well as American-born Iranians who have a vested personal interest in Persian and Iranian culture and wish to speak with older relatives or recent arrivals, but have no further academic aspirations with the language. The vocabulary, dialogues and readings herein are designed for learners somewhere in the middle of these two categories--that is, for students of the humanities and social sciences, such as history, literature, sociology, ethnomusicology,

Introduction

political science, and the like, who will eventually need to speak Persian with colleagues, as well as to read relevant textual material in their own disciplines. Most students study Persian out of a genuine interest in modern Iran and may in addition have Iranian friends or acquaintances either on campus or beyond the academic environment. Because no two language classes will have the same mix of students, individual teachers must tailor certain aspects of this text to the needs of their classes.

Many students in our classes come to Persian with knowledge of a second or even third language, such as French, Arabic, or another Islamic language. Therefore, we have made a special effort to "overstuff" lessons with Persian vocabulary coming from Arabic, English, and French. This extra material is presented on an optional basis with the hope that students with prior knowledge of these words will find this vocabulary useful and easy to master. These words may then be added to drills or omitted according to the needs and composition of the class.

Culture

In the context of language learning, culture refers to how people interact when they are speaking to each other, what the givens and assumptions common to most speakers of that language are within that society, and how people use their language. A conversation between two people is a microcosm of their society. In this sense, culture might involve the following among a multitude of other possibilities:

- developing friendships and interacting socially with a group of people you do not know very well
- asking questions of, and talking about yourself with, new acquaintances
- interacting with various types of people in different social situations
- dealing with the unique situational needs for respect, equality, age difference, same-gender/cross-gender interactions, friendliness, intimacy, gratitude, and so on

Introduction

Culture is the context in which the language is spoken. Iranian culture in the context of this course involves how to use Persian for interpersonal exchanges with Iranians, based on the expectations and norms of Iranian society.

In this vein, we introduce students to certain important Iranian cultural areas at some length, for example, politeness and respect in greetings, addressing people, asking permission, and other contexts; food and accompanying behaviors and expectations; the use and importance of gestures; formal, informal, and intimate ways of speaking to people; attitudes about family relations; making and responding to compliments, requests, favors, and so forth. In addition to this material, we also provide students with background information on Shiite Islam, Iranian calendars and festivals, Iranian educational systems, Iranian names, the geography of Iran, money, poetry and proverbs, humor, sarcasm and irony with friends, and many other cultural topics.

While we try to have students communicate in the terms of their own realities quickly, and relate to the language as something they can actually speak, we also expose them to Iranian culture from day one. We start out with what is familiar to the students, by enabling them to talk first about their own backgrounds; next they ask and talk about the same issues with other students, and eventually with Iranian friends and Iranians on campus, and for some students, in the community at large. There is a large Iranian presence in the United States, including many recent arrivals and visitors from Iran. Most university environments have attracted Iranian students and professors and usually their families as well. Urban centers have an additional asset in having even larger, more varied Iranian communities, bringing with them a wide variety of personal and general cultural styles of interaction. In addition, more and more American-born Iranians are attending Persian-language courses on the university level, some to learn the script and increase their vocabulary and others to learn Persian from the very beginning. Classroom interaction allows for students with more contact with, and insights into, Iranian culture and to share their own experiences, further enriching the students' understanding and learning of Iranian culture. We do not mean to imply here, however, that students will learn to speak Persian only if

Introduction

they meet Iranians outside of class. This course is set up to provide the maximum number of opportunities for them to use the language patterns learned in class. This is accomplished through classroom interaction and peer teaching, valuable tools in the learning process. Thus the relationships students form in class will play an important role in their language learning process throughout this course. Since structured and open-ended conversation time with classmates is built into this course, students will begin to use Persian for real communication and at the same time have fun as they learn.

Transcription

In Lesson 1 through Lesson 5, we have used English-based transcription to represent Persian, for several reasons. First and most important, the use of transcription allows us to teach complete sentences from the first lesson, thereby emphasizing the spoken language from the start. Commencing with the Persian writing system would inevitably place the written language and the individual word at the center of the course. Second, transcription represents the sounds of spoken Persian more accurately and unambiguously than does the Persian alphabet. Finally, using the transcription system for colloquial Persian and the writing system for written language in the initial lessons allows us to clearly distinguish between these two language forms until students have gained some familiarity with them. One side benefit of this approach is that Arabic-speaking students are less tempted to pronounce Persian as Arabic when they see it in transcription.

Most of the transcription system used in this text should be fairly obvious to English speakers, except for Persian sounds not existing in English. The main exception to an English-based spelling is the vowel /æ/. Since it is the most common vowel in Persian and even though it is almost identical to the English "a" vowel in "cat," Americans tend to pronounce it like "ah" in "Kahn." We have used a special vowel symbol here to remind students constantly that it must be clearly distinguished from Persian /a/.

Additional Signs

Intonation contours will not be indicated everywhere, but they will be marked precisely in the dialogues and in the sections on pronunciation. A number of additional signs are used to indicate word stress, sentence stress, and intonation. These include the following:

Word Stress

(´)   acute accent: primary word stress

(`)   grave accent: secondary word stress (generally reserved for compound verbs)

Note: Because word stress falls on the final syllable of most words (except verbs and certain adverbs), final stress is not marked and is considered the norm. Stress marks are employed for all cases where stress falls on any syllable but the last.

Intonation and Sentence Stress

In the first two lessons, the contours of sentence intonation are marked by lines that run below, through and above the sentence:

```
           ___
        |  |
        |  |
     ___|  |                        statement intonation
           |
           |___


           ___
        |  |
        |  |
     ___|  |___                     question intonation
```

(_) Occasionally, this symbol is illustrated by using **bold** letters. However, after the first two lessons, we have used the *italic*, **bold**, or underline to mark the one syllable receiving the principal stress in a sentence. (mæn inja far<u>si</u> míkhunæm.)

Introduction

⸘ The barred question mark is used as a reminder that questions formed with question words normally take statement intonation instead of question intonation. (See below, Lesson 1, Sections 1.3.1 "Notes," and 1.5 "Question Intonation.")

To demonstrate the way these signs work, here follows an English sentence marked as we would mark a Persian sentence.

My friend téachès màthemátics in Shìráz.

The difference between sentence stress and intonation can be confusing at first. To see how it works, move the stress to different words in the sentence. As you do, the meaning of the sentence will change slightly, but the sentence as a whole will continue to receive statement intonation, which in English is a level contour that drops off at the end.

<u>My</u> friend téachès màthemátics in Shìráz.	(Not someone else's friend.)
My <u>friend</u> téachès màthemátics in Shìráz.	(Not my sister, for example.)
My friend <u>té</u>achès màthemátics in Shìráz.	(And does not study it.)
My friend téachès màthe<u>má</u>tics in Shìráz.	(Not some other subject.)
My friend téachès màthemátics in Sh<u>ìrá</u>z.	(Not some other city.)

Audio CD

Certain sections in Volume 1 and Volume 2 are accompanied by audio components, the beginning of which will be marked with this symbol: 🔊. This symbol also appears in the Contents proceding the sections that contain audio components. The following sections have an audio component: Lesson 1--1.4 Dialogue 1, 1.10 Numerals; Lesson 2--2.4 Dialogue 2, 2.15 Phonology Review; Lesson 3--3.4 Dialogue 3, 3.11.3 Past Roots of Verbs; Lesson 4--4.4 Dialogue 4, 4.11.5 The Ending Pronoun; Lesson 5--5.4 Dialogue 5, 5.16 Translation Practice; Lesson 6--6.4 Dialogue 6, 6.13 Long Dialogue, last Reading Text in the lesson (end of 6.15); Lesson 7--7.4 Dialogue 7, 7.13 Long Dialogue, 7.13.1 Reading and Writing (text about Suzan); Lesson 8--8.4 Dialogue 8, Optional Reading: Islam (end of 8.12); Lesson 9--9.4 Dialogue 9, 9.13.1 Longer Narrative in Colloquial; Lesson 10--10.4 Dialogue 10, 10.14.1 Fereydun

Introduction

Mohammadi; Lesson 11--11.4 Dialogue 11, 11.13 Long Dialogue, 11.14 (11.14.1) Reading and Writing; Lesson 12--12.4 Dialogue 12, 12.13 Long Dialogue, 12.14.1 Geography of Iran Lesson 1, 12.16 Composition; Lesson 13--13.4 Dialogue 13, 13.14.1 Geography of Iran, Lesson Two; Lesson 14--14.4 Dialogue 14: Formal Speech, 14.14.1 Geography of Iran, Lesson Three; Lesson 15--15.4 Dialogue 15, 15.14.1 Geography of Iran, Lesson Four; Lesson 16--16.4 Dialogue 16, 16.13 (16.13.1, 16.13.2, 16.13.3) Reading and Writing, 16.14.1 Reading.

Important Note

Italic type is used to indicate formal written Persian terms when they first appear in vocabulary lists. **Bold** (and in some cases **bold** and *italic*) type is used in the drills to indicate which words or phrases need to be substituted.

| Lesson One | درس یکم |

TOPICS COVERED IN THIS LESSON

- Basic Greetings: Hello, how are you? Fine, thanks / Not bad.
- Basic Classroom Expressions
- Names of People and Places
- Friends and Relatives
- Famous People: Where does Bill Clinton (etc.) live?
- Politeness: Please. Thank You.

RESOURCES AND BACKGROUND: INFORMATION AND ACCURACY

Phonology

Contrast of /æ/ and /a/

Contrast of vowels without glides (Persian) and vowels with glides (English)

Question intonation

Contrast of unreduced vowels (Persian) and reduced vowels (English)

Grammar Patterns to be Drilled

Verbs

Present tense of verbs (suffix): mí-

Third person singular (ending): ("He/she/it") -e

Nouns

Possessive ending: -æm "my"

Preposition of location: dær "in, at "

Optional deletion of full subject

Sentence Pattern

(subject) + location + verb

Grammar Discussion

The Persian Verb and Basic Sentence Word Order

Lesson One   *MODERN PERSIAN*   درس یکم

1.1   Phonology: Contrast of /æ/ and /a/

The sounds /æ/ and /a/ must be clearly distinguished in Persian, because many words differ in meaning only on the basis of the contrast between them. Examples:

/æ/		/a/	
/chæp/	"left"	/chap/	"print"
/dæsht/	"field, plains"	/dasht/	"had"
/sæf/	"line, queue"	/saf/	"smooth, clear"

Even though English has a sound very similar to /æ/ and another not too different from the Persian /a/, English speakers tend to confuse these two vowel sounds when speaking Persian. Because Persian makes heavy use of this vowel contrast, you will be frequently misunderstood if you don't pronounce them as clearly distinct sounds. We discuss each of these sounds separately:

/æ/: English has a near approximation of the Persian /æ/ in the vowel of words like "cat," "sack," etc. Be careful, however. The English /æ/ in most people's speech changes quality somewhat before the sounds /m/ and /n/. Compare your own usual pronunciation of "mat" vs. "man." You will also notice that for some English speakers, the quality of this vowel also changes before English "b," "d," and "g" and before "f," "s," and "sh," as in "sat" vs. "sad" or "match" vs. "mash." Do you notice a slightly different quality in the vowel of the second word in each of these pairs? The same change in quality does not occur in Persian. Listen to the following words pronounced by an Iranian and compare them to your own pronunciation of similar English words:

Persian	**English**		**Persian**	**English**
/chæp/	"chap"	but:	/hæm/	"ham"
/æks/	"axe"		/mæn/	"man"
/æz/	"as"		/dæsht/	"dashed"
/sæbt/	"sapped"		/sæd/	"sad"

2

Lesson One **MODERN PERSIAN** درس یکم

Be careful to pronounce the Persian words like the native speaker's model and not use the equivalent English vowels.

/a/: It is harder to approximate the Persian /a/ with an English vowel. The closest English vowel is the "ah" sound of "got," "odd," or "Kahn." The Persian /a/ is pronounced farther back in the mouth and thus may sound deeper to you. If you have Iranian friends who are nonnative speakers of English, you will notice this very distinctive vowel in their English pronunciation. Listen to the following words pronounced by an Iranian and compare them with your own pronunciation of similar English words:

Persian	**English**	**Persian**	**English**
chap	"chop"	shad	"shod"
bam	"bomb"	jash	"Josh""

Alternatively, the Persian /a/ sounds a little like the "aw" sound in "paw" for some speakers. Again, this is not exactly the Persian sound. It is only an approximation. Listen to the difference in the following Persian and English words:

Persian	**English**	**Persian**	**English**
pa	"paw"	mad	"Maude"
gaz	"gauze"	fal	"fall"
kaf	"cough"	tas	"toss"

We introduce the /æ/ — /a/ contrast in the first lesson so that you will be able to learn the difference in pronunciation early and thus avoid numerous misunderstandings.

Pronunciation Drill 1

| næm | nam | bæd | bad | chæp | chap | zad | zæd | az | æz | dasht | dæsht |
| pæs | pas | mad | mæd | bam | bæm | sæf | saf | næ | na | dam | dæm |

Lesson One   *MODERN PERSIAN*   درس یکم

Pronunciation Drill 2

| kæmal | damad | sæmæd | bæradær | kæmærbænd | færiba |
| chæmæn | chæran | hæsæn | sælam | abadan | æbædæn |

Pronunciation Drill 3 (/a/ — /o/ distinction)

mad   mod   na   no(h)   dam   dom   shad   shod   kasht   kosht

Pronunciation Drill 4 (Persian /a/ — /o/ before /r/)

bar   bor   dar   dor(r)   lar   lor   sar   sor   par   por

1.2 Glides

The element that makes the English pronunciation of "man" different from that of the Persian /æ/ in /mæn/ is called a glide. A glide is made by moving the tongue gradually from the articulation of one vowel into position for another short but different vowel. The main vowel and the following glide together are often called diphthongs. Many glides are automatic in English, and certain vowels are never pronounced without a glide. By this, we mean that although you may not realize it, /i/, /o/, and /u/, as in "read," "road," and "rude," are always pronounced /iy/, /ow/, and /uw/ /riyd/, /rowd/, /ruwd/. In addition, the /æ/ vowel in some positions in English is automatically followed by a glide, as is the case of the word "man" discussed above in section 1.1.

In some cases, of course, the English diphthong contrasts with the plain vowel, as in /met/ "met" vs. /meyt/ "mate" or /prad/ "prod" vs. /prayd/ "pride." Because of the phonetic rule of one-symbol-per-sound, diphthongs are transcribed with two separate symbols. Persian has only one commonly used diphthong, /ey/, as in /heyf/, /heys/, or /beyzi/. As in English, this sound contrasts with the unglided /e/: /heys/ vs. /hes(s)/.

Note carefully that Persian /i/, /o/, and /u/ do not include glides as English does automatically. If you pronounce these vowels with glides, you will immediately be detected as

Lesson One MODERN PERSIAN درس یکم

having a foreign accent in Persian (and many other languages as well). These automatic glides of English should be "unlearned" in order to attain a good Persian accent. The lack of glide after the Persian /æ/ has already been drilled. The glided English vowels /iy/, /ow/, and /uw/ and their unglided Persian equivalents are each discussed separately below.

English /iy/ and Persian /i/

In English, as the /i/ is articulated, there is a slight glide to a higher tongue position (and the lower jaw may move up somewhat accordingly), producing a y-sound after the vowel. Compare these Persian vowels with the corresponding English vowels that have glides and are often lengthened:

Persian		**English**		**Persian**		**English**	
/bid/	"bead"	/biyd/		/niz/	"knees"	/niyz/
/did/	"deed"	/diyd/		/bist/	"beast"	/biyst/
/sin/	"seen"	/siyn/		/tiz/	"tease"	/tiyz/

Pronunciation Drill 5

bid	did	sin	niz	bist	miz
pip	div	si	rast	sænjid	bæsti
dídim	simi	shimi	sib	ziba	mina
vizit	iran	irani	mídidim	mídidid	míbinim

English /uw/ and Persian /u/

As the sound /u/ is articulated in English, the tongue automatically moves into position for a w-sound after the vowel, yielding a diphthong /uw/. Since this glide is made automatically or unconsciously, you are probably unaware that you make it. It will, however, become obvious to you when you contrast the pronunciation of the word "soup" (/suwp/) with the Persian equivalent /sup/, which as you see has no glide. Compare these Persian vowels with the

Lesson One　　　　　*MODERN PERSIAN*　　　　　درس يكم

corresponding English vowels that have glides and are somewhat longer than in Persian.

Persian	**English**		**Persian**	**English**	
/sup/	"soup"	/suwp/	/lus/	"loose"	/luws/
/sut/	"suit"	/suwt/	/su/	"Sue"	/suw/
/dud/	"dude"	/duwd/	/duz/	"dues"	/duwz/

Pronunciation Drill 6

sup	sut	dud	lus	su	sud
bud	ku	zud	buf	mum	fut
mush	nun	luti	sufi	puran	tu-hæm
susmar	doluks	shampu	liverpul	yuta	

Imam Khomeini mosque, Tehran

Lesson One   *MODERN PERSIAN*   درس يكم

English /ow/ and Persian /o/

The glided o-sound of English is the easiest way to spot an American accent, not only in Persian but in many languages, because of two changes in the English /o/. For this reason special attention should be given to this vowel. First of all, depending on your particular dialect of English, the o-vowel of the diphthong usually sounds like the uh-sound of "up," or even like the /e/ of "met." Then, in addition, this vowel is followed by a w-glide. Very few dialects of English actually pronounce a true o-vowel, and even when they do, the vowel is still followed by the w-glide. Thus, the true o-vowel of Persian sounds quite different from the average o-sound of English, and it has no w-glide following it. Compare these Persian vowels with the corresponding English vowels, which have glides and sound somewhat longer:

Persian	**English**	
/bot/	"boat"	/bowt/
/kot/	"coat"	/kowt/
/mod/	"mode"	/mowd/
/bon/	"bone"	/bown/

Pronunciation Drill 7

bot	kot	mod	bon	dom	kosh
kosht	mosht	kond	post	som	kobra
shoma	jóstid	konj	moc	moft	motor
telefon	shokolat	radio	diplom	holænd	
motshækéræm					

We would like to remind you that there are some glides in Persian, but they do not occur in any of the cases we have discussed here. /ey/, which was mentioned above, is the most common Persian diphthong. There are one or two others, but they need not be mentioned here.

Lesson One   *MODERN PERSIAN*   درس يكم

1.3 Greetings and Cultural Expressions

1.3.1 Cultural Materials: Greetings

tekrar konid	repeat (it)!
sælam	Hello (in Arabic, literally: "Peace")
hal	health, condition
chetor	how
hál-e shoma chetór-e?	How are you? (literally: "How is your health?")
mérsi	Thanks
motshækér-æm	Thank you (literally: "I am thankful.")
khub	good, well
bæd	bad
khub-e	Fine (good) (literally: "It is good/fine.")
bæd nist	Not bad (literally: "It is not bad.")

Discussion

In glossing Persian words and phrases, we have given idiomatic equivalents where possible — what we would say in the same situation. Sometimes such idiomatic renderings differ in syntax or literal meaning from the Persian. Where this is true, a literal translation will be given in parentheses. The usual Persian greeting is /sælam/, a word that literally means "peace" in Arabic and is a shortened form of the Arabic Islamic greeting formula /sælam æleykom/, "Peace (be) upon you." Where Iranians would say /sælam/, however, we would normally say "Hello" or "Hi." Similarly, when Iranians ask politely how you are, both question and reply make /hal/, "health/condition," the subject of the sentence, while in English we make the person the subject. Thus Iranians literally say the equivalent of "How is your health?" and "It is good," but this would be translated into English as, "How are you?" and "I am fine" in more normal conversation. (There is a variant form in Persian that is more similar to the

8

Lesson One MODERN PERSIAN درس يكم

English "How are you?" without *hal,* but this form is used between people with more familiar relationships. See Lesson 3 -- 3.11.2.)

You will note also from the sample greetings in section 1.3.3 below that it is perfectly acceptable — in fact quite common — to answer an inquiry about your health simply with any of the equivalents of "Thank you" (a). There is no need to include the equivalent of "Fine" as we do in English. When it is included, however, it usually comes second, not first as it does in English -- see(b) and (c):

(a) hál-e shoma chetór-e?   (b) hál-e shoma chetór-e?   (c) hál-e shoma chetór-e?
    mérsi   mérsi. khub-e.   mérsi. bæd nist.

In the greeting /hál-e shoma chetór-e?/, note that:

- a. The major stress (i.e., sentence stress) is on the first syllable of the sentence.
- b. There is a flat intonation contour for the rest of the sentence.
- c. Even though the sentence is a question, there is no special question-type intonation because of the presence of a question word, /chetor/ "how":

```
___
há |
    | l-e shoma chetór-e?
```

Note that questions with question words (who? what? etc.) in Persian — as well as in English — usually take statement intonation. As mentioned in the discussion of our transcription system in the Introduction, all questions with question words will be punctuated with the special question mark /?/ to indicate the intonation of this type of sentence. The question mark /?/ is reserved for questions with question intonation, which you will encounter in this lesson. (See also this lesson, section 1.5 for a fuller discussion of question intonation.)

Notes on alternate forms, intonation, and transcription in this text

In informal discourse, the pronunciation of /motshækér-æm/ is as we have given it. In slower, more studied pronunciation ("recitation form"), it gains an extra syllable and the /k/ is doubled: /motæshækkér-æm/.

Lesson One   *MODERN PERSIAN*   درس یکم

Note that falling intonation is used on all complete utterances even if they consist of one word (see further discussion of intonation in section 1.5 of this lesson):

```
 ___              ___          ___               ___
| á |           mér |        khú |            | ké |
sæl |   I am   | si          | be   motshæ|   | ræm
```

Note: In the intonation contours you see here and in future lessons, we had to split up the vowel of final stressed closed syllables, for example, the -/lám/ of /sælám/, in order to show you that the intonation falls on that syllable. We are not implying that there are really two vowels here, but just that in the space of time in which that vowel is pronounced, the intonation moves from high to low:

Regular Transcription   **Transcription with Sentence Contour**

```
                                        ___
                                       | lá |
                                       |    |
          sælám                        sæ |  | ám


                                        ___
                                       | rá |
           irán                        |    |
                                        i |  | án
```

1.3.2   Classroom Expressions: lotfæn tekrar konid, please repeat

tekrár konìd	repeat (it)!
tælæffoz	pronunciation
tælæffóz konìd	pronounce (it)!
gúsh konìd	listen!
jæváb bèdid	answer!

Lesson One   *MODERN PERSIAN*   درس یکم

sælám konìd (be ___)	greet, say hello (to ___)!
dobare	again
mígæm	I say, I'll say, I'll say (it)
dobare mígæm	I'll say it again, I'll repeat it
lotfæn	please
hæme	everyone, all
ba-hæm	together, with each other
hæme ba-hæm	all together, everyone at the same time
yæ:ni chi?	what does that/it mean?
yæ:ni _____	it means _____, that means _____
khub-e	it's fine, that's good
doróst-e	that's correct, it's right
bæd-e	it's bad, that's bad

1.3.3 Sample Greetings

gúsh konìd: (Students, listen but do not repeat.)   گوش کنید:

sæ<u>lam</u>. h<u>á</u>l-e shoma chetór-e?

<u>mér</u>si. <u>khub-e</u>.   (dobare mígæm)

sæ<u>lam</u>. h<u>á</u>l-e shoma chetór-e?

<u>mér</u>si. bæd <u>nist</u>.   (dobare mígæm)

sæ<u>lam</u>. h<u>á</u>l-e shoma chetór-e?

<u>mér</u>si.   (dobare mígæm)

sæ<u>lam</u>. h<u>á</u>l-e shoma chetór-e?

<u>mér</u>si. motshæ<u>kér</u>-æm.   (dobare mígæm)

Lesson One   *MODERN PERSIAN*   درس یکم

1.3.4 Exercises

a. lotfæn tekrár konìd: لطفا تکرار کنید

Repeat the above greetings after your teacher, first in unison, then individually. In this exercise, the teacher says /dobare/ or /dobare tekrár konìd/ instead of /dobare mígæm/.

b. lotfæn jæváb bèdid: لطفا جواب بدید:

No cue is given. Answer the teacher's greeting with any form you like.

c. lotfæn sælám konìd: Greet and answer each other.   لطفا سلام کنید:

    Teacher: "Bill," lotfæn be "Suzanne" sælám konìd:
    Bill: sæ<u>lam</u>. <u>hál</u>-e shoma chetór-e?
    Suzanne: mé<u>r</u>si. motshækér-æm.

🔊 1.4 Dialogue 1

The following is a conversation between Hasan and George, who have just been introduced by a mutual Iranian acquaintance. The conversation takes place in the United States.

lotfæn gúsh konìd: لطفا گوش کنید:

    George: bæradæræm dær <u>iran</u> zendegí mìkone.   My brother lives in Iran.
    Hasan: <u>rást</u> mìgid? unja cheká<u>r</u> mìkone?   Really? What does he do there?
    George: dær shiraz <u>dærs</u> mìde.   He teaches in Shiraz.

1.4.1 Intonation   dobare gúsh konìd: (Note intonation patterns.)   دوباره گوش کنید

George: <u>bæradæræm dær i</u>/ \<u>ran</u>/ \<u>zendegí mìkone</u>./   My brother lives in Iran.
Hasan: \<u>rást</u>/ \<u>mìgid?</u>/ \<u>unja</u>/ \<u>cheká</u>r/ \<u>mìkone</u>/   Really? What does he do there?
George: \<u>dær shiraz</u>/ \<u>dærs</u>/ \<u>mìde.</u>/   He teaches in Shiraz.

Lesson One *MODERN PERSIAN* درس یکم

1.4.2 Vocabulary List 1 **lotfæn tekrár konìd** لطفا تکرار کنید

bæradær	brother	chekár mìkone	what does he/she do?
bæradæræm	my brother	dærs mìde	he/she teaches
dær	in	pedær	father
zendegí mìkone	he/she lives	madær	mother
rást mìgid?/mìgin?	really?	dust	friend
unja	there	koja?	where?

Iranian Place Names: **lotfæn tælæffóz konìd** (See accompanying map.) لطفا تلفظ کنید

iran	tæbriz	ræsht	tehran
yæzd	æhvaz	kerman	bakhtæran/kermanshah
esfæhan	shiraz	abadan	mæshhæd
hæmædan	zabol	zahedan	bændær æbbas

Azadi Square, Tehran

Lesson One   MODERN PERSIAN   درس یکم

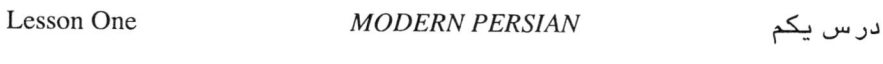

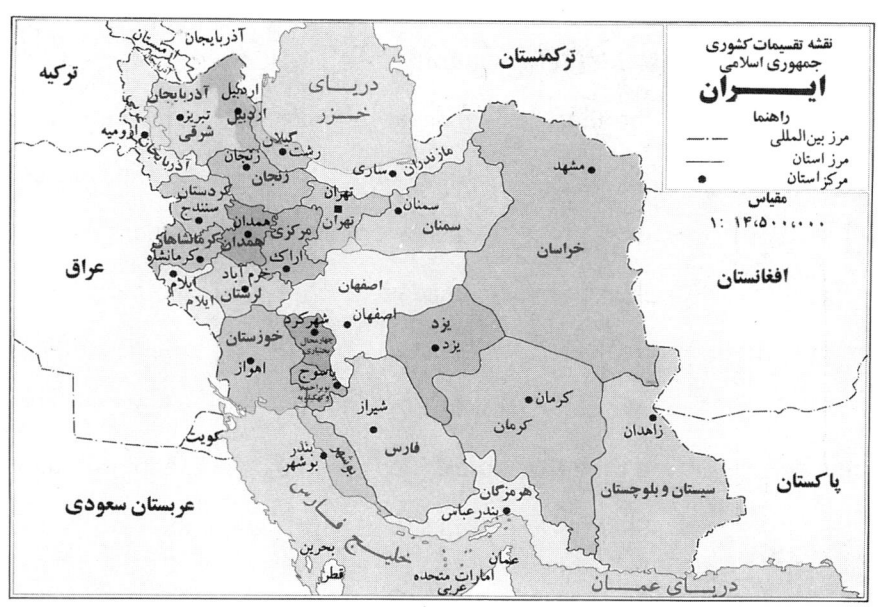

Map of Iran

North American Place Names: **lotfæn tælæffóz konìd**   لطفا تلفظ کنید

(Remember to stress the last syllable.)

kaliforniá	nio york	tegzás	kanadá
vashængtón	yutá	arizoná	los anjelés
tusán	filadelfiá	perinstón	siatél
ohayó	kolombús	pensilvaniá	nio jerzí
torontó	shikagó	bostón	san feransiskó

Iranian Personal Names: **lotfæn tekrár konìd**   لطفا تکرار کنید

| **Men's Names:** | jæmshid | æli | fereydun |
| **Women's Names:** | shæhla | pærvin | shirin |

Be prepared to use additional names of Iranian friends or acquaintances for class drills.

Lesson One   *MODERN PERSIAN*   درس یکم

Note that when the sentence stress falls early in the sentence, or at the beginning in cases of special emphasis on specific words, the following level contour characteristic of questions is maintained regardless of length:

\rást/   \mìgid?/   \pe/ /dǽr\ /etun míkhad biad inja\   (special emphasis)

On the other hand, sentence stress will occasionally fall on the final syllable of the sentence. If the sentence stress falls on the last syllable of a question, the intonation is slightly different from the normal question intonation: the final syllable rises in a way not altogether different from the English question intonation, but slower and longer:

$$n?$$
$$a$$
$$r$$

shoma færda mírid teh

Listen to your teacher read the following sentences and identify whether they are statements or questions:

shoma farsi khub hærf mìzænid	rast mìgid
bæradæræm dær iran zendegí mìkone	pedæresh ziad kár mìkone
shoma khudnevis darid	madæresh rusi mídune
shoma farsi mídunid	næfæhmidid
æli færda míad inja	æli færda míad inja
æli dær shiraz zendegí mìkone	madæresh rusi mídune

(Review 1.3, "Greetings and Cultural Expressions," and 1.4, "Dialogue 1")

Lesson One   *MODERN PERSIAN*   درس یکم

1.5 Question Intonation

The question intonation in Persian has a different contour than that in English. The English question intonation generally rises at the end of the sentence:

Is he a new student?   Do you have a pen?

In all Persian sentences, including both statements and questions, the stress falls on <u>one</u> particular syllable in the sentence. In sentences with multiple clauses, there is generally one stressed syllable per clause. This stressed syllable is also accompanied by a rise in pitch, which forms part of the intonation contour of the sentence (see Lesson 3, section 3.11.1).

The intonation for both statements and questions begins with a level contour, then both contours rise in pitch at the point of the sentence stress. At this point, statement and question intonations differ:

Statement Intonation   Question Intonation

The statement intonation falls to   The question intonation falls from the

a pitch lower than that in the original pitch high pitch of the sentence stress back

in which the sentence began and   to the <u>same</u> pitch in which the sentence

terminates with a level contour: began and terminates with a level contour:

\bæradæræm dær i/ \ran/ \zendegí mìkone./   \bæradæræm dær i/ \ran/ \zendegí mìkone?/

As you can see, the question intonations of English and Persian are quite different, and it will not suffice simply to use English question intonation when making a Persian question. In addition to a different contour, the Persian question usually has a lengthened final syllable.

Listen to the following sentences read twice, once as a statement and once as a question. Note that a statement is converted to a question <u>only</u> by intonation. There are no accompanying grammatical changes.

pedæresh un<u>ja</u> zendegí mìkone.   pedæresh un<u>ja</u> zendegí mìkone?

shoma darid <u>kár</u> mìkonid.   shoma darid <u>kár</u> mìkonid?

jæmshid <u>né</u>mikhad bíad inja.   jæmshid <u>né</u>mikhad bíad inja?

bæradæretun shi<u>mi</u> dærs mìde.   bæradæretun shi<u>mi</u> dærs mìde?

1.6 Substitution Drills

Drill 1: Substitution

| ran |

\bæradæræm dær i | | zendegí mìkone.

cues: responses:

    pedær   pedæræm dær iran zendegí mìkone.

    madær   madæræm dær iran zendegí mìkone.

    dust   dústæm dær iran zendegí mìkone.

    pedær   etc.

    madær

    (bæradær)

Drill 2: Substitution

(The sentence stress here is on /shiraz/ and represents the normal pattern. The stress is on /dærs/ in the context of the dialogue since it answers the question /unja chekár mìkone?/)

bæradæræm   \dær shi /\raz/ \dærs mìde./

    cues: responses:

       esfæhan   dær esfæhan dærs mìde.

       kalifornia   dær kalifornia dærs mìde.

       tehran   dær tehran dærs mìde.

(vashængton, abadan, nio york, iran, (shiraz))

(Have a place name in mind and be ready to use it when called on.)

Lesson One MODERN PERSIAN درس یکم

Drill 3: Substitution (Be ready to supply names of your own choice.)

\jæmshid dær teh/ \ran/ \dǽrs mìde./

æli	shæhla
shirin	pærvin
fereydun	(jæmshid)

Drill 4: Free Substitution

Teacher: æli (etc.) chekár mìkone?

Student: dær- _____ dǽrs mìde.

Drill 5: Substitution (Intonation as in Drill 3)

    pedæræm   dær tehran   zendegí mìkone.

  cues: responses:

dǽrs mìde	pedæræm dær tehran dǽrs mìde.
zendegí mìkone	pedæræm dær tehran zendegí mìkone.
chekár mìkone	pedæræm dær tehran chekár mìkone?
dǽrs mìde	etc.

Drill 6: Substitution (Intonation as in Drill 3)

    bærádæræm   dær   iran   zendegí mìkone.

  cues: responses:

jæmshid	jæmshid dær iran zendegí mìkone.
vashængton	jæmshid dær vashængton zendegí mìkone.
esfæhan	jæmshid dær esfæhan zendegí mìkone.
nahid	nahid dær esfæhan zendegí mìkone.
æli	æli dær esfæhan zendegí mìkone.
kalifornia	æli dær kalifornia zendegí mìkone.

Lesson One *MODERN PERSIAN* درس يكم

                dærs mìde   æli dær kalifornia dærs mìde.

shæhla   etc.

          tehran

fereydun

          shiraz

madæræm

          nio york

dústæm

                zendegí mìkone

          tehran

shirin

pedǽræm

          iran

(bæradǽræm)

(Now insert names of your own choice into the pattern.)

Drill 7: Substitution

      jæmshid dær <u>tehran</u>   chekár mìkone?

cues: responses:

æli   æli dær tehran chekár mìkone?

       esfæhan   æli dær esfæhan chekár mìkone?

shæhla   etc.

       tehran

       nio york

(cues: fereydun, shiraz, arizona, æli, ohayo, jæmshid, (tehran))

Lesson One MODERN PERSIAN درس یکم

Drill 8: Substitution

(Intonation as in Drill 3, Two cues are given simultaneously)

Example: <u>jæmshid</u> dær <u>tehran</u> zendegí mìkone. (æli/esfæhan)

<u>æli</u> dær <u>esfæhan</u> zendegí mìkone. (shæhla/iran)

<u>shæhla</u> dær <u>iran</u> zendegí mìkone.

(cues: pærvin/nio york, fereydun/shiraz, shirin/kalifornia, (jæmshid/tehran))

(Have a friend's name and a place name in mind and be ready to use them when called on.)

1.7 Question and Answer Drills

Drill 9: Cued Question/Answer

In the following exercise the first two cues are given to Student 1; the third is given to Student 2.

Student 1: <u>jæmshid</u> dær <u>tehran</u> chekár mìkone?

Student 2: unja <u>zendegí mìkone</u>. (cues: S1 æli/shiraz, S2 dærs mìde)

Student 1: <u>æli</u> dær <u>shiraz</u> chekár mìkone?

Student 2: unja <u>dærs mìde</u>.

(cues: **S1** fereydun/esfæhan, **S2** dærs mìde; **S1** shæhla/nio york, **S2** zendegí mìkone; **S1** pærvin/kalifornia, **S2** zendegí mìkone (**S1** jæmshid/tehran, **S2** zendegí mìkone))

(Find a partner and continue practicing this pattern in pairs using names and verbs of your own choice.)

Drill 10: Question and Answer

a. "George Bush" koja zendegí mìkone?

"Bill Clinton" koja zendegí mìkone?

(Governor of your state) koja zendegí mìkone?

(Persian teaching assistant) koja zendegí mìkone? unja chekár mìkone?

Lesson One MODERN PERSIAN درس یکم

(Persian professor) koja zendegí mìkone? unja chekár mìkone?

(Student's name) koja zendegí mìkone?

(Another student's name) koja zendegí mìkone?

(Iranian friend of student) koja zendegí mìkone?

b. Break up into pairs or small groups and ask each other the type of questions in section a, using names of famous people, famous Iranian names in current events, and other familiar names, e.g.,

"Meryl Streep" koja zendegí mìkone?

"Clint Eastwood" dær kalifornia chekár mìkone?

"Benazir Bhutto" koja zendegí mìkone? (be farsi: binæzír butó)

rást mìgid? unja chekár mìkone? etc.

1.8 Situational and Practical Drills

Greetings and Classroom Expressions

\há/ \l-e shoma?	A common abbreviated form of /hál-e shoma chetór-e?/
hál-e shoma chetór-e?	(And) how are you?
	(note change in sentence stress for the response only)
yævashtær	slower
tondtær	faster
tæmrín konìd	practice (command form)
bégid	say, say it (command form)
béporsid	ask (command form)

Greetings: **lotfæn gúsh konìd** لطفا گوش کنید

sælam. hál-e shoma chetór-e?

mérsi. khub-e. hál-e shoma chetór-e?   (note change in sentence stress)

mérsi. bæd nist.

sælam. hál-e shoma?

Lesson One   *MODERN PERSIAN*   درس یکم

motshæ<u>ké</u>r-æm. hál-e sho<u>ma</u> chetór-e?

<u>mér</u>si. <u>kh</u>ub-e.

sæ<u>lam</u>. <u>h</u>ál-e shoma chetór-e?

motshæ<u>ké</u>r-æm. <u>kh</u>ub-e. hál-e sho<u>ma</u> chetór-e?

<u>mér</u>si. <u>kh</u>ub-e.

sæ<u>lam</u>. <u>h</u>ál-e shoma chetór-e?

<u>mér</u>si. motshæ<u>ké</u>r-æm. hál-e sho<u>ma</u> chetór-e?

<u>mér</u>si. <u>kh</u>ub-e.

lotfæn tekrár konìd: The above greetings are drilled orally.   لطفا تکرار کنید:

lotfæn tæmrín konìd: لطفا تمرین کنید:

Greet each other using any of the possible combinations desired.

Drill 11: Exercises

     a.   **lotfæn gúsh konìd:**   لطفا گوش کنید:

yævash<u>tær</u> bégid	yævash<u>tær</u> mígæm
yævash<u>tær</u> tælæffóz konìd	tond<u>tær</u> mígæm
tond<u>tær</u> tæmrín konìd	doba<u>re</u> bégid
doba<u>re</u> béporsid	tond<u>tær</u> jæváb bèdid

     b.   **lotfæn jæváb bèdid:**   لطفا جواب بدید:

The sentences in section a are repeated and then you will be asked to respond to /yæ:ni chi?/

     c.   **lotfæn tekrár konìd:**   لطفا تکرار کنید:

The sentences of section a are drilled.

(Review Pronunciation Drills, Dialogue 1, Drills, Greetings)

Lesson One MODERN PERSIAN درس يكم

1.9 Reading Persian

The reading and writing material of the first five lessons is divided into three parts. In the first part — which includes Lessons 1 and 2 — you will learn to read (sections 1.9 and 2.9) and write well over half of the thirty-two letters and eight diacritical marks that make up the Persian writing system, but with little or no regard for the meaning of what you are reading or writing. Instead the emphasis will be on the mechanics of recognizing and forming letters. In the second part — Lessons 3, 4, and 5 — you will learn to read (sections 3.9, 4.9, and 5.9) and write the remainder of the letters and diacritical marks, but in words, phrases, and sentences that will already be meaningful or familiar to you. These sections will present the Persian equivalents of all those words you have already learned orally and seen only in transcription.

The sequence in which the letters and other signs of the writing system are presented here is determined by particular features of individual letters, not by the sequence of the Persian alphabet. The alphabet will be given in sequence in Lesson 5, section 5.9.7, together with the name and sound value or values of each letter. The alphabet is also given at the beginning of the accompanying Persian-English glossary.

In the third part of the reading and writing material, starting with Lesson 6, the principal differences between colloquial and Formal Written Persian (FWP), and the rules for transforming your colloquial speech to writing, will be described.

1.9.1 Reading Persian: The Alphabet (*ælefba*)

The Persian alphabet is simply the Arabic alphabet with four additional letters. These additional letters represent sounds that occur in Persian but not in Arabic — at least not in classical Arabic. Persian, like Arabic and all other languages that use the Arabic alphabet, is written from right to left. For example, the word <u>daru</u> (medicine) is written <u>urad</u>. In its native dress, <u>urad</u> looks like this: دارو The letters used to write this word are:

Lesson One *MODERN PERSIAN* درس یکم

Sound	Shape	Name
/d/	د	dal
/a/	ا	ælef
/r/	ر	re
/u/	و	vav

There are a number of other words that can be written with these same four letters, as you can see from the following exercise. In doing this exercise, first spell each word aloud, then read it. (There is a key to all the exercises after Lesson 16.)

Since the script is so new to you, you may feel it necessary to write in the transcription over each of the words to help you sound them out. This is a perfectly natural practice at this point. However, if you leave the words in the exercises below unmarked, it will give you a fresh chance to practice your reading skills again in class.

Reading Exercise 1: Spell and read aloud. Example: رود (re vav dal /rud/)

دور	رادار	راد	را
دارا	دادار	داد	دا
رودار	دود	رود	رو

Note: Print/Typescript vs. Handwriting: Before proceeding further it is important to make clear that the handwritten and printed forms of the Persian alphabet differ in a number of significant ways. You cannot learn to write Persian correctly by simply copying the printed forms. Print and typescript are virtually identical, however. The discussion of the forms of the letters of the alphabet that follows is restricted to print and is designed to prepare you only to recognize and read these letters.

1.9.2 Connecting and Nonconnecting Letters

The letters of the Persian alphabet are divided into two groups, those that may be joined to a **following** letter, and those that may not. As you can see ا ، د ، ر and و are nonconnecting letters. There are only three other letters in the alphabet that are also

nonconnecting, and they all have the shape of either د or ر. They are distinguished by the addition of dots. Note that a nonconnecting letter may connect to a preceding letter, but never to a following letter.

Sound	Shape	Name
/z/	ذ	zal
/z/	ز	ze
/zh/	ژ	zhe

1.9.3 Duplicate Letters

Note that both ز and ذ have the sound of /z/ in Persian. This is so because the original sound of ذ in Arabic does not occur in Persian and was therefore assimilated to what was to Persian ears the nearest equivalent — /z/. There are a number of sounds in Arabic — each represented by a separate letter — which, like ذ, do not occur in Persian. These sounds have also been assimilated to the nearest Persian equivalent. This means that the Persian alphabet has a number of duplicate letters for the same sound. These duplicate letters will be dealt with more fully in Lesson 4.

All the letters of the Persian alphabet other than ا، د، ذ، ر، ز، ژ and و are connecting letters. That is, they must be joined to the letter that immediately **follows** them. Here are three quite common connecting letters.

Sound	Shape	Name
/s/	سـ	sin
/m/	مـ	mim
/i/	یـ	ye

Before illustrating how connecting and nonconnecting letters are joined together in words, it will be necessary to explain another aspect of the Persian alphabet — that of how the position of a letter in a word can affect its shape.

Lesson One MODERN PERSIAN درس یکم

1.9.4 Shape and Position

There are no capital or lower case distinctions in Persian. However, a number of letters have different shapes for the beginning, middle, or end of a word. In final position a few even have two shapes depending on whether the letter that precedes them is connecting or nonconnecting. These shape-changers are all connecting letters. Printed nonconnecting letters have a single shape, regardless of their position or of the preceding letter.

Of the three connecting letters just introduced, the first two have two shapes — one for initial and medial positions and a second for final position. This is a common pattern. The third letter also has one shape for initial and medial positions, but two slightly different shapes for word-final position.

Final	Medial	Initial
س	ـسـ	سـ
م	ـمـ	مـ
ـی / ی	ـیـ	یـ

Notice how a letter changes according to position and whether or not it is connected to a previous letter:

سیر	/sir/	سور	/sur/	سار	/sar/
ریس	/ris/	روس	/rus/	راس	/ras/
رام	/ram/	رومی	/rumi/	ریما	/rima/

The following exercise illustrates these changes in the letters you have learned so far.

Reading Exercise 2: Spell and read aloud. Example: روسی (re vav sin ye /rusi/)

زا	ما	مار	رام	ذو
سو	سوز	سار	راس	روس
ژاژ	ساز	ریس	ریسی	روز
مام	ماسی	دامی	مادی	داماد
روسی	مور	موری	مومی	سامی
ماساژ	سوزید	داری	دارید	میدید

26

Lesson One　　　　　　　*MODERN PERSIAN*　　　　　　　درس یکم

داد	دادی	دوز	میدوز	میدوزی
موذی	داریم	میریم	میر	میز
میری	میرزا	سیر	سیز	موسیر
سیما	سیمی	سیری	سیروس	سیم

Damavand, highest point in Iran, Tehran

1.9.5 Digraph

In the initial position in a word, the three vowels /a/, /i/, and /u/ are indicated by a combination of two signs, the vowel sign preceded by an initial *ælef*. For initial /i/ and /u/, the sequences of *ælef* and the letters *ye* and *vav* are written sequentially: ای /i/ and او /u/. For initial /a/, however, one of the two *ælef*'s is written horizontally above the other as a curved

Lesson One　　　MODERN PERSIAN　　　درس یکم

line called a *kolah* or *mædde* : آ.　This digraph has the name *ælef mædde* or *ælef ba koleh*. In these three digraph vowels, the extra *ælef* elements have no sound of their own. They simply represent an orthographic convention for vowels in initial position. Remember that it is only in initial position that these vowels must be written with digraphs. In medial and final position the letter itself is enough, as you can see from the following contrasts:

ساری	/sari/	vs.	آری	/ari/
راد	/rad/	vs.	آرد	/ard/
روس	/rus/	vs.	اوس	/us/

Reading Exercise 3: Spell and read aloud. Example آرام (ælef mædde re ælef mim /aram/)

آ	آس	آسا	آر	آرا
آرام	او	اوس	ای	ایراد
ایرادی	ایماژ	رام	اورا	آرامی

Reading Exercise 4, Review: Be prepared to spell and read these words aloud in class.

دارو	آسا	اوس	داماد	ساری
آرام	ایراد	سامی	داریم	میرید
سارا	سیروس	ماساژ	روسی	رادار
ایماژ	موذی	رودار	اوس	میدوزی

1.9.6 Dots

As you have already seen, Persian letters are distinguished from each other both by shape and by the use of one, two or three dots over or under letters with the same shape: د vs. ذ on the one hand, and ر vs. ز vs. ژ on the other. Hypothetically, a single shape could be used to make seven separate letters by the use of subscript and superscript dots. In fact, the largest number of letters to be generated from a single shape by the use of dots is six. The

Lesson One   *MODERN PERSIAN*   درس یکم

prolific shape is *ye* (ـی) which you have so far encountered only in that letter. This shape never stands alone but when combined with dots, it produces five additional letters. While all of these letters have the **same shape in initial and medial** positions, there are **three distinct final shapes** — one for *nun*, one for *ye*, and one for the other four:

Sound	Name	Final	Medial	Initial
		(after nonconnector)		
/b/	be	ب	ـبـ	بـ
/p/	pe	پ	ـپـ	پـ
/t/	te	ت	ـتـ	تـ
/s/	se	ث	ـثـ	ثـ
/n/	nun	ن	ـنـ	نـ
/i/	ye	ی/ـی	ـیـ	یـ

The final shapes for all of these letters (as well as all other letters) when following a **connector** have a little stroke connecting them to the previous letter:

Letter		Final After nonconnector		As in:	Final After connector		As in:
					(note extra stroke)		
be	ب	تاب	tab	->	...ب	سیب	sib
pe	پ	پاپ	pap	->	...پ	پیپ	pip
te	ت	تات	tat	->	...ت	پیت	pit
se	ث	ثاث	sas	->	...ث	ثیث	sis
nun	ن	سان	san	->	...ن	سین	sin
ye	ی	بودی	budi	->	...ی	سینی	sini

The shape used for *sin* has only one dotted variant, *shin*:

Sound	Name	Final	Medial	Initial
/s/	sin	س	ـسـ	سـ
/sh/	shin	ش	ـشـ	شـ

Lesson One MODERN PERSIAN درس یکم

Do not confuse the two shapes with three dots over them that have been introduced so far: one is ش *shin*, a *sin* with three dots and represents the sound /sh/; the other is ث *se*, a *te* with three dots and represents another /s/ sound. There have been two duplicate letters introduced so far, two for /z/ (ز and ذ), and two for /s/ (س and ث). In both cases only one of these letters is commonly used and the other is quite uncommon and can be effectively ignored at this point. Whenever you are given transcription work to do, **always depend on س for /s/ and ز for /z/**. The other two letters — ذ and ث — will be important when you get to the stage of needing to spell specific words.

Reading Exercise 5: Spell and read aloud.

با	باب	بابا	آب	آبی
پا	پاپ	پاس	سوپ	پیپ
تا	تات	ذات	تاتی	توت
ثا	باث	ثیار	ایثار	میراث
نا	نان	نون	آن	آنان
بان	ناب	بانو	ناباب	آبان
نور	بور	تور	تابان	تابوت
آباد	آبادی	آبادان	آبادانی	آرامی
توری	توران	تورانی	تورانیان	ایران
آثار	آبشار	ثانی	تابی	شادی
سور	شور	سوری	شوری	آش

30

Lesson One　　　　　　　*MODERN PERSIAN*　　　　　　　درس یکم

Caspian shore, Bandar-e Anzali

Reading Exercise 6, Review: Be prepared to spell and read aloud in class.

سیمین	شیمی	سامان	ساسان	ماساژ
سوزان	ایران	توران	بو	بودی
میبودی	میدوزی	میسوزی	میبازی	میسابی
میآبی	میرانی	میسازی	آمار	آثار
ایراد	داروساز	اورانوس	زیبا	ریزی
پیپ	تیپ	تیم	توپ	آمین
ایماژ	ذاتی	شورید	بازار	آزار

Reading Exercise 7, Transcription:

Transcribe from Persian to phonetic characters and from phonetic characters to Persian. This work is to be done as homework but may also be **read** (Persian to phonetics) or **written**

Lesson One *MODERN PERSIAN* درس یکم

(phonetics to Persian) on the blackboard or in pairs/small groups. Other words that conform to the rules learned so far may be given spontaneously in class.

Persian to Phonetics			**Phonetics to Persian**	
آبادی	=>	abadi	میسابی => misabi	
سیمین		شورید	namus	ziba
ایراد		ذاتی	abadan	budim
ریزی		ایماژ	shiraz	dadid
سوزان		میبازی	iran	darid
آثار		آمار	azar	ash
میتابید		مومیا	niaz	mandana

Perisan Gulf, Bandar-e Abbas

Lesson One MODERN PERSIAN درس یکم

🔊 **1.10 Numerals**

The printed version of the Persian numerals are the following:

1	2	3	4	5	6	7	8	9	0
۱	۲	۳	۴	۵	۶	۷	۸	۹	۰

Now that we have gotten you accustomed to the fact that Persian is written from right to left, you will be surprised to learn that the Persian numerals are read from left to right (like English)! If you see a number such as 497 in your chart work, remember to read it as 497 and not 794. For the time being, we will ask you to study these figures for recognition purposes only, since the handwritten forms look somewhat different. The handwritten forms of "three" and "four" are especially different from the printed form; "four," in fact, has two printed forms. The words for the numbers from one to ten are presented in the next lesson at the end of the vocabulary for Lesson 2 (section 2.2).

1.11 Grammar Discussion: The Persian Verb and Basic Sentence Word Order

The discussion of Persian verb structure begins in Lesson 2. Here we would simply like to draw your attention to a few elementary points about Persian syntax. In contrast to English, the basic Persian sentence puts the verb last. That is, both the subject and the object precede the verb, as does generally everything else that might be lumped under the title "predicate phrase." This word order, however, is flexible in Persian. In the context of extended speech, of course, elements of the sentence do move around, especially for purposes of emphasis. The drills in section 6 above provide many examples of the most common pattern of the simple sentence in Persian, and various dialogues in early lessons show the flexibility of word order in discourse. It is worth pointing out that the Persian verb contains an indication of the person and number of its subject in its conjugation. The ending /-e/, which you have seen on all the verbs in this lesson, indicates that the subject of the verb is third person singular ("he," "she" or "it"). The Persian sentence does not need a separate subject to be a complete utterance, and thus, in the context of extended discourse, a subject that has been mentioned

Lesson One   MODERN PERSIAN   درس یکم

may be dropped:

    example: bæradæretun chekár mìkone?   "What does your brother do?"

                 dær shiraz dærs mìde.   "He teaches in Shiraz."

Put another way, the Persian verb by itself in some contexts may serve as a "complete" sentence. English requires that a sentence have a separate subject as well as a verb. "Teaches" by itself is not a sentence in English, but /dærs mìde/ by itself is a complete grammatical utterance in Persian. There is a specific sequence in the placement of verbal modifiers such as adverbs ("well, "slowly"), question words ("where," "when," etc.) and prepositional phrases ("in Shiraz," etc.). The order of these elements will be discussed in later lessons, starting with Lesson 4 (4.11).

1.15 Vowel Reduction in English

An English vowel changes its quality according to the amount of stress it receives. Notice that the second "a" in "anátomy" receives the regular pronunciation of the English "a" sound since it is also the stressed syllable in that word. In the adjectival form of the same word—"anatómical"—the stress shifts to the third syllable with the consequence that the sound value of the second "a" is reduced from the a-sound of "cat" to a sound rather like "uh." This change is more accurately indicated thus:

    anatomy /ínætīmiy/   anatomical /ænītámīkīl/

This type of vowel change or vowel reduction does not occur in Persian, and you should take care to give vowels the same quality in all syllables. Observe the following Persian vowels as they occur in stressed position and in unstressed position (all stresses here are on final syllables):

bæd	bædi	bædia	sob	soba	sobane
dust	dusta	dustane	bin	bini	binia
nam	name	namei	mes	mesi	mesia
som	sombol	sombolchini	div	divar	divari

34

Lesson One *MODERN PERSIAN* درس يكم

dan	danesh	daneshmænd	daneshmændan
div	divist	divísto-chel	divísto-chélo-char

The only place where a similar type of vowel reduction occurs in Persian is when unstressed /æ/ or /e/ precedes stressed /ha/ sequence:

næhár esfæhán bæhár bæchehá

Pronunciation Drill 9

bænd	míbænde	némibænde	chek	mícheke	némicheke
dun	mídune	némidune	kosh	míkoshe	némikoshe
bin	míbine	némibine	bash	míbashe	némibashe
chek	chekíd	chekaníd	chekanidé		míchekanide
kesh	míkeshim	némikeshim	némikeshunim		némikeshunimesh

Pronunciation Drill 10

zæban	ashpæz	simin	chini	forush	boros
hæmdæm	festival	pelastik	zabol	kabol	shorævi
rusie	zhapon	telefon	telegraf	kapitalist	sosialist
komunist	demokrat	kapitalisti	sosialisti	liberal	fanatik
vitamin	epizod	televizion	toyota	mersedes	kompiuter
kampiuteri	vezheteriæn	nikson	janson	kenedi	reygæn
karter	shirak	cherchil	estalin	moskow	berlæn
paris	vashængton	lændæn	tehran	esfæhan	tæbriz
zænjan	shiraz	hæmædan	mæshhæd	abadan	æhvaz
kærachi	dehli	pekæn	tokio	pakestan	bæluchestan
æræbestan	hendustan	uganda	suis	norvezh	chekoslovaki

Lesson One *MODERN PERSIAN* درس يكم

Pronunciation Drill 11

mídune	míkhabe	mítabe	míkoshe	míjænge	míbine
míkube	mízæne	bédune	békhabe	bétabe	bókoshe
béjænge	bébine	békube	bézæne	némidune	némikhabe
némitabe	némikoshe	némijænge	némibine	némikube	némizæne

| Lesson Two | درس دوم |

TOPICS COVERED IN THIS LESSON

- Family Background: What does your brother (etc.) do? He studies biology in the university, teaches French in a school, practices the guitar, studies in Arizona, etc.

- Family, Friends, and Languages: Does your sister (etc.) know Persian? Does she study Arabic?

- More Basic Greetings: More on Hello. Good-bye.

- More Classroom Expressions

- Is it easy? Hard? Right / correct? Yes, it is. No it's not.

- Numbers 1 to 10

- More Iranian Names

Listening Materials

Listening Comprehension: George and Hasan

RESOURCES AND BACKGROUND: INFORMATION AND ACCURACY

Phonology

The Persian /kh/

Contrast of Persian and English /t/ and /d/

The Persian /r/

Grammar Patterns to Be Drilled

Verbs

Command Forms: *bé-,* — *konid*

Nouns

Possessive Ending "your": *-etun*

Sentence Patterns

(subject) + (location) + object + verb

Lesson Two MODERN PERSIAN درس دوم

Question words

    subject — *ki*

    location — *koja*

    object — *chi*

Reading and Writing Persian

    The letters ج - چ - ح - خ

    Silent و

    Syllabification

Grammar Discussion

    Verbs

        Simple vs. Compound

        Present Tense

        Command Form

        Person

        Verb Roots

Cultural Materials

    Variations on Greetings

    Good-bye

    Classroom Expressions

Lesson Two   *MODERN PERSIAN*   درس دوم

2.1 Phonology /kh/ sometimes as /x/

This unit introduces the new sound /kh/ or /x/. In this text we transcribe it as /kh/ since Americans are more familiar with this convention than they are with /x/ to represent this sound. Because this sound is not found in English, English speakers sometimes substitute /k/ or /h/ for it. It is like a strong German *ch* — as in *Bach* — or the Scottish *Loch*. The following drills contrast /kh/ first with /k/, then with /h/. Note that this sound does not soften according to the vowels that precede or follow it.

Pronunciation Drill 1

| khub kub | khar kar | khash kash | khal kal | khord kord | khosh kosh |

Pronunciation Drill 2

| khan han | khæm hæm | khe he | khal hal | khæste hæste | khosh hosh |

Pronunciation Drill 3

| har khar kar | khud hud kud | kol khol hol | han khan kan |

Pronunciation Drill 4

khan	khish	khud	khab	khun	khæt
bækht	rokh	sukht	shukh	shukhi	khoshab
khoshkhæt	khodkar	khoshbækht	khoshhal	khoshkhænde	khoshkhab

2.1.1 Phonology: /t/ and /d/

The sounds "t" and "d" are pronounced very rapidly in American English when they occur between vowels. For example:

| better | butter | kitty | latter | ladder | kidding |

Lesson Two *MODERN PERSIAN* درس دوم

This reduction of "t and "d" does not occur in Persian. Moreover, the normal American pronunciation of these consonants is rather similar to the Persian /r/. Care should therefore be taken to give Persian /t/ and /d/ their full pronunciation at all times to avoid their being heard as /r/. Listen to the following pairs of words:

mídune	mírune	mítune	mírune
dídi	díri	pít-e	pír-e
bódo	bóro	mát-i	már-i

Pronunciation Drill 5

mídune mírune	dídi díri	bódo bóro	bédun bérun
míde míre	dúd-e dúr-e	mád-e már-e	sæd-e sær-e
bæd-i bæri	dídæm dír-æm	bædesh bæresh	mídæme míræme

Pronunciation Drill 6

| mítune mírune | pít-e pír-e | mát-e már-e | khætesh khæresh | tút-e túr-e |
| tát-e tár-e | zatí zarí | bétune bérune | tutí turí | tutiá turiá |

2.2 Vocabulary

Vocabulary for Section 2.3 (Greetings, Cultural Materials)

lotfæn tekrár konid لطفا تکرار کنید

khoda	God
khodá ha<u>fez</u>. (full form 1)	Good-bye	(May <u>God</u> be your <u>Protector</u>.)
kho<u>dá</u>fez. (short form 1)	Good-bye	
khodá ha<u>féz</u>-e shoma. (full form 2)	Good-bye	(May <u>God</u> be <u>your</u> <u>Protector</u>.)
kho<u>dá</u>fez shoma. (short form 2)	Good-bye	

Lesson Two MODERN PERSIAN درس دوم

Note: The short forms listed here are the forms usually heard in normal colloquial speech. The full forms are recitation forms and tend to sound stilted in everyday usage. The form 2's listed above are frequently, though not necessarily, used as answers to form 1's.

Vocabulary for Dialogue 2

chi	what	mídune	he, she knows
inglisi	English	bǽle	yes
bæradǽretun	your brother	daneshgah¹	university
farsi	Persian	míkhune	he, she studies

Note:

1. Pronunciation of the Final /h/: In normal speech, the consonant /h/ is usually elided at the end of a word, after both consonants and vowels. Thus, the word for "university" is regularly pronounced /daneshga/. (See 4.1, 7.1, and 8.1 below.)

Vocabulary for Drills Part 1

khahær	sister	espanioli	Spanish
fizik	physics	rusi	Russian
shimi	chemistry	ærӕbi	Arabic
		chini	Chinese

Place Names (not all necessarily used in drills)

Stress marks are used here as a reminder to place stress on the final syllable.

moskó	Moscow	rom	Rome
megzík	Mexico	beyrút	Beirut
emriká/amriká	America	æmmán	Amman
parís	Paris	lændæn	London

Lesson Two   *MODERN PERSIAN*   درس دوم

| muníkh | Munich | ankará | Ankara |

Vocabulary for Section 2.8, Situational and Practical Drills: Classroom Expressions

dorost	correct, right	yævash	slow, slowly
do<u>rós</u>t-e?	Is it correct? Is it right?	tond	quick, quickly, fast
do<u>rós</u>t-e.	It's correct. It's right.	mæn	I
dorost <u>nist</u>.	It's not right. It's not correct.	shoma	you[1]
khub <u>nist</u>.	It's not right. It's not correct.	ki	who
moshgel	difficult, hard	be farsi	in Persian[2]
mosh<u>gél</u>-e?	Is it hard/difficult?	be inglisi	in English[2]
mosh<u>gél</u>-e.	It is hard/difficult.	khodafezí konìd	say good-bye
moshgel <u>nist</u>.	It's not hard/difficult.	(command form)	
asun	easy	hǽrf bèzænid	speak
a<u>sún</u>-e?	Is it easy?		
a<u>sún</u>-e.	It's easy.	æz SSS béporsid	ask SSS
asun <u>nist</u>.	It's not easy.	mæn míporsæm	I ask, I'll ask
næ.	no.	jæváb mìde	he/she answers,
<u>né</u>midunæm	I don't know.		will answer

Notes:

1. shoma indicates you plural or polite singular, as vous in French.

2. dær farsi, dær inglisi, etc. are not correct in the sense of an adverb, i.e. "I'll say it in Persian," etc. This phrase would only be correct in the sense of location: "there are six vowels in Persian," i.e., in the Persian language, etc.

Numerals through Ten

yek	one	shish	six
do	two	hæft	seven
se	three	hæsht	eight

Lesson Two MODERN PERSIAN درس دوم

| char | four | no(h) | nine |
| pænj | five | dæ(h) | ten |

Vocabulary for Drills Part II

tæmrín mìkone	he, she practices	mædrese	school
gitar	guitar	khabgah	dormitory
piano	piano (stress: pianó)	khune	house; at home,
biolozhi (zistshinasi)	biology₁	hærf mìzæne	he, she speaks

2.3 Cultural Materials: Greetings

2.3.1 Variations on Greetings

lotfæn gúsh konìd: لطفا گوش کنید:

sælam. hál-e shoma chetór-e?

mérsi. khub-e. hál-e shoma chetór-e?

mérsi. bæd nist.

sælam. hál-e shoma khub-e? (new form with question intonation)

mérsi. hál-e shoma chetór-e?

mérsi. khub-e.

sælam. hál-e shoma. (Note: no question intonation)

mérsi. hál-e shoma chetór-e?

motshækér-æm. khub-e.

sælam. hál-e shoma. hál-e shoma khub-e?

mérsi. khub-e. hál-e shoma chetór-e?

mérsi. motshækér-æm.

43

Lesson Two MODERN PERSIAN درس دوم

sælam. hál-e shoma chetór-e? hál-e shoma khub-e?

mérsi. motshækér-æm. hál-e shoma chetór-e?

motshækér-æm. khub-e.

lotfæn tekrár konìd (repeat the above patterns) لطفا تکرار کنید

2.3.2 Good-bye

lotfæn tekrár konid: لطفا تکرار کنید:

| S1: | khodáfez. | S1: | khodáfez. |
| S2: | khodáfez. | S2: | khodáfez-e shoma. |

Note: Watch your intonation in saying /khodáfez/. Americans tend to use the same intonation here that they use for the English "Bye, now," which, of course, sounds similar to the Persian question intonation. Listen to your teacher's model and get used to saying this expression with a falling intonation, just like the statement intonation.

2.4 Dialogue 2

The following is a continuation of the dialogue begun in Lesson 1 (1.4). The two parts should be learned as a continuous unit.

lotfæn gúsh konìd: (complete dialogue: Dialogue 1 and Dialogue 2) لطفا گوش کنید:

George:	bæradæræm dær iran zendegí mìkone.
Hasan:	rást mìgid? unja chekár mìkone?
George:	dær shiraz dærs mìde.
Hasan:	chi dærs mìde?
George:	inglisi.
Hasan:	bæradæretun farsi mídune?
George:	bæle. dær daneshgah farsi míkhune.

dobare gúsh konìd: (Dialogues 1 and 2 are repeated.) دوباره گوش کنید:

Lesson Two   MODERN PERSIAN   درس دوم

lotfæn gúsh konìd: (Note intonation patterns.)   :لطفا گوش کنید

Hasan:	\chi/ \dærs mìde?	What does he teach?
George:	\ingli/ \si/ \i./	English.
Hasan:	bæradæretun far/ \si/ \mídune?	Does your brother know Persian?
George:	\bæ/ \le./ dær daneshgah farsi \mí/ \khune.	Yes, he studies Persian at the university.

Note: "bæle" is both formal and informal. "are" is very informal.

Persian Question Intonation

     Persian question intonation was introduced in Lesson 1 (section 1.5). You also learned (Notes, section 1.3.1) that questions with question words in Persian take statement intonation. Also turn to Pronunciation Drill 9 of this lesson for a review drill of question intonation. Compare the examples and their intonations in Persian and English. Note the punctuation used for each type of sentence in the Persian transcription. The examples given below are presented in the following order:

a. statement   **b. question with question word**   **c. question without question word**

    a. dær daneshgah farsi míkhune.   a. khúb-e.

    b. bæradæretun chi dærs mìde?   b. hál-e shoma chetór-e?

    c. bæradæretun farsi mídune?   c. hál-e shoma khúb-e?

2.5 Phonology: /r/

The Persian /r/ is different from the English /r/. Listen to the following list of words:

| færanse | dær | dar | roman | hærf | shiraz | dærs mìde |
| bord | særv | shir | rish | ræsht | rusi | bæradær |

The letter /r/, which is somewhat similar to the Spanish simple "r," especially between vowels, is made by a short flap of the tongue against the alveolar ridge (gum ridge) behind the front

45

Lesson Two *MODERN PERSIAN* درس دوم

teeth. Do not confuse this sound with the English "l" or "d." The /r/ becomes shorter before consonants and is often voiceless at the end of a word.

Pronunciation Drill 7

    dir   dur   rus   rast   bóro   rish   ræng

    ruh   bord   dar   hærf   særv   dærs   nærm

(Be careful not to change the quality of the vowel before or after /r/)

Pronunciation Drill 8:(/æ/ and /a/before /r/)

    dær dar   tær tar   sar sær   bær bar   mar mær

Pronunciation Drill 9: Review of question intonation. Convert the following statements to questions:

    dústæm dær iran zendegí mìkone.   khahæræm rusi míkhune.

    bæradæræm farsi míkhune.   pærvin dar emrika dærs mìde.

    pedæræm fizik míkhune.   dústæm dær shiraz zendegí mìkone.

    æli dær daneshgah zendegí mìkone.   pedæretun æræbi mídune.

Remember that question intonation is not normally used with sentences with question words. Note the intonation on the following sentences:

    pedæretun chekár mìkone?   khahæretun chi míkhune?

    bæradæretun chi dærs mìde?

2.6 Drills: Part I

Drill 1: Substitution

    bæradæræm farsi míkhune.

    (cues: rusi, fizik, æræbi, espanioli, inglisi, (farsi))

Lesson Two　　　*MODERN PERSIAN*　　　درس دوم

Drill 2: Substitution

    a. <u>bǽradǽræm</u> fizik míkhune.

       (cues: pedær, khahær, bæradær, dust, khahær, madær, (bæradær))

    b. Make up sentences according to this pattern, substituting two nouns of your choice.

       S1: <u>bæradǽræm farsi</u> míkhune. **S2**: <u>pedæræm espanioli</u> míkhune.

       (possible substitutions: pedær, khahær, bæradær, dust, madær — fizik, æræbi, rusi, espanioli, shimi)

Drill 3: Substitution

    a. <u>bǽradǽretun</u> farsi mídune?

       (cues: madær, bæradær, dust, khahær, pedær, (bæradær))

    b. Ask questions of each other according to this pattern. If the answer is affirmative, the answer should be a full sentence. If it is in the negative, the answer may simply be /næ/ "no" or /némidunæm/ "I don't know."

       S1: <u>bæradǽretun</u> farsi mídune? **S2**: bæle. <u>bæradǽræm</u> farsi mídune.

                or: **S2**: næ.

(Note the change in the attached possessive pronoun in this and the next few drills.)

Drill 4: Substitution

    dær <u>daneshgah</u> farsi mìkhune.

    (cues: tehran, esfæhan, amrika, iran, (daneshgah))

Drill 5: Substitution

    bæradǽræm dær <u>daneshgah farsi</u> míkhune.

    (cues: amrika/inglisi, nio york/fizik, æmman/æræbi, iran/farsi, tehran/shimi, mosko/rusi, megzik/espanioli, shiraz/inglisi, (daneshgah/farsi))

Lesson Two   *MODERN PERSIAN*   درس دوم

Drill 6: Cued Question/Answer

(Note the change in the attached possessive pronoun in the next two drills):

    S1:   khahǽretun chekár mìkone?   S2:   khahǽræm <u>inglisi</u> dærs mìde.

    (cues: farsi, shimi, rusi, fizik, æræbi, (inglisi))

Drill 7 Cued Question/Answer

(Continue the pattern of Drill 6, substituting nouns and verbs of your own choosing.

    S1:   <u>khahær</u>etun chekár mìkone?   S2:   <u>khahæræm dær daneshgah farsi míkhune</u>.

    S1:   <u>dúst</u>etun chekár mìkone?   S2:   <u>dústæm dær daneshgah chini dærs mìde</u>.

2.8 Situational and Practical Drills

Cultural Materials: Classroom Expressions

Drill 8 Exercises

    a.   **lotfæn gúsh konìd:**   لطفا گوش کنید:

    mæn <u>mí</u>porsæm. shoma jæ<u>váb</u> bèdid. (shoma lotfæn jæ<u>váb</u> bèdid.)

    mæn <u>mí</u>porsæm. ki jæ<u>váb</u> mìde?

    S1, lotfæn æz <u>S2</u> béporsid. S2, lotfæn æz S1 béporsid.

    S1, mæn æz shoma <u>mí</u>porsæm. shoma lotfæn æz S2 béporsid. (*shoma* here means one person)

    mæn æz shoma <u>mí</u>porsæm. ki jæ<u>váb</u> mìde? (*shoma* here means you, plural, i.e., the whole class)

    lotfæn fa<u>rsi</u> hærf bèzænid. (Please speak <u>Persian</u>.)

    lotfæn be fa<u>rsi</u> jæváb bèdid. (Please answer <u>in Persian</u>.)

    lotfæn khodafe<u>zí</u> konìd. lotfæn be farsi khodafezí konìd.

    <u>khú</u>b-e? bǽle. <u>khú</u>b-e.

    do<u>rós</u>t-e? b<u>ǽ</u>le. do<u>rós</u>t-e.

    do<u>rós</u>t-e? næ. dorost <u>nist.</u>

Lesson Two   *MODERN PERSIAN*   درس دوم

    moshgél-e? bǽle. moshgél-e.

    moshgél-e? næ. moshgel <u>nist</u>.

    a<u>sú</u>n-e? bǽle. a<u>sú</u>n-e.

    a<u>sú</u>n-e? næ. asun <u>nist</u>.

    dorόst-e? <u>né</u>midunæm

b. **lotfæn jæváb bèdid**:   لطفا جواب بدید:

    The above sentences of section a are drilled

c. **lotfæn tekrár konìd**:   لطفا تکرار کنید:

    The above sentences of section a are repeated, and you should respond to the teacher's /yǽ:ni chi?/.

Drill 9 Numerals One through Ten

lotfæn tekrár konìd: لطفا تکرار کنید:

yek   do   se   char   pænj   shish   hæft   hæsht   no(h)   dæ(h)

2.9 Reading Persian: The Alphabet (*ælefba*)

The shape ح is used for four letters in Persian: ج چ ح خ

                               connected/unconnected

Sound	Name	Final	Medial	Initial
/j/	jim	ج‍ /ج	‍ج‍	ج‍
/ch/	che	چ‍ /چ	‍چ‍	چ‍
/h/	he	ح‍ /ح	‍ح‍	ح‍
/kh/	khe	خ‍ /خ	‍خ‍	خ‍

49

Lesson Two *MODERN PERSIAN* درس دوم

2.9.1 Reading Exercise 1: Spell and read aloud.

باجی	باج	جیم	جار	جا
چین	چاچی	ماچ	چار	چا
حین	حاج	حاجی	حار	حا
خار	خیم	خاچی	خاچ	خا
خان	جاجیم	چاخان	جا	خانان
بیچیز	بیجان	بیخار	ریح	راح
جیمی	چینی	خامات	روحی	ریخو
میچین	چین	میچینیم	میچینید	میچینی
میخیزی	میخیزی	میخیز	خیز	میخیزیم

2.9.2 Silent و

In a few words و is silent after خ. In these words the combination خو is pronounced as though it was simply خ /kh/ as in خواب /khab/ "sleep" and خوار /khar/ "vile, base." Words containing a silent و are always followed by ا, with one exception, the word خویش /khish/ "one's own (classical/poetic)." Such words cannot be distinguished by pronunciation alone from words spelled without the silent و — such as خاب /khab/ "rejected," خار /khar/ "thorn," and خیش /khish/ "plowshare." Words that are spelled with silent و are few but common. They follow no particular pattern and must simply be memorized. There are no other silent letters in Persian. You may also think of او as a form of ا that occurs in the following words.

Reading Exercise 2: Spell and read aloud.

خاب	خواب	خار	خوار
خان	خوان	خیش	خویش

Lesson Two MODERN PERSIAN درس دوم

2.9.3 Syllabification

Syllables in Persian follow one of the following patterns: 1. a single vowel (V), 2. a vowel followed by a consonant (VC), 3. a vowel followed by two consonants (VCC), 4. a consonant followed by a single vowel (CV), 5. a consonant followed by a vowel and a second consonant (CVC), 6. a consonant followed by a vowel and a cluster of two consonants (CVCC).

Examples:

1. vowel (V)	آ
2. vowel + consonant (VC)	آش
3. vowel + consonant cluster (VCC)	ایست
4. consonant + vowel (CV)	را
5. consonant + vowel + consonant (CVC)	راد
6. consonant + vowel + consonant cluster (CVCC)	داشت

Words of more than one syllable are made up of combinations of these patterns.

Examples:

CV-CV	ماما
CV-CVC	رادار
CV-CVCC	میداشت

Note that while a syllable in Persian may end in two consonants, and rarely in three, no Persian syllable can begin with more than a single consonant. When Persian borrows a word that begins with a consonant cluster, except in the case of Iranians who speak the source language as well as Persian, it must alter its pronunciation to suit Persian phonology. English "plastic" and "student," for example, become "pelastik" and "estudent." That is, a vowel either is inserted between the two initial consonants (*pelastik, perinston ,boros* "brush") or is added at the beginning (*estudent, espageti*) to break up the cluster. The usual pattern is that an /e/-vowel is added before an initial /s/ (and sometimes /sh/), but a vowel (/e/, or sometimes /o/) is inserted after the first consonant in all other cases. With the addition of this extra vowel, a

new syllable is created and the Persian patterns of syllabification are preserved: pe-las-tik; es-tu-dent. The rule that no syllable may begin with a consonant cluster also means that the initial consonants of a **syllable** are always divided by a vowel wherever they occur in the word. The word دوستی /dustí/ "friendship" will be divided into syllables in Persian as دوس-تی /dus-ti/ not /du-sti/ as might be possible in English. Similarly داشتیم /dashtim/ "we had" will be divided داش-تیم /dash-tim/ not /da-shtim/. Thus in foreign words with initial clusters in internal syllables, there is often an alternation depending on how the syllables are divided. That is, "telegraph" can be divided "tele-graph" or "teleg-raph," yielding Persian *te-le-ge-raf* or *te-leg-raf*. When three consonants come together, as in "ostralia," divided either "os-tralia" or "ost-ralia," the result is *osteralia* or *ostralia*. When more than three consonants come together, as in "Einstein" (*aynshtayn* — the y-glide is also a consonant), it will be divided *ayn-shtayn* yielding: *ayn-eshtayn*.

Reading Exercise 3: Read aloud.

A. CVCC

چیست	دوست	داشت	راست
خواست	ساخت	سوخت	ریخت
راند	خواند	ماند	بیخت

B. CVC-CV

داشتی	ریختی	دوستی	بیختی
راندی	ماندی	خواندی	ساختی

C. CVC-CVC

چارچوب	سوسمار	شاخدار	روحدار
راندید	ریختیم	ساختیم	سوختید

D. CV-CVC-CVC

میراندیم	میداشتیم	میخواندیم	میساختیم
میراندید	میداشتید	میخواندید	میساختید

Lesson Two　　　　　　　　　　*MODERN PERSIAN*　　　　　　درس دوم

Reading Exercise 4, Review:

حاجی	چاخان	جانان	بیچیز	ریخو
خویش	خان	خوار	ریح	روحدار
میخیزیم	میساختیم	چینی	بیخار	سوسمار
داشت	سوخت	بیخت	باشید	پاشید
میداشت	میذاشت	میخواند	میبیخت	دوستدار

Reading Exercise 5: Transcription

Transcribe from Persian to phonetic characters and from phonetic characters to Persian. This work is to be done as homework but may also be read (Persian to phonetics) or written (phonetics to Persian) on the blackboard or in pairs/small groups. Other words that conform to the rules learned so far may be given spontaneously in class.

Persian to Phonetics　　　　　　　　　　**Phonetics to Persian**

آبادی =>	abadi	misabi =>	میسابی
بیچیز	میخواندید	in	sukht
خوار	پاشید	an	haji baba
سوختیم	دوستدار	khan	carcub
بیجا	بیجان	hin	dashtim
چینی	خامات	cakhan	mikhizi

2.10 Drills: Part II

Drill 10: Cued Question/Answer

(Note the change in the attached possessive pronoun in this and the next few drills.)

　　a. **S1:** bæradæretun koja zendegí mìkone?　**S2:** bæradæræm dær <u>tehran</u> zendegí mìkone. (cues: esfæhan, iran, khabgah, amrika, (tehran))

　　b. **S1:** khahæretun koja farsi míkhune?　**S2:** khahæræm dær <u>tehran</u> farsi mìkhune. (cues: shiraz, vashængton, mæshhæd, iran, mædrese, daneshgah, (tehran))

Lesson Two   *MODERN PERSIAN*   درس دوم

Drill 11: Cued Question/Answer

S1: <u>bæradǽretun</u> koja zendegí mìkone?   **S2:** <u>bæradǽræm</u> dær <u>tehran</u> zendegí mìkone.

(khahær, emrika)

S1: khahǽretun koja zendegí mìkone?   **S2:** khahǽræm dær <u>emrika</u> zendegí mìkone.

(cues: pedær/iran, dust/æmman, bæradær/nio york, khahær/lændæn, madær/mosko,

dust/ankara, (bæradær/tehran))

(Continue asking questions according to this pattern, using nouns of your own choice.)

Drill 12: Cued Question/Answer

S1: <u>bæradǽretun</u> koja dærs mìde?   **S2:** <u>bæradǽræm</u> dær tehran dærs mìde.

S1: unja chi dærs mìde?   **S2:** <u>inglisi</u> dærs mìde.

(cues: khahær/farsi, dust/biolozhi, pedær/shimi, bæradær/æræbi, madær/fizik,

dust/farsi,(bæradær/inglisi))

Drill 13: Cued Question/Answer

S1: <u>bæradǽretun</u> <u>farsi</u> mídune?   **S2:** bæle. bæradǽræm <u>farsi</u> mídune.

(cues: dust/rusi, khahær/inglisi, pedær/æræbi, madær/espanioli, (bæradær/farsi))

(Continue asking questions according to this pattern, using nouns of your own choice.)

Drill 14: Substitution

dústetun farsi <u>mídune</u>?

(cues: dærs mìde, míkhune, hærf mìzæne, tæmrín mìkone, (mídune))

Drill 15: Substitution

dær <u>daneshgah</u> farsi <u>míkhune</u>.

(cues: khune/dærs mìde, tehran/tæmrín mìkone, mædrese/dærs mìde,

khabgah/míkhune, esfæhan/hærf mìzæne, mædrese/míkhune, khune/tæmrín mìkone)

Lesson Two   *MODERN PERSIAN*   درس دوم

Drill 16: Cued Question/Answer

    S1:   khahǽretun chi <u>míkhune</u>?

    S2:   khahǽræm <u>farsi</u> míkhune.

    (cues: dærs mìde/fizik, tæmrín mìkone/gitar, hærf mìzæne/inglisi, míkhune/shimi,

    tæmrín mìkone/piano, (mìkhune/farsi))

Continue asking questions according to this pattern, using nouns of your own choice.

Drill 17: Question/Answer

    Answer the following questions with complete sentences. If the answer is negative, simply answer /næ/ "no" or /némidunæm/ "I don't know." Names of students in the class should be used where SSS is indicated:

pedǽretun koja zendegí mìkone?	unja chekár mìkone?
SSS koja farsi míkhune?	SSS koja zendegí mìkone? unja farsi tæmrín
mìkone? dústetun farsi mídune?	<u>mædrese</u> yæ:ni chi?
<u>daneshgah</u> yæ:ni chi?	<u>hæft</u> yæ:ni chi?
ki espanioli mídune?	SSS koja farsi tæmrín mìkone?
khahǽretun inglisi míkhune?	koja?
ki farsi hærf mìzæne?	SSS dær khabgah zendegí mìkone?
<u>yævashtær</u> yæ:ni chi? (to S2: doróst-e?)	
<u>pænj</u> yæ:ni chi?	SSS inglisi míkhune?
koja?	SSS farsi dærs mìde?
koja dærs mìde?	ki æræbi míkhune? koja æræbi míkhune?
ki gitar tæmrín mìkone?	lotfæn be SSS sælám konìd.
<u>jæváb bèdid</u> yæ:ni chi?	<u>tælæffoz</u> yæ:ni chi?
<u>noh</u> yæ:ni chi?	SSS biolozhi míkhune? (doróst-e?)

Lesson Two   *MODERN PERSIAN*   درس دوم

2.11 Grammar Discussion: Verbs

Thus far in Lessons 1 and 2 you have seen the following verbs in the present tense and /or in the command form (imperative):

Present		**Command/Imperative**	
		tekrár konìd	repeat!
		tælæffóz konìd	pronounce!
		gúsh konìd	listen!
		sælám konìd	greet, say hello!
		khodafezí konìd	say good bye!
tæmrín mìkone	practices	tæmrín konìd!	practice!
zendegí mìkone	live		
chekár mìkone	what does X do?		
jæváb mìde	answers	jæváb bèdid	answer!
dærs mìde	teaches		
hærf mìzæne	speaks	hærf bèzænid	speak!
rást mìgid?/rást mìgin?	really*		
mígæm	I say	bégid	say!
míporse	he/she asks	béporsid	ask!
mídune	he/she knows		
míkhune	he/she studies		
khahésh mìkonæm	please (literally: I plead, beg, implore)		

* (literally "Do you <u>say</u> the truth?")

We will analyze the following grammatical points in these verbs:

1. Simple vs. Compound Verbs

Verbs that consist of one word are called simple verbs. Those verbs that consist of two words are called compound verbs and function grammatically as a single verb unit:

Lesson Two   *MODERN PERSIAN*   درس دوم

Simple Verbs	**Compound Verbs**
mídune	zendegí mìkone
mígæm	dǽrs mìde
béporsid	hǽrf mìzæne
	tekrár mìkone
	jæváb bèdid

Compound verbs usually consist of a noun or noun-like element (the compounding element) and a purely verbal form as the second element. Although the two elements are separate words and at times behave grammatically as separate entities, **they are a single lexical and syntactic unit**. That is, together they have a meaning that is different from the meanings of the separate words — /dærs/ "lesson," /mìde/ "he/she gives," but /dærs mìde/, "he/she teaches." There is an analogous pattern in English. The verb "to pay" means one thing by itself and another in the compound "to pay attention." In Persian, as in this English example, the meaning of the compound is determined by the compounding element, not the verbal. The Persian compound verb occupies the same position in the sentence as the simple verb.

2. Present Tense

    a.   **form** — The present tense of all verbs listed above has the prefix /mi-/. This prefix is always attached to the verbal element — /mídune/, /dærs mìde/. Primary stress normally falls on the first syllable of a verb. (See /be-/, next point below.) In simple verbs the prefix /mi-/ always receives primary stress — /mídune/, /míkhune/, /mígæm/. In compound verbs primary stress is placed on the appropriate syllable of the compounding element — /dǽrs/, /tæmrín/, /zendegí/ — and the verbal prefix /mì-/ receives secondary stress.

Simple Verbs	**Compound Verbs**
mídune	dǽrs mìde
mígæm	hǽrf mìzæne

Lesson Two *MODERN PERSIAN* درس دوم

        míkhune   zendegí mìkone

Further information on the rules for stress will be given in Lesson 3.

  b.   **meaning** — The present tense form has more than one usage:

- It may indicate a <u>habitual</u> <u>action</u> or an action done on a regular, usually repetitive, basis:

    /jan dær khabgah farsi tæmrín mìkone./ "John practices Persian in the dorm."

- <u>Future</u> <u>time</u> may also be indicated by the present tense. (Although there is a formal future tense in Persian, it is used only occasionally in colloquial speech.):

    /mæn tælæffóz mìkonæm, shoma tekrár konìd./ "I'll pronounce (it), you repeat."

- The present tense can sometimes have, though **not on a regular basis**, a <u>present</u> <u>progressive</u> (continuous, on-going) meaning: /farsi míkhune/ "He is studying Persian."

    (There is a special verb form to indicate the present progressive, which will be introduced in Lesson 11.)

- The present tense is used to describe states as well as actions:

            mídune   "he/she knows"

            zendegí mìkone   "he/she lives"

3. Command Form (Imperative)

You have encountered two types of command forms — one with a verbal prefix /bé-/ and one without this prefix, which we call a "zero" prefix and designate with a barred zero (Ø).

bé-	**Ø**
béporsid	gúsh konìd
bégid	tælæffóz konìd
hærf bèzænid	tekrár konìd

Lesson Two MODERN PERSIAN درس دوم

        jæváb bèdid   khodafezí konìd

The imperative is formed from the present tense of the verbs you know by the following rules:

    a.   If the verb is a compound verb in which the second element is /míkonæm/, drop the /mí-/ and change the /-æm/ to /-id/.

                tæmrín mìkonæm   tæmrín konìd

    b.   For the other verbs you have learned, both simple and compound, change the /mi-/ to /be-/ and the /-æm/ to /-id/.

mígæm	bégid
dǽrs mìdæm	dǽrs bèdid
mikhoræm	bekhor
minvisæm	benvis
minvisid (in)	benvisid (in)
mibinæm	bebin
mibinid (in)	bebinid (in)

Note that the stress on the /bé-/ follows the same rules as for /mí-/: it is primary in simple verbs and secondary in compound verbs. Further discussion of the imperatives can be found in section 5.11.7 and complete rules for their formation are given in Lesson 11 (sections 11.2 and 11.3).

4. Person

Unlike English, the Persian verb includes the person of the subject in the verbal suffixes. The present suffix /-e/ indicates the third person singular ("he/she/it').

        khahǽræm mídune   "My sister knows."

        mídune   "(He/She/It) knows."

The second person plural ending of the verb is the same in both the present indicative and the imperative. So far you have encountered it only in the imperative /-id/ — (bégid, hærf bèzænid, tekrár konìd, etc.). In the present tense the personal suffix is the same (*mígid* "you

Lesson Two *MODERN PERSIAN* درس دوم

say," *hǽrf mìzænid* "you speak," *tekrár mìkonid* "you repeat," etc.). This second person plural ending and the accompanying pronoun, *shoma,* "you," can mean either formal/polite (singular or plural) or plural familiar. There is an alternate form of this ending that predominates in colloquial Persian — /-in/. The two forms may be used in both the present tense and the imperative:

> hǽrf mìzænid or hærf mìzænin   "you speak"
> hǽrf bèzænid or hærf bèzænin   "speak!"

The /-id/ ending is slightly more formal than the /-in/, although they are often used interchangeably or concurrently in speech, depending on the individual and the social situation. We have tried to give some sense of how these constraints operate in the dialogues to follow. We have also used the /-id/ for the first classroom commands we taught since an additional degree of formality seemed appropriate there. It would not be right to think of the /-id/ ending as the formal one, and the /-in/ as the informal, however, since the degree of overlap between them is large and not altogether predictable. Some Iranians will insist that /-in/ is the **only** colloquial form and that /-id/ is used only in the written language, but in fact if you observe people's normal speech, especially in polite situations, you will find both /-in/ and /-id/ in conversation. The safest rule is to follow the example of your teacher — especially what your teacher actually **does**, rather what he/she says he/she does.

The full conjugation of the present tense of simple and compound verbs is given below, together with a listing of personal endings alone.

Simple Verb	**Compound Verb**
mídunæm	hærf mìzænæm
míduni	hærf mìzæni
mídune	hærf mìzæne
mídunim	hærf mìzænim
mídunin/mídunid	hærf mìzænin/hærf mìzænid
mídunænd/mídunæn	hærf mìzænænd/hærf mìzænæn

Lesson Two   *MODERN PERSIAN*   درس دوم

man farsi hǽrf mizænæm.	ma farsi hǽrf mizænim.
to farsi hǽrf mizæni.	shoma farsi hǽrf mizænid.
u farsi hǽrf mizæne	una farsi hǽrf mizænæn.

The verb suffixes ("personal endings") separately:

-æm	first person, singular
-i	second person, singular (familiar form)
-e	third person, singular
-im	first person, plural
-in/-id	second person, plural (formal singular)
-ænd/æn	third person, plural

As you have noticed, the third person plural ending has two forms: /-ænd/ and /-æn/. The alternation between these two endings is similar to that of /-id/ and /-in/. /-ænd/ is slightly more formal than the /-æn/, and many people will insist that only /-æn/ is used in colloquial Persian. But in fact both endings are heard in speech all the time, depending on the individual and the social situation. Again, follow the example of your teacher.

Personal pronouns

mæn	(I)		ma	(we)
to [shoma in formal]	(you)		shoma	you (plural)
u	(he/she/it)		una [anha]	they
mæn farsi hærf mizænæm.			ma farsi hærf mizænim.	
to farsi hærf mizæni.			shoma farsi hærf mizænid.	
u farsi hærf mizæne			una farsi hærf mizænæn.	

5. Separate Subject

Although verbs include a personal ending, separate or overt subjects are used as required by the context or the intention of the speaker. The difference between Persian and English here is that English always requires an overt subject, and Persian often does not. That is, "speaks" and "teaches" cannot stand alone in English, but /hærf mìzæne/ and /dærs mìde/

Lesson Two   *MODERN PERSIAN*   درس دوم

may be considered complete grammatical utterances in Persian. Usually the overt subject is omitted when the context is already established and the subject has already been mentioned in the conversation:

• khahǽretun farsi hǽrf mìzæne?	"Does <u>your sister</u> speak Persian?"
• bǽle. khub hǽrf mìzæne.	"Yes, <u>she</u> speak<u>s</u> it well."
• koja zendegí mìkone?	"Where does <u>she</u> live?"
• dær iran zendegí mìkone.	"<u>She</u> live<u>s</u> in Iran."
• unja chekár mìkone?	"What does <u>she</u> do there?"
• shimi dǽrs mìde.	"<u>She</u> teach<u>es</u> chemistry."
• khahǽretun inglisi mídune?	"Does <u>your sister</u> know English?"
• bǽle. mídune.	"Yes, <u>she</u> does."

You will note that in most of the sentences after the introductory question, the subject is not explicitly repeated. Of course, it could be if the speaker so chooses. In the course of a long conversation about the same subject, the subject noun or pronoun will be overtly expressed from time to time for essentially stylistic reasons, as it is in the last question above (/khahǽretun farsi mídun-e/). This rule about the optional nature of an explicit subject holds true for all persons of the verb:

• <u>shoma</u> farsi mídun<u>in</u>?	"Do <u>you</u> know Persian?"
• bǽle. farsi mídun<u>æm</u>.	"Yes. <u>I</u> know Persian."
• inglisi dǽrs mìd<u>in</u>? "	"Do <u>you</u> teach English?"
• næ. shimi dǽrs mìd<u>æm</u>.	"No, <u>I</u> teach chemistry."
• farsi mídun<u>in</u>?	"Do <u>you</u> know Persian?"
• bǽle. mídun<u>æm</u>.	"Yes, <u>I</u> do."

Languages in general have mechanisms for omitting words that have already been mentioned in any given discourse. What they omit and how they do it varies a good deal. It is interesting to note that in Persian the overt subject is deleted but the verb is retained whereas in English, the opposite is true. The overt subject is required while the verb is deleted and

Lesson Two MODERN PERSIAN درس دوم

replaced by the auxiliary verb "do."

- farsi mídun<u>in</u>? "Do <u>you</u> know Persian?"
- bǽle. mídun<u>æm</u>. "Yes, <u>I</u> do."

(subject deleted, verb retained) (subject obligatory, verb replaced)

The use of the other persons of the verb are drilled in Lessons 3 and 4.

6. Present Root of the Verb

All Persian verbs have two stems. By convention these are known as the present root and the past root because one is used in forming the present tense and the other the past. The terms are misleading. Both stems have a number of functions beyond the formation of these two tenses. Moreover, neither is associated exclusively with past or present time. The "past" root, for example, is used to form the formal future tense and the infinitive, and the "present" root is the basis of the imperative and the subjunctive. Both can function at times as nouns, and so on. We will follow the established convention in this textbook, however we urge you to keep in mind that the terms "past" and "present" here are simply terms of convenience. What is important is that you learn both stems of each new verb, and learn them as a pair.

Present tense and present root — To derive the present root of verbs you have already learned, subtract the prefixes and suffixes we have discussed in this grammar lesson and the form that is left is the present root. In the case of compound verbs, the present root consists of two elements:

	Present Tense/Command Form	**Present Root**
Simple Verbs	mí-dun-e "he, she, it knows"	-dun-
	bé-pors-id "ask"	-pors-
Compound Verbs	dærs mì-d-e	dærs -d-
	hærf mì-zæn-e	hærf -zæn-
	hærf bè-zæn-id	
	gúsh kon-ìd	gush -kon-

The past stems for all verbs you have learned through Lesson 3 will be presented at the

63

Lesson Two   *MODERN PERSIAN*   درس دوم

end of that lesson and beginning with Lesson 4 all verbs will be introduced in the glossary of each lesson in the present tense and past root forms. Again, you will be expected to memorize the present and past stems of all verbs from that point throughout the textbook.

7. Present Tense and Command Form of Verbs in Lessons 1 and 2

With the knowledge of the stems and affixes (i.e. prefixes and suffixes) of Persian verbs, we may fill in the present tenses, command forms and present stems of all verbs presented in the beginning of this discussion:

	Present Tense	**Command Form**	**Present Stem**
Compound	tekrár mìkone	tekrár konìd	tekrar -kon-
	tælæffóz mìkone	tælæffóz konìd	tælæffoz -kon-
	gúsh mìkone	gúsh konìd	gúsh -kon-
	sælám mìkone	sælám konìd	sælám -kon-
	khodafezí mìkone	khodafezí konìd	khodafezi -kon-
	tæmrín mìkone	tæmrín konìd	tæmrin -kon-
	zendegí mìkone	zendegí konìd	zendegi -kon-
	chekár mìkone	(no command form)	chekar -kon-
	khahésh mìkonæm	*	khahesh -kon-
	dærs mìde	dærs bèdid	dærs -d-
	jæváb mìde	jæváb bèdid	jæváb -d-
	hærf mìzæne	hærf bèzænid	hærf -zæn-
Simple	míporse	béporsid	-pors-
	míge	bégid	-g-
	rást mìgid	*	rast -g-
	mídune	*	-dun-
	míkhune	békhunid	-khun-

* These forms are rarely used.

Lesson Two　　　　　MODERN PERSIAN　　　　　درس دوم

2.15　Phonology Review: lotfæn tekrár konìd:　　　لطفا تکرار کنید:

mikh	kakh	sheykh	shukh	dokhtær	mokh	ækhtær
nækhab	bókhorid	khers	khan	sakhtæn	khish	khis
khiar	khianæt	hend	hænuz	rækht	nækhæridæm	hæva
hush	khosh	hich	haj	khaj	khænde	hendi
hæd	khæt	nokhud	nahid	nækh	nækhshe	khaviar
bækhshesh	rish	reshte	rial	rivas	rædif	reza
ræsht	roshd	rokh	ræsm	ru	rænj	rud
rok	dir	sær	shur	mar	tar	nilufær
sir	shir	bíarid	bébærid	æræbi	barun	bord
chærm	gorz	gorbe	chærkh	pært	arayeshgah	khud

Lesson Three   درس سوم

TOPICS COVERED IN THIS LESSON

- Conversation: What languages do you know? Do you speak Spanish? Yes, I do / No, I speak English. Does your friend know Persian? No, she speaks Arabic and English. How do you say _____? What does _____ mean? Do you work? Yes, I do/No, I don't.

- More Questions about Family: Where does your husband work? Does your wife know English?

- Addressing People. More Iranian First and Last Names.

- Politeness: Excuse me/I'm Sorry. Offering Food/Handing Objects. After You. The Polite Way to Handle a Compliment. You're Welcome

RESOURCES AND BACKGROUND: INFORMATION AND ACCURACY

- Basic Islamic Expressions Used in Context of Politeness.
- Starting to Explain or Define Words in Persian.

Listening Materials

    Narrative Passage

Phonology

    Phonemic vs. Phonetic

    Palatal Variants of /k/ and /g/

    Intonation Accompanying Forms of Address

    The Persian /q/

Grammar Patterns to Be Drilled

    Verbs

First Person Singular:	*mæn mídunæm*
Second Person Plural:	*shoma mídunin*
Negative Form of the Verb:	*némidunæm*

Lesson Three   *MODERN PERSIAN*   درس سوم

    Past Roots

Other

    "and"

Sentence Patterns

    (subject) + (object) + adverb-manner + verb

    optional alternative: (subject) + adverb-manner + object + verb

Vocabulary Building

    Words of Western Origin in Persian

Reading and Writing Persian

    The letters ه - ع - ف - ق - گ - ک - ل

Grammar Discussion

    Word and Sentence Stress

    The Pronouns of Persian

    Formal and Familiar Pronouns of the Second Person

    Past Roots of Verbs

Cultural Materials

    Forms of Address

    Taarof

    Classroom Expressions

    The Persian Language

Lesson Three   *MODERN PERSIAN*   درس سوم

3.1 Phonology Preface: Phonemic vs. Phonetic

Thus far in our discussion of Persian phonology and the contrast of English and Persian pronunciation, we have been referring to vowels or consonants simply as "sounds." Actually the consonants and vowels in our transcription — /p/, /sh/, /æ/, /a/, etc. — are more precisely termed "phonemes." If you exchange one phoneme for another in a language, you normally will have a different word. For example, if we change the /æ/ in English "sack" to /a/, we have the word "sock"; if we change the /k/ of "sack" to /g/ we will have "sag." Persian /næm/ "damp" is distinct from /nam/ "name" because /a/ and /æ/, as you have seen, are different phonemes.

A phoneme, therefore, is a sound that native speakers of a language perceive as an independent sound. Each phoneme is distinct from every other phoneme in the language.

Some phonemes in a language, however, are not always pronounced identically in every word. A phoneme can have its own variants, depending on how the sounds next to it affect it. This type of alternation in pronunciation, however, does not produce a change in the word or its meaning, because the variant pronunciations are still parts, in a sense, of the same phoneme. They are variations on the same entity.

We have already introduced examples of how certain sounds are affected by the sounds that surround them. For example, you have seen how the English "a" is slightly different in the two words "cat" vs. "man." In Lesson 1 (1.1 and 1.2) you learned that the difference involves a glide (or diphthongization) in the word "man" but not in "cat." We told you that this glide shows up in English usually before /m/ and /n/ and for most speakers of American English also before /b/, /d/, /g/, /s/, /f/, and /sh/ as in "sat" vs. "sad" or "match" vs. "mash." The use of one or the other sound depends on the following consonant. Functionally speaking, in English these are two variants of one and the same phoneme. In fact, most native speakers of English never notice the difference in these two variants until they are confronted with learning a foreign language where the same variants do not occur. As we mentioned in Lesson 1 (1.2), if you transfer the English variants to Persian, you will not be making a real mistake in

Lesson Three　　　　　　　　*MODERN PERSIAN*　　　　　　　درس سوم

communication but will simply appear to have a foreign accent.

This type of variation is called *subphonemic* or *phonetic* variation. That is, under the influence of surrounding sounds, a phoneme in a language may change — sometimes quite a bit — but these variants are still perceived as the same sound.

Let us show you another example in English before we go on to the Persian example for this lesson. The American English /t/ changes drastically in <u>normal</u> speech in the following words:

<u>t</u>op; bu<u>tt</u>on or moun<u>t</u>ain; Be<u>tt</u>y or Ri<u>t</u>a; <u>t</u>ree or <u>t</u>rue; ca<u>t</u>

One of these variant sounds, the /t/ of "Betty" was already discussed and contrasted with Persian in Lesson 2 (2.1.2).

We will not discuss all these phonetic variants of /t/ in detail. We simply ask that you pronounce the above words with /t/ in a normal, everyday fashion and to pay attention to your pronunciation. In fact, if you contrast your normal unselfconscious pronunciation of these words with a careful, clearly enunciated style, you will notice that the differences between the two sets are all in the pronunciation of the /t/. Can you hear the difference? Have you perceived that the /t/ in careful speech may sound almost the same in each word but sounds drastically different when pronounced in the usual conversational manner? Have you noticed that you were never aware of these drastic changes and that all the "different" /t/'s above were actually perceived as the same?

Have you also noticed that people learning English as a second language often have trouble with the phonetic variants of /t/ and may prefer to pronounce them all the same? Their pronunciation of these words is completely intelligible but by not using the variants the way an American does their foreign accent is easily detected.

Henceforth phonemes in Persian will be presented between slashes (/æ/), and phonetic or subphonemic variants will be presented between square brackets ([ ]). Words presented in standard orthography will be placed between double quotes.

Lesson Three   *MODERN PERSIAN*   درس سوم

So far we have asked you either to learn Persian phonemes that are new to you, such as /kh/, or to notice the phonetic variations in your English speech in order not to transfer them automatically to Persian, as in English "man" vs. Persian /mæn/. In this lesson, we introduce a Persian subphonemic variation in the phonemes /k/ and /g/. Remember, because the following is a Persian subphonemic variation, a native speaker of Persian will not perceive the variant sounds as different sounds and will probably not even be aware that they are varying the pronunciation from one word to another.

3.1.1 Phonology: Variants of /k/ and /g/

The sounds /k/ and /g/ in both Persian and English are produced when the tongue contacts the back part of the soft palate. In both languages, as well, the /k/ and the /g/ phonemes have phonetic variants that are affected by the vowel following them. If you sound out the difference in "cool" and "keep," you will discover that /k/ is made farther back in the mouth if it precedes /u/ and farther forward if it precedes /i/.

The Persian /k/ is also made in a relatively fronted position before the Persian vowels /i/, /e/, and /æ/ and is made farther back in the mouth before /u/, /o/, and /a/. There is, however, an additional difference between these two variations of the Persian /k/. The front part of the tongue is slightly raised toward the hard palate while saying /k/ before /i/, /e/, and /æ/. This raising of the tongue tip results in what sounds like an additional "y" sound between /k/ and the vowels, as in the English sequence "cue" (/kyuw/). This phenomenon is called "palatalization" and is represented by a superscript "y":

/kæm/   [k^{y}æm]   "a little"

Since these palatal variants are subphonemic, the failure to palatalize /k/ and /g/ before front vowels will not make your Persian unintelligible, but it will mark your accent as foreign. Listen to the following words that contrast the two variations of /k/ in Persian:

| kæm | kam | kæf | kaf | kesh | kosh | kamran |
| ketab | kotob | ki | ku | kise | kuse | kashan |

Lesson Three   *MODERN PERSIAN*   درس سوم

The Persian /k/ that occurs at the end of a syllable is also automatically palatalized:

pak   tæk   læk   nik   lik   khuk

The same kind of variation is true of the Persian /g/. The /g/ is always palatalized before /i/, /e/, and /æ/ and at the end of a syllable. The /gy/ sequence in the English word "Montague" /mántəgyuw/ or "figure" is similar to the Persian palatalized /g/.

Pronunciation Drill 1

kæm kam   kæf kaf   kesh kosh   ketab kotob   ki ku   kise kuse

Pronunciation Drill 2

gæz gaz   gær gar   gæv gav   gel gol   gerd gord   giah guya   gir gur

Pronunciation Drill 3

pak   tæk   læk   nik   lik   khuk

sæg   ræg   dig   rig   ræng   bærg

3.1.2 Cultural Materials and Phonology: Forms of Address and Intonation Used When *Addressing People*

aqa   sir; mister

khanum/khanum   madam; Miss, Mrs. (Ms.); wife

(/khanum/ is used in ordinary speech, and /khanum/ in more formal or deferential contexts.)

The polite forms of address, /aqa/ and /khanum/, occur far more frequently in Persian than in English. They are used alone to call someone's attention or to refer to someone whose name the speaker does not know, as equivalents of English, "Oh, Sir/Madam/Miss!" or "What does this gentleman/lady want?" They are also used in combination with the last name, as follows:

Lesson Three   *MODERN PERSIAN*   درس سوم

aqá-ye shærifi	Mr. Sharifi
khanúm-e shærifi	Ms. Sharifi
khanóm-e shærifi	Ms. Sharifi

The normal stress for these words is on the last syllable, as it is for all personal names in Persian. However, when they are used like Mr. or Ms./Mrs. with a family name, they lose that stress and are pronounced as part of the name:

\kha/ \nú/ \úm   \khanúm-e shæri/ \fí/ \í

The form a name takes when used to address a person directly is indicated in Persian by a shift in stress and intonation to the first syllable of the form of address used. This holds true for names, the forms of address introduced above, or a combination of the two. Note also that in addressing someone, the intonation used is the question intonation rather than statement intonation:

Form Used When:

Speaking about Someone			**Addressing Someone**	
\jæm/	**\shí/**	\íd/	**\jæm/**	\shid/
\pær/	**\ví/**	\ín/	**\pær/**	\vin/
\kha/	**\nú/**	\úm/	**\khá/**	\num/

or slightly more deferentially:

\kha/	**\nó/**	\óm/	**\khá/**	\nom/
\khanóm-e shæri/	**\fí/**	\í /	**\khá/**	\nom-e shærifi/
\ a /	**\qá/**	\á/	**\á/**	\qa/
\aqá-ye shæri/	**\fí/**	\í/	**\á/**	\qa-ye shærifi/

Lesson Three   *MODERN PERSIAN*   درس سوم

3.2 Vocabulary

Dialogue 3

shoma	you	máshallah	Wonderful! Good
æz	from		for you! (see 3.3)
æz koja	how, how come	khéyli	very
	(literally, from where)	khub	well, good
mídunin	you know	kha(h)ésh mìkonæm	please (see also 3.3
mídunæm	I know		and Dialogue 3)
inja	here	hænuz	still, yet
míkhunæm	I study	kæm ([kʸæm])	little, not very
aqa	sir, Mr.; gentleman		much [1]
khanum/	ma'am, madame, Ms. Mrs.; lady		
khanom			

Drills Parts I and II

færanse	French (language); France	nækhér/nækhéyr	no (polite)
almani	German	hala	now
zhaponi	Japanese	bébækhshid	"Excuse me!"
-o/væ [2]	and	torki	Turkish and/or
shohær	husband		Azerbaijani
yád mìgiræm	I learn	mífæhmæm	I understand
aqa	sir; mister	kár mìkonæm	I work
khanum	ma'am, madame, Ms. Mrs.;	ziad [3]	very, much, a lot;
khanom	wife,		too, too much (see
			also section 3.1.2)

Vocabulary, Situational and Practical Drills

bolænd	loud
bolændtær	louder

73

Lesson Three   *MODERN PERSIAN*   درس سوم

mæsælæn	for example
yævash (2)	quiet, quietly, softly
behtær	better
soal	question
jævab	answer, reply
bishtær	more; mostly, for the most part
____ chi míshe?	How do you say ___?
	(literally: "What does __ become?")
"book" be farsi chi míshe?	How do you say "book" in Persian?
"book" be farsi míshe /ketab/.	"Book" is *ketab* in Persian.
ketab	book
ketabáro bébændid.	close your (the) books.
áfærin/afærín	excellent, bravo! (a word of praise)

Iranian First Names (remember, stress falls on the last syllable)

fereshte	woman's name (literally: angel)
kamran	man's name (literally: one who achieves his desires)

Iranian Last Names (remember, stress falls on the last syllable)

shærifi	from *sharif* "noble" (Arabic)
shirazi (esfæhani, tehrani, tæbrizi, yæzdi, khomeini, ræfsænjani, etc.)	from/native to Shiraz: Family names are often formed by adding an /í/ to the names of cities, towns and villages, such as Esfahan, Tehran, Tabriz, Yazd, Khomein, Rafsanjan, etc.

There is a full discussion of Iranian names in Lesson 7 (7.12).

Lesson Three   *MODERN PERSIAN*   درس سوم

Vocabulary Notes

1. *kæm* The word *kæm* means "little" in the sense of "not very much," not in the sense of "small." It is not an adjective. It is generally an adverb. *mæn farsi kæm hærf mìzænæm* means "I speak (very) little Persian/I don't speak much Persian." *kæm* can also be an adverb of time, in which case it means "seldom." The above sentence can also mean "I seldom speak Persian."

2. *-o/-vo/væ* The conjunction "and" has three pronunciations, /-o/, /-vo/, and /væ/. The first appears most commonly. It only occurs when joined to the preceding word and cannot be pronounced alone or begin a phrase (/mǽno shoma/, /æræbío farsi/ — see drill 17 of this lesson). After vowels (except /i/) the /-o/ for many speakers becomes /-vo/ (/tæmrín mìkonevo dærs mìkhune/, /tæmrín mìkoneo dærs mìkhune/ — see drill 18 of this lesson). /væ/ occurs only when the conjunction begins a phrase or clause — *væ shoma chi míkhunin?* "And what do you study?" *væ hǽsæn?* "And Hasan?" Even though /væ/ is heard in speech, it is not the preferred form and you should not get in the habit of using it on a regular basis. It is more literary than colloquial.

3. *ziad* means both "very much" and "too much"; these meanings are often not distinguished in Persian. For this reason, Iranians learning English frequently use "too" when they only intend to express the idea of "a lot, very much." Thus, "I liked that movie too much" — meaning that he/she liked it very much — or "You study too much" — meaning only that you study a great deal.

Cultural Material

Taarof

   Taarof (/tæ:arof/) is the general term for the Iranian conception of politeness and social grace. *Taarof* is pervasive in Iranian culture, and hard to describe outside of it. It covers a wide variety of social situations, both formal and informal, and sometimes is as much a matter of gesture as of language. *Taarof* consists of the polite phrases that are appropriate to a wide variety of specific situations, but it includes actions as well, such as offering guests food and

Lesson Three   MODERN PERSIAN   درس سوم

drink however short their visit, standing up as a sign of respect when someone enters a room, or, when a friend or guest has admired something in your home, offering it to them as a gift. As a part of deferential behavior, it even includes body posture, such as standing or sitting in an attitude of deference in the presence of someone who is older or your senior in some other respect.

Perhaps the best way to understand this very complex and important term is through consideration of particular phrases special to *taarof* and the situations in which they are used. We have chosen several illustrations to describe here. Your teacher will be able to provide you with many others.

befærmaid- befærmain

befærmain, literally means "Command it!" The message it gives, however, might be better rendered into English by "Please" followed by the appropriate verb — "Please help yourself," "Please sit down," "Please come in," "Please have another," and so on. It is an invitation to express or do what is pleasing and appropriate in virtually any situation. It is the most common and useful of the many terms special to *taarof*. For example *befærmain* is said in the following situations:

1. When offering someone food or drink that has been placed on the table. In this situation, *befærmain* is roughly equivalent to the English "Help yourself" but is usually said several times, along with other phrases, to coax guests out of their shyness and self-restraint. Shyness and reticence in these situations are in a way part of the behavior associated with *taarof* and people, even if they are hungry will usually not take food offered to them the first or second time. Iranians, therefore, often find Americans crass or socially ungraceful for their "dig right in" directness when food is offered to them.

2. When you open the door to guests who have arrived, *befærmain* is said to invite them into your house.

3. When giving someone whatever he or she has requested — a pen, the salt shaker, an

Lesson Three   *MODERN PERSIAN*   درس سوم

object off a shelf or out of a display case — *befærmain* is the term used where we might say "Here you are."

4.   *befærmain* is said as a rough equivalent of "after you" when people arrive simultaneously at a doorway. It is often repeated several times. But the question of who precedes whom through a door is a touchy one, and it will not be settled by the simple repetition of this one phrase. It is generally understood that ultimately those who are more respected, dignified, and worthy should go first. In the case of strangers or people who are not peers, social position, age, or respect will decide who will pass through the doorway first. In the case of peers or friends, polite persistence or physical strength will win out, and in this case the winner is the one who goes last!

5.   If someone addresses you by name to ask a question or request, *befærmain* expresses your readiness to listen and respond.

To repeat, *befærmain* is the polite form of virtually any request: "sit down," "stand up," "enter," "speak," "wait," "have some more," "go right ahead." The list is, quite literally, endless.

kha(h)ésh mìkonæm

This phrase means literally, "I request, I plead," but it translates best as "Please," "You're welcome," or "Please don't mention it" as a polite disclaimer:

1.   As you can see in Dialogue 3 below, when a compliment is made it usually is not merely acknowledged with a "thank you" as in English, but is answered with some phrase that implies polite disagreement with the speaker's high opinion. In the dialogue this disagreement is made explicit — *kha(h)esh mikonæm. hænuz khéyli kæm mídunæm* — however, in many cases a simple *kha(h)ésh mìkonæm* would be enough. In short, it is considered polite to refute a compliment whereas saying "thank you" means you accept it, tantamount to saying, "Yes, you are right. I am wonderful."

Lesson Three   MODERN PERSIAN   درس سوم

2. kha(h)ésh mìkonæm and *lotfæn* are the most common ways to say "Please":

> kha(h)ésh mìkonæm tekrár konìd.
>
> lotfæn tekrár konìd.
>
> kha(h)ésh mìkonæm yævashtær hærf bèzænid.
>
> lotfæn yævashtær hærf bèzænid.
>
> kha(h)ésh mìkonæm ketabátuno bébændid.
>
> otfæn ketabátuno bébændid.

3. In a related usage, *kha(h)ésh mìkonæm* is the most common way to say "You're welcome." Many other languages — Russian and Italian to mention two — also use the same word for "Please" and "You're welcome." Thus, of the sequence "Please--Thank you--You're welcome," the first and the last elements are both expressed in Persian by *kha(h)ésh mìkonæm*:

kha(h)ésh mìkonæm tekrár konìd.	"Please repeat (it)."
mérsi.	"Thanks."
kha(h)ésh mìkonæm.	"You're welcome."

4. *kha(h)ésh mìkonæm* may also be used in place of or in combination with *befærmaid* as a simple reinforcement of its meaning.

> befærmaid. khah<u>ésh</u> mìkonæm.
>
> khahésh mìkonæm be<u>fær</u>maid.
>
> (note the difference in intonation)

The combination of these two phrases is especially commonly used when offering someone food or drink or when asking them to make themselves comfortable.

énshallah, máshallah, ælhæmdollah

Three expressions that function as part of Persian *taarof* and are pious in origin but have also come to be used in everyday speech with only slightly religious connotation are:

1. *énshallah* "If God wills." This expression must be used when referring to any future action, on the assumption that nothing will or can occur without His approval. Depending on

the tone of the speaker, it can express pious hope, profound skepticism, or anything in between. This expression is the usual equivalent of English "I hope (so)."

2.   *máshallah* "What God wills." This expression was originally used to ward off the evil eye. It was said, and is still used, when praising a person or thing of value, beauty, or excellence, in the belief that whatever God has willed into being is protected by Him and should not occasion envy. From this, it has come to be used as an general expression of wonder and approval as well, equivalent of something like "Bravo!" "Good for you!"

3.   *ælhæmdolellah* or *ælhæmdolla* "Praise (be) to God." This is a pious phrase inserted after an expression of well-being ("I am well, praise God") and has come to abbreviate the whole phrase. A perfectly acceptable response to *hál-e shoma chetór-e?* is simply, *ælhæmdolellah*. It is also used on occasions when an American might say, "Thank God!" "Thank Heaven!"

3.4 Dialogue 3

(In this new format the vocabulary for each dialogue sentence is given first and should be introduced before the sentence is given.)

shoma	you
æz	from
æz koja	from where (here: how, how come)
mídunin	you know

Hasan: \shoma æz koja far/ \si/ \mídunin?   How do you know Persian?
(literally: where do you know Persian from?)

mæn	I
inja	here
míkhunæm	I study

George: \mæn inja farsi/ \mí/ \khunæm./   I study Persian here.

Lesson Three MODERN PERSIAN درس سوم

	máshallah	(term of approval, see 3.3)
	khéyli	very
	khub	well, good
Hasan:	\má/ \shallah./ \khéy/ \li khub hærf mìzænin.	Marvelous! You speak it very well.
	kha(h)ésh mìkonæm	please (response to a compliment)
	hænuz	still, yet
	kæm	little
	mídunæm	I know
George:	khal **(h)ésh** mìkonæm.	Oh no, I still know very little.
	hænuzl **khéy** l li kæm mídunæm.	

dobare gúsh konìd دوباره گوش کنید

Hasan:	shoma æz koja far<u>si</u> mídunin?
George:	mæn inja farsi <u>mí</u>khunæm.
Hasan:	<u>má</u>shallah! <u>khéy</u>li khub hærf mìzænin.
George:	kha(<u>h</u>)ésh mìkonæm. hænuz <u>khéy</u>li kæm mídunæm.

3.5 Phonology: /q/

Phonetic Information on /q/:

The Persian sound /q/ is pronounced by making a "g"-like sound, but with the farthest part back of the tongue in contact with the uvula. If you are familiar with Arabic pronunciation, you should know that, unlike Arabic, /qaf/ and /qeyn/ fall together in standard Iranian Persian as /q/. This sound is a voiced stop (not voiceless as in most forms of Arabic).

The /q/ is regularly pronounced as a stop only in initial position. There is a different pronunciation to the /q/ sound when it occurs between vowels or before certain consonants. In these positions, it is pronounced as a voiced fricative (as /qeyn/ in Arabic), not as a stop. This sound is the voiced equivalent of /kh/ and should not be confused with it.

Lesson Three   *MODERN PERSIAN*   درس سوم

A **stop** sound is one that is held for a brief instant and released and cannot be continued once released. Voiceless stops in Persian and English are /p/, /t/, and /k/ (see separate discussion of "the glottal stop"); voiced stops are /b/, /d/, /g/, and Persian /q/. A **fricative** is a sound that is created by forcing air through a very narrow area in the mouth; it also has continued articulation (as opposed to a stop, which does not). The voiceless fricatives of Persian are /f/, /s/, /sh/, and /kh/; the voiced fricatives of Persian are /v/, /z/, /zh/, /h/, and, in the phonetic positions mentioned below, [q];

Listen to the following words with both variants of /q/:

The Stop Variant of /q/:

    qaf   qaz   qænd   qævi   qol   qom   qu   qir   qebres

The Fricative Variant of /q/:

    aqa   oqat   roqæn   hæqiqi   tæqdim   eqbal   eqdam   baqban   tæqyir

Drills with the Stop Variant of /q/:

Pronunciation Drill 4: /q/ - /g/ Contrast

    qol gol   qom gom   qaf gaf   qaz gaz   qar gar   qir gir   qu gu

Pronunciation Drill 5: /q/ - /k/ Contrast

    qol kol   qaf kaf   qar kar   qal kal   qu ku

Pronunciation Drill 6: /q/ - /kh/ Contrast

    qol khol   qar khar   qali khali   qu khu   qænd khænd

Pronunciation Drill 7

    qatel qafel qazi quri quz quti qesse qermez qorub

    qiafe qors qæt qeble qodræt qias qeyr qæmgin qæblæn

Lesson Three *MODERN PERSIAN* درس سوم

Drills with the Fricative Variant of /q/:

Pronunciation Drill 8

    aqa   oqat   tæqlid   roqæn   baqela   oqab   zoqal   hæqiqi   tæqdim

    siqe   eqbal   eqdam   baqban   tæqyir   soqati   næqme   tæqribæn   fæqir

Pronunciation Drill 9: Medial /q/ - /g/ Contrast

    bærqi bærgi   aqa aga(h)

Pronunciation Drill 10: Medial /q/ - /kh/ Contrast

    tæqribæn   tækhribæn   bærqi   bærkhi   tæqyir   tækhyir

Pronunciation Drill 11: Contrast of Stop and Fricative Variants of /q/:

    qati   soqati   qab oqab   gal zoqal   qænd roqæn   qe siqe   qir fæqir

When /q/ occurs at the end of a word, either pronunciation (stop or fricative) will be heard. Variation depends on the individual speaker, and some people use the stop and the fricative interchangeably in final position.

Pronunciation Drill 12

    otaq   ojaq   daq   sholuq   hoquq   tæriq   toroq

    sadeq

Note: For another important phonetic variation of /q/, see Lesson 4 (4.1).

Tongue Twisters

--qurío qænd qéyr-e qabél-e moqayes<u>æst</u>. "A teapot and a sugar lump are not comparable."

--<u>bé</u>bækhshin, khánom. ye qædri <u>qænd</u> míkham. "Excuse me, Ma'am, I'd like a little (lump of) sugar."

--bef<u>ær</u>main, aqa. qænd tu qænd<u>dún</u>-e "Help yourself, sir, the sugar is in the sugar bowl."

Lesson Three　　　　　*MODERN PERSIAN*　　　　　درس سوم

3.6　Drills: Part I

Drill 1: Imitation　(see Lesson 2, Section 2.11, Part 4, "Person" for discussion of -id/-in)

	a.		b.
	mæn hǽrf mìzænæm		shoma hǽrf mìzænin
	mæn mídunæm		shoma mídunin
	mæn tæmrín mìkonæm		shoma tæmrín mìkonin
	mæn mífæhmæm		shoma mífæhmid
	mæn yád mìgiræm		shoma yád mìgirin
	mæn míkhunæm		shoma míkhunin
	mæn míporsæm		shoma míporsid
	mæn kár mìkonæm		shoma kár mìkonid
	mæn mígæm		shoma mígin
	mæn chekár mìkonæm?		shoma chekár mìkonin?
	mæn tekrár mìkonæm		shoma tekrár mìkonid
	mæn jæváb mìdæm		shoma jæváb mìdin
	mæn gúsh mìkonæm		shoma gúsh mìkonin

Drill 2: Cued Question/Answer

　　S1:　shoma æz koja <u>farsi</u> mídunin?

　　S2:　mæn inja <u>farsi</u> míkhunæm.

　　(cues:　inglisi, torki, almani, espanioli, færanse, chini, æræbi, rusi, zhaponi, (farsi))

　　(alternatives to S1:　khánum-e SSS/áqa-ye SSS, shoma æz koja <u>farsi</u> mídunin?

　　　　　　　　　　áqa-ye SSS/khánum-e SSS, bébækhshid, shoma æz koja <u>farsi</u> mídunin?)

Lesson Three   *MODERN PERSIAN*   درس سوم

Drill 3: soálo jævab (= porsesh pasokh)

(For a negative answer, use *næ, nækheyr* or *némidunæm* "I don't know." Those sentences that are punctuated with periods are statements. They are compliments and are included here to elicit the response *khahesh mìkonæm*. See Lesson 3, Section 3.3.)

S1:

áqa, hál-e shoma chetór-e? hál-e shoma khub-e?

shoma koja zendegí mìkonin?

shoma kár mìkonin? (koja kár mìkonin?)

shoma inja chi yád mìgirin?

(shoma farsi khéyli khub hǽrf mìzænin.)

mæn farsi hǽrf mìzænæm?

koja farsi hǽrf mìzænæm?

S2:

shoma inja chekár mìkonin?

mæn farsi tond hǽrf mìzænæm?

(tælæffózetun khéyli khub-e. máshallah.)

shoma koja farsi tæmrín mìkonin?

(Iranian friend) farsi khub hærf mìzæne?

inglisi khub hǽrf mìzæne?

S3:

mæn koja zendegí mìkonæm?

mæn inja chekár mìkonæm?

mæn chi dǽrs mìdæm?

mæn æz shoma be farsi míporsæm?

farsi moshgél-e?

qaf moshgél-e?

tælæffózetun khub-e?

S4:

shoma piano yád mìgirin?

koja tæmrín mìkonin?

shoma inja chi míkhunin?

shoma koja farsi míkhunin?

mæn inja chi hǽrf mìzænæm?

Drill 4: Substitution

<u>shoma</u> farsi khub hǽrf mizænin. (shæhla)

<u>shæhla</u> farsi khub hǽrf mìzæn<u>e</u>.

(cues: shohǽræm, mæn, shoma, khahǽræm, shoma, æli, mæn, ki, shoma, dústæm, mæn, (shoma))

Lesson Three MODERN PERSIAN درس سوم

Drill 5 : Substitution

<u>mæn</u> dær <u>daneshgah</u> <u>inglisi</u> <u>míkhunæm</u>.
------------------emrika------------------------------------
---dǽrs mìdæm (yæ:ni chi?)
dústæm---
-----------------------------------espanioli--------------------
--yád mìgire---
------------------paris------------------------------------
---míkhune----
shoma--
----------------------------------almani---------------------
------------------khabgah-----------------------------------
------------------khune------------------------------------- (yæ:ni chi?)
--tæmrín mìkonin
-----------------------------------piano-----------------------
mæn--
------------------mædrese---------------------------------- (yæ:ni chi?)
-------------------------------inglisi-----------------------
---míkhunæm----
-----------------(daneshgah)-------------------------------

Drill 6 : soálo jævab (porsesh pasokh)

(For a negative answer, use *næ, nækheyr* or *némidunæm.*)

S2:

ki kár mìkone?

koja kár mìkonin?

S4:

khánum, bébækhshin, shoma inglisi mídunin?

Lesson Three　　　　　*MODERN PERSIAN*　　　　　درس سوم

mæn koja kár mìkonæm?　　　　　shoma inja chi míkhunin?

shoma farsi yád mìgirin?　　　　　shoma farsi dær khabgah tæmrín mìkonin?

shoma farsi tæmrín mìkonin?　　　　shoma almani hærf mìzænin?

S2, S1 koja farsi tæmrín mìkone?　　SSS farsi khub tælæffóz mìkone?

S2:　　　　　　　　　　　　　　**S4:**

khaháretun dær mædrese chi míkhune?　　ki farsi mídune?

bæradæretun fizik míkhune?　　　shoma farsi míkhunin?

madæretun rusi dærs mìde?　　　shoma æz koja farsi mídunin?

khanúmetun piano yád mìgire?

khaháretun færanse mídune?　　(Now continue asking questions of each other)

Daneshju

Drill 7: Question/Answer

In this drill the teacher asks a student a question about another student. The first student must then elicit the information from the second student and report it to the teacher. For example:

The teacher asks:　　　　　　　　"Jo Anne" farsi mídune?

The student addresses Jo Anne and asks:　　"Jo Anne," shoma farsi mídunin?

86

Lesson Three *MODERN PERSIAN* درس سوم

    She replies: bǽle. farsi mídunæm.

    The student then reports this to the teacher: bǽle. "Jo Anne" farsi mídune.

SSS farsi mídune?	SSS koja farsi míkhune?
SSS inglisi hǽrf mìzæne?	SSS inja chekár mìkone?
SSS koja farsi tæmrín mìkone?	SSS kár mìkone?
SSS færanse mídune?	SSS koja zendegí mìkone?
SSS dǽrs mìde?	SSS farsi yád mìgire?
SSS dær khune farsi tæmrín mìkone?	SSS koja kár mìkone?
SSS be farsi jæváb mìde?	SSS inglisi khub mífæhme?

Drill 8: Substitution

    shoma khéyli <u>tond</u> <u>hǽrf mìzænin</u>. (yævash/jæváb mìdin)

    shoma khéyli <u>yævash</u> <u>jæváb mìdin</u>.

(cues: kæm/kár mìkonin, bæd/tælæffóz mìkonin, ziad/tekrár mìkonin, kæm/yád mìgirin, bolænd/mígin, (tond/hǽrf mìzænin))

Drill 9: Substitution

    <u>shoma</u> <u>farsi</u> <u>khub</u> <u>hǽrf mìzænin</u>. (æræbi)

    shoma æræbi khub <u>hǽrf mìzænin</u>. (tælæffóz mìkonin)

    <u>shoma</u> æræbi khub tælæffóz mìkonin. (kamran)

    kamran æræbi <u>khub</u> tælæffóz mìkone. (bæd)

    kamran <u>æræbi</u> bæd tælæffóz mìkone.

(cues: torki, hǽrf mìzæne, mæn, yævash, shoma, bolænd, tond, fereshte, ziad, tæmrín mìkone, farsi, mæn, kæm, shoma, hǽrf mìzænin, dorost, pærvin, inglisi, tond, yád mìgire, færanse, khub, mífæhmæm, hǽrf mìzænæm, farsi, ziad, shoma, (khub))

Lesson Three MODERN PERSIAN درس سوم

Drill 10: soálo jævab

(Sentences that are punctuated with periods are statements. They are compliments and are included here to elicit the response *khahesh mìkonæm*. See Lesson 3, Section 3.3.)

shoma farsi khub hǽrf mìzænin?	shoma farsi ziad tæmrín mìkonin?
mæn farsi tond hǽrf mìzænæm?	ki farsi tond hǽrf mìzæne?
SSS dorost jæváb mìde?	shoma koja zendegí mìkonin?
mæn koja dǽrs mìdæm?	shoma farsi khub hǽrf mìzænin.
bæradǽretun kæm hǽrf mìzæne?	shoma ziad kár mìkonin.
SSS yævash farsi hǽrf mìzæne?	shohǽretun inglisi khub mídune?
áqa-ye SSS, shoma khub tælæffóz mìkonin.	mæn farsi ziad míporsæm?
khanúm-e SSS farsi khub mífæhme?	SSS farsi bolænd tekrár mìkone?

3.7 Review

At this stage of learning, you know how to say many things. You can talk about different people, actions those people do, and places where the actions occur. You know words for languages, some university courses, and skills. You also learned adverbs to describe actions and skills and adjectives to describe the quality of things. The following list is a brief reminder of some things you know how to say. Use this list to help you practice and to converse about the various things you know how to say. You will probably surprise yourself with how much you can actually say in only Lesson 3!

People Family members, husband, wife, friend, friends' names, Iranian first names (m, f), last names, Mr., Mrs., famous people

you, I, he/she; your, my

everyone

who

Places, Location university, school, dormitory, house/home

here, there

Lesson Three MODERN PERSIAN درس سوم

	Iranian, American, Canadian, European, Middle Eastern place names, where, in / at, from
Things to Practice, Study	chemistry, biology, physics, piano, guitar, pronunciation
Languages	German, Spanish, Persian, French, English, Russian, Turkish, Arabic, Japanese
Nouns	book, answer, question, what
Numbers from One to Ten	
Letters of the Alphabet	ælef, ælef mæædde, be, pe, te, se, jim, che, khe, he, dal, zal, re, ze, zhe, sin, shin, mim nun, vav, ye (so far)
Verbs	ask, answer, know, don't know, learn, listen, live, practice, pronounce, repeat, say, say good-bye, say hello, speak, study, teach, understand, do what, work, close the books
Adjectives/Adverbs	good/better/bad, a lot/more/little/very, loud/louder/quiet, fast/faster, slow/slower, difficult/easy, correct together, in Persian, again, now, still, yet, mostly, for example, really
Language Learning	How do you say X, what does that/it mean, it means X
Polite Expressions	excuse me, please, greetings and good-bye, áfærin, befærmaid, énshallah, máshallah, ælhæmdollah

3.8 Situational and Practical Drills

Drill 11   Classroom Expressions

a. gúsh konìd:

    lotfæn yævashtær hǽrf bèzænid.　　　　　yæ:ni chi?

    lotfæn bolændtær hǽrf bèzænid.　　　　　yæ:ni chi?

    lotfæn bishtær hǽrf bèzænid.　　　　　　yæ:ni chi?

    lotfæn tondtær hǽrf bèzænid.　　　　　　yæ:ni chi?

Lesson Three   *MODERN PERSIAN*   درس سوم

      lotfæn ketabáro bébændid.   yæ:ni chi?

      lotfæn behtær tælæffóz konìd.   yæ:ni chi?

b.   **jæváb bèdid:**

      <u>mæsælæn</u> be inglisi chi míshe?

      <u>bébækhshin</u> be inglisi chi míshe? (to another student: /dorόst-e?/)

      "question" be farsi chi míshe?

      "mister" be farsi chi míshe? (be espanioli chetor?)

Drill 12: Taarof (read Section 3.3)

    An object (book, pen) is passed around the room from student to student. As each student passes the object to the next person, he/she says *befærmain*. The one who receives it thanks him/her, and the first student responds with *kha(h)esh mìkonæm*. Alternatively, this exercise may be done in pairs:

S1:   befærmaid. (befærmain) (as he/she extends the object)

S2:   mérsi.

S1:   kha(h)ésh mìkonæm.

3.9   Reading Persian: The Alphabet (*ælefba*)

3.9.1 ک /kaf/, گ /gaf/, and ل /lam/

    The shape ک is used to represent two letters: *kaf*, which is the primary shape, and *gaf*, which is the primary shape with an additional bar: گ. A letter with an initial and medial shape similar to that of ک and گ is *lam* ل. It has no cross-bar ("hat"), however, and its curve in final position goes below the line of writing. The special ligature for ل (first) and ا (second) is the printed form لا, pronounced *la*.

90

Lesson Three *MODERN PERSIAN* درس سوم

Sound	Name	Connected Final	Unconnected Final	Medial	Initial
/k/	kaf	ک	ک	ک	ک
/g/	gaf	گ	گ	گ	گ
/l/	lam	ل	ل	ل	ل

Note: When ل (lower case L) is followed by ا (long a) we should have لا (La), however, many fonts as well as most handwriting styles will show this combination as لا and this is what you will see in this book.

Reading Exercise 1: Spell and read aloud.

کوشک	کوک	کاکا	کاش	کار
گوشت	دیگ	گاگا	گور	گار
کیلو	گیل	لیلی	لال	لیمو
خالکوب	خالی	حال	کال	خال
میخکوب	میکوبی	میگیری	گیری	گیر

3.9.2 ق /qaf/ and ف /fe/

These two letters are distinguished in initial and medial positions only by the number of dots they take. In final position, however, the curve of the *qaf* is deep like that of ن while that of *fe* is flat like that of ب.

Sound	Name	Connected Final	Unconnected Final	Medial	Initial
/f/	fe	ف	ف	ف	ف
/q/	qaf	ق	ق	ق	ق

Lesson Three   *MODERN PERSIAN*   درس سوم

Reading Exercise 2: Spell and read aloud.

فال	فیل	قال	قیل	ناف
قاف	فاق	بوف	کاف	گاف
روفت	بافت	کافور	فالگیر	فالگیری
قالی	آقا	قورت	فیلقوس	قیفال
قاپ	قاپید	میقاپید	میقاپیدی	میقاپیدید
بافتید	ریزباف	فیلم	فیلمساز	فیلمسازی

Reading Exercise 3: Review.

لاک	لیک	کیل	کیلو	گیل
گیلان	مالامال	آلمان	آلمانی	چالاک
میخکوب	خالکوب	خاکروب	فالگیر	لاستیک
آقا	قانون	آفاق	اوستاخ	قوچان
قاف	کاف	گاف	لام	جیم

3.9.3 The Glottal Stop. ع (glottal stop) and ه /he/

The pronunciations and functions of the glottal stop are described in Lesson 5 (5.1). There are two ways of representing the glottal stop in writing: either by the letter *eyn* ع or by the *hæmze*. See Lesson 5 (5.9.2) for the forms and functions of the *hæmze*.

Below we introduce only the *eyn* ع. Note that it is one of the letters that has two different shapes in the final position and distinctively different shapes in initial and medial position as well.

Duplicate /he/

The sole duplicate letter for the sound /h/ is ه. Both *he* letters —ه and ح— are quite different in appearance, but are pronounced exactly alike. There are several names that people use to help them distinguish which *he* they are referring to when needed. There is even

Lesson Three　　　　　　　　*MODERN PERSIAN*　　　　　　　درس سوم

a mnemonic occasionally used to remind people of the shape of these two letters:

Letter	"Nikname"	Meaning	Mnemonic
ح	he (-ye) jimî	The he shaped like a jim	
	he (-ye) bozorg	The big he	
	he (-ye) hæmmali	The he in hæmal "porter" curves like the back of a porter	
ـه	he (-ye) do cheshm	The he with two eyes	
	he (-ye) kuchik	The small he	
	he (-ye) hendune	The he in hendune "watermelon" looks like a watermelon	

he (-ye) do cheshm also has distinctively different shapes in medial and final positions but a single shape in initial position.

		Unconnected		Connected		
Sound	Name	Final	Final	Medial	Initial
/h/	he	ه	ـه	ـهـ	هـ
/:/	eyn	ع	ـع	ـعـ	عـ

Reading Exercise 4: Spell and read aloud.

عاد	عیسا	عود	ریع	جوع
عالی	شیمی	داعی	ساعی	میعاد
هات	هوش	هین	بیهوش	ایهام
پیه	دیه	آگاه	آگاهی	گاهگاه

Lesson Three   *MODERN PERSIAN*   درس سوم

Reading Exercise 5: Review.

میقاپید	خوابگاه	پیک نیک	حاجی	چاپی
شاهکار	ناپاک	میعاد	عادی	توپ بازی
داروها	آماق	آفاق	روحی	ناکام
ذال	قالی	کانادا	لامپ	شیمی

Reading Exercise 6: Transcription.

Transcribe between Persian and phonetic characters. This exercise is to be done as homework but may also be **read** (Persian to phonetics) or **written** (phonetics to Persian) on the blackboard or in pairs/small groups. Other words that conform to the rules learned so far may be given spontaneously in class.

Persian to Phonetic

کانادا	عود
داعی	بیهوش
آگاه	گاهگاه
شاهکار	پیک نیک
داروها	آفاق

Phonetic to Persian

kargah	lastik
kilu	kah
iham	lal
fars	míkubid
alman	kala

3.10 Drills, Part II

Drill 13: Imitation

míkhune	némikhune
míporsæm	némiporsæm
mígæm	némigæm
mífæhmin	némifæhmin
mídunin	némidunin
zendegí mìkone	zendegì némikone
hǽrf mìzænæm	hǽrf némizænæm

Lesson Three   *MODERN PERSIAN*   درس سوم

    gùsh mìkonæm   gùsh némikonæm

    yàd mìgirin   yàd némigirin

    kàr mìkone   kàr némikone

    jæváb mìdin   jævàb némidin

Drill 14: Transformation

(First repeat the cue, then transform it to the negative. For sentence stress, see Section 3.11.1, Level 4.)

    ex: æli færanse khub mídune. ==========> æli færanse khub némidune.

mæn dær iran zendegí mìkonæm.   dústæm dær khune gitar tæmrín mìkone.

mæn æræbi dærs mìdæm.   khahæretun inja kár mìkone.

jæmshid ziad tæmrín mìkone.   mæn farsi khub tælæffóz mìkonæm.

shohæræm torki mífæhme.   mæn dær khabgah zendegí mìkonæm.

shoma rusi hærf mìzænin.   pærvin færanse yád mìgire.

ki gúsh mìkone?   shoma yævash hærf mìzænin.

mæn bishtær míporsæm.   shahla behtær tælæffóz mìkone.

shoma dorost mígin.   shoma bolænd tekrár mìkonin.

Drill 15: soálo jævab

shoma færanse mífæhmin?   shahla khéyli khub tælæffóz mìkone?

mæn tond hærf mìzænæm?   (fereshte) inglisi khub tælæffóz mìkone?

shoma dær (abadan) kár mìkonin?   shoma dorost jæváb mìdin?

(aqá-ye shærifi) dær daneshgah dærs mìde?   SSS fizik míkhune?

shoma almani míkhunin?   mæn yævash hærf mìzænæm?

dústetun yævash kár mìkone?   (khanúm-e shirazi) dær mædrese dærs mìde?

Lesson Three *MODERN PERSIAN* درس سوم

mæn æz shoma ziad míporsæm?   (fereydun) inglisi bæd tælæffóz míkone?

shoma kár míkonin?   bébækhshid, aqa, shoma inja chekár míkonin?

SSS æræbi yád mìgire?   (to SSS: rást mìge?)

SSS farsi ziad tæmrín míkone?   (lotfæn æz SSS béporsid)

shoma espanioli mídunin?   <u>dust</u> mæsælæn be espanioli chi míshe?

inja rusi hǽrf mìzænæm?   mæn chi hærf mì zænæm?

<u>ketab</u> be inglisi chi míshe?   khéyli motæshækkér-æm.

bébækhshid, khanum, shoma inglisi mídunin?

(Now continue asking questions of your own.)

Drill 16: *Substitution*

<u>fereydun</u> inglisi khub <u>mídune</u>.

shoma

          (negative)   (shoma inglisi khub <u>némidunin</u>)

          hǽrf némizænin

mæn

          yàd némigiræm

          (affirmative)   (mæn inglisi khub <u>yád mìgiræm</u>)

ki

          dærs mìde

(cues: shoma, (negative), shohǽretun, hærf némizæne, mæn, némifæhmæm, shoma, (affirmative), dústæm, hærf mìzæne, fereydun, (mídune))

Lesson Three   *MODERN PERSIAN*   درس سوم

Drill 17: Substitution

Note: Words that end in /k/ or /g/ have the palatalized variants of these phonemes in final position (see Lesson 3, Section 3.1) but have the non-palatalized variant when the word is followed by /-o/, since /o/ is not a front vowel, i.e. fizik^j but (fizíko shimi).

   a.   pedǽræm fizíko <u>shimi</u> dærs mìde.

         (cues: zistshinasi, inglisi, farsi, (shimi))

   b.   khanúmæm <u>farsí</u>o inglisi hærf mìzæne.

         (cues: æræbi, rusi, torki, chini, almani, (farsi))

Drill 18: Imitation

(The /-o/ form of the conjunction "and" is attached directly to the word that precedes it. When the final sound of the word preceding "and" is a vowel other than /i/, a /v/ is frequently inserted in speech between the vowel and /o/ (/aqávo khanum/). (See Section 3.2 above, vocabulary note 2)

   a.   færanséo espanioli   færansévo espanioli

         aqáo khanum   aqávo khanum

         pianóo gitar   pianóvo gitar

   b.   soálo jævab   pedǽro madǽræm

         khúbo bæd   kío ki

         aqávo khanum   mǽno bæradǽræm

         chinío zhaponi   shomávo khahǽretun

         mǽno shoma   injávo unja

         ælío fereshte   kǽmo bish ("more or less")

         fereshtévo reza   radióvo televizion/radióo televizion

         sælámo khodáfez   televizióno sinema

         fizíko shimi   telefóno teleg(e)raf

         khahǽro bæradær   saládo deser

Lesson Three MODERN PERSIAN درس سوم

Drill 19: Substitution

    mæn <u>farsío æræbi</u> míkhunæm.

    (cues: shimi/biolozhi, inglisi/færanse, rusi/fizik, færanse/almani, (farsi/æræbi))

Drill 20: soálo jævab

(Those sentences that are punctuated with periods are statements. They are compliments and are included here to elicit /khahesh mìkonæm/. See section 3.3)

shoma fizik míkhunin?	"behtær" yæ:ni chi?
madǽretun espanioli mídune?	aqa, bébækhshid, pedǽretun koja zendegí mìkone?
shoma koja zendegí mìkonin?	shoma dær khabgah zendegí mìkonin?
"jævab" yæ:ni chi?	(máshallah tælæffózetun khéyli khub-e.)
dústetun farsi hǽrf mìzæne?	khéyli khub hǽrf mìzæne?
khahǽretun koja zendegí mìkone?	unja kár mìkone?
(máshallah khub hǽrf mìzænin.)	mæn taaróf mìkonæm?
shoma chini mídunin?	koja chini míkhunin?
khanúmetun farsi mídune?	khanúmetun koja farsi yád mìgire?
shoma farsi tæmrín mìkonin?	shoma koja farsi tæmrín mìkonin?
mæn hala rusi dǽrs mìdæm?	rusi mídunin?
shoma biolozhi míkhunin?	mæn inja chi dǽrs mìdæm?
shoma zhaponi mífæhmin?	shoma hala færanse yád mìgirin?
(shoma farsi khéyli khub mídunin.)	khahǽretun kár mìkone? koja?
inja ki gitar mízæne? khéyli khub mízænin?	khanum, bébækhshin. "still, yet" be farsi chi míshe?

Lesson Three MODERN PERSIAN درس سوم

The following questions require a more extended answer:

Teacher: bébækhshin, khanum, "ælhæmdolellah" yǽ:ni chi?

Student: mæsælæn mæn mígæm *hál-e shoma chetór-e?* væ shoma jæváb mìdin, *ælhæmdolellah.*

bébækhshin, aqa, "máshallah" yǽ:ni chi? mæsælæn...

khanum, bébækhshin "taarof" yǽ:ni chi? mæsælæn...

khanum, bébækhshin "befærmaid" yǽ:ni chi? mæsælæn...

3.11 Grammar Discussion

3.11.1 Word and Sentence Stress

As you have already seen in Lessons 1 through 3, there are two types of stress in Persian: <u>word stress</u> — indicated in this text by / ´/ for primary (main) stress and / `/ for secondary stress — and <u>sentence stress</u> — indicated by the underlining of the stressed syllable. There is a certain hierarchy as well as some general rules for determining or predicting where these stress types appear in any given word or sentence.

1. Word Stress: Nouns, Adjectives, etc.

The stress of most words in their basic forms, specifically words that are not conjugated forms of verbs, falls on the last syllable in Persian. For this reason, all words that take word-final stress are unmarked in this text (with certain exceptions, such as /pianó/, etc., as a reminder):

Nouns			**Adjectives**	**Adverbs**	**Other**
ketáb	inglisí	tehrán	bolænd	mæsælǽn	pænjáh
jæváb	khanúm	bærádær	bolændtær	lotfæn	ziád
soál	aqá	daneshgáh	yævásh	dobaré	sælám
pianó	taaróf	amriká	behtær	hænúz	shomá
radió	shærifí	mædresé	sinemá	jæmshíd	lændǽn

The stress does not fall on the last syllable in words other than verbs in the following

99

Lesson Three *MODERN PERSIAN* درس سوم

cases you have encountered:

A. When the last syllable is one of several types of ending added to the root.

1. The possessive endings attached to nouns do not take stress. When these are added, the stress remains on the last syllable of the base form:

    bæradǽr   bæradǽræm
               bæradǽretun
    dúst   dústæm
               dústetun

2. In nouns and adjectives to which the verb "to be" is attached, stress remains on the base form:

    doróst   khúb
    doróst-e   khúb-e   motshækér-æm

3. The form /-o/ of the word "and" is attached directly to the end of a word and does not take stress; the stress remains on the base form:

    mæno shomá   soálo jæváb   kæmo bish

Note: not all endings added to a root are unstressed as you have seen with the comparative form of adjective/adverbs:

    tónd tondtǽr   bolǽnd bolændtǽr

B.

1. Many interjections and certain adverbs and conjunctions of two or three syllables take the stress on the first syllable. Also the marginal verb form /yǽ:ni/ belongs in this category. These words must simply be memorized as they are encountered:

    bæle   khodáfez   khéyli
    nækheyr   énshallah   væli
    mérsi   máshallah   áfærin

100

The stress is on the fourth syllable from the end in the word /ælhæmdolellah/.

2. Some of these words have alternate emphatic forms with the stress on the final syllable:

        nækhéyr!   enshalláh!   afærín!

        mashalláh!   ælhæmdolelláh!

C. The stress shifts to the first syllable of personal names and titles when used in addressing someone (see Section 3.1.2 for a discussion of the intonation used when addressing people):

        féreydun   áqa   khánum-e shirazi

2. Simple Verbs

In verbs, particularly conjugated forms, the stress usually shifts forward in the word to any of various elements that occur before the verb root. Therefore in the examples of simple verbs encountered so far, the stress is on the first syllable of the verb:

        mídunæm   némige

        némidunæm   béporsid

        mífæhmin?   bégid

3. Compound Verbs

In the case of compound verbs the stress again shifts forward to the compounding element. Since compound verbs are technically two words, each word must have its own stress. Thus in compound verbs, the compounding element receives primary stress that follows the rules for nouns and adjectives and receives stress on the last syllable. The first prefix of the verbal element receives secondary stress. If these two words should be pronounced separately, i.e. not as a unit, each word will receive primary stress:

        jæváb   compounding element

        míde   verbal element

        jæváb mìde   compound verb

Lesson Three *MODERN PERSIAN* درس سوم

    jæváb   compounding element

    bédid   verbal element

    jæváb bèdid   compounding verb

In the case of compound verbs with the verbalizer /mìkone/ in which there is no prefix to indicate the command form, the secondary stress falls on the last syllable of the verbal element:

    tæmrín mìkone ———> tæmrín konìd

When compound verbs are in their negative forms, the negative prefix takes precedence over the compounding element. Primary stress is then on the negative prefix and secondary stress on the compounding element:

    jæváb mìde —————> jævàb némide

4. Sentence Stress

As is the case with single words, each sentence (or clause) has only one major stress. It occurs on one syllable in the sentence and is higher in pitch and intensity than the rest of the sentence and is an important factor in determining the intonation contour of a sentence. See Lesson 1 (Section1.5, the notes to Section 1.3.1, and the notes to Dialogue 2) for further discussions of sentence intonation. The stress of a sentence depends on the content or the context of conversation in which the sentence appears. The following general rules — as well as a hierarchy of rules — can be made for determining or predicting sentence stress:

Level 1

In the majority of sentences in a conversation or discourse, or in a single sentence in isolation, the sentence stress appears on the word just before the verb (simple or compound):

    shoma farsí mídunin?   shomá chí míkhunin?

    mæn dær tehrán zendegí mìkonæm.   mæn injá farsí yád mìgiræm.

In the word that takes sentence stress, the rules for word stress must be observed to determine which syllable in that word will receive the sentence stress. Thus, in a usual type of sentence as presented above, the stress will fall on the word before the verb but not necessarily

Lesson Three *MODERN PERSIAN* درس سوم

on the syllable before the verb:

word in isolation	**word with sentence stress**
tondtǽr	lotfǽn tondtǽr jæváb bèdid.
bæradǽretun	mæn æz bæradǽretun míporsæm.

Level 2

Context — In the context of conversation, the word that is the focus of an answer to a question receives the sentence stress. Thus if we take a sentence such as /mæn inja farsí míkhunæm/, it will have the expected sentence stress pattern when it is out of context. However, the stress in this sentence will definitely be determined by the context of what precedes it and will thus change. As an answer to three different questions, the stress on this same sentence may appear in three different places accordingly:

1. shoma inja chí míkhunin? — What are you studying here?
   mæn inja farsí míkhunæm. — I'm studying Persian here.

2. shoma æz koja farsi mídunin? — How do you know Persian?
   mæn inja farsi míkhunæm? — I'm studying Persian here.

3. shoma koja farsi míkhunin? — Where are you studying Persian?
   mæn injá farsi míkhunæm. — I'm studying Persian here.

Also in the context of conversation, that word that is in contrast with a previous sentence or clause receives the sentence stress:

1. shoma dær khabgah farsí tæmrín mìkonin?
   næ. dær azmayeshgáh farsi tæmrín mìkonæm. (special emphasis on place)

2. shoma inglisi tónd hærf mìzænin væli farsi yævásh hærf mìzænin.
   (emphasis on adverbs instead of /hærf/)

Level 3

/khéyli/ usually takes sentence stress wherever it occurs in a sentence:

shoma khéyli khub farsi hærf mìzænin.

Note the change in stress in the expansion of the following basic sentence:

103

Lesson Three MODERN PERSIAN درس سوم

shoma farsí hærf mìzænin.

shoma khúb farsí hærf mìzænin.

shoma khéyli khúb farsí hærf mìzænin.

Level 4

The negative prefix of the verb not only takes highest precedence in the rules of word stress but sentence stress also <u>almost</u> <u>always</u> falls on the negative particle:

mæn farsí <u>né</u>midunæm.

shomá dær daneshgáh farsí <u>né</u>mikhunin.

The negative particle usually takes precedence over all other words that normally take sentence stress:

shomá <u>kæm</u> farsí tæmrín mìkonin.

shomá kæm farsí tæmrìn <u>né</u>mikonin.

shomá <u>khéyli</u> khúb farsí hærf mìzænin.

shomá khéyli khub farsí hærf <u>né</u>mizænin.

3.11.2 The Pronouns of Persian

Formal and Familiar Pronouns of the Second Person

As discussed in Lesson 2, /shoma/ is used either as a polite pronoun of the second person, "you (polite, singular)" or as a familiar pronoun of the plural. It may also be used as a polite plural pronoun:

shoma ko<u>ja</u> zendegí mìkonin? (singular polite, plural familiar or polite)

There is, in addition, the pronoun /to/ which is second person singular **familiar**, "you (familiar)." /to/ is used only with intimate friends, children, and people of lesser social status. It should by no means be used with strangers, with older and respected people, or in new social situations, where it would represent a definite faux pas. /to/ agrees with the second person singular of the verb: *to míduni?* (familiar)

The pronoun, however, as with other pronouns may be unexpressed:

Lesson Three   MODERN PERSIAN   درس سوم

farsi khéyli khub hærf mìzæni.

There are a few different ways of greeting and asking about people's health in the familiar forms. These variations, again, must be used carefully. Here are two ways to ask "how are you?" in varying levels of informality:

Informal	**More Informal/Casual**
hálet chetór-e?	chetór-i?
mérsi. khub-e.	mérsi. khúb-æm.

Note that in the more informal version, the question is asked more directly — "how are you?" rather than "how is your health?" — and the answer follows suit — "I am fine" rather than "it is fine." Both of these versions agree with the pronoun *to*, and therefore, should not be used except with classmates or friends with whom you are familiar. Do not assume, as one might in American culture (Americans are known universally for rapidly addressing people on a familiar basis), that a new Iranian acquaintance is automatically a friend or someone with whom you can allow yourself to be familiar. The use of these two alternates to *hál-shoma chetór-e* with the wrong person is just as much a faux pas as using the pronoun *to* with the wrong person, as mentioned above.

You will encounter the following pronouns for other persons:

Third Person Singular

/u/ third person singular human pronoun meaning "he" or "she" (but not "it"). This pronoun is used mostly in the literary (written) language although it is sometimes used in speech.

/un/ the pronoun most commonly used in speech for the third person singular. It refers to animates as well as inanimates ("he," "she," "it"). This pronoun is also the demonstrative pronoun ("that one"). /in/ ("this one") can also be used to mean "he," "she," or "it" in colloquial speech, depending on the location of the person or thing you are speaking about.

Lesson Three	*MODERN PERSIAN*	درس سوم

The new learner should be careful in the usage of the third person pronouns since /un/ and /in/ have serious social constraints. Used in the wrong context, they will sound insulting. They should not be used when referring politely to someone, especially if that person is present or if you are referring to a member of the family of the person to whom you are speaking. On the other hand, the pronoun /u/ is not used commonly in speech and sounds awkward when it is. In these cases, the deferential pronoun /ishun/ is used and takes a third person plural verb (even though referring to one person). Use of the deferential form will be discussed at length in Lesson 9 (9.3.1).

Third Person Plural

/una/ or /unha/ and /in/ or /inha/ are the pronouns for "they." They are the plural forms of the pronouns /un/ and /in/ respectively. /una/ is commonly used in speech — somewhat more so than /ina/ — but both forms have the same social constraints of usage as /un/ and should be avoided if you are speaking about people present, unless they are friends or peers.

The Full Set of Persian Pronouns

The pronouns that have been discussed thus far are:

singular	mæn	I
	to	you (familiar)
	u	he, she (literary)
	un, in	he, she, it (colloquial)
plural	ma	we
	shoma	you (plural, familiar; singular/plural, polite)
	una/unha, ina/inha	they
	ishun	he, she, they (polite, deferential)

The pronouns /ma/, /un/, /in/, /una/, and /ina/ will be drilled in Lesson 4.

Lesson Three   *MODERN PERSIAN*   درس سوم

3.11.3 Past Roots of Verbs

As mentioned in Lesson 2 (2.11, part 6), all Persian verbs have a present and a past root. Both roots are very important in the formation of tenses. Since the past root will be required for the formation of several forms introduced later in this text, they will be used as cues in drills in the remainder of this text. All newly introduced verbs will also be accompanied by their past roots in the vocabulary sections. Memorize the following past roots of those verbs you have already learned in Lessons 1 through 3. The present forms as well as the present roots are also listed as an aid to memorization:

Compound Verbs

Present Tense	Present Root	Past Root
tekrár mìkone	tekrar -kon-	tekrár kærd
tælæffóz mìkone	tælæffoz -kon-	tælæffoz kærd
gúsh mìkone	gush -kon-	gush kærd
sælám mìkone	sælam -kon-	sælam kærd
khodafezí mìkone	khodafezi - kon-	khodafezi kærd
tæmrín mìkone	tæmrin -kon-	tæmrín kærd
zendegí mìkone	zendegi -kon-	zendegi kærd
chekár mìkone	chekar -kon-	chekar kærd
khahésh mìkone	khahesh -kon-	khahesh kærd
dærs mìde	dærs -d-	dærs dad
jæváb mìde	jævab -d-	jævab dad
hærf mìzæne	hærf -zæn-	hærf zæd
yád mìgire	yad -gir-	yad gereft
rást mìge	rast -g-	rast goft

Simple Verbs

míporse	-pors-	porsid
míge	-g-	goft

Lesson Three *MODERN PERSIAN* درس سوم

mídune	-dun-	dunest
míkhune	-khun-	khund
mífæhme	-fæhm-	fæhmid

3.11.4 The Negative

As mentioned in Lesson 2 (2.11, part 1) and in the preceding section, Persian verbs are either simple or compound. Compound verbs consist of a compounding element (noun, etc.) and a purely verbal form that function together as a unit. To form the negative of a present tense of the verbs you have learned so far, the particle /né-/ is prefixed to the /mí-/ of the present tense. /mí-/, as you know, is prefixed directly to a simple verb and prefixed directly to the second member — the purely verbal element — of a compound verb. Thus, the negative present of all the simple verbs and of all the second members of the compound verbs you have learned so far (except "to be") will all begin with the sequence /némi-/:

mídune	némidune
zendegí mìkone	zendegì némikone

The change in stress from /mídune/ and /zendegí mìkone/ to /némidune/ and /zendegì némikone/ are discussed above in Section 3.11.1, parts 1 and 4. Here are the negative forms of the verbs you have learned so far:

	Present Affirmative	**Present Negative**
Compound Verbs	tekrár mìkone	tekràr némikone
	tælæffóz mìkone	tælæffòz némikone
	gúsh mìkone	gùsh némikone
	sælám mìkone	sælàm némikone
	khodafezí mìkone	khodafezì némikone
	tæmrín mìkone	tæmrìn némikone
	zendegí mìkone	zendegì némikone
	chekár mìkone	cekàr némikone

	khahésh mìkone	khahèsh némikone
	dærs mìde	dærs némide
	jæváb mìde	jævàb némide
	hærf mìzæne	hærf némizæne
	yád mìgire	yàd némigire
	ràst mìge	ràst némige
Simple Verbs	míporse	némiporse
	míge	némige
	mídune	némidune
	míkhune	némikhune
	mífæhme	némifæhme
To Be	-e	nist

The negative of "to be" will be drilled in Lesson 4 (4.8) and Lesson 6 (6.6). You will also see in future lessons that the negative particle /né-/ takes this form only when it occurs before the verbal prefix /mi-/. When it occurs directly before the root, without an intervening /mi-/, it is pronounced /næ-/. You will encounter this form of the negative in the past tense (see Note in Lesson 4, Section 4.3 for the expression /næfæhmidæm/) and in all negative forms of "to have" (see Lesson 5, beginning with Drill 17).

3.12 The Persian Language

Persian is an Indo-European language. More specifically, it is a member of the Iranian group of Indo-European languages, which consists of a large number of genetically related languages including Baluchi, Kurdish, Pashto (or Pushtu), and Ossetic. Iranian languages are spoken by various communities of Iran, Afghanistan, Central Asia and the Caucasus, Pakistan, Turkey, Iraq, Syria, and throughout the Persian Gulf.

There are several schools of thought among historical linguists and archaeologists regarding the dates and routes of migration of Indo-European peoples into central, southern,

Lesson Three   *MODERN PERSIAN*   درس سوم

and western Asia. Some scholars date their arrival in the area in the third and second millennia B.C., whereas other evidence points to a possibility of their appearance in the area two to four millennia prior to those dates. Some specialists identify their route into southern and western Asia from the northern steppes through Central Asia, others through the Caucasus, and still others claim that they were indigenous to Asia Minor and did not move very far to reach their present-day distribution throughout southern Asia.

At an early point a group we now call the Indo-Aryans split off from the rest of the Indo-European peoples and then further divided in two with one group remaining on the Iranian plateau, and the other moving into the Indian sub-continent. By roughly the ninth century B.C., Iranian peoples had penetrated to the western rim of the plateau. There they came into conflict with the Assyrians and so entered recorded history. In the sixth century one Iranian tribe from the western rim of the plateau, the Medes, overthrew the Assyrians as rulers of Mesopotamia, and shortly thereafter a second tribe, the Persians, under the leadership of Cyrus the Great (*kurósh-e kæbir*) overthrew the Medes. Cyrus and his most eminent successor, Darius (*dariush*), conquered and ruled over an empire that extended from Egypt and Greece in the west to Central Asia and the Indus Valley in the east.

The Persian empire endured until well into the fourth century B.C., when it was conquered by Alexander the Great in 333 - 330 B.C. The rulers of this early Persian royal house, known collectively as the Achaemenids (*hækhamæneshian*), had brief accounts of their accomplishments carved into stone foundation tablets and the sides of mountains in Old Persian, and sometimes in Elamite and Old Babylonian as well. These monumental inscriptions and tablets provide us with the only surviving examples of this earliest form of Persian. Old Persian, which was written in cuneiform, was a contemporary and near relation of Avestan—the language of the Zoroastrian scriptures—and Sanskrit. It was a highly inflected language, with seven cases, three genders, and dual form in addition to a singular and plural. Its relation to modern Persian is only historic, and Cyrus would be equally at a loss for words in present-day Tehran or New York.

Lesson Three MODERN PERSIAN درس سوم

The linguistic relationship between a later form of the language known as Middle Persian and Modern Persian is much more transparent. Middle Persian, a term used to describe a number of closely related dialects, was current in various parts of Iran from the third century B.C. to the ninth century A.D. Middle Persian languages were written in a variety of scripts and one of them, called Dari, seems to have been the court language of the Sassanian Dynasty (224 - 652 A.D.). The rulers of this dynasty revived much of the lost glory of the Achaemenids. The dialects that made up Middle Persian were all grammatically simpler than Old Persian. In them, as is the case in Modern Persian, gender and case have been lost as has the dual number. There was an extensive literature in Middle Persian, which has now, alas, been almost entirely lost.

After the Arab and Islamic conquest of Iran, which began in the middle years of the seventh century and went on for nearly a century, Middle Persian survived unaltered for a time in a few centers of Zoroastrian culture, such as the province of Fars (former Pars). But throughout most of the country the Arabic language gained currency among the elite and had a profound and far-reaching impact on the language of ordinary daily life. Modern Persian, or New Persian as it is sometimes called, is essentially an Arabized and Islamized development of a Middle Persian language that is written in the Arabic script. It grew up as a camp and court language that served as the means of communication between Arabs and Iranians, and between the speakers of various Iranian languages and dialects who came together in the courts of the Arab rulers and their Muslim Iranian clients.

The earliest examples of Modern Persian date from the eighth century. By the end of the tenth century it was already a richly varied literary language, and it has remained so down to the present day. There have been significant alterations in the grammar, syntax, and lexicon of Modern Persian throughout this period, as is inevitable in any living language. The language of classical Persian literature is enough unlike the language of present day Iran to be better described as a different dialect—much as the language of Shakespeare is a different dialect from that of twentieth-century America. Different, that is, but widely studied,

Lesson Three MODERN PERSIAN درس سوم

understood, and quoted.

At present Modern Persian is the official language in three countries: Iran, where it is called *farsi* and is the native language of nearly half the population; Afghanistan, where it is called *dari,* or *farsi dari,* and shares official status with Pashto; and the (ex-Soviet) Republic of Tajikistan, where it is called *tojiki*. Tajik has been written in a modified Cyrillic alphabet, but there is a recent movement in post-Soviet Tajikistan to revive the use of the Arabic script. In addition, Persian is studied as one of the major vehicles of Islamic culture in universities from Morocco to Indonesia, and enjoys particular esteem in Pakistan and in India where it was displaced by English as the official language of education and government only in the late nineteenth and twentieth centuries.

3.13 Narrative Passage

Listen to the following paragraph recorded on tape. Look at the new words and try to listen only and not follow along with your eyes until you feel you have understood most of the paragraph.

mæn inja farsi dærs mìdæmo shoma farsi yád mìgirin. bolænd tekrár mìkonino ziad tæmrín mìkonin. shoma inja inglisi hærf némizænin. inja farsi mìporsæmo shoma be farsi jævább mìdin. khub mífæhmino khub hærf mìzænin. mæn ziad kár mìkonæm væli[1] shoma bishtær kár mìkonin. shoma khune khéyli farsi míkhunin. míkhunino tæmrín mìkonin. dær azmayeshgah[2] tælæffoz tæmrín mìkonino tælæffózetun khéyli khub-e.

    1.   væli "but"
    2.   azmayeshgah "laboratory;" here, "(language) lab"

Reading

sælam. esme mæn jæmshid-e. mæn dær tehran zendegi mikonæm. mæn daneshju-am va dær daneshgah tehran farsi mikhunæm. Pedar o madæræm dær tehran zendegi mikonæn. mæn yek khahær or do ta bærader daræm. khaharæm daneshamuz-e va bærædæram dær esfahan kar mikonan.

Lesson Four   درس چهارم

TOPICS COVERED IN THIS LESSON

- Conversation: What is your name? What is this? Who is that?

- Find out where Karen's parents live.

- Whom do you study with?

- Why? Because.

- Do you speak Persian? I'm learning. How about you? I Speak Only a Little.

- Do you work out? Of course!/Yes, but…

- Asking and talking about reading and writing

- Classroom items: Pen, pencil, notebook, paper, chair, table, etc.

- More Iranian Names

- More Greetings: Good Morning, Good Night

Listening Materials

Listening Comprehension: "Jo Anne, Robyn, and Vida"

RESOURCES AND BACKGROUND: INFORMATION AND ACCURACY

Phonology

Syllable-Final /h/: /tehran/

Initial Consonant Groups: /kelas/ "class"

/q/ before voiceless consonants: -*qt* = *[-kht]*

ya "or" — intonation and usage

Tongue Twisters

Grammar Patterns to Be Drilled

Verbs

First Person Plural: *ma mídunim*

Third Person Plural: *una mídunænd*

"To Be" (stage one):   *un chi-e? un kí-e? ésmetun chi-e?*

Lesson Four   MODERN PERSIAN   درس چهارم

    Past Roots and the Present Tense

Nouns

    Possessive Ending "his/hers": *-esh*

Prepositions

    ba　　　　　　"with"

    sær-e kelas　　"in class"

Sentence Patterns

    Coordination:

        ya　　"or"

        væ li　"but"

        Comparative Degree (Type One: *tær + ya*)

        Double Negatives: *hich -væqt* + negative verb

        What is this? Who is this?　*in chi-e? in kí-e?*

    Word Order:

        (subject) + (adverb-time) + preposition + (object) + verb

        ma　　　　hichvæqt　　sær-e kelas　　inglisí　　hærf némizænim

Vocabulary Building

    Words of Western Origin Used in Persian

Reading and Writing

    Diacritics

        Representing Unwritten Vowels

        Doubled Consonants

        Transcribing Foreign Words

        Full Sentence Questions and Answers

Grammar Discussion

    Word Order

Lesson Four *MODERN PERSIAN* درس چهارم

    Parts of Speech and Elements of the Sentence

    Question Order: Persian vs. English

    Prepositions and Pronouns

    The Ending Pronouns (Possessive Pronouns)

Cultural Materials

    Meals and Food: Part 1 (in English)

Lesson Four   *MODERN PERSIAN*   درس چهارم

4.1 Phonology

4.1.1 Syllable-Final /h/

Although the sound /h/ occurs in both English and Persian, the distribution of this sound in Persian differs from that in English. In English, "h" is pronounced only at the beginning of a syllable—ho-tel, in-ha-bitant—and never at the end. In Persian, however, /h/ occurs both at the beginning and the end of syllables—both hæsæn, es-fæ-han, hal *and* teh-ran, fæh-mí-din, shæh-lá, da-nesh-gah.

The trend in colloquial Persian is to drop /h/ in most positions, particularly in rapid speech. Thus kha*hésh mìkonæm* and *khabgah* are usually pronounced *khaésh mìkonæm* and *khabga*. On a more careful, but still normal level of speech, however, the /h/ is clearly enunciated. It is also retained slightly more in word-initial position. The rules governing the dropping of the /h/ are described below in Lesson 5 (5.15), Lesson 7 (7.1), and Lesson 8 (8.1). The following exercise drills the syllable-final /h/ in its enunciated form:

Pronunciation Drill 1

khers	tæh	dæh	beh	kuh	ænduh	tæfrih	noh	rah
mah	tehran	behtær	kæhroba	æhmæd	æhsæn	mæhtab	bæhsi	tohmæt
sæhne	ehsas	ehya	mehri	æhli	læhje	sæhvi	ehsan	ohde
fæhmid		mífæhmin?	fæhmídin?			bókhorid		ehtemal

Pronunciation Drill 2: -qt /-kht/, -qs /-khs/

When /q/ is followed by a voiceless consonant, most notably /t/ or /s/, it is pronounced as [kh]. This is true both when the combination *-qt* or *-qs* comes at the end of a syllable and when a syllable division falls between them:

hichvæqt [hichvækht]	"never"	eqtesad [ekhtesad]	"economics"
ræqs [rækhs]	"dance"(noun)	æqsam [ækhsam]	"kinds, sorts"

Lesson Four MODERN PERSIAN درس چهارم

This change occurs in very few words, but some of them are quite common. Whenever such a word occurs in this text its pronunciation will be noted in the vocabulary.

Pronunciation Drill 3:   Review (Imitation)

mikh	sheykh	shukh	dokhtær	mokh	ækhtær	nækhab	bókhorid
khælq	qayeq	qashoq	hakem	qurt	khord	khahær	ækhlaq
khoshækhlaq	khaqani	khaneqa	khanegi	khak	khaloqli	qiloqal	khoshqælb
khoshqælæm	khoshqoli	jiq	khiki	kæbk	qæhqæh	hæq	hoquq
mohæqqeq	qalebgir	tæhqi	qods	qærb	mæqreb	shærq	mæshreq
qændshekæn	qelqelæk	qerqere	qurbaqe	qæhti	qæhve	quti	æmiq
kaqæz	ahæk	qæshqai	kæshki	kakh	khaleq		

4.1.2 *ya* "or" — Intonation and Usage

The use of the conjunction "or" with nouns in Persian is slightly different from that of English. One of the usages of "or" is between two subjects or two objects of an interrogative sentence.

Does <u>Ahmad</u> or <u>Reza</u> speak English? (subject)

Do you study <u>Persian</u> or <u>Arabic</u>? (object)

In Persian, the conjunction *ya* appears between two **clauses**, the second of which is elliptic. That is, most of the elements of the second clause are the same as those of the first clause and become deleted. Thus for the Persian equivalent of the above two English sentences, there are two forms, the underlying (or full) form and the usual or (short) form:

Lesson Four   *MODERN PERSIAN*   درس چهارم

Underlying (Full)	**Usual (Short)**
subject:	
æhmæd inglisi hærf mìzæne ya reza inglisi hærf mìzæne?	æhmæd inglisi hærf mìzæne ya reza?
object:	
shoma farsi míkhunin ya æræbi míkhunin?	shoma farsi míkhunin ya æræbi?

The full form is sometimes heard in speech.

The intonational contour used in this type of sentence is of interest. The intonation of the first clause does not drop before *ya* and thus resembles the regular question intonation. The second clause, whether the long form or the short form is used, receives statement intonation. Each clause, as expected, has one sentence stress which falls on the word that is contrasted:

subject:

\æh/ **mæd**/   \inglisi hærf mìzæne ya re/ **za**/   \inglisi hærf mìzæne?

\æh/ **mæd**/   \inglisi hærf mìzæne ya re/ **zá**/   **á**

object:

\shoma/ far/ **si**/   \míkhunin ya æræ/ **bi**/   \míkhunin?

\shoma far/ **si**/   \míkhunin ya æræ/ **bí**/ í

In the remainder of this text all sentences of the above type will be punctuated with a question mark in parentheses after the first clause (and before *ya*) and with a period after the second clause to represent the intonation on both clauses:

shoma farsi míkhunin (?) ya æræbi.

The full (underlying) form of the second clause is generally used when the identical verb of the clauses is "to be":

in medád-e (?) ya khodkár-e? "Is this a pencil or a ballpoint (pen)?"

Lesson Four   *MODERN PERSIAN*   درس چهارم

Tongue Twisters (/kh/, /q/, /k/, /g/)

khaloqlí-e khanúm-e khaqani dær khaneqa kha<u>ne</u> dasht.   "Mrs. Khaqani's cousin lived in a khaneqah."

hoqúq-e aqá-ye gorgani khéyli <u>k</u>æm-e.   "Mr. Gorgani's salary is very small."

4.2 Vocabulary (All words that you will be able to spell by the end of this lesson have been included in Persian script.)

Vocabulary, Dialogue 4

ælbæte/ælbætte		of course, certainly
chetor? (2)		how about, what about
ma	ما	we, us
hær do	هر دو	both
ba	با	with
moællem	معلم	teacher
fæqæt[1] tanha	فقط (تنها)	only
sær-e[2] dar	سر (در)	in, at
hichvæqt[3]		never (pronunciation: [hichvækht], see 4.1.2)

Drills, Part I

shæb	شب	evening, night
shæba		evenings, in the evening(s)
ruz	روز	day
ruza		days, during the days, in the daytime
mokaleme	مکالمه	conversation, dialogue
	گفتگو ، گفت و شنود	
kelas	کلاس اتاق درس	class

119

Lesson Four *MODERN PERSIAN* درس چهارم

tærjome	ترجمه	translation
tærjomé mìkonæm	ترجمه میکنم	I translate
tærjome kærd	ترجمه کرد	past root of /tærjomé mìkonæm/
værzesh		exercise, calisthenics; athletics, sports
værzésh mìkonæm		I exercise, play sports, get exercise
værzesh kærd		past root of /værzésh mìkonæm/
mínevisæm		I write
nevesht		past root of /mínevisæm/
neveshtæn		writing
khundæn		reading
míkhunæm (2)		I read
khund (2)		past root of /míkhunæm/
bæche	بچه	child
dokhtær	دختر	girl, daughter
pesær	پسر	boy, son
un		that, those (he, she, it — See 3.11.2)
in	این	this, these (he, she, it — See 3.11.2)
bimarestan	بیمارستان	hospital
væli		but
ya		or
chéra?	چرا	why?
bæràye ínke	برای اینکه	because

Lesson Four　　　*MODERN PERSIAN*　　　درس چهارم

Bacheha

Vocabulary, Situational and Practical Drills and Drills Part II

dæftær	دفتر	notebook
kaqæz		paper
mashin (خودرو)	ماشین	car, automobile
medad	مداد	pencil
miz	میز	table, desk
pul	پول	money
saæt	ساعت	watch, hour
sændæli		chair
khodkar	خودکار	ballpoint pen (literally "automatic")
esm (nam)	اسم (نام)	name
una		they, them (See 3.11.2); those people/things

Lesson Four MODERN PERSIAN درس چهارم

ina they, them (See 3.11.2); these people/things

Iranian Personal Names

Men's First Names   **Women's First Names**

reza   رضا   vida   ویدا

mæhmud محمود   giti   گیتی

hoseyn حسین   mehri   مهری

Last Names/Family Names

firuzi   فیروزی

sadeqi   صادقی

esfæhanian اصفهانیان

Vocabulary Notes

1. *fæqæt* — "only": Note the usage of the word *fæqæt* with a negative verb:

   mæn fæqæt inglisi mídunæm.   "I know only English."

   mæn fæqæt inglisi némidunæm.   "I don't know only English."

The implication in the second sentence is that you do not only know English but another language (or languages) as well. This implication in the use of the word *fæqæt* may apply to other words in the sentence, e.g. subject, verb, or adverbs, etc:

   mæn fæqæt hærf némizænæm.   mínevisæmo míkhunæm.

   "I don't only speak.   I read and write."

   fæqæt mæn gush némikonæm.   shomávo bærádæretun gúsh mìkonin.

   "Not only I listen.   You and your brother listen."

In the above examples, the sentence stress is on the negative particle as expected. If, however, the sentence stress is placed on the word to which *fæqæt* applies, the sentence usually takes on the connotation of "except."

   mæn fæqæt inglisi némidunæm.   (The implication in both these

   fæqæt mæn inglisi némidunæm.   sentences is that everyone but me

Lesson Four MODERN PERSIAN درس چهارم

"Only I don't know English."   knows English.)

mæn fæqæt inglisi némidunæm.   (I know whatever else is necessary.)

"It's only English that I don't know."

Note: Some Persian speakers substitute *fæqæt* (only) with *tænha* (alone, only)

    mæn tanha yek sib khordæm   I ate only an apple.

2. *sær-e:* There are two prepositions that mean "in": *dær* and *sær-e*. The choice between these two prepositions is made by the choice of the noun that follows. Certain nouns, most notably *kar* "work" and *kelas* "class" require *sær-e* but the majority require the familiar *dær*. It is also not uncommon, especially in more formal written styles, to have *dær* occur with all nouns. That is, *dær kelas* is acceptable in writing but *sær-e kelas* is preferred in speech. (See also the drills of Lesson 7)

3. *hichvæqt—ma sær-e kelas hichvæqt inglisi hærf némizænim*: As you can see from this sentence, when there is a negative word in a sentence, the verb in Persian is also in the negative. You will encounter more sentences with the double negative later in this course. Instead of *hichvæqt*, you may also use *hærgez* or *hichhgah*,.

4. For the intonation and usage of clauses joined by *ya*, "or," see Section 4.1 above:

4.3 Cultural Material and Classroom Expressions

sob (bamdad)	morning
sob bekhéyr/sob bekhér.	Good morning.
shæb	evening, night
khosh	happy, merry, good
shæb bekhéyr/shæb bekhér.	Good night.
shab khosh	Good night.
ruz khosh	Good day.
mærhæmæt-e shoma ziad	(taarof) Polite, formal form of good bye (literally "May you enjoy great mercy/favor")

Lesson Four *MODERN PERSIAN* درس چهارم

tækhte (also: tækhte-siah)	blackboard
pá-ye tækhte	to the blackboard
lotfæn befærmaid pa-ye tækhte	Please go to the blackboard.
bénevisid	write (command form)
békhunid	read (command form)
fæhmídid/fæhmídin?	Do you understand?
fæhmídæm (past tense)	I understand.
næfæhmidæm (past tense)	I don't understand.

Note: Many expressions in Persian that are in the past tense have English equivalents that are in the present tense. For example, in English when we want to ask if someone understands what we are saying to them we say, "Do you understand?" And the response would be, "Yes. I understand," or "No. I don't understand." The Persian equivalents are in the past tense:

fæhmídin?   "Did you understand?"   bǽle. fæhmídæm.   "Yes. I understood."

næ. næfæhmidæm   "No. I didn't understand."

"Understand" in the present tense in Persian has a more general meaning than in English. "mífæhmid?," for example, is used when you wish to say something like "Do you understand French?" A statement like æli mífæhme means that Ali is intelligent and understands things in general. The negative, æli némifæhme, suggests that Ali doesn't understand much of anything.

(Although the past tense will not be introduced formally until Lesson 12, some expressions that use that tense will appear from time to time in the next few lessons, and the past stem of the verb is introduced below in 4.6)

4.4 Dialogue 4

The following conversation occurs when Vida, who has just arrived in the United States, runs into two women studying Persian at a university in California. Robyn is interested in Iranian folklore, music, and dance. She has dark hair and looks as if she might be Iranian.

Lesson Four   *MODERN PERSIAN*   درس چهارم

Jo Anne is a language major, studying French and Italian and has taken an interest in Persian. She is tall and blonde. At this point, Jo Anne is intently studying her Persian spelling, nervously preparing for a quiz, and Robyn is practicing a new Persian song she has learned. Vida is confused when she first sees them, thinking that they might be Iranians born in the United States. Because she is curious, she approaches Robyn first:

Vida: khánum, bébækhshid. shoma farsi mídunid?   Excuse me, Miss, do you know Persian?

     ælbæte   of course, certainly

     ye kæmi   a little

Robyn: ye kǽmi mídunæm. ælbæte khéyli kæm.   I know a little. Of course, very little.

     chetor   what about, how about

Vida: dústetun chetor?   How about your friend?

     ma   we

     hær do   both

     míkhunim   we read, study

Jo Anne: bǽle. ma hær do hala farsi míkhunim.   Yes, we are both studying Persian now.

     mídunænd   they know

Vida: pedæro madæretun farsi mídunæn(d)? *   Do your parents know Persian?

     fæqæt   only

     hærf mìzænænd   they speak

Jo Anne: nǽkheyr. fæqæt inglisi hærf mìzænæn(d).*   No, they speak only English.

     ba   with

     ba ki   with whom

     moællem   teacher

     moællémetun   your teacher

Lesson Four   *MODERN PERSIAN*   درس چهارم

Vida:	ba ki tæm<u>rín</u> mìkonid? ba moæl<u>lé</u>metun?	Whom do you practice with? Your teacher?
	sǽr-e	in, at
	híchvæqt	never
	hǽrf némizænim	we do not speak
Robyn:	b<u>ǽ</u>le. ma sǽr-e kelas híchvæqt inglisi hǽrf n<u>é</u>mizænim.	Yes, we never speak English in class.

dobare gúsh konìd   دوباره گوش کنید

Vida:	khánum, <u>bé</u>bækhshid. shoma far<u>si</u> mídunid?
Robyn:	ye <u>kǽ</u>mi mídunæm. ǽlbæte <u>khéy</u>li kæm.
Vida:	<u>dús</u>tetun chetor?
Jo Anne:	b<u>ǽ</u>le. ma hær <u>do</u> hala farsi míkhunim.
Vida:	pedǽro madǽretun far<u>si</u> mídunænd?
Jo Anne:	n<u>ǽ</u>kheyr. fæqæt ingli<u>si</u> hǽrf mìzænænd.
Vida:	ba ki tæm<u>rín</u> mìkonid? ba moæl<u>lé</u>metun?
Robyn:	b<u>ǽ</u>le. ma sǽr-e kelas híchvæqt inglisi hǽrf n<u>é</u>mizænim.

* In this dialogue we have opted for /-id/ over /-in/ for two reasons. The first is that the context is slightly more formal because Vida is introducing herself to two strangers. The second, and more important reason is that we wish to make clear that /-id/ and /-in/ may both be heard in normal conversation and you should not get into the habit of thinking one or the other is preferable.

As mentioned earlier in Lesson 2 (2.11, Part 4), the third person plural ending {-ænd} has a variant {-æn} that you will hear from time to time. Both of these forms are heard in colloquial speech, but the contrast between {-ænd} and {-æn} is less noticeable than the contrast of {-id} and {-in}. This is the case because a final /d/ is often automatically dropped after an /n/. The situation is similar to that in English where the final /d/ that is usually

dropped when "and" connects a pair of words (i.e., "John an' Mary"). On the other hand, it is not uncommon to hear the final /-d/ pronounced in this ending, even in colloquial speech.

4.5 Vocabulary Building

4.5.1 Introduction

In the vocabulary building sections we will demonstrate how you can enlarge your Persian vocabulary by becoming familiar with certain types of words or families of words. A knowledge of how words are formed and of how categories of words are related to each other speeds up the process of acquiring vocabulary. The words presented in these sections are, except where noted, optional, but you should be familiar with the principles they illustrate. This first section analyzes the ways in which words from English and French have made been incorporated into Persian. Subsequent sections will be devoted to important features of Persian word construction and to the large Arabic element in Persian.

4.5.2 Words of Western Origin in Persian

English and Persian both belong to the category of languages that prefer to borrow words to describe new things rather than make up or redefine words of their own. German and Arabic, by contrast, are both languages that prefer invention to importation. Recently Persian has also given preference to words formed from pure Persian roots, such as *zistshenasi,* to replace the older (and still used) term, *biolozhi.* While English and Persian both solved the problem of what to call a self-propelled vehicle with flanged metal wheels that ran on rails and drew cars behind it by borrowing the French word *train,* German used a native word *Zug* from the verb that means "draw or pull," and Arabic added a new meaning to the existing term *qitâr* "a string of camels" (Persian: *qetar, qætar*).

English began as a hybrid of Germanic Anglo-Saxon and Norman French. During the Renaissance it substantially increased its vocabulary by the large-scale importation of Latin words, and in subsequent centuries it went on to borrow words from virtually every language

Lesson Four *MODERN PERSIAN* درس چهارم

with which it came in contact, including Persian — orange *(narænj)*, cummerbund *(kæmærbænd)*, jungle *(jængæl)*, khaki *(khakí)* — and Arabic — sherbet, camel, alcohol, algebra. Similarly, what we call Modern Persian began in the centuries after the Islamic invasion of Iran as a hybrid of Middle Persian (Indo-European), and Arabic (Semitic). In the centuries that followed it borrowed very heavily from Arabic, beginning with the alphabet itself, and, to a much more limited extent, from Turkish as well. Since the mid-nineteenth century, the principal sources of new borrowings in Persian have been the languages of Europe, especially French and English.

The following are examples of the many words of Western European origin that have made their way into Persian. Many of these words are now part of the lexical compositions of most languages of the modern world:

adres	address	*salad*	salad
chek	check	*deser*	dessert
telefon	telephone	*shokolat*	chocolate
pasport	passport	*vanil*	vanilla
vitamin	vitamin	*sigar*	cigarette
aspirin	aspirin	*kaset*	cassette, (c. player)
alerzhi	allergy	*motor*	motor
bank/bang	bank	*garazh*	garage
televizion	television	*albom*	album
radio	radio	*negativ*	negative (film)
film	film	*sinema/sinæma*	cinema, movies
modern	modern	*metod*	method
mazhik	magic marker	*biolozhi*	biology
pakæt	envelope, paper bag	*entomolozhi*	entomology

Lesson Four MODERN PERSIAN درس چهارم

The following words are of purely English origin in Persian:

parking	parking lot	*shampu*	shampoo
jaz	jazz	*pelastik*	plastic
super	supermarket	*keraker*	crackers
telefon-e hamrah	cellular phone	*kuler*	air conditioner ("cooler")

The following words are of purely French origin in Persian and will be familiar to those students who know French.

pasazh	arcade	*dikte*	dictation, spelling
tæmbr	stamp	*kado*	gift
mayo	bathing suit	*okazyon*	bargain
papiyon	bowtie	*aparteman*	apartment
doktora	doctorate	*rezhim*	diet
diapositiv	slide (film)	*motorsiklet*	motorcycle
kart	card	*shans*	luck
kart postal	post card	*dekurazhe*	discouraged
lastik	tire (of car)	*moble*	furnished
lamp	light bulb	*dush*	shower
balkon	balcony	*mobl*	furniture (couch)
fóq-e lisans	Master's Degree	*diplom*	high school diploma
lisans	Bachelor's Degree		*(mixed/French and Arabic)*

When foreign words are borrowed into Persian, they must conform (for most speakers, at least) to Persian phonology. The following rules are observed:

Lesson Four *MODERN PERSIAN* درس چهارم

1. Stress is placed on the final syllable of the word. This rule also happens to correspond to the rules of French.

English	**French**	**Persian**
vítamin	vita**mi**ne	*vitamín*
sálad	sa**la**de	*saláb*
dóctorate	docto**rat**	*doktorá*
sécretary	secré**taire**	*sekreter*

Even words borrowed from languages that do not have the stress on the last syllable must change it to the last in Persian:

Source Language	**Persian**	
tárjuma (Arabic)	*tærjomé*	"translation"
eklésia (Greek)	*kelisiá/kelisá*	"church"

Motorseklet

2. Because English with its eight to eleven non-glided or "pure" vowels (depending on the analysis), has more than Persian, with six, the vowels of an English word must change to accommodate the Persian vowel system:

Lesson Four　　　　　　　　*MODERN PERSIAN*　　　　درس چهارم

English and English Phonology	Persian
puncture (British: "flat tire")	*pæncær*

3. French nasal vowels (transcribed in phonetics with a /~/) are converted to vowel plus nasal consonant. The "ü" and "ö" vowels of French are converted to Persian /u/ and /o/ respectively:

French and French Phonology	Persian	
balcon /bælkõ/	*balkón*	"balcony"
Juin /zhüæ~/	*zhuæn*	"June"
de luxe /dö lüks/	*dolúks*	"deluxe; fancy"

4. Persian phonology does not permit any two consonants to come together in the beginning of a word (or a syllable), so a vowel is inserted between the two initial consonants of a borrowed word (see also discussion in Lesson 2, Section 2.9.3). This inserted vowel is usually /e/, although other vowels occur under conditions that will be described in future lessons:

Kleenex	*kelinéks*	
clutch (of car)	*kelác / kælác*	
crème caramel (French)	*kerém karamél*	"creme caramel, flan"
plage (French)	*pelázh*	"beach"
cracker(s) / class	*kerakér / kelás*	

When the first consonant in the word is an /s/, the additional Persian vowel is placed in the beginning of the syllable:

stadium	*estadióm*
Scotland	*eskotlænd*
spaghetti	*espagetí*
stereo	*esterió*

The rule of vowel insertion between two initial consonants also applies for the beginning of a syllable:

"English" (En-glish) changes in Persian to <u>ing-li-si</u> or <u>in-ge-li-si</u>.

It is important to remember that these rules are also applied to proper names. The

Lesson Four MODERN PERSIAN درس چهارم

Persian pronunciation of the names of two authors of this book is /estiló/ and /kelintón/. /estokholm/ is also one of the largest cities in /eskandinaví/, and so on. Of course, as we have mentioned, bilingual Persian speakers will very likely pronounce the initial clusters as they are in their original languages.

4.6 Using Past Stems as Verb Cues

From this point on, the past roots of verbs will be used as cues in substitution drills. The past roots of all the verbs you have encountered through this lesson are listed below opposite the third person singular present form of the same verb. You should learn the past roots and be able to transform them into the present tense before you begin the drills in this section.

Past Root	**Present Tense**	**Past Root**	**Present Tense**
zendegi kærd	zendegí mìkone	dunest	mídune
tekrar kærd	tekrár mìkone	fæhmid	mífæhme
gush kærd, etc. *	gúsh mìkone	goft	míge
dærs dad	dærs mìde	nevesht	mínevise
jævab dad	jæváb mìde	porsid	míporse
hærf zæd	hærf mìzæne	rast goft	rást mìge
yad gereft	yád mìgire	khund	míkhune

* (sælam kærd, chekar kærd, tælæffoz kærd, tærjome kærd, khahesh kærd, værzesh kærd, tæmrin kærd)

Drill 1: Imitation

    ma fæqæt inglisi hærf mìzænim.

    ma hænuz inja zendegí mìkonim.

    ma sær-e kelas mokaleme tæmrín mìkonim.

    ma inglisi behtær mídunim?

Lesson Four　　　　*MODERN PERSIAN*　　　　درس چهارم

ma hichvæqt tærjomè némikonim.

ma dær daneshgah farsi yád mìgirim.

ma ruza dǽrs mìdim.

ma farsi khéyli yævash mínevisim.

ma dær mædrese inglisi míkhunim.

ma shæba dær khabgah farsi tæmrín mìkonim.

ma fæqæt rusi némifæhmim.

ma ruza inja værzésh mìkonim.

mæno shoma némidunim?

mæno pedǽro madǽræm inja zendegí mìkonim.

mæno to hala chekár mìkonim?

mæno shǽhla æz moællem míporsim.

ma khéyli tond jæváb mìdim?

Drill 2:　Substitution

<u>ma</u> farsi <u>yád mìgirim</u>.

tæmrin kærd　　　　　　　　　(ma farsi tæmrín mìkonim.)

shoma

mæn

pedǽræm

fæhmid　　　　　　　　　　　(pedǽræm farsi mífæhme.)

ma

khund　　　　　　　　　　　　(ma farsi míkhunim.)

tærjome kærd　　　　　　　　(ma farsi tærjomé mìkonim.)

mæn

mæno bæradǽræm

dærs dad　　　　　　　　　　(mæno bæradǽræm farsi dǽrs mìdim.)

Lesson Four *MODERN PERSIAN* درس چهارم

ma

nevesht (ma farsi mínevisim.)

hærf zæd (ma farsi hærf mìzænim.)

reza

tæmrin kærd (reza farsi tæmrín mìkone.)

yad gereft (reza farsi yád mìgire.)

dunest (reza farsi mídune.)

ma

(yad gereft)

Drill 3: Substitution

a. ba <u>moællémæm</u> fæqæt farsi hærf mìzænæm.

(cues: un pesær, shohæretun, khanúm-e shærifi, un dokhtær, fereshte, hæsæn, un bæche, jan (moællémæm))

b. Break up into pairs and continue making sentences of your own using this pattern.

Drill 4: Substitution

ba <u>moællémetun</u> farsi hærf mìzænin (?) ya ba <u>jæmshid</u>.

(cues: un pesær/un dokhtær, shohæretun/dústetun, ma/una, khanúm-e shærifi/aqá-ye firuzi, un dokhtær/jæmshid, fereshte/in pesær, hæsæn/khanúmetun, un bæche/ki, (moællémetun/jæmshid))

Drill 5: soálo jævab

ma inja fæqæt farsi yád mìgirim?

ma dær iran zendegí mìkonim?

ma inja værzésh mìkonim?

134

Lesson Four MODERN PERSIAN درس چهارم

ma inja ketab míkhunim? chéra?/chéra næ?

ma koja zendegí mìkonim?

ma dær daneshgah kár mìkonim?

ma inja khundǽno neveshtæn yád mìgirim?

ma inja khéyli hærf mìzænim vǽli hænuz ziad néminevisim. chéra?

dær daneshgah chi míkhunim?

ma ruza farsi tæmrín mìkonim (?) ya shǽba. chera?

mǽno shoma chi hærf mìzænim?

ma farsi be inglisi tærjomé mìkonim?

ma dorost tælæffóz mìkonim?

ma hala tondtær yád mìgirim (?) ya yævashtær. chera?

mǽno (T.A., etc) farsi hærf mìzænim vǽli ba shoma khéyli tond hærf némizænim. chéra?

ma ba shohǽretun farsi hærf mìzænim? ba mehri chetor?

ma farsi mínevisim (?) ya fǽqæt hærf mìzænim.

ma sær-e kelas chekár mìkonim?

ma ba ki ærǽbi hærf mìzænim?

ma inja zhaponi tæmrín mìkonim? farsi chetor?

mǽno shoma ziad kár mìkonim (?) ya kæm. chera?

Drill 6: Cued Question/Answer

    S1: shoma <u>færanse</u> mídunin?   S2: bǽle aqa. <u>færanse</u> mídunæm.

    S1: <u>almani</u> chetor?   S2: bǽle. almanío færanse mídunæm.

(cues: farsi/inglisi, rusi/almani, færanse/espanioli, torki/æræbi, chini/zhaponi,

(færanse/almani))

Lesson Four MODERN PERSIAN درس چهارم

Drill 7: Substitution (use of /hichvæqt/)

<u>reza</u> hichvæqt inglisi <u>hǽrf némizæne</u>.

ma--(<u>ma</u> hichvæqt inglisi <u>hǽrf némizænim</u>.)

-------------------------tærjome kærd----------(ma hichvæqt inglisi <u>tærjomè némikonim</u>.)

mǽno khahǽræm-------------------------------

-----------------------------------tekrar kærd-------------(<u>mǽno khahǽræm</u> hichvæqt inglisi <u>tekràr</u>

---<u>némikonim</u>.)

-------------------------dærs dad-----------------

vida---

-------------------------khund-------------------

-------------------------nevesht-----------------

mæno bæradæræm-----------------------------

-------------------------ketab khund-------------

-------------------------hærf zæd---------------

shoma--

(reza)---

Drill 8: soálo jævab

shoma farsi yád mìgirin? æræbi chetor?

shoma almani (rusi, torki, chini) mídunin (?) ya færanse.

mæn (torki, etc.) mídunæm væ̀li khéyli khub némidunæm. shoma chetor?

mæn inja chi dǽrs mìdæm?

shoma farsi khub hǽrf mìzænin? færanse chetor?

ma inja fæqæt mokaleme yád mìgirim? neveshtæn yád némigirim?

shoma ketab míkhunin? be inglisi míkhunin (?) ya be farsi. (chéra be farsi ketab némikhunin?)

<u>yævash</u> yæ:ni chi? <u>tond</u> chetor?

Lesson Four MODERN PERSIAN درس چهارم

shoma inglisi dærs mìdin? mokaleme dærs mìdin?

shoma inja chi míkhunin? shoma farsi khub hǽrf mìzænin. (statement)

mæn almani dǽrs mìdæm? farsi chetor?

shoma farsi khub tælæffóz mìkonin? inglisi chetor?

mæn ba shoma farsi hǽrf mìzænæm? farsi khub mífæhmin?

shoma ziad kár mìkonin? shohǽretun chetor?

shoma ba bæradǽretun inglisi hǽrf mìzænin?

shoma ba ki farsi hǽrf mìzænin? væli (that person) inglisi mídune?

shoma be inglisi ketab míkhunin? tond míkhunin?

shoma farsi tond hǽrf mìzænin? mæn chetor?

ma farsi dǽrs mìdim (?) ya yád mìgirim.

shoma farsi tond mínevisin? chera?

ma inja ziad tærjomé mìkonim? væli tærjomé mìkonim, næ?

shoma khune værzésh mìkonin? koja værzésh mìkonin? chera?

ma sær-e kelas khundǽno neveshtæn tæmrín mìkonim? mokaleme chetor?

ma sær-e kelas hichvæqt inglisi hǽrf némizænim?

4.8 Situational and Practical Drills: Classroom Expressions

A chart or actual props must be used in the following drills.

Drill 9: in chi-e? (Teacher points to objects or holds them up in turn.)

    a.   **T:** in chi-e? **S:** un <u>ketáb</u>-e.

(cues: medad, saæt, mashin, khodkar, sændæli, dæftær, pul, kaqæz, miz, (ketab))

(optional extra cues: pasport, telefon, mazhik, kaset, salad, sigar, keraker, kart postal, lamp, vitamin, tæmbr, aspirin, pakæt, telefon-e hamrah, etc.)

    b.   Pictures or objects held up may optionally be in groups (a number of watches, books, etc.). Plural nouns are not needed for such questions. Third person

Lesson Four MODERN PERSIAN درس چهارم

plural pronouns, however, should be used, but the verbs do not need to be pluralized:

T: ina chí-e?   **S:** una <u>ketáb</u>-e.

Drill 10: in chi-e?

T: in <u>kaqæz</u>-e?   **S:** bǽle. un <u>kaqæz</u>-e.

(cues: use a few of the cues in Drill 9)

Drill 11: in chi-e?

T: in <u>míz</u>-e?   **S:** næ(kher). un <u>miz</u> nist. un <u>sændælí</u>-e

(cues: use a few of the cues in Drill 9)

Drill 12: in chi-e? (In this drill the you will ask each other questions using the props and the above patterns.)

Drill 13: Cued Question/Answer

S1: áqa/khánum, <u>bé</u>bækhshin. <u>é</u>smetun chi-e?   **S2:** ésmæm _____-e.

Drill 14: un kí-e?

T: un kí-e? (aqá-ye shærifi)   **S:** un aqá-ye shærifí-e.

(cues: dústæm, moællémæm, mehri, jæmshid, etc.)

Lesson Four　　　MODERN PERSIAN　　　درس چهارم

4.9 Reading and Writing
4.9.1 Diacritics حَرَكات (واكه ها)

For westerners, the most striking feature of the Persian alphabet system, after the direction in which it is written, is that not all the sounds are written. In particular, the vowel sounds /e/, /æ/, and /o/ are not represented by specific letters, as are /i/, /a/, and /u/. What sounds like /bæradær/ is written in Persian characters as *bradr* (برادر), /doktor/ as *dktr* (دكتر), and /chekar/ as *chkar* (چكار).

Of course there are diacritical marks, called حركات that can be used to indicate these vowels or, when there is a consonant cluster, the absence of a vowel. They are as follows:

Sound	Persian Name		Arabic Name	Shape and Position
/æ/	zebær	زِبَر	fæthe	◌َ
/e/	zir	زیر	kæsre	◌ِ
/o/	pish	پیش	zæmme	◌ُ
no vowel	sokun	سُكون	sokun	◌ْ

Using the حركات the pronunciation of the words used as examples so far in this subsection would be indicated like this:

حَرَكات　چِكار　دُكْتُر　بَرادَر

And the names of the individual diacritical marks like this:

زیر　زِبَر　پیش　سُكون

These signs are a nuisance to print since they don't fit comfortably on the line like the letters of the alphabet. They are also difficult to read both because they are smaller than regular letters and because the *zir* of one line overlaps with the *zebær* of the next. As a consequence they do not appear in the normal run of printing or in correspondence. They are used in fine editions of literary classics and, to some extent, in elementary school texts to indicate the pronunciation of new or rare words. We will use them quite sparingly in here for the same purposes.

Lesson Four   *MODERN PERSIAN*   درس چهارم

The absence of حرکات or some other means of indicating all the vowels in a new word can make it difficult to be sure of its pronunciation. However, as you have already seen, many Persian words are spelled rationally, with a sign for every sound, and the pronunciation of many more is either rational in large part, or conforms to patterns that will become familiar to you as you progress in the language. To help you in your mastery of first-year Persian, we will indicate the pronunciation of all new vocabulary at the beginning of the lesson in which it occurs. The Glossary also contains all the vocabulary used in the text together with Latin transcriptions.

Reading Exercise 1: Spell and read aloud.

Example: pe zir dal zebær re /pedær/   پِدَر

بَرادَر   بَرادَرَم   پِدَر   مِرسی   بَد
دوسْت   تِکْرار   دُرُسْت   زِنْدِگی   سَلام

4.9.2 (ّ) تَشدید

There are a number of words in Persian — mostly of Arabic origin — that contain doubled or geminated consonants. The doubling of a consonant is called تشدید *tæshdid* in Persian. It is not indicated in the script by writing the consonant twice, as it would be in any of the languages using the Latin alphabet, but by placing a special sign — also called a تشدید — over the appropriate character. Thus, the Persian word for "teacher" is written:

مُعَلِّم not مُعَلْلِم

The (ّ) looks like a small ـس without the connecting line, or, to switch alphabets, like a small script "w." As you have surely guessed already, the تشدید is rarely used in printing or correspondence, but, like the حرکات, appears only in fine editions and school texts. Further explanation of doubled consonants is given below in Lesson 6(6.1).

Here are further examples of words with doubled (geminated) consonants:

Lesson Four   *MODERN PERSIAN*   درس چهارم

/motæshækker-æm/ "I am thankful; thank you"   مُتَشَکِّرَم

/næqqash/ "painter"   نَقّاش

/mæhæll/ "location, place"   مَحَلّ (جا)

4.9.3 Vocabulary Review. Spell and Read Aloud.

Here is a selection of words from Lessons 1 through 3 for which the pronunciation has been indicated by the use of حرکات and تشدید. They are given in alphabetical order, although all letters of the alphabet are not represented.

Example: pe zir dal zebær re /pedær/ پِدَر

بَد	تَهْران	تَبْریز	اینْجا	آمْریکا	آلْمان
تِکْرار کُنید	پِدَر	بِهْتَر	بِبَنْدید	بِبَخْشید	بَدْنیسْت
حَرْف بِزَنید	اِمْشَب	چِکار	جَمْشید	تُنْدْتَر	تُنْد
میکُنَم	خواهِش	خواهَر	خوابْگاه	خُدا	حَرَکات
ژاپُنی	رَشْت	راسْت	دوسْت	دُرُسْت	دانِشْگاه
عَلی	عَرَبی	شَهْلا	سَلام	سَلام	شَریفی
مُتَشَکِّرَم	لَنْدَن	کَم	گَرْما	کُجا	فارْسی
هَنوز	میکُنَم	میفَهْمَم	میپُرْسَم	مُعَلِّم	مَشْهَد

4.9.4 Representing the Unwritten Vowels

Although there are no letters in the Persian alphabet that are used exclusively to represent /æ/, /e/, and /o/, in certain situations, the letters ا, و, and ه are made to do double service by representing one or another of them.

In initial position, all three of these vowels are represented by ا. Any word that begins with an ا followed by any letter but و or ی must be read as beginning with one of these vowels. (Both و and ی, however, can also be read as consonants, as you will see in Lesson 5, Section 5.9.)

141

Lesson Four   *MODERN PERSIAN*   درس چهارم

The حرکات are sometimes used to indicate which vowel is appropriate, but by and large at this stage in your learning, you simply will have to guess which to read, unless it is a word you already know.

Examples:

اِنْگِلِسْتان	/engelestan/	"England"	اَز	/æz/	"from"
اَمْریکا	/emrika/	"America"	اَز کُجا	/æz koja/	"how"
اِسْپانیا	/espania/	"Spain"	اَرْمَنِسْتان	/ærmænestan/	"Armenia"
اِسْم	/esm/	"name"	اُسْتُرالیا	/ostralia/	"Australia"
			اُسْتاد	/ostad/	"professor"

You should note that words that begin with an *eyn* ع and one of these vowels are indistinguishable in pronunciation from those that begin with an *ælef* ا. That is, you cannot tell by ear that the first column of words given below all begin with ع and the second with ا:

آل	/al/	"family"	عالی	/ali/	"excellent"
اَلْبُرْز	/ælborz/	"Elburz"	عَلی	/æli/	"Ali"
الیاس	/elias/	"Elias"	عِلْم	/elm/	"science"
اُرْدو	/ordu/	"camp"	عُرْف	/orf/	"tradition"

The letter ـه is used to represent /e/ or /æ/ when either sound occurs at the end of a word. Thus نه /næ/ "no" and به /be/ "to, toward." Of course, ـه can also have a consonantal value in this position, and نه and به are in fact homographs for /noh/ "nine" and /beh/ "quince." Such occasions for misunderstandings are quite rare, fortunately, and it is worth emphasizing that in the vast majority of cases, ـه at the end of a word stands for the vowel /e/.

Examples:

مَدْرِسه	/mædrese/	"school"	مُکالِمه	/mokaleme/	"conversation"
فِرِشْته	/fereshte/	"angel"	تَرْجَمه	/tærjome/	"translation"
بَله	/bæle/	"yes"	فَرانْسه	/færanse/	"France"

Lesson Four　　　　　　　　*MODERN PERSIAN*　　　　　　درس چهارم

| سه | /se/ | "three" | تُرکیه | /torkie/ | "Turkey" |
| بَچه | /bæche/ | "child" | لَهْجه | /læhje/ | "dialect, accent" |

In the very few cases where /o/ occurs in final position, it is represented by و. Note that whenever the word دو /do/ "two" appears as part of a compound word the و is retained even though by the rules of the Persian writing system it might be dropped.

Examples:

تو	/to/	"you (familiar)"	پیانو	/piano/	"piano"
پالتو	/palto/	"overcoat"	دو	/do/	"two"
دو باره	/do bare/	"again"	دو چَرْخه	/do chærkhe/	"bicycle"

While /æ/ and /e/ are never represented by any letter in medial position, medial /o/ is sometimes represented by the letter و. Several of the words for which this is true are quite common, as: خود /khod/ "self" خوش /khosh/ "good" خور/خورد /khor-khord/ "eat." In order to indicate which vowel sound is represented by medial و، حرکات may be used. The convention is that زبر is used before و if it stands for /o/ and پیش if it stands for /u/. In some cases the /o/ in a word you have learned is really pronounced as an /ow/ glide in Formal Written Persian (FWP), in which case it is also represented by زبر:

| خوشه | /khushe/ | "bunch" but | خوش | /khosh/ | "good, happy" |
| رُو | /ru/ | "face" but | روشن | /ro(w)shæn/ | "light" |

This orthographic convention derives from the fact that و (and ی) are sometimes consonants and sometimes vowels. Consonantal و and ی will be discussed below in Lesson 5 (5.9).

Reading Exercise 2: Transcribe into phonetic script.

خوشْگِل　　اُتُو　　اِش　　اَنْد　　اَسْت　　دَه
گُذَشْتَه　　کُمیته　　خوراک　　خودْکار　　با هوش　　خوشه

143

Lesson Four MODERN PERSIAN درس چهارم

4.9.5 Transcribing Foreign Words

As the pronunciation of foreign words must be adapted to the phonology of Persian, so their spelling must be adapted to its writing system. Because this writing system is weak in vowel signs, the results of such adaptations are often quite surprising.

Examples:

تِلِفُن	/telefon/	"telephone"	آی بی ام	/ay bi em/	"IBM"
نیو جِرْزی	/nio jerzi/	"New Jersey"	سیا	/sia/	"CIA"
کافه تِریا	/kafeteria/	"cafeteria"	زیراکْس	/ziraks/	"Xerox"

4.9.6 Writing Practice

Answer the following questions. Note that the only second person plural ending used in writing is ید — /-id/. (cf. Lesson 2, Section 2.11, part 4)

۱. من فارسی تند حرف میزنم؟   ۷. شما عربی میفهمید؟
۲. شما فارسی زیاد تمرین میکنید؟   ۸. من با شما چینی حرف میزنم؟
۳. من در آمریکا زندگی میکنم؟   ۹. من از شما زیاد میپرسم؟
۴. شما کجا زندگی میکنید؟   ۱۰. شما با معلّم مکالمه تمرین میکنید؟
۵. شما در دانشگاه چکار میکنید؟   ۱۱. ما اینجا ژاپنی حرف میزنیم یا فارسی؟
۶. ما اینجا زیاد ترجمه میکنیم؟   ۱۲. شما در کلاس چِکار میکنید؟

4.10 Drills, Part II

Drill 15: Substitution   (with use of past roots of verbs)

a. fereydúno pærvin koja <u>zendegí mìkonænd</u>?

(cues: kar kærd, dærs dad, tæmrin kærd, værzesh kærd, (zendegi kærd))

b. hoséyno vida chi <u>míkhunænd</u>?

(cues: yad gereft, dunest, hærf zæd, fæhmid, tekrar kærd, dærs dad, porsid, tærjome kærd, goft, nevesht, (khund))

Lesson Four MODERN PERSIAN درس چهارم

Drill 16: soálo jævab

    pedǽro madǽretun koja zendegí mìkonænd? kár mìkonænd? koja?

    pedǽro madǽretun inglisi mídunænd? færanse chetor?

    pedǽro madǽretun dǽrs mìdænd? (chi dǽrs mìdænd?)

    SSSo SSS (two students from class) inja almani hǽrf mìzænænd? chi hǽrf mìzænænd?

    SSSo SSS æræbi yád mìgirænd? farsi chetor?

    SSSo SSS værzésh mìkonænd? (æz una béporsid.) sær-e kelas værzésh mìkonænd?

    SSSo SSS tondtær farsi mínevisænd (?) ya hǽrf mìzænænd. chéra?

    (You may continue to ask a few of your own questions according to this pattern)

Drill 17: Substitution

    <u>pedǽro madǽræm</u> fæqæt inglisi hǽrf mìzænænd.

    (cues: pedǽræm, shoma, ælío reza, ma, una, jæmshid, un pesæro un dokhtær,

    shohæretun, gitío mehri, giti, mæn, un bæche, ma, hoseyn, (pedǽro madǽræm))

Drill 18: Substitution

    a. <u>bæradǽræm</u> <u>shæba</u> <u>inglisi</u> <u>dǽrs mìde</u>.

        mæhmúdo kamran -----------------------------------

        --tæmrin kærd

        un pesær---

        ----------------------------piano-------------------

        mæn--

        ----------------------------almani------------------

        ---tærjome kærd

        shiríno vida---------------------------------------

        ---yad gereft

        una---

Lesson Four *MODERN PERSIAN* درس چهارم

```
-------------------------------------------nevesht
---------------------------inglisi----------------------
bæradǽræm-------------------------------------------
---------------------------------------------(dærs dad)
```

b. <u>fereydúno giti</u> dær <u>iran</u> <u>zendegí mìkonænd</u>.

```
dústæm---------------------------------------------
una------------------------------------------------
------------------------------------------kar kærd
ma-------------------------------------------------
---------------------------bimarestan----------------
pedǽro madǽræm-------------------------------------
---------------------------daneshgah------------------
---------------------------dærs dad-------------------
```
(pedæro madæræm dær daneshgah dærs mìdænd.)
```
fereydun--------------------------------------------
------------------------------------------værzesh kærd
---------------------------khune----------------------
---------------------------mædrese--------------------
fereydúno giti---------------------------------------
-----------------iran---------------------------------
-----------------------------------------(zendegi kærd)
```

Drill 19: soálo jævab

shoma dær bimarestan kár mìkonin? ba ki kár mìkonin? una farsi mídunænd?

shoma chetor? koja kár mìkonin?

SSSo SSS kár mìkonænd?

Lesson Four MODERN PERSIAN درس چهارم

shoma ba pedǽro madǽretun zendegí mìkonin?

ma inja chi yád mìgirim? sær-e kelas chekár mìkonim? mokaleme yád mìgirim?

mæn sær-e kelas tond hærf mìzænæm? shoma chetor? (chéra?)

bæradǽro khahǽretun chekár mìkonænd? koja zendegí mìkonænd?

shoma inja khundǽno neveshtæn yád mìgirin? farsi ya inglisi?

ma inja taaróf mìkonim? taarof yǽ:ni chi?

khánum, bébækhshid. in medád-e? (chi-e?)

mǽno mehri* inja farsi hærf mìzænim? ba ki hærf mìzænim?   *(name of teaching
                                                                            assistant)

mehrío pærvin farsi hærf mìzænænd (?) ya torki.

Drill 20: Substitution - /dústesh/ "his/her friend" (see Section 4.11.5 below)

    a.   <u>dús</u>tesh farsi mídune.

        (cues: pesær, khahær, moællem, madær, dust, dokhtær, pedær, (dust))

    b.   ba <u>dús</u>tesh hichvæqt <u>inglisi</u> hærf némizæne.

        (cues: pedær/farsi, khahær/espanioli, moællem/chini, dokhtær/almani,

        dust/torki, madær/rusi, pesær/færanse, (dust/inglisi))

Drill 21: Substitution

(See Section 4.1 for a discussion of the intonation used in sentences that use *ya* "or.")

    a.   <u>shoma</u> farsi <u>tondtær</u> hærf mìzænin (?) ya <u>reza</u>.

        ("Do you speak Persian faster or does Reza?")

        (cues: una/shoma, mæn/æli, bolændtær, shoma/Tom o Shæhla, bishtær,

        fereydúno mehri/æli, behtær, mæn/shoma, tondtær (shoma/reza))

    b.   shoma farsi <u>tondtær</u> <u>hærf</u> <u>mìzænin</u> (?) ya inglisi.

        (cues: behtær, nevesht, tælæffoz kærd, bishtær, dunest, tekrar kærd, bolændtær,

        behtær, tærjome kærd, hærf zæd, (tondtær))

Lesson Four   MODERN PERSIAN   درس چهارم

Drill 22: Free Conversation

The class breaks up into groups of three or four to ask each other questions — with or without their textbooks — and carry on a conversation using the kinds of questions they have been practicing.

4.11 Grammar Discussion

4.11.1 Parts of Speech and the Elements of a Sentence

You have been learning implicitly in the drills of the first four lessons that there is a specific order to the elements of a Persian sentence. The most striking characteristic of this order — in its difference from English — is that the verb generally occurs at the end of the sentence. As you will see throughout this text there are only very few exceptions to this rule. That is, Persian is a verb-final language but it is not rigidly so.

Since the verb (V) occurs finally, sentences that contain a direct object will place both the subject (S) and the object (O) before the verb (V), yielding SOV:

mæn	farsi	míkhunæm.
S	O	V
shoma	gitar	tæmrín mìkonin.

To expand upon the subject-verb or subject-object-verb minimum, other elements are then added to the sentence. Each of these elements appears in a specific place in the sentence, granted, of course, that there is a certain degree of flexibility in this order.

These additional elements include adverbs of time, place, and manner; prepositional phrases of time, place, and manner, etc.; question words; sentence adverbials; and various miscellaneous words. Each of these elements can be expanded and of course elements of different categories can occur in a sentence, potentially yielding a long sentence with various types of elements. Before we give you the specific rules for their placement, let us discuss the elements themselves.

Lesson Four   *MODERN PERSIAN*   درس چهارم

Note: Verbs of motion behave differently from other verbs. See the Note to Dialogue in Lesson 7 (7.9), Colloquial/FWP Transformations.

Adverbs

You have learned the following adverbs that belong to various adverb types:

Adverbs of Time

    shæba, ruza, hala, hænuz, hichvæqt, hæmishe ("always")

Adverbs of Place

The English category of Adverbs of Place, which includes such words as "here" and "there," does not have an equivalent in Persian. The equivalent words in Persian are all nouns and words such as /inja/, /unja/, and /khune/ in a Persian sentence are actually truncated forms of prepositional phrases (/dær inja/, etc.) and should therefore be considered with prepositional phrases of place.

Adverbs of Manner

Most adverbs of manner double as adjectives. As adverbs, however, they do have a specific position in the sentence as discussed below in Section 4.11.2. The adverbs of manner that you have encountered so far are:

    khub, tond, tondtær, yævash, yævashtær, bolænd, bolændtær, behtær, bishtær, ziad

Prepositional Phrases

Prepositional Phrases of Time

    None encountered so far. (an example is *bæ:d æz zohr* "afternoon")

Prepositional Phrases of Place

    dær daneshgah, dær shiraz, etc.   dær shiraz dærs mìde.

    sær-e kelas, etc.   sær-e kelas fæqæt farsi hærf mìzænim.

Prepositions deleted:

    inja, unja, khune   mæn khune farsi tæmrín mìkonæm.

Lesson Four   *MODERN PERSIAN*   درس چهارم

Other "place-like" phrases:

    be farsi, be inglisi, etc.   lotfæn be farsi tærjome konid

Prepositional Phrases of Manner

    None encountered so far. (an example is *békhubí* "well")

Other Prepositional Phrases

    Accompaniment: ba _____: mæn ba æli farsi tæmrín mìkonæm

                                    ba moællémetun farsi hærf mìzænin?

Question Words

    Question words and their position in the sentence have been given an independent treatment below in Section 4.11.2.

Sentence Adverbials

    There are several types of sentence adverbials but for our present purposes, we shall say that they generally occur in the beginning of the sentence and modify or contribute to the sentence **as a whole**. This category includes the following words you have learned:

    lotfæn, mæsælæn

    máshallah

    bǽle, nǽ(kher)

    Sometimes a whole phrase or a shortened sentence may have the same function, as in the case of /khahésh mìkonæm/, which can have the same meaning as /lotfæn/.

    khahésh mìkonæm yævashtær hærf bèzænid.

4.11.2 Word Order

    The word order of a Persian sentence — including the various optional elements — can be represented in the following formula:

    Sentence Adverbials + Subject + Time + Place + Other Prepositional Phrases + Accompaniment or Manner + Object + Verb

    For the present discussion, adverbs and prepositional phrases that express the same

Lesson Four   *MODERN PERSIAN*   درس چهارم

function (e.g., adverbs of time and prepositional phrases of time) are considered one category (e.g., time).

So far you have not encountered any sentence with all these elements simultaneously. However, you have seen many sentences with various combinations of these elements:

Sent Adv	Sub-ject	Time	Place	Other Prepositional Phrases	Manner	Object	Verb
	ma		sær-e kelas	mokaleme		tæmrín mìkonim.
	ma	shæba	dær khabgah			farsi	tæmrín mìkonim.
	ma	hala			tondtær	farsi	yád mìgirim.
	ma	hænuz	dær bimarestan				kár mìkonim.
	ma			ba shohæretun		farsi	hærf mìzænim.
	ma		inja		ziad		tærjomé mìkonim?
bæle	ma	hala			fæqæt	farsi	hærf mìzænim.

Or, for example, a sentence with all the elements present:

bæle   mæn   hala   sær-e kelas   ba moællémæm   ziad   farsi   tæmrín mìkonæm.

بله، من حالا سر کلاس با معلمم فارسی تمرین میکنم (می کنم).

بله، من هرگز سر کلاس با شهلا فارسی تمرین نمیکنم (نمی کنم) ولی با او بازی میکنم.

Expansion of Elements

Within each element more than one constituent can occur at a time, or any given element may be expanded, yielding potentially even longer sentences. You have seen, for example, that a subject can be expanded from *pedæretun* to *pedæro madæretun* or from *mæn* to *mæno shoma* or even *mæno pedæro madæræm*. The object, of course, may also be expanded, e.g., *almanío færanse*.

So far you have not encountered more than one time word or manner word in a sentence, but they occur frequently, as you will see when we introduce time word phrases.

Lesson Four MODERN PERSIAN درس چهارم

Soon it will seem to you that the sentences of Lesson 4 were not only easier but so much shorter than sentences you will be making automatically.

In the expansion of phrases you will notice that some words such as *fæqæt* and *khéyli* can be used to expand more than one kind of element in a sentence:

ma ruza dær khabgah farsi tæmrín mìkonim	"In the daytime we practice Persian in the dorm."
fæqæt ma ruza dær khabgah farsi tæmrín mìkonim.	"Only we practice Persian in the dorm in the daytime."
ma fæqæt ruza dær khabgah farsi tæmrín mìkonim.	"We practice Persian in the dorm only in the daytime."
ma ruza fæqæt dær khabgah farsi tæmrín mìkonim.	"In the daytime we practice Persian only in the dorm."
ma ruza dær khabgah fæqæt farsi tæmrín mìkonim.	"In the daytime in the dorm we practice only Persian."

Flexibility of Word Order

There is, of course, a certain flexibility in the word order formula. For reasons of emphasis or focus, certain elements will move forward — sometimes only one element farther forward and sometimes to the beginning of the sentence. A very common switch accompanying only slight emphasis will place the direct object before the adverb of manner, or the place word before the time word, as in the following sentences you have learned:

Object + Manner	**Normal** (Manner + Object)
shoma farsi khub hærf mìzænin.	(shoma khub farsi hærf mìzænin.)
shoma farsi tondtær hærf mìzænin, ya inglisi?	(shoma tondtær farsi hærf mìzænin, ya inglisi?

Place + Time	**Normal** (Time + Place)
ma sær-e kelas hichvæqt inglisi hærf némizænim.	(ma hichvæqt sær-e kelas inglisi hærf

némizænim.)

Further grammatical rules concerning word order and changes in word order for emphasis, focus, and other reasons will be discussed in future lessons.

4.11.3 Question Order: Persian vs. English

Persian and English both have two types of questions: those with question words and those without. You have already seen that these two types of questions have different patterns of intonation.

Question words — also known as WH-words in English — in Persian and English are the following:

Persian	**English**
ki	who
chi	what
koja	where
key	when
chéra	why
kodum	which, which one
chetor (cheguneh)	how (usually "how" of description, "like what")
chetorí	how (by what means)
cheqædr	how much
chænd-ta	how many
etc.	

There are several differences in question structure between English and Persian:

1. *Position of the Question Word*

The English question words tend to be moved forward in the sentence, usually to the first position:

Lesson Four *MODERN PERSIAN* درس چهارم

(a) I live <u>with George</u>.

<u>Who</u> do you live with? (usual, everyday speech)

<u>With whom</u> do you live? (more formal style)

(b) I went to London <u>by train</u>.

<u>How</u> did you get to London?

In Persian question words usually do not shift places but instead occupy the same position in the sentence that their non-question counterparts (e.g., their answers) occupy. The question word may even replace the verb, which is sentence-final:

base sentence:	<u>dústæm</u>	<u>ruza</u>	<u>dær daneshgah</u>	<u>farsi</u>	<u>tæmrín mìkone?</u>
Subject =	<u>ki</u>	ruza	dær daneshgah	farsi	tæmrín mìkone.
Time =	dústæm	<u>key</u>	dær daneshgah	farsi	tæmrín mìkone?
Place =	dústæm	ruza	<u>koja</u>	farsi	tæmrín mìkone?
Object =	dústæm	ruza	dær daneshgah	<u>chi</u>	tæmrín mìkone?
Verb =	dústæm	ruza	dær daneshgah		<u>chekár mìkone?</u>

Notice, however, that the question words are fronted in the equivalent English sentence:

	Who	**Verb**	**What**	**Where**	**When**
	<u>My friend</u>	<u>practices</u>	<u>Persian</u>	<u>at the university</u>	<u>in the daytime</u>.

Subject	**Who** practices Persian at the university in the daytime?
Verb	**What** does my friend do at the university in the daytime?
Object	**What** does my friend practice at the university in the daytime?
Place	**Where** does my friend practice Persian in the daytime?
Time	**When** does my friend practice Persian at the university?

2. *Inversion*

In addition to fronting the question words, English also inverts word orders in certain tenses, and where modals do not already exist, it introduces them in order to perform this inversion:

Lesson Four MODERN PERSIAN درس چهارم

    (c)   You are studying Persian <u>for good reasons</u>.

           <u>Why</u> are you studying Persian?   (<u>You are</u> becomes <u>are you</u>.)

           but notice the introduction of a modal word for (<u>does</u>) purposes of inversion:

    (d)   He lives <u>in Tehran</u>.

           <u>Where</u> does he live?   (<u>He lives</u> becomes <u>does he live</u>.)

Equivalent changes do not occur in Persian. There is no inversion of subject and modal and as mentioned above, the question words are not fronted to the first position:

    He is studying Persian <u>in Tehran</u>.   dústetun <u>dær tehran</u> farsi míkhune.

    <u>Where</u> is he studying Persian?   dústetun   <u>koja</u>   farsi míkhune?

    (2 word order changes)   (no word order changes)

3.   *Questions with Prepositional Phrases*

    Notice that in English questions that contain a preposition before the question word, only the question is fronted in everyday speech and the preposition is left behind:

        <u>What</u> does he write <u>with</u>?

Because fronting does not occur in Persian questions in the first place, this situation does not occur. Just remember never to split a preposition from the following question word:

    æli <u>ba bæradæresh</u>   zendegí mìkone.   æli <u>ba medad</u>   mínevise.

    æli   <u>ba ki</u>   zendegí mìkone?   æli   <u>ba chi</u>   mínevise?

4.11.4 Prepositions and Pronouns

In English, pronouns — and only pronouns — change form after prepositions and in certain other positions:

        "<u>I</u> know." but "Sit with <u>me</u>."

This change in form of pronouns is known as "case". Other languages, such as Latin or Russian, have a full case system for nouns as well as pronouns. Persian has no case forms. As a result — in contrast with English — Persian pronouns remain unchanged after prepositions:

    mæn "I"   ba mæn, æz mæn   "with me, from me"

Lesson Four　　　　　　*MODERN PERSIAN*　　　　درس چهارم

ma "we"　　　　ba ma, æz ma　　　　"with us, from us"

etc.

This is just another example of how English and Persian contrast and how the resulting difference is more a problem of English grammar and English categories than of Persian. Note the discussion of the possessive forms in Lesson 5 (5.11.1).

4.11.5 The Ending Pronoun, -esh "his, her, its"

Persian has a full complement of suffixed (attached, unstressed) pronouns as well as the separable pronouns that you have already encountered. Suffixed pronouns are attached directly to the nouns they modify and function much as "possessive" pronouns do in English. Here is the full set of suffixed pronouns for colloquial and formal (FWP) Persian:

Meaning	**Colloquial**	**FWP**	**Colloq. Ex.**	**FWP Ex.**
my	-æm	-æm	medadæm	medadæm
your (familiar)	-et	-at	medadet	medadat
his, her, its	-esh	-ash	medadesh	medadah
our	-emun	-eman	medademun	medademan
your (plural, familiar/polite;singular polite)	-etun	-etan	medadetun	medadetan
their (also singular third person polite)	-eshun	-eshan	medadeshun	medadeshan

The suffixed pronouns are also discussed at length below in Lesson 5 (5.11.8).

4.12 Meals and Food: Part 1

Iranians eat their three meals a day at about the same times that Americans do. But the traditional Iranian diet and the Iranian rhythms of food and work differ substantially from those of Americans. The Iranian work day begins quite early, often at seven or eight o'clock, and continues until one or two in the afternoon when there is often a midday break. Most

Lesson Four MODERN PERSIAN درس چهارم

government offices close for the day at this time. Elsewhere, work resumes in late afternoon and continues until early evening. In this pattern, the morning hours predominate. Work may stop in the early afternoon and resumes at a reduced pace in the late afternoon.

sobhane is the first meal of the day. In its simplest form it consists of bread and tea with sugar. White cheese and jam are often included and, possibly, a soft-boiled egg. It is a light meal, taken early in the day. Office workers may supplement it with a sandwich (cheese, boiled egg, chicken or tongue) in midmorning — the Tehran equivalent of coffee and pastry. More commonly, hunger is staved off by drinking several cups of hot, sweet tea throughout the morning.

Traditionally, the principal meal of the day is *nahar*. Ideally, people return from work and children from school so that all members of the family can be home then. The centerpiece of the meal will be a *khoresht* or *polo* (see Lesson 5, Section 5.12 for descriptions of foods mentioned here) or, on special occasions, *kæbab*, but bread, fresh green herbs, yogurt, and onions will also be served. In very traditional households, this meal, like all meals, is served on a cloth *(sofre)* spread on the floor in the main room of the house, with the members of the family seated around it. Many workmen either bring their lunch with them, or some member of the family will take it to where they work. Others will purchase a lunch of a sandwich (*sandvich*) or of stew (*abgusht*) from a nearby coffeehouse (*qæhvekhane*) — so named although the principal beverage served is tea. Tea comes in small, individual pots that have been simmering on the back of the stove all morning and is served with large loaves of bread and a handful of onions and fresh herbs.

Sham is a lighter meal than *nahar*, but more substantial than *sobhane*. It may be no more than a sandwich, an egg dish called *kuku*, stew, or a dish called *kotlet*, which consists of meat, bread, onions and spices ground up together and fried in patties. It may also be the leftovers from *nahar*, and it is eaten after nightfall. The only time that *sham* is the major meal of the day is when guests have been invited. Then, many dishes are prepared and the meal is served quite late.

Lesson Four　　　　*MODERN PERSIAN*　　　　درس چهارم

Iran's incorporation into the world economy has gradually imposed a more western style of work schedule on some sectors of the Iranian workforce so that at present there is a modern, western pattern of work and meals that exists alongside the traditional one, and often overlaps with it. In this pattern, there are two roughly equal periods of work, one before and one after the midday meal. Lunch must be a light meal because digesting a heavy one would interfere with the afternoon's work. The lunch break is also so brief and the distance from work or school to home so great that it is not practical for workers and school children to return there for a meal. The evening meal is the only one where the whole family may sit down together. The pull of the traditional pattern is strong, however, and the tendency is to eat a substantial meal both at noon and in the evening.

A spread of Persian sweets

nan, mast, pænir, sæbzi

Although Iran is justly famous for its savory pilaffs, rice is often a luxury. *nan* (colloq. *nun*) "bread" made from wheat flour is the real staple of the Iranian diet and is a part of most meals. For most Iranians a meal without bread just isn't a meal. Until quite recently, bread was cooked only in small bread bakeries (*nunvaí*) scattered through every neighborhood. And, since each bakery made only one type of bread, there were often several *nunvais* in fairly close

proximity. Recently, the government has encouraged the production of bread in factory ovens (*nán-e mashini*) as an economy measure. There are almost infinite regional variations in bread but the most common types are the following:

nún-e taftun. It is a flat, round loaf, a foot to a foot and a half in diameter, cooked on the inner wall of a large, dome shaped ceramic oven (*tænur*). The baker *(nunva)* slaps on the loaf with a convex wooden paddle, and peels it off with tongs when it is ready.

nún-e sængæk The word for "stone" in Persian is *sæng,* and a small stone or pebble is a *sængæk*. *nún-e sængæk* is cooked on a heap of small pebbles that has been heated by a gas jet. The loaf is shaped like a rough isosceles triangle. It is crispy and delicious when hot, and the bread of choice for breakfast. The bakers shake most of the stones loose from the loaves when they bring them out of the oven, but a few wind up on the scale with your bread, too. You can crack a tooth on those stones if you are not careful.

nún-e bærbæri. This is also rectagular, like *sængæk,* but it is thicker, marked by parallel ridges that run the length of the loaf, and is cooked in an oven like a pizza oven. It is also sprinkled with sesame seeds. Afghan bread, now available in some American cities, is the same as *nún-e bærbæri*.

nún-e lævash This word means ordinary bread in Arabic, but in Persian it refers to a thin, delicate kind of *taftun* that is baked principally by Armenians and is found basically in Tehran.

nún-e sefid. "White bread" is the term used for the slender, tubular loaves that are used for sandwiches.

Yogurt (*mast*) is usually eaten plain and is a common part of *nahar* and *sham*.[1] When it is mixed with water and served as a beverage, it is known as *abduq* or simply *duq*. Two other dishes made from *mast* are especially popular in summer. The first, *másto khiar,* is a side dish made by adding grated cucumbers (*khiar*), a little onion and salt to it. *Másto khiar* is served with a few ice cubes in the bowl. *Abduq khiar* is a summer soup that starts out like *másto khiar*, but to this are added water (*ab*), finely chopped fresh herbs— *næ:na* "mint,"

Lesson Four *MODERN PERSIAN* درس چهارم

tærkhun "tarragon," *ræyhan* "Iranian basil," *jæ:færi* "flat leaf parsley," *shevid* "dill," *tære* "small, Iranian leeks," *geshniz* "coriander,"-- finely chopped walnuts (*gerdu*), and raisins (*keshmesh*).

There is really only one kind of cheese (*pænir*) commonly found in Iran. It is white, is made from the milk of sheep or cows, and served either freshly made (unaged, *pænir-e taze*) — called farmer's cheese in the United States — or pickled in brine like Greek feta cheese.

One other common side dish is simply a plate of fresh green herbs — the same ones used in the preparation of *abduq khiar* with the addition of scallions (*piazce*) and radishes (*toropche*). These are eaten with fresh bread and a little *pænir* — delicious!

1. Note that yogurt is never eaten with jam or honey. The idea of mixing the two is abhorrent to most Iranians because yogurt and jam belong to two conflicting food categories — "cold" and "hot" — and they mix the two only in cooking.
(See Lesson 5, Section 5.12 for a description of the principal dishes served at *nahar* and *sham*.)

شما امشب(tonight) شام چی میخورید؟
من امشب برای(for) شام چلوکباب، ماست و خیار، و بستنی(ice cream) میخورم.
شما صبحانه چی میخورید؟

Reading

sælam. Nam-e (esm-e) mæn Jæmshid-e. mæn dær tehran zendegi mikonæm. æn daneshju hasam va dær daneshgah-e tehran ædæbiyat-e farsi mikhunæm. pedar va madæræm dær tehran zendigi mikonæn. mæn do ta khahær be esm-e puran va parivn va do ta bæradær be esm-e farzad va farhad daræm. puran daneshamuz-e dabirestan-e. parvin daneshamuz-e dabestan-e. bæradærham dær esfahan kar mikonan. farzad dar ketabkhaneh-ye daneshgah-e esfahan kar mikone va farhad pezheshk-e.

Lesson Five   درس پنجم

TOPICS COVERED IN THIS LESSON

- Talk about Daily Activities: Playing Games/Sports, Taking a Bath, Cooking, Eating, Resting, Reading the Newspaper, Smoking, Having Coffee/Tea, Sleeping.

- Ask More About Family and Personal Life: Do you have a car/bicycle? How many children do you have?

- Begin Offering, Accepting and Refusing Food in Formal Situations.

- Say Good-bye to a New Acquaintance: It was nice meeting you.

- Give or Ask for Descriptions: What kind of book is this? It's a Persian book/a language cassette/a telephone book/a Persian test, etc.)

- Talk about People's Relations (Mehri's Sister/Jay's Teacher) or People's Objects (Ahmad's book/ Denise's Persian exam), etc.

- Use the Higher Persian Numbers

- Start Giving Opinions: I think (that)..., I don't think so.

- Begin Explaining and Defining Words in Persian.

- Use Classroom Expressions: Whose Turn is It? We have a test tomorrow. Do we have homework tonight? I forget/I don't remember. don't know what I'm supposed to do. You're kidding! etc.

RESOURCES AND BACKGROUND: INFORMATION AND ACCURACY

Phonology

    The Glottal Stop and Lengthened Vowels

    The Loss of /h/ and Lengthened Vowels

    Final Consonant Clusters (A)

Grammar Patterns to Be Exercised

    Verb Phrase

        "to have"   ***dasht-dar***

Lesson Five MODERN PERSIAN درس پنجم

    The Negative Form of "to have"   ***nædaræm***

    Verbs that Require Direct Objects   ***khund-khun*** "to read, study, sing,"

        khord-khor: "to eat, drink"

    "What is this?" "Who is this?"   in chi-e? in kí-e?

Noun Phrase

    Possession: The *Ezafe* Construction

    Indefinite Article   *ye*

    Counting Nouns   chænd-ta sib? se-ta.

    Possessive Endings   *-emun* "our," *-eshun* "their"

    Numbers

Adjectives and Adverbs

    "also"   *(h)æm*

    "both___and"   *hæm ___hæm*

Vocabulary Building

    Noun + Verbalizer = Verb

Reading and Writing Persian

    Consonantal و and ى

    More Duplicate Letters: /t/: ط, /s/: ص, / z/: ض, ظ, /q/: غ, /n/: أ, and /:/: ع

    Read and Translate: Full Sentences

    Written Representation of the *ezafe*

Grammar Discussion

    Noun Phrase

        The *ezafe* construction

        Extended Noun Phrases

        Counting and Counting Nouns, Time Words, Money

        The Second Person Familiar Pronoun

        Short Pronominal Endings for Nouns

Lesson Five　　　　*MODERN PERSIAN*　　　　درس پنجم

Verb Phrase

    dasht/dar "to have" (Affirmative and Negative)

    The Infinitive

    Verbs with Obligatory Objects: *qæza míkhoræm/dærs mìkhunæm*

    The Command Form (Imperative)

    Personal Endings for Verbs

Cultural Materials

    Two Persian Compliments

    Saying Good-bye

    Meals and Food, Part 2

    Food and Taarof

Listening Materials

    Listening Comprehension: Vida and Jo Anne

    be læhjé-ye mæshhæd

Lesson Five   *MODERN PERSIAN*   درس پنجم

5.1 Phonology

5.1.1 The Glottal Stop and Lengthened Vowels

The sound that phoneticians call the glottal stop /:/ is that sound that is heard in the English colloquial negatives, *uh-uh* or *hm-hm* or the sound representing /t/ in the word *button* when pronounced quickly in normal speech. This sound also exists in Persian where it is represented by *:eyn* and *hæmze* (see Lesson 3, Section 3.9.3 and also Lesson 5, Section 5.9.2). The pronunciation of /:/ in Persian varies according to the phonetic context in which it is found. When it is the first consonant of a word or syllable (:V or :VC — where V is any vowel and C is any consonant), the glottal stop is simply not pronounced. In this position we use no phonetic sign to represent the glottal stop. In writing, a *hæmze* in initial position is usually omitted. The written *:eyn* (ع), however, is never omitted.

Examples:

اکبر /ækbær/ but عالی /ali/ عبری /ebri/

When the glottal stop occurs after a vowel and before a consonant /V:C/, it is dropped but not without effect: the preceding vowel is lengthened in compensation for the lost glottal stop. We indicate this vowel lengthening by the use of a /:/; thus /V:C/ becomes /V:C/. Only in very carefully enunciated speech, such as that used in formal addresses or in reading aloud from a written text, is the Persian glottal stop pronounced in this position. The glottal stop as it occurs in other phonetic environments will be discussed in later lessons.

Pronunciation Drill 1: Imitation of Vowel Length

بد	/bæd/	بعد	/bæ:d/	صد	/sæd/	سعد	/sæ:d/
بدش	/bædesh/	بعدش	/bæ:desh/	صدی	/sædi/	سعدی	/sæ:di/
دوا	/dæva/	دعوا	/dæ:va/	بدن	/bædæn/	بعداً	/bæ:dæn/
علم	/ælæm/	اعلم	/æ:læm/	شله	/shole/	شعله	/sho:le/

Lesson Five MODERN PERSIAN درس پنجم

Pronunciation Drill 2: Final Consonant Clusters (A)

کفش kæfsh	بنفش bænæfsh	کشف kæshf	نصف nesf	اشک æshk
کبک kæbk	سرو særv	صرف særf	قلب qælb	ارج ærj
گرم gærm	قرن qærn	کوشک kushk	لطف lotf	ربط ræbt
عضو ozv	زرشک zereshk	نبش næbsh	لفظ læfz	مرگ mærg

5.2 Vocabulary

Since you will have learned all of the Persian alphabet by the end of this lesson, we have begun to include the Persian form of all new words that have the same written and colloquial spelling. Starting in Lessons 6 and 7, both colloquial and written forms will be given. Any words not spelled out in this lesson involve a change from colloquial to FWP.

Vocabulary, Dialogue 5

dáræm (occasionally /daræm/)	دارم	I have
dasht	داشت	to have (past stem)
pæs	پس	then (not in a temporal sense); in that case, so
tænha	تنها	alone; lonely; only
(h)æm	هم	also, too; neither
dærs mikhunæm [1]		I study
dærs khund		to study (past stem)

Vocabulary, Exercises Part I

esterahæt mìkonæm	استراحت میکنم	I rest
esterahæt kærd	استراحت کرد	to rest (past stem)
míkhoræm	میخورم	I eat, I drink (N.B.: no distinction in Persian)

165

Lesson Five MODERN PERSIAN درس پنجم

khordı	خورد	to eat, to drink (past stem)
bæ:d-æz-zo(h)r	بعد از ظهر	afternoon
bæ:d-æz-zo(h)ra[2]		afternoons, in the afternoon(s)
chai mìkhoræm	چای میخورم	I drink tea
pæs-æz-zohr,	پس از ظهر	afternoon, after the midday
pæs æz nimruz		
bazí mìkonæm	بازی میکنم	I play (games, sports - not music)
bazi kærd	بازی کرد	to play (past stem)
dush mìgiræm	دوش میگیرم	I take a shower
hæmum/hæmam	حمام	bath, public bath (Turkish style)
hæmúm mìkonæm	حمام میکنم	I bathe, take a bath
hæmum kærd	حمام کرد	to bathe (past stem) (also: hæmum mìgiræm; hæmum gereft) = dush migiram, dush gereft.
taaróf mìkonæm	تعارف میکنم	see Lesson 3, Section 3.3.2
míkhabæm	میخوابم	I sleep
khabid	خوابید	to sleep (past stem)
sob(h), bamdad, pegah	صبح (بامداد، پگاه)	morning
soba[2]		mornings, in the morning(s)
sob(h)ane/sobune[2]	صبحانه (چاشت، ناشتایی)	breakfast
valibal	والی بال	volleyball (also spelled: والیبال)
kæbab	کباب	kebab, (charcoal-) broiled meat
qæhve	قهوه	coffee
karkhune	کارخانه	factory
avaz	آواز	song, Persian classical singing

166

Lesson Five *MODERN PERSIAN* درس پنجم

italiai	ایتالیائی	Italian (language, person, adjective)
ebri	عبری	Hebrew
dæri	دری	Dari (Afghan Persian)
tajiki	تاجیکی	Tajik (the Persian of Tajikistan)
ozbæki	ازبکی	Uzbek
ordu	اردو	Urdu
hendi	هندی	Hindi; Indian (adjective or person)
name	نامه	letter (*book*)
shagerd	شاگرد	pupil, student (through high school); apprentice
ab	آب	water, juice
doróst mìkonæm	درست میکنم	I prepare, make, cook; correct, repair
dorost kærd	درست کرد	to prepare, make, cook; correct, repair (past stem)
emtehan	امتحان	examination, test
futbal	فوتبال	soccer
mæjælle	مجله	magazine
nun	نان	bread
portoqal/porteqal	پرتقال	orange
qæza	غذا	food, meal
ruzname	روزنامه	newspaper
sib	سیب	apple
zæban	زبان	language; tongue
sigar	سیگار	cigarette
sigár mìkeshæm	سیگار میکشم	I smoke

Lesson Five　　　　*MODERN PERSIAN*　　　　درس پنجم

Vocabulary, Situational and Practical Exercises

no(w)bæt	نوبت	turn (e.g. "my turn")
mærd	مرد	man
zæn	زن	woman, wife
væqt (pronounced: /vækht/)	وقت	time
emtehán mìdæm	امتحان میدم	I take a test (what the student does)
emtehán mìkonæm (+ æz)	امتحان میکنم (+ ان)	I test, examine (what the teacher does)
emtehan kærd	امتحان کرد	to test, examine (past stem)
emruz	امروز	today
emshæb	امشب	tonight
færda	فردا	tomorrow
tæklíf-e shæb	تکلیف شب	homework
khoshvæqt (/khoshvækht/)	خوشوقت	pleased, glad
fék(r) mìkonæm [3]	فکر میکنم	I think, I think so
miændishæm (formal)	فکر میکنم	I think,
fekr kærd	فکر کرد	to think (past stem)
færansævi	فرانسوی	French (adj.)

Words of Western Origin

restoran (=qæza khori)	رستوران	restaurant
otobus	اتوبوس	bus
bilit /belit (alternate spelling)	بلیت	ticket
sandvich	ساندویچ	sandwich
hotel (= mosafer khaneh)	هتل	hotel

168

Lesson Five *MODERN PERSIAN* درس پنجم

Village women

The following words of western origin are optional but may be used easily in Situational Exercises)

kompot	کمپوت	compote, fruits cooked in syrup
benzin	بنزین	gasoline
pómp-e benzin	پمپ بنزین	gas station
not	نت	notes (musical)
kurs (=dærs)	کورس (درس)	course (academic)
keyk	کیک	cake

Obligatory Vocabulary from Section 5.5: To be used in Situational and subsequent exercises

soál mìkonæm (=míporsam)	سئوال میکنم	I ask, I question
zendegi	زندگی	life
kar	کار	work, job, occupation; chore, task, endeavor; behavior, act
tæmrin	تمرین	drill, exercise, practice

Lesson Five   *MODERN PERSIAN*   درس پنجم

dærs	درس	lesson
hærf (=sokhæn)	حرف	speech, utterance, discourse
fekr (=andisheh)	فکر	thought
shukhi	شوخی	joking, kidding, joke (but not in the sense of "story, anecdote" as in "to tell a joke")
telefon	تلفن	telephone
telefón mìkonæm	تلفن میکنم	I call, phone (up)
post	پست	mail
póst mìkonæm	پست میکنم	I mail (a letter)
fotokopi	فتوکپی	photocopy
fotokopí mìkonæm	فتو کپی میکنم	I photoduplicate, Xerox
dikte	دیکته	dictation, spelling
dikté mìkonæm	دیکته میکنم	I dictate spelling words

Vocabulary, Exercises Part II

læhje	لهجه	accent, dialect
khæt(t)	خط	handwriting, line
dochærkhe	دوچرخه	bicycle
ketabkhune	کتابخانه	library
shune	شونه	comb; (also means "shoulder")
kebrit	کبریت	match(es)
chænd?	چند	how many?

Numbers; (see Drills 20 and 21 of this lesson for the use of numbers in counting nouns)

yek/ye	یک	۱	char		۴
do	دو	۲	pænj	پنج	۵
se	سه	۳	shish		۶

Lesson Five   *MODERN PERSIAN*   درس پنجم

hæft	هفت	٧	chardæh	١۴	
hæsht	هشت	٨	punzdæh	١۵	
noh	نه	٩	shunzdæh	١۶	
dæh	ده	١٠	hivdæh	١٧	
yazdæh	یازده	١١	hizhdæh	١٨	
dævazdæh	دوازده	١٢	nuzdæh	نوزده	١٩
sizdæh	سیزده	١٣	bist	بیست	٢٠

bísto yek	بیست و یک	٢١	pænjah	پنجاه	۵٠
bísto do, etc.	بیست و دو	٢٢	pænjá(h)o yek/pænjávo yek	پنجاه و یک	۵١
si	سی	٣٠	pænjá(h)o do/pænjávo do	پنجاه و دو	۵٢
sío yek	سی و یک	٣١	shæst	شصت	۶٠
sío do, etc.	سی و دو	٣٢	hæftad	هفتاد	٧٠
chel	چهل	۴٠	hæshtad	هشتاد	٨٠
chélo yek	چهل و یک	۴١	nævæd	نود	٩٠
chélo do, etc.	چهل و دو	۴٢	sæd	صد	١٠٠
sædo yek, etc.	صد و یک	١٠١	sædo sío hæft	صد و سی و هفت	١٣٧
sædo sizdæh	صد و سیزده	١١٣	sædo shæsto se	صد و شصت و سه	١۶٣
sædo bísto pænj	صد و بیست و پنج	١٢۵			
sædo hæshtádo hæsht	صد و هشتاد و هشت	١٨٨			

sæd	صد	١٠٠	shishsæd		۶٠٠
divist		٢٠٠	hæftsæd	هفتصد	٧٠٠
sisæd	سیصد	٣٠٠	hæshtsæd	هشتصد	٨٠٠
charsæd		۴٠٠	nohsæd	نه صد	٩٠٠
punsæd		۵٠٠	hezar	هزار	١٠٠٠

Lesson Five MODERN PERSIAN درس پنجم

Vocabulary Notes

1. Certain verbs usually require a direct object and do not generally stand alone. See Section 5.11.6 of this lesson).

2. صبحها /soba/ صبحانه /sobane/ The /h/ sound is elided in many environments, especially after consonants. This phenomenon is discussed in this lesson in Section 5.15, Lesson 7 (7.1 and 7.9.1), and Lesson 8 (8.1).

3. Final /r/ is often not pronounced after certain consonants, such as /k/, and before another word beginning in a consonant. For example, the verb *fékr mìkonæm* becomes [fék mìkonæm] in ordinary speech. When a final vowel is added to the noun form *fekr*, the /r/ is pronounced. Thus, *fék mìkonæm* "I think," but *fekra* "thoughts" or *fékr-e khub* "a good thought." We have indicated the pronunciation of such words by putting parentheses around the /r/ thus *fek(r)*. See Lesson 10 (10.1) for a fuller discussion of the loss of /r/ and other sounds in word-final position.

4. In colloquial Persian, both /ye/ and /yek/ will be heard for the number "one." The form /ye/, however, is considered more colloquial and, although heard frequently, it is never uttered alone. /ye/ must always be followed by another word: /ye saæt/ "one hour," etc.

5.2.1 Classroom Expressions and Cultural Materials (Optional Material)

no(w)bæt-e kí-e?	Whose turn is it?
no(w)bæt-e mæn-e.	It's my turn.
fék(r) mìkonæm no(w)bæt-e jórj-e.	I think it's George's turn.
mæn færda æz shoma emtehán mìkonæm.	I'm going to test you tomorrow.
mæn emruz emtehán mìdæm.	I'm going to take a test today.
ma emshæb tæklíf-e shæb darim?	Do we have homework tonight?
dige	Else, in addition.
dige chi?	What else?
dige chi darim?	What else do we have?

Lesson Five MODERN PERSIAN درس پنجم

dige ki?	Who else?
dige koja?	Where else?

Other Useful Expressions

The following are additional possible answers you may wish to use in the "soálo jævab" sessions and other classroom situations.

válla(h)	honestly, really
válla(h) némidunæm.	I honestly don't know.
khodá mídune.	God (only) knows.
dorost némidunæm.	I don't know exactly.
yádæm ræft.	I forget. (past tense used as present equivalent in English. See Lesson 4 (4.3, note)
yádæm nist.	I don't remember.
momkén-e.	Maybe, possibly; It's possible. (For now, use this as an independent utterance only)
momken nist.	It's not possible.
fék(r) mìkonæm.	I think so.
fèk(r) némikonæm.	I don't think so.
shoma chi fék(r) mìkonin?	What do you think?
shoma chi mígin?	What do you say?
chi bégæm?	What should I say? What am I supposed to say?
chekár konæm?	What should I do? What am I supposed to do?
némidunæm chi bégæm.	I don't know what to say. I don't know what I'm supposed to say.
némidunæm chekár konæm.	I don't know what to do. I don't know what I'm supposed to do.
dige chi bégæm?	What else should I say?
dige chekár konæm?	What else should I do?

Lesson Five   *MODERN PERSIAN*   درس پنجم

di<u>ge</u> chi fék(r) mìkonin?	What else do you think? etc.
so<u>á</u>l kon<u>ǽ</u>m?	Should I ask? Am I supposed to ask?
jæ<u>vá</u>b bèdæm?	Should I answer? Am I supposed to answer?
so<u>á</u>l kon<u>ǽ</u>m (?) ya jæ<u>vá</u>b bèdæm.	Should I ask or answer?
shu<u>khí</u> mìkonin.	You're joking/kidding!
shu<u>khí</u> mìkonin?	Are you joking/kidding?
khejal<u>æt</u> mìkeshæm.	I'm embarrassed. I'm (too) shy.
chéra <u>mǽn</u>?	Why me?

5.2.2 Two Persian Compliments (Optional)

In Persian poetry the full moon symbolizes perfect beauty. To compare a woman's face to the moon is to say that, like the moon, her face is perfect in its roundness, that her skin is pale, and that her beauty is set off by dark lustrous hair as the moon's is set off by the darkness of the night sky. In colloquial speech, the terms "moon" *mah* and "like the moon" *mésl-e mah* have become general purpose compliments that are used to describe anything or anyone that is exceptionally fine or beautiful. To say that someone speaks Persian "like the moon" sounds comic in English, but in Persian it means that his or her Persian is perfect, like the moon, and so very beautiful.

In Persian poetry as well, the song of the nightingale, *bolbol,* is proverbial for its melodious sweetness. Should someone say that you speak Persian like a "nightingale" they are paying you a high compliment indeed. Or, perhaps, it would be truer to say that they are offering you a fine piece of *taarof*, since you will hear such compliments long before you have attained the fluency of the nightingale or the perfection of the moon.

mésl-e	مِثل	like (preposition)
mah	ماه	moon
bolbol	بُلبُل	nightingale

Lesson Five   *MODERN PERSIAN*   درس پنجم

shoma farsi mésl-e <u>mah</u> hǽrf mìzænin!	You speak Persian beautifully!
shoma farsi mésl-e bo<u>l</u>bol hǽrf mìzænin!	You speak Persian like a nightingale!
reply: khahésh mìkonæm.	Please! (Don't embarrass me.) Thank you.

🔊 5.4 Dialogue 5

The following dialogue is a continuation of the situation introduced in sections 4.4 and 4.13.

dárÍd	you have
Robyn: vída, shoma khahǽro bæra<u>d</u>ǽr darid?	Vida, do you have any sisters and brothers?
Vida: <u>bǽ</u>le. ye khahǽro ye bæra<u>d</u>ǽr daræm	Yes, I have one sister and one brother,
vǽli inja zendegí <u>né</u>mikonænd.	but they don't live here.
pæs	therefore, then
tænha	alone
Robyn: pæs shoma tæ<u>nha</u> zendegí mìkonid?	Then do you live alone?
Vida: næ. ba khahǽr-e meh<u>ri</u> zendegí	No, I live with Mehri's sister.
mìkonæm.	
-(h)æm	also, too
dǽrs mìkhune	he/she studies (general sense)
Robyn: khahǽr-e mehrí-æm <u>dæ</u>rs mìkhune?	Does Mehri's sister study too?
Vida: næ. dær bimarestán-e	No, she works at the university hospital.
daneshga(h) <u>ká</u>r mìkone.	

Complete Dialogue

Robyn:	vída, shoma khahǽro bæra<u>d</u>ǽr darid?
Vida:	<u>bǽ</u>le. ye khahǽro ye bæra<u>d</u>ǽr daræm vǽli inja zendegí <u>né</u>mikonænd.
Robyn:	pæs shoma tæ<u>nha</u> zendegí mìkonid?
Vida:	næ. ba khahǽr-e meh<u>ri</u> zendegí mìkonæm.
Robyn:	khahǽr-e mehrí-æm <u>dæ</u>rs mìkhune?
Vida:	næ. dær bimarestán-e daneshgah <u>ká</u>r mìkone.

Lesson Five MODERN PERSIAN درس پنجم

Notes to Dialogue:

Let us examine the following sentence and its meanings:

    mæn ye bæradǽro ye khahær daræm.

Grammatically, this pattern can have two different meanings, each with its own intonational pattern:

mæn ye bæradǽro ye kha/   **hær**/   \daræm.   I have a brother and a sister.

\mæn/   ye   \bæradǽro/   ye   \khahær daræm.   I have one brother and one sister.

In the first sentence, the word /ye/ functions as the indefinite article and does not receive any special emphasis. In the second sentence, the word /ye/ functions as the number "one" and receives a special sentence stress of its own. This stress contrast is not always consistent and sometimes /ye/ may be interpreted as either the indefinite article or the number "one." /ye/ as the indefinite article may often be omitted from the sentence completely, in which case the noun appears unmodified. Grammatically, it is still an indefinite noun and is ambiguous concerning number/plurality and also coincides with the generic form of the noun:

shoma bæradǽro khahær darin?	Do you have a brother and a sister?
	Do you have brothers and sisters?
mæn soal daræm.	I have a question./I have questions.
shoma portoqal míkhorin?	Would you like an orange? (indefinite, singular)
	Would you like some oranges? (indefinite, plural)
	Do you eat oranges? (generic)

You will find a more detailed discussion of number and the use of plurals in relation to noun categories (indefinite, generic, etc.) in Lesson 9 (9.11).

Lesson Five   *MODERN PERSIAN*   درس پنجم

5.5 Vocabulary Building: Verbalizers

As you can see from the list of verbs that you have learned so far, there are more compound verbs than simple verbs in Persian. Of the compound verbs, most are formed with the verbalizer *kærd/kon*. You have learned several noun/verb pairs in which the verb is simply formed by adding *kærd/kon* to the noun:

Noun			**Verb**
tælæffoz	"pronunciation"	tælæffóz mìkonæm	"I pronounce"
værzesh	"exercise, sports"	værzésh mìkonæm	"I exercise, play sports"
tærjome	"translation"	tærjomé mìkonæm	"I translate"

New verbs are easily made from nouns you already know according to this pattern. Sometimes the meaning of the derived verb is slightly different (or more extended) than the original noun form as you have seen in this example:

sælam	"hello"	sælám mìkonæm	"I greet, say hello"

The following are some new verbs formed by the addition of kærd/kon to nouns you already know:

soal	"question"	soál mìkonæm	"I ask, I question"
taarof	(see 3.7.2)	taaróf mìkonæm	(see 3.7.2)
mashin	"car"	mashín mìkonæm	"I type, type up"
shohær	"husband"	shohǽr mìkonæm	"I marry, get married"
			(said of women only)

As mentioned in the discussion of compound verbs (Lesson 2, Section 2.11.1), the first element may also be a form other than a noun:

dorost	"right, correct"	doróst mìkonæm	"I fix, make, cook"
kæm	"little"	kǽm mìkonæm	"I lessen, reduce, turn down" (radio, etc.)
ziad	"much, a lot"	ziad mìkonæm	"I increase, turn up" (radio)

By the reverse process, you already know many nouns derived from verbs you have learned:

177

Lesson Five   *MODERN PERSIAN*   درس پنجم

zendegí mìkonæm	"I live"	zendegi	"life"
kár mìkonæm	"I work"	kar	"work"
tæmrín mìkonæm	"I practice"	tæmrin	"exercise, drill"
khahésh mìkonæm	"I ask /beg (of)"	khahesh	"favor, request"
gúsh mìkonæm	"I listen"	gush	"ear"
khodafezí mìkonæm	"I say goodbye, bid farewell"		
khodafezi	"good-bye, farewell"		

The verbalizer need not always be *míkonæm* as you have seen with:

    jævab   "answer"   jeváb mìdæm   "I answer"

Here are some new nouns derived from other compound verbs you have learned:

dærs mìdæm	"I teach"	dærs	"lesson"
hærf mìzænæm	"I speak"	hærf	"words, utterance, something said"

The following are new nouns or verbs derived from verbs and nouns introduced in Lesson 5:

Verbs   **New Nouns**

esterahǽt mìkonæm	"I rest"	esterahæt	"rest"
fék(r) mìkonæm	"I think"	fekr	"thought, idea"
hæmúm mìkonæm	"I bathe"	hæmum	"bath, public bath" ("Turkish" style)
shukhí mìkonæm	"I joke, kid"	shukhi	"joking, kidding, joke (but not 'story, anecdote')"

Nouns   **New Verbs**

emtehan	"test, exam"	emtehán mìkonæm	"I test, examine, try out/on "
shune	"comb"	shuné mìzænæm	"I comb"
kæbab	"broiled meat"	kæbáb mìkonæm	"I broil, charcoal-broil"
zæn	"woman"	zæn mìgiræm	"I marry, get married"
			(said of men only)

Nouns of western origin that are used in Persian also are formed into compound verbs with the addition of *míkonæm* and other verbalizers:

Lesson Five MODERN PERSIAN درس پنجم

Nouns		New Verbs = Nouns + mìkonæm	
telefon	"telephone"	telefón mìkonæm	"I call, phone"
post	"mail"	póst mìkonæm	"I mail"
fotokopi	"photocopy"	fotokopí mìkonæm	"I photoduplicate, Xerox"
polikopi	"mimeograph"	polikopí mìkonæm	"I mimeograph, ditto"
dikte	"dictation"	dikté mìkonæm	"I dictate spelling words"

Nouns		New Verbs = Nouns + Other Verbalizer	
telegeraf	"telegraph"	telegeráf mìzænæm	"I telegraph, send a telegram."
sigar	"cigarette"	sigár mìkeshæm	"I smoke"
rezhim	"diet"	rezhím mìgiræm	"I go on a diet"

5.6 Drills, Part I

Drill 1 Substitution   (The *ezafe* Construction)

a. <u>khahǽr</u>-e mehri koja inglisi míkhune?

   (cues: shohær, pesær, shagerd, dust, (khahær))

b. khahær-e <u>mehri</u> chai míkhore?

   (cues: reza, giti, hoseyn, vida, (mehri))

c. <u>pedǽro madǽr</u>-e reza bæ:d-æz-zohra esterahǽt mìkonænd.

   (cues: pesǽro dokhtær, khahǽro bæradær, pedǽro bæradær, (pedǽro madær))

Drill 2 Substitution   (The *ezafe* Construction - Continued)

a. <u>pedǽr-e shæhla</u> bolænd hǽrf mìzæne.

   (cues: khahær/jæmshid, bæradær/mæhmud, dokhtær/fereshte, shohær/giti, (pedær/shæhla))

b. dúst-e <u>bæradǽræm</u> hichvæqt hæmùm némigire.

   (cues: moællémetun, un pesær, ælío reza, aqá-ye firuzi, (bæradæræm))

c. <u>pedǽro madǽr-e dústæm</u> khéyli taaróf mìkonænd.

Lesson Five MODERN PERSIAN درس پنجم

(cues: shagerd/fereshte, khahǽro bæradær/un pesær, pesǽro dokhtær/khanúm-e shirazi, moællem/ælío reza, (pedǽro madær/dústæm))

Drill 3 Expansion   (The *ezafe* Construction - Continued)

T: æli farsi mídune. (cue: moællem)

S: moællém-e æli farsi mídune.

mehri nun némikhore. (khahær)	reza vitamin míkhore? (dust)
moællémetun chekár mìkone? (madær)	giti shimi dærs mìde? (shohær)
reza shæba dær bimarestan kár mìkone. (bæradær)	fereshte chi míkhune? (shagerd)
mehri ba shoma valibal bazí mìkone? (pesær)	SSS khéyli ab míkhore? (dust)
ælío reza sobane némikhorænd. (pedǽro madær)	pærvin ruza aváz mìkhune. (shohær)
vida bæ:d-æz-zohra esterahǽt mìkone. (pesær)	hæsæn sigár mìkeshe? (khanum)
nahid shæba qæza doróst mìkone? (shohær)	mæhmud soba míkhabe. (dokhtær)
SSS dær khune mæjælle míkhune? (moællem)	kamran æz mæn míporse. (pedær)

Drill 4 Cued Question/Answer

T to S1:   <u>pedǽr-e S2 kár mìkone?</u> (T refers to the teacher and S to a student)

S1 to T: némidunæm. æz S2 míporsæm

S1 to S2:   <u>pedǽretun kár mìkone?</u>

S2 to S1:   <u>bǽle. pedǽræm dær (nio york, etc.) kár mìkone.)/(næ. pedǽræm kàr némikone.</u>

S1 to T: <u>pedǽresh dær nio york kár mìkone./(næ. pedǽresh kàr némikone.)</u>

T to S1:   mérsi.

(Once you have worked through a few of the following cues to understand the order, you may break up into groups of three or four to ask each other the questions.)

Cues:

pedǽro madær-e S2 sobane míkhorænd?   moællém-e S2 ruza dærs mìde(?) ya shæba.

madær-e S2 sigár mìkeshe?   madær-e S2 chai míkhore (?) ya qæhve.

khahær-e S2 soba ruzname míkhune?   khahǽr-e S2 aváz mìkhune? bolænd míkhune?

hál-e S2 chetór-e?   hál-e pedǽr-e S2 chetór-e?

dúst-e S2 valibal bazí mìkone?   dúst-e S2 khub tærjomé mìkone (?) ya bæd.

dúst-e S2 kæbab doróst mìkone?   dúst-e S2 æræbi yád mìgire (?) ya ebri.

dúst-e S2 ruza chekár mìkone?   dúst-e S2 qæza doróst mìkone?

shohǽr-e S2 nun míkhore? khéyli míkhore?   pedær-e S2 bæ:d-æz-zohra esterahæt mìkone?

khanúm-e S2 farsi hǽrf mìzæne?   (chera?/chera næ?)

bæradær-e S2 værzésh mìkone?   koja værzésh mìkone?

dúst-e S2 dær karkhune kár mìkone (?) ya dǽrs mìkhune?

moællém-e S2 sær-e kelas mokaleme tæmrín mìkone (?) ya fæqæt tærjomé mìkone?

Drill 5 Cued Question/Answer

a. **S1:** <u>shoma</u> soba chekár mìkonin?   **S2:** <u>mæn</u> soba <u>hæmúm mìkonæm</u>.

(cues: æli/ebri khund, ma/sobane khord, nahído dústesh/futbal bazi kærd, vida/nun khord, shoma/farsi tærjome kærd, mæn/name nevesht, aqá-ye shirazi/dærs dad, (shoma/hæmum kærd))

b. **S1:** <u>shoma</u> bæ:d-æz-zohra chekár mìkonin?   **S2:** <u>mæn</u> bæ:d-æz-zohra <u>dǽrs mìkhunæm</u>.

(cues: kamran/kar kærd, shoma/ruzname khund, mæn/esterahæt kærd, ma/khabid, shoma/qæza dorost kærd, una/værzesh kærd, giti/avaz khund, mæn/qæhve dorost kærd, ma/tæmrin kærd, (shoma/dærs khund))

(Now continue asking questions according to these patterns)

Lesson Five *MODERN PERSIAN* درس پنجم

Drill 6 Cued Question/Answer ("ALSO")

S1: shoma <u>fizik</u> míkhunin?   **S2:** bǽle, áqa. (bǽle, khánum)

S1: <u>shimí</u>-æm míkhunin?   **S2:** nǽkher. <u>shimi</u> némikhunæm.

(cues: farsi/æræbi, færanse/espanioli, ebri/æræbi, rusi/almani, (fizik/shimi))

Drill 7 Cued Question/Answer

S1: <u>æli fæqæt farsi hǽrf mìzæne?</u>   **S2:** næ. <u>inglisi</u>-æm <u>hǽrf mìzæne</u>.

(cue: pedǽro madǽresh fæqæt qæhve míkhoræend? chai)

S1: <u>pedǽro madǽresh fæqæt qæhve míkhoræend?</u>   **S2:** næ. <u>chaí</u>-æm <u>míkhoræend</u>.

cues: una fæqæt sib míkhoræend? portoqal   mæn fæqæt inglisi yád mìgiræm? ebri   SSS fæqæt dær apartemánesh míkhabe? sær-e kelas jæmshído bæradǽresh fæqæt ruzname míkhunænd? mæjælle   ma fæqæt nun míkhorim? ab   reza fæqæt færanse mídune? almani   dústetun fæqæt dær karkhune kár mìkone? dær bimarestan   una fæqæt æz mæn míporsænd? æz mehri   shoma fæqæt ba bæradǽretun zendegí mìkonin? ba dústæm   mæno shǽhla fæqæt be farsi tærjomé mìkonim? be inglisi   hoseyn fæqæt inja kár mìkone? dær daneshgah   shoma fæqæt qæzá-ye irani dorósht mìkonin? qæzá-ye italiai   mæhmúdo fereydun fæqæt valibal bazí mìkonænd? futbal   shoma fæqæt chaí-e chini míkhorin? chaí-e zhaponi   mæn fæqæt ba pærvíno khahǽresh farsi hǽrf mìzænæm? ba giti   ma fæqæt mokaleme tæmrín mìkonim? khundǽno neveshtæn   shoma name fæqæt be æræbi mínevisin? be espanioli

5.8 Situational and Practical Exercises

Polite Expressions: Saying Goodbye to Someone You've Just Met

The following expressions with kh*oshvæqt* are said upon saying good-bye to a person you have just met. They are in the past tense, another example of a Persian past tense usage equivalent to an English present. In the present tense with the verb "to be," kh*oshvæqt* is also

Lesson Five *MODERN PERSIAN* درس پنجم

used upon being introduced to someone (See Lesson 7, Section 7.8).

khéyli khosh<u>væqt</u> shodæm.	I am very happy /pleased to have met you.
mǽn-æm khoshvæqt shodæm.	I'm also happy/pleased to have met you; "likewise"
fe:læn	for now, for the time being

Memorize:

khob. fe:læn kho<u>dá</u>fez.	Well, goodbye for now.
kho<u>dá</u>fez. khéyli khosh<u>væqt</u> shodæm.	Goodbye. I am very pleased to have met you.
mǽn-æm khoshvæqt shodæm.	I am very pleased to have met you, too.
kho<u>dá</u>fez(-e) shoma. khéyli khosh<u>væqt</u> shodæm.	Goodbye. I am very pleased to have met you.
mǽn-æm khoshvæqt shodæm.	I am very pleased to have met you, too.
fe:læn kho<u>dá</u>fez.	Goodbye for now.
khodáfez. mærhæmæt-e shoma zi<u>ad</u>.	Goodbye. It's been a real pleasure.
khéyli khosh<u>væqt</u> shodæm.	I am very pleased to have met you.
mǽn-æm khoshvæqt shodæm.	I am very pleased to have met you, too.

Drill 8: in chi-e?

  T: in <u>chi-e</u>?

  S: un <u>ketáb-e farsí-e</u>. mal-e dost-e mæne.

(cues: dæftær-e telefon, míz-e moællem, tæmrín-e farsi, dærs-e pænj, emtehán-e farsi, kasét-e muzik, dæftær-e not, pómp-e benzin, kúrs-e zæban, pakæt-e sigar, bilít-e otobus, kéyk-e shokolati)

Lesson Five   *MODERN PERSIAN*   درس پنجم

Drill 9: be farsi yæ:ni chi?

fæqæt be farsi jæváb bèdid!   فقط به فارسی جواب بدید!

    Teacher: "kelás-e inglisi" yæ:ni chi?

    Student: mæsælæn, unja inglisi míkhunim. dær kelás-e inglisi inglisi yád mìgirim. dær un kelas shekespir míkhunim.

"moællém-e zæban" yæ:ni chi?   "ésm-e zæn" yæ:ni chi?

"emtehán-e farsi" yæ:ni chi?   "ésm-e mærd" yæ:ni chi?

"restorán-e khabgah" yæ:ni chi?   "zæbán-e ebri" yæ:ni chi?

"væqt-e sobane" yæ:ni chi?   "ruzname-ye daneshga" yæ:ni chi?

optional:

"motór-e mashin"   "restorán-e hotel"   "albóm-e tæmbr"   "kúrs-e zæban"

Drill 10: lotfæn be inglisi tærjomé konid.

áb-e porteqal	kompót-e sib	be væqt-e tehran
míz-e moællem	væqt-e kelas	dærs-e pænj, tæmrín-e se
kasét-e muzik	bilít-e sinema	kúrs-e zæban
emtehán-e shimi	tæmrín-e gitar	væqt-e qæza
mæjællé-ye "People"	adrés-e mædrese	

optional:

| be væqt-e nio york | sandvíc-e zæban | sigár-e færansævi |
| tím-e futbal | púl-e taksi | konsért-e jaz |

Drill 11: in ketab-e chi-e?

    T: in ketab-e ki-e   S: un ketab-e moaleme

(cues: dæftær, medad, sændæli, sæt, kaqæz, pul, fotokopi, sigar, adres, bilit, kaset, sandvich)

Lesson Five MODERN PERSIAN درس پنجم

Drill 12, in ketáb-e kí-e?

In this exercise the teacher points to objects that belong to students in the classroom.

T: in <u>ketáb</u>-e kí-e?   **S:** un <u>ketáb</u>-e <u>SSS</u>-e

(cues: dæftær, medad, sændæli, khodkar, saæt, kaqæz, pul, fotokopi, sigar, adres, bilit, kaset, sandvich)

Drill 13, in ketáb-e chi-e?

In this exercise the teacher points to objects in the room or holds up pictures brought into class and asks what the object is.

T: in <u>ketáb</u>-e chi-e?   **S:** un <u>ketáb</u>-e <u>farsí</u>-e (bilit)

T: in <u>bilít</u>-e chi-e?   **S:** un <u>bilít</u>-e <u>otobús</u>-e.

(cues: kelas, dæftær, dærs, tæmrin, kaset, sandvich, pakæt, albom, kurs, sigar, keyk)

Drill 14: un kí-e?

a. **S1:** un <u>aqa</u> kí-e?   **S2:** vállah, némidunæm.

(cues: khanum, pesær, dokhtær, mærd, zæn, bæche, moællem, emrikai)

b. **S1:** un <u>aqa</u> kí-e?   **S2:** <u>bæradær-e hæsæn-e</u>.

(cues: dokhtær/khahær-e nahid, mærd/shohær-e khahæræm, zæn/dúst-e shirin, aqa/moællém-e dariush, khanum/madær-e hoseyn, zæn/zǽn-e aqá-ye shærifi, pesær/shagérd-e khanúm-e firuzi)

5.9 Reading and Writing

5.9.1 Consonantal و and ى

The two signs that have been used thus far to represent /u/ (and /o/) and /i/ are also respectively used to represent the consonants /v/ and /y/, and the glides /ow/ and /ey/. Since there is usually nothing in medial or final position to tell you which sound is intended, the context is the only guide to the proper reading. Both *rud* "river" and *rævæd* "goes (poetic

185

Lesson Five MODERN PERSIAN درس پنجم

form)" are spelled رود and سیر represents three words — *sir* "full," *seyr* "journey," and *seyær* "conduct." English provides many examples of similar ambiguity in spelling, as: "read" (present tense) vs. "read" (past tense); "tear" (i.e., "rip") vs. "tear" (as in "tear gas"), "bow" (i.e., "to bow down") vs. "bow" (as in "rainbow"), etc.

There are two contexts in which و and ی can only stand for /v/ or /y/:

1. When they begin a word:

| یاد | /yad/ | "mind" | ولی | /væli/ | "but" |
| یک | /yek/ | "one" | ورزش | /værzesh/ | "sport" |

2. When they follow (ا) *ælef* in medial or final position:

| پایان | /payan/ | "end, finish" | باور | /bavær/ | "believing" |
| چای | /chay/ | "tea" | گاو | /gav/ | "cow, bull" |

When حرکات are used with و and ی to distinguish consonant from vowel, the conventions are as follows:

Consonant: As with any other consonant.

سَیَر	/seyær/	"conduct"	اوِسْتا	/ævesta/	"Avesta"
هَجْو	/hæjv/	"satire"	اَیَّام	/æyyam/	"days"
رَهْی	/ræhy/	"slave"	رَوَد	/rævæd/	"goes"

Vowel: (ُ) plus و = /u/. (ِ) plus ی = /i/

اِیمن	/imæn/	"safe, secure"	اوست	/ust/	"it, he/she is"
مِیل	/mil/	"mile"	روح	/ruh/	"spirit"
اِیرانی	/irani/	"Iranian"	سُو	/su/	"direction"

Vowel: (َ) plus ی = /ey/ (َ) plus و = /ow/.*

| اَیمن | /eymæn/ | "auspicious" | اَوراق | /owraq/ | "pages" |
| مَیل | /meyl/ | "desire" | رَوح | /rowh/ | "ease" |

186

Lesson Five   *MODERN PERSIAN*   درس پنجم

/pærtow/ پَرتَو "ray"   /ri/ ری "Ray (city)"

Note: The سکون is often left off the و or یـ when indicating a glide.

The chart below presents in tabular form the information just given about the various pronunciations of و , یـ , او , and ایـ:

Sign	Initial	Medial	Final
و	/v/	/u/ /o/ /ow/ /v/	/u/ /o/ /ow/ /v/
یـ	/y/	/i/ /ey/ /y/	/i/ /ey/ /y/
او	/u/ /ow/ /æv/	/av/	/av/
ایـ	/i/ /ey/ /æy/	/ay/	/ay/

Reading Drill 1: Transcribe into the phonetic alphabet.

أواخِر   والی بال   دُوَل   سَهْو
اَیادی   یابو   بَیَل   نَهْی
بُوق   دَولت   بیل   زانو

5.9.2 Duplicate Letters

There are seven sounds in Persian that are represented by more than one letter or sign — /t/, /s/, /h/, /z/, /q/, /n/, and /:/. You have already learned duplicate letters for /s/ (س and ث), /z/ (ز and ذ), and /h/ (ه and ح). In this section you will review those and learn all of the remaining letters and signs. Here are all of them in a single table.

Letter/Sign	Name		Sound
ت تـ	ته	te	/ t /
ط	طا	ta	
ث ثـ	ثه	se	/ s /
س سـ	سین	sin	

187

Lesson Five   *MODERN PERSIAN*   درس پنجم

صـ ص	صاد	sad	
حـ ـحـ ح	حه (حمّالی)	he (-ye hæmmali)	/ h /
هـ ـهـ ه	هه (دو چشم)	he (-ye do cheshm)	
ز	زه	ze	/ z /
ذ	ذال	zal	
ضـ ض	ضاد	zad	
ظ	ظا	za	
عـ ـعـ ع/ـع	عین	eyn	/ : /
ئـ ؤ أ	همزه	hæmze	
غـ ـغـ غ/ـغ	غین	qeyn	/ q /
ق قـ	قاف	qaf	
ن نـ	نون	nun	/ n /
أ	تنوین	tænvin	

Duplicate Letter for /t/: ط ta /t/

ط has exactly the same shape in initial, medial, and final positions. It appears in a number of common words:

اطاق /otaq/ "room"   فقط /fæqæt/ "only"   شطرنج /shætrænj/ "chess"

In an effort to "de-Arabize" the language, Iranian educators began to spell a number of words of non-Arabic origin that had come to be spelled with a ط with a ت instead. Thus, you will encounter both اطاق and اتاق. Our preference is for the older spelling, but both are correct.

Another Duplicate Letter for /s/: صاد sad /s/

صاد is a new shape. It is a connecting letter like both سین and ثه. It is less common than the former but more common than the latter. You have already encountered it in the words:

188

Lesson Five   *MODERN PERSIAN*   درس پنجم

صندلی	/sændæli/	"chair"	اصفهان	/esfæhan/	"Isfahan"
اصفهانیان	/esfæhanian/	"PN"	صادقی	/sadeqi/	"PN"
صبح	/sob(h)/	"morning"	صبحانه	/sobhane/	"breakfast"

Do not let the "tooth" (dændune) here confuse you. It is part of the letter and has no accompanying dot(s).

Ruins of the Temple of Anahita

Two More Duplicate Letters for /z/: ضاد zad/, *and* ظا za

The additional letters for /z/ are all dotted forms of other letters. As ذال and زه are dotted forms of دال and ره, so ضاد and ظا are dotted forms of صاد and طا.

رضا	/reza/	"PN"	تلفظ	/tælæffoz/	"pronunciation"
اضافه	/ezafe/	"*ezafe*"	حافظ	/hafez/	"preserver, memorizer (of Qor:an), PN"

Remember, ص and ض have the dændune incorporated into the letter but this is <u>not</u> the case for ط and ظ; there is no dændune in the latter.

Lesson Five   *MODERN PERSIAN*   درس پنجم

A Duplicate Letter for the Glottal Stop: همزه

(See descriptions of the glottal stop in Phonology sections)

Like همزه، تشدید must be written in conjunction with a letter of the alphabet. The تشدید may be written over any letter except *ælef,* but the همزه, except when at the end of a word, must only be written over ـیـ (without the dots), و and ا. These letters are called "the chair for hæmze" *(sændælí-e hæmze).*

سوئد /sued/ "Sweden"   سؤال /soal/ "question"

Lesson Five MODERN PERSIAN درس پنجم

متأهل /motææhhel/ "married"

In writing, the همزه is usually omitted when its "chair" is ا (and sometimes و). That is, both متأهل and متاهل are normal and acceptable spellings, but سوئد would be impossible without the *hæmze*.

Latterly, ئـ has become the chair of preference for همزه in Persian, and it is used in words where — by the rules of Arabic orthography — either و or ا would be correct. For example:

سؤال /soal/ "question" instead of سئوال

and

مسأله /mæs:æle/ "problem" instead of مسئله .

Remember the "chair" for همزه is only that; it is not pronounced as a vowel. That is, متأهل is pronounced /motææhhel/, not /motahhel/ or /motaahhel/. When a همزه occurs before an /a/ vowel (ا) in the middle of a word, it is written as a *mædde* or *kolah* (~) over the *ælef* (آ):

الآن /æl:an/ "now"   قرآن /qor:an/ "Koran"

Because the glottal stop is generally not pronounced in Persian, you may find it amazing that so much attention is paid to the writing of a letter that is not even pronounced. If such is the case, take a moment to think about all the English words spelled with silent "gh," as in "bough," "thought," "through," "dough," etc., not to mention the additional problem of "rough," and "cough."

Duplicate Letter for /q/: غین qeyn غ

The غ is simply a dotted ع

کاغذ /kaqæz/ "paper"   جغرافیا /joqrafia/ "geography"

Duplicate Letter for /n/: تنوین; tænvin /-æn/

The *tænvin* is not exactly a duplicate for /n/, but represents the whole syllable /-æn/ which has an /n/ in it. Persian regularly makes use of the Arabic adverbial ending /-æn/. You have already encountered it in *lotfæn* "please," *fe:læn* "for now," and *mæsælæn* "for

Lesson Five   *MODERN PERSIAN*   درس پنجم

example," and you will shortly learn معمولاً *mæ:mulæn* "usually" and تقریباً *tæqribæn* "approximately." The process of adding the /n/ sound to a word ("nunation" in Arabic grammar) is called تنوین *tænvin*, as is the sign used to indicate it. The تنوین is, like همزه and تشدید, a diacritic not a letter, and so must be written over a letter. The sole letter that is used as a chair for تنوین in Persian is ا and the sign itself consists of two parallel diagonal lines, (ً). Examples:

لطفاً   مثلاً   فعلاً   معمولاً   تقریباً

The تنوین is not always written and these same words are often printed without it:

لطفا   مثلا   فعلا   معمولا   تقریبا

We must point out to you that the use of *tænvin* in any given word is a matter of spelling and the words that contain a *tænvin* must be memorized. Do not assume that all syllables that have an *æn* in final position are spelled this way. Common words such as *mæn*, *khundæn*, *neveshtæn*, etc., are spelled with *nun*:

نوشتن   خواندن   من

Reading Drill 2, Review Vocabulary: Be prepared to read in class.

کار	کاش	کاکا	کوک	کوشک
جواب	پروین	یواش	نوشت	نوشتن
هیچ وقت	ورزش	ورزش کردن	مینویسم	مینویسید
مینویسیم	مینویسند	ولی	یا	یاد
یاد گرفت	یاد میگیرم	یاد میگیرید	یاد میگیریم	یاد میگیرند
یعنی	یک	بیروت	نخیر	شب بخیر
فریدون	تلفظ	تلفظ کنید	حافظ	خدا حافظ
لطفا	مثلا	الآن	قرآن	سئوال
بفرمائید	سوئدی	خیلی	حسین	ویدا

192

Lesson Five *MODERN PERSIAN* درس پنجم

With the conjunction و

| فیزیک و شیمی | برادر و خواهر | پدر و مادر | من و شما |
| فریدون و پروین | فارسی و عربی | شب و روز | خوب و بد |

Students of the Persian language, Michigan

Lesson Five MODERN PERSIAN درس پنجم

5.9.3 Alphabetization

Here are all the letters of the Persian alphabet in their normal sequence.

الفبای فارسی
Persian Alphabet

example		name	pronunciation	shape	
مثل		نام	تلفّظ	شکل چاپی الفبا	
far	ælef ba kolah	الف با کلاه	a	ا	آ
rat		ælef	الف	æ	ا	ا
bob		be	بِ	b	ب	ب
pen		pe	پِ	p	پ	پ
table		te	تِ	t	ت	ت
sand		se	ثِ	s	ث	ث
jack		jim	جیم	j	ج	ج
chair		che	چِ	ch	چ	چ
habit		he	حِ	h	ح	ح
Scottish loch		khe	خِ	kh	خ	خ
dog		dal	دال	d		د
zoo		zal	ذال	z		ذ
Persian ruz		re	رِ	r		ر
zoo		ze	زِ	z		ز
pleasure		zhe	ژِ	zh		ژ
sand		sin	سین	s	س	س
shoe		shin	شین	sh	ش	ش
sand		sad	صاد	s	ص	ص
zoo		zad	ضاد	z	ض	ض

194

Lesson Five   *MODERN PERSIAN*   درس پنجم

table	ta	طا	t	ط	ط
zoo	za	ظا	z	ظ	ظ
no	ayn	عین	long vowel sound	عـ ـعـ ـع ع	ع
French /r/	qeyn	غین	q	غـ ـغـ ـغ غ	غ
fat	fe	ف	f	ف ف	
French /r/	qaf	قِ	q	قـ ق	
kick	kaf	کاف	k	ک ک	
gate	gaf	گاف	g	گ گ	
late	lam	لام	l	ل ل	
minimum	mim	میم	m	م ـم	
nun	none	نون	n	ن ـن	
very	vav	واو	v	و و	
hospital	he	هِ	h	هـ ـهـ ـه ه	
yes	ye	یِ	y	ی ی	
uh-uh	hamzeh	همزه	/ ' / , / : /	أ ئ ؤ ء	

The vowels (Long, and Short):

    short   (اَ ـَ)   (اِ ـِ ـه ه)   (اُ ـُ و)

    long   (آ،ا)   (ای ـیـ ی)   (او و)

    compound   (اِیـ)   (اُو)

Alphabetization Exercise

The following list of words is taken from the English to Persian glossary and are therefore alphabetized in the left-hand column according to the English alphabet. Write the Persian words out in the right-hand column according to Persian alphabetical order:

195

Lesson Five	MODERN PERSIAN	درس پنجم

silent, extinguished	khamush	خاموش
silent, quiet	saket	ساکت
simple	sade	ساده
since	æz in ke	از اینکه
to sing; to read, study (with object)	khandæn	خواندن (خوندن)
single, unmarried	mojærræd (mojæræd)	مجرد
singly, one by one	yeki yeki	یکی یکی
singular	mofræd	مُفْرَد
sir (polite)	qorban (qorbun)	قربان (قربون)
Sir, Mister	aqa	آقا
Sirus "Cyrus"	sirus	سیروس
sister	khahær	خواهر
sister-in-law	khahær zæn	خواهر زن
sit	neshæst/neshin	نشست/نشین
to sit	neshæstæn	نشستن
night	shæb	شب
sixty	shæst	شصت
skirt	damæn	دامن
sleep	khabid/khab	خوابید/خواب
to sleep; to lie down	khabidæn	خوابیدن
sleep; asleep; dream	khab	خواب

Lesson Five　　　MODERN PERSIAN　　　درس پنجم

Reading Drill 3, Translation Practice:

After you have completed the handwriting exercises for Lesson 5, read and translate the following sentences:

۱. سلام آقای صادقی. بفرمائید اینجا.

۲. پروین و رضا الآن عربی یاد میگیرند.

۳. بله، آقای اصفهانیان، «چیر» یعنی «صندلی.

۴. من خوب مینویسم ولی یواش مینویسم.

۵. ما خیلی کم صبحانه میخوریم.

۶. این سئوال زیاد سخت (difficult) نیست.

۷. فریدون و محمود عربی و عبری یاد میگیرند.

۸. خدا حافظ خانم صادقی. من خیلی خوشوقت شدم.

۹. لطفا خوب تلفظ کنید. لطفا بنویسید «آذربایجان».

۱۰. چرا ویدا و حسین فقط مکالمه تمرین میکنند؟

5.10　Drills, Part II

Drill 14:　Substitution

    a.　<u>do</u>chærkhé-ye <u>mæ</u>hmud khub-e.

(cues: færanse/pærvin, ketabkhune/daneshgah, qæza/in restoran, mædrese/shæhla, khune/un zæn, læhje/reza, khabga(h)/daneshgah, ruzname/daneshgah, sobane/in hotel, (dochærkhe/mæhmud))

    b.　<u>shuné</u>-ye <u>reza</u> khub nist.

(cues: tælæffoz/dústetun, ketabkhune/un aqa, soal/moællémetun, qæza/kafeteria, ab/inja, ebri/un mærd, hæmum/khabgah, væqt/emtehan, læhje/un khanum, khæt/mehri, torki/kamran, gitar/giti, restoran/bimarestan, qæhve/in restoran, hal/dústetun, tærjome/æli, moællem/vida, (shune//reza))

Lesson Five *MODERN PERSIAN* درس پنجم

Drill 15: Substitution

aqá-ye esfæhanian dær daneshgáh-e <u>tegzas</u> dærs mìde.

(cues: perinston, kolombia, harvard, yuta(h), tehran, kalifornia, arizona, ohayo, esfæhan, paris,(tegzas))

Drill 16: Cued Question/Answer (dasht/dar "to have":Present Tense)

a. Actual objects passed from student to student may be used as cues

S1: shoma <u>medad</u> darin?   **S2:** bæle. befǽrmaid.

S1: mérsi.   **S2:** khahésh mìkonæm.

(cues: kaqæz, ketáb-e farsi, khodkar, mæjælle, ruzname, (medad))

b. **S1:** shoma <u>medad</u> darin?   **S2:** næ. væli kh<u>odkar</u> daræm.

(cues: mashin/dochærkhe, khune/aparteman, piano/gitar, soal/jævab, pul/væqt, kaqæz/pakæt, televizion/radio, mæjælle/ruzname, sigar/kebrit, chai/qæhve, emtehan/kelas, qæza/pul, polo/nun, sib/portoqal, ab/chai, sandvich/keyk, (medad/khodkar))

Drill 17: Cued Question/Answer (Negative of dar/dasht, "either, neither")

a. **S1:** mæn <u>mashin</u> nǽdaræm. shoma chetór?

S2: mæn-æm nǽdaræm.

(cues: pul, kelás-e inglisi, khodkar, tæklíf-e shæb, bilít-e otobus, (mashin))

b. soálo jævab

S1: shoma <u>mashin</u> darin?

(**S2:** bǽle. mæn <u>mashin</u> daræm. shoma chetór?)

S1: mæn-æm (daræm/nǽdaræm).

(**S2:** mæn <u>mashin</u> nǽdaræm. shoma chetór?)

(cues: pul, kelás-e inglisi, khodkar, tæklíf-e shæb, bilít-e otobus, saæt, kar, dæftær-e telefon, ketáb-e farsi, dochærkhe, hæmum, name, shune, dæftær-e not, albóm-e tæmbr,

Lesson Five   *MODERN PERSIAN*   درس پنجم

kasét-e muzik, emtehán-e farsi, (optional: benzin, aspirin, televizion, kebrit, (mashin))

Drill 18   Cued Question/Answer   ("our" and "their")

   a.   **tekrár konid**:   تکرار کنید:

        dústemun kelas dare.   dústemun kelas nǽdare.

        dústetun kelas dare.   dústetun kelas nǽdare.

        dústeshun kelas dare.   dústeshun kelas nǽdare.

   b.   "our"

       jæváb bèdid: جواب بدید:

       S1:   dústetun kelas dare.

       S2:   jæváb-e azad (e.g, bæle. dústemun kelas dare.)

(dærs/mokaleme, moællem/mashin, emtehan/neveshtæn, kelas/mǽrdo zæn, (moællem/kelas))

   c.   "their"

       jæváb bèdid: جواب بدید:

       S1:   dústeshun kelas dare.

       S2:   jæváb-e azad (e.g. bǽle. dústeshun kelas dare.)

(cues: moællem/mashin, emtehan/neveshtæn, dust/kebrit, kelas/dæstyar,* (dust/kelas))

     * /dæstyar/ = Teaching Assistant, T.A.

Drill 19: Transformation

   The cue given is not included in the answer. Example:

       ba dústæm sobane míkhoræm. (un)

       ba dústesh sobane* míkhore.

       (cues: shoma, mæn, una, shoma, ma, un, (mæn))

   * (depending on the teacher's preference: *sobhane, sobane, sobhune, sobune*)

Lesson Five　　　　　　　*MODERN PERSIAN*　　　　　درس پنجم

Drill 20: Repetition and Substitution

    a.   **tekrár konid**:　　　　　　　　　　تکرار کنید:

        chænd-ta medad, pænj-ta medad, car-ta medad, se-ta medad, do-ta medad

        N.B.: ye dune medad chænd-ta shagerd, bist-ta shagerd, punzdæh-ta shagerd,

        dæh-ta shagerd, N.B.: ye shagerd/ye dune shagerd; chænd-ta bæradær, pænj-ta

        bæradær, car-ta bæradær, se-ta bæradær, do-ta bæradær, N.B.: ye bæradær/ye

        dune bæradær.

    b.   **gúsh konid**:　　　　　　　　　　گوش کنید:

        do ta sæet = "two watches"

        do sæet = "two hours"

        tekrár konid:　　　　　　　　　　تکرار کنید:

        "watches": pænj-ta sæet, car-ta sæet, se-ta sæet, do-ta sæet

        N.B.: ye dune sæet

        "Time elements and money": pænj sæet, char sæet, se sæet, do sæet, ye sæet;

        bist ruz, punzdæh ruz, dæh ruz, ye ruz; bist dolar, punzdæh dolar, dæh dolar,

        ye dolar;

    c.   **tekrár konid** (counting objects without naming them):

        ye dune, do-ta, se-ta, car-ta, pænj-ta, dæh-ta, punzdæh-ta, bist-ta

    d.   (cue: do/mashin) ========> mæn <u>do-ta mashin</u> daræm.

        (cues: se/name, do/emtehán-e farsi, ye/shune, dæh/shagerd, char/kaqæz,

        ye/ketáb-e farsi, se/bæche, do/qæhve, se/dolar, ye/chai, dæh/bilít-e otobus,

        do/khahær, se/soal, hæsht/sændæli, ye/khodkar, (do/mashin))

Drill 21: Cued Question/Answer

    a.   **S1:** shoma chænd-ta <u>mæjælle</u> darin?   **S2:** mæn <u>do</u>-ta <u>mæjælle</u> daræm.

        (cues: name/pænj, sib/ye, pakæt/punzdæh, kelás/char, mashin/se, dæftær-e telefon/do,

        bilít-e opera/ye, (mæjælle/do))

Lesson Five　　　　　　MODERN PERSIAN　　　　　　درس پنجم

b.　　S1: shoma chænd-ta <u>mæjælle</u> darin?　　　S2: jæváb-e azad

(cues: moællém-e farsi, dæftær, kasét-e farsi, bæradær, sib, kelás, mashin, dæftær-e telefon,(mæjælle))

(Continue this pattern with words of your own choice for two or three minutes with a partner.)

Drill 2: Soálo Jævab

(The following questions do not need to be done all in one session. Questions that are placed in parentheses are intended to be asked only if you feel comfortable asking them. Some questions may be too personal depending on your relationship with the person you are asking.

 ma sær-e kelas chekár mìkonim?

 ma sær-e kelas fæqæt farsi hǽrf mìzænim? chera?

 ma sær-e kelas khéyli kár mìkonim? ma tæklíf-e shæb darim? emtehán-æm darim? ma inja værzésh mìkonim?

 ma emshæb tæklíf-e shæb darim? fék mìkonin tæklíf-e shǽbemun khéyli ziád-e?

 ma færda emtehan darim? mæn færda æz shoma chi míporsæm?

 ma inja fæqæt farsi hǽrf mìzænim? chéra? shoma inglisi behtær hǽrf mìzænin (?) ya farsi. chéra?

 inja chænd-ta shagerd darim? chænd-ta mærd darim? chænd-ta zæn? (nowbæt-e kí-e?)

 ketábemun chænd-ta dærs dare? in dærs chænd-ta tæmrín-e tælæffoz dare? vidio-e in dærs sækht-e?

 inja ki æræbi mídune? bishtær æræbi hǽrf mìzænin (?) ya mínevisin.

 æli æræbi mídune? shoma chetor? — æræbi mídunin?

 sara o æli æræbi mídunænd? æræbi behtær hǽrf mìzænænd(?) ya farsi. (khob. béporsin.)

 inja ki værzésh mìkone? shoma soba værzésh mìkonin? (to another: shoma chetor?) koja værzésh mìkonin?

Lesson Five   *MODERN PERSIAN*   درس پنجم

S1, shoma mashin darin? chænd-ta mashin darin? (mashínetun khub kár mìkone?)

(S2, mashín-e S1 khub kár mìkone?)

shoma chænd-ta khahǽr-o bæradær darin?

shoma dúst-e irani darin? ésmesh chi-e? u fæqæt farsi mídune?

(inglisi khub hǽrf mìzæne?) u bæradær o khahær dare?

bæradæresh/khahæresh dær emrika zendegí mìkone?

shoma bæradær darin? ésmesh chi-e? koja zendegí mìkone? unja chekár mìkone?

shoma alerzhi darin? shoma aspirin míkhorin? shoma chi fék mìkonin? aspirin bæráye* alerzhi khub-e? vitamin se chetor? vitamin se bæráye* alerzhi khub-e?

(/bæráye/ yæ:ni "for")

áb-e portoqal vitamin se ("C") dare? áb-e sib chetor?

sina inglisi hærf mìzæne? læhjé-ye rusi dare? shoma rusi hǽrf mìzænin?

shoma dæftær-e telefón-e (city) darin? dæftær-e telefon chænd-ta esm dare?

dæftær-e telefón-e shikago bozorgtær-e (?) ya dæftær-e telefón-e (Tucson, Phoenix, etc.). rást mìgid? shoma fék mìkonin dæftær-e telefón-e los anjeles chænd-ta ésm-e irani dare?

shoma emruz sandvich darin? chænd-ta? sær-e kelas sandvich míkhorin? shokolat chetor? (chéra? rezhim darin?)

shoma khoresh doróst mìkonin? khorésh-e chi?

(shoma soba hæmúm mìkonin? dær hæmum aváz mìkhunin?)

shoma albóm-e tæmbr darin? tæmbr-e irani darin?

shoma khune darin? garazh chetor?—garazh darin?

shoma aparteman darin? apartemánetun telefon dare?

(shoma tænha zendegí mìkonin? ba ki zendegí mìkonin?)

shoma dær khabgah zendegí mìkonin? khabgah restoran dare? restorán-e khabgah khúb-e?

202

Lesson Five　　　　*MODERN PERSIAN*　　　　درس پنجم

shoma televizion darin?　khub kár mìkone?

shoma khéyli dærs mìkhunin?　koja dærs mìkhunin?

(shoma dær bank pul darin?　khéyli pul darin?)

shoma ebri mídunin?　æræbi chetor?

shoma farsi tond mínevisin?　ba chi mínevisin?　ma sær-e kelas khundæno neveshtæn tæmrin mìkonim?　mokaleme chetor?

shoma kasét-e muzik darin?　chænd-ta?　kasét-e jaz darin?

shoma kár mìkonin?　koja kár mìkonin?

shoma lisans darin?　fóq-e lisans chetor?

shoma mashin darin?　dochærkhe chetor?

shoma medad darin?　chænd-ta medad darin?　khudkár-æm darin?

shoma keravat darin?　chænd-ta?　papiyon chetor?

shoma pasport darin?　vizá-ye iran chetor?

shoma sigar darin?　kebrit chetor?　sigár-e chi darin?

S1, shoma mæjælle darin?　chænd-ta mæjælle darin?　ruzname míkhunin?　ésm-e ruzname chi-e?

S1-o S2 kár mìkonænd?　SSS1 koja kár mìkone?　S2 chetor?

S1-o S2 værzésh mìkonænd?　koja værzésh mìkonænd?

"mæhmud" ésm-e pesær-e (?) ya dokhtær-e.

"vida" ésm-e dokhtær-e?

in chi-e?　(kaqæz, medad, khodkar)/(miz, sændæli, sæt, ...)　inja chænd-ta (sændæli, ...) darim?

in ketáb-e chi-e?　in dæftær-e chi-e?

ésm-e mæn chi-e?

ésm-e in aqa chi-e?　un aqa chetor?

ésm-e in khanum chi-e?　in khanum chetor?

203

Lesson Five — *MODERN PERSIAN* — درس پنجم

5.11 Grammar Discussion

5.11.1 The Noun Phrase: The *Ezafe* Construction

The *ezafe* اضافه construction in Persian is the means used to express the genitive and other similar relationships between a noun and its modifiers. The *ezafe* is formed by placing an unstressed /-e/ between the noun and the word that modifies it. By convention, this unstressed /-e/ is represented as being attached to the noun modified, not to the noun, pronoun, or adjective that modifies it:

Persian		Grammatical Relationship	Translation
ketáb-e æli	کتاب علی	Possession (N + N)	Ali's book
hál-e shoma	حال شما	Possession (N + Pro)	your health
mædær-e dústæm	مادر دوستم	Possession (N + N)	my friend's mother
kelás-e farsi	کلاس فارسی	Description (N + N)	Persian class

The *ezafe* construction is used in all cases where various types of modifiers normally follow what they modify, as is the case with noun + noun, as shown above, as well as noun + adjective combinations:

ketáb-e irani	کتاب ایرانی	(an) Iranian book
dæftær-e siah	دفتر سیاه	(a) black notebook
khodkær-e abi	خودکار آبی	(a) blue pen
gol-e zærd	گل زرد	(a) yellow flower
ræng-e sefid	رنگ سفید	white color

When the modifier comes first, the *ezafe* is not used. Adverbs, for example, regularly precede adjectives, and demonstratives always precede what they modify. In these cases, the *ezafe* is not used:

khéyli khub	خیلی خوب	very good
in pesær	این پسر	this boy

There are cases in which the adjective precedes the noun, although none has yet occurred in these lessons. The superlative degree of an adjective regularly precedes the noun it

modifies. In addition, an adjective may occasionally be placed before a noun for special emphasis:

| behtærin ketab | بهترین کتاب | the best book |
| bæd fékri nist | بد فکری نیست | That's not a bad idea! |

However, to repeat, when the modifier follows what it modifies, the *ezafe* is obligatory. Moreover, this rule is not affected by the fact that a noun may be modified by a series of modifiers. Generally each of these modifiers in a string of noun modifiers gets an *ezafe* marker:

kelás-e farsi	کلاس فارسی	a / the Persian class
kelás-e farsí-e emruz	کلاس فارسی امروز	today's Persian class
kelás-e farsí-e emrúz-e shoma	کلاس فارسی امروز شما	your Persian class for today

The Written Representation of the *Ezafe*

1. After all consonants, the *ezafe* is not written, although it is sometimes indicated by the *zir:*

ketáb-e æli	کتابِ علی	Ali's book
dærs-e do	درسِ دو	Lesson 2
kelás-e farsi	کلاسِ فارسی	Persian class

2. After ا and و , the *ezafe* is always represented by *ye*:

   | aqá-ye firuzi | آقایِ فیروزی | Mr. Firuzi |
   | daneshjú-ye irani | دانشجویِ ایرانی | Iranian student |

3. After ی, the *ezafe* is never written (except by an optional zir)

   | farsí-e mæn | فارسیِ من | My Persian |
   | zhaponí-e mandana | ژاپنیِ ماندانا | Mandana's Japanese |

4. After final ه, the *ezafe* is represented by *hæmze* (ء) over the ه although it is not usually written. It is also occasionally represented by the use of ی:

205

Lesson Five   *MODERN PERSIAN*   درس پنجم

        khuné-ye pærvin   خانه پروین   Parvin's house

or: خانه ی پروین   خانهء پروین   خانه پروین

Uses of the *Ezafe*

The *ezafe* construction encompasses what would be a variety of grammatical relationships in English. Some of these uses of *ezafe* and their English translations are illustrated below. Since English has nothing quite like the *ezafe*, idiomatic translations often require a rearrangement of the elements of the Persian, or a paraphrase of them, as in the example given above (*kelás-e farsí-e emrúz-e shoma*), which can be put in acceptable English only by moving the elements around in translation: "Your Persian class today." Remember, the differences in translation below are generally an <u>English</u> translation problem. Persian treats all of these relationships grammatically in the same way:

    HEAD NOUN + *ezafe* + modifier

English has different ways of expressing these relationships. It will not take you long to accustom yourself to the *ezafe* construction and to form new phrases with it.

I.   Possession or intimate association

Ezafe Construction		**English Equivalent**
a. **possessor/modifier is animate**		**noun + 's (possessive s)**
ésm-e bæradæræm	اسم برادرم	my brother's name
ruznamé-ye hæsæn	روزنامه حسن	Hassan's newspaper
nowbǽt-e ki	نوبت کی	whose turn

Here are some other noun combinations in this relationship:

soál-e daneshju	سئوال دانشجو	the student's question
mædresé-ye shæhla	مدرسه شهلا	Shahla's school
khǽt-e mæhmud	خط محمود	Mahmud's handwriting
mashín-e madæræm	ماشین مادرم	my mother's car

                                                                     English Equivalent:

Lesson Five MODERN PERSIAN درس پنجم

    b. **possessor/modifier is inanimate**   **noun + of + noun**

    be læhjé-ye mæshhædi به لهجه مشهدی   in the accent of Mashed

    English Equivalent:

    noun + of/in/at + noun

    qæhvé-ye in restoran قهوه این رستوران   the coffee at this restaurant

    kúrs-e shimi درسِ شیمی   a course in chemistry

II. The modifier describes or further qualifies the noun it modifies:

    moællém-e zæban معلم زبان   language teacher

    ketáb-e farsi کتاب فارسی   Persian book

    (What kind of teacher? What kind of book?)

Here are some other noun combinations in this relationship:

    English Equivalent

    noun-nóun compound

    (with stress usually on second noun)

khorésh-e bademjun	خورش بادمجان	eggplant stew
tæmrín-e pænj	تمرین ۵	drill (exercise) 5
dærs-e pænj	درس ۵	lesson 5
telefón-e daneshgah	تلفن دانشگاه	university telephone
ruznamé-ye daneshgah	روزنامه دانشگاه	university newspaper
ketabkhuné-ye daneshgah	کتابخانه دانشگاه	university library
bimarestán-e daneshgah	بیمارستان دانشگاه	university hospital

    English Equivalent

    nóun-noun compound

    (with stress often on first noun)

áb-e sib	آب سیب	ápple juice
kasét-e muzik	کاست موزیک	músic cassette
emtehán-e farsi	امتحان فارسی	Pérsian test

Lesson Five   *MODERN PERSIAN*   درس پنجم

kúrs-e zæban	درس زبان (کورس)	lánguage course
albóm-e tæmb	آلبوم تمبر	stámp album
bilít-e otobus	بلیط اتوبوس	bús ticket
dǽftær-e farsi	دفتر فارسی	Pérsian notebook

III. The modifier explains the head noun or is a specific name for it

zæbán-e færanse	زبان فرانسه	the French language
mæjællé-ye taym	مجله تایم	<u>Time</u> magazine

Here are some other noun combinations in this relationship:

hotél-e hilton	هتل هیلتون	Hotel Hilton
sinemá-ye pasifik	سینمای پاسیفیک	Pacific Theater
sigár-e kent	سیگار کنت	Kent cigarettes
daneshgá-ye tehran	دانشگاه تهران	Tehran University

Adjectives

In Lesson 6 you will encounter another important use of the *ezafe* construction: Nouns are followed by the adjectives that modify them and are connected to them by the *ezafe*:

ketáb-e khub	کتاب خوب	(a) good book
læhjé-ye bæd	لهجه بد	(a) bad accent

As mentioned above, there is a minority of adjectives that precede the nouns they modify. These adjectives do not take the *ezafe*. Other uses of the *ezafe* construction will be discussed as they are encountered in future lessons.

5.11.2 Extended Noun Phrases

Noun phrases you have encountered so far are of either of two types — **noun-ezafe-noun/pronoun** or **noun-personal possessive ending** — or a combination of both:

ketáb-e æli	کتاب علی	Noun1-ezafe-Noun2
hál-e shoma	حال شما	Noun1-ezafe-Pronoun

Lesson Five   *MODERN PERSIAN*   درس پنجم

bæradǽræm	برادرم	Noun1-possessive ending
ésm-e bæradǽræm	اسم برادرم	Noun1-ezafe-Noun2-possessive ending

Noun phrases may also be longer and more complex as you have seen with:

shagérd-e khanóm-e shirazi	شاگرد خانم شیرازی	Mrs. Shirazi's student.
moællém-e ælío reza	معلم علی و رضا	Ali and Reza's teacher
pedæro madær-e dústæm	پدر و مادر دوستم	my friend's mother and father
dúst-e in pesær	دوست این پسر	the friend of this boy
pesær-e aqá-ye firuzi	پسر آقای فیروزی	Mr. Firuzi's son

Here are some additional longer noun phrase strings. Note that English doesn't really string words together in the same way Persian does.

moællém-e dúst-e aqá-ye shirazi   معلم دوست آقای شیرازی

The teacher of Mr. Shirazi's friend (Mr. Shirazi's friend's teacher)

pesær-e dúst-e moællém-e ælío reza   پسر دوست معلم علی و رضا

The son of Ali and Reza's teacher's friend (Ali and Reza's teacher's friend's son)

væqt-e emtehán-e kelás-e farsi   وقت امتحان کلاس فارسی

The time of the exam of the Persian class (the Persian class exam's time)

Any of the noun phrases in a string may also be modified by an adjective:

bærádær-e bozórg-e in pesær   برادر بزرگ این پسر   this boy's big (older) brother

Here are some additional noun phrase strings consisting of three nouns in which the third noun is modified by a personal possessive ending or a demonstrative pronoun — /in/-/un/.

ésm-e dúst-e bæradǽræm   اسم دوست برادرم   the name of my brother's friend

qæzá-ye restorán-e in hotel   غذای رستوران این هتل   the food in this hotel's restaurant

And an example of the fourth noun in a string modified by /in/:

mokalemé-ye dærs-e pænj-e in ketab   مکالمه درس ۵ این کتاب

The dialogue of Lesson 5 of/in this book

In the expansion of a noun phrase, modifiers of a noun may include both the demonstrative /in/ or /un/ and the personal endings simultaneously:

Lesson Five　　　　　　　MODERN PERSIAN　　　　　درس پنجم

in dústæm	این دوستم	This friend of mine
un dústetun	اون دوستتون	That friend of yours

Noun phrases in any language can get inordinately long. Witness the the name of the following document from the New York State Tax Commission: New York State Real Property Transfer Gains Tax Clearance Certificate. This "officialese" name forms <u>one</u> noun phrase that is ten words long; it is the name of one type of certificate, hence one noun phrase. German is famous not only for long noun phrases but also for writing them as one word.

5.11.3 The Noun Phrase: Counting Nouns

As you saw in the exercises of this lesson (Lesson 5, exercises 20 and 21), when counting most nouns, a counting particle is inserted between the number and the noun. This counting particle is usually *dune* for "one" and *ta* for all other numbers as well as the question word *chænd*:

چند تا سیب؟　　دو تا سیب،　　سه تا سیب،　　چار تا سیب

How many apples? Two apples, three apples, four apples, etc.

Whenever you count objects, even if the object is not stated, the appropriate counting particle is necessary:

چار تا.　　چند تا کتاب؟　　How many books? Four.

If the objects are in front of you and you are counting them off, you will not need to say the noun, but will need to use the counting particle.

Example (counting the number of apples in front of you while you point to each one to keep track of how many you are counting):

*یه دونه، دو تا، سه تا، چار تا، پنج تا، شیش تا، هفت تا،

هشت تا، نه تا، ده تا ـ من ده تا سیب دارم

"One, two, three, four, five six, seven, eight, nine, ten — I have ten apples."

Note: in counting like this, you will also hear /yeki, do-ta, .../ instead of /ye dune, do-ta, .../

Lesson Five   *MODERN PERSIAN*   درس پنجم

Exceptions:

a. Counting particles are not used with time words, money and a few other categories of nouns:

    Time elements: pænj saæt, char saæt, se saæt, do saæt, ye saæt; bist ruz, punzdæh ruz, dæh ruz, ye ruz

    Money: bist dolar, punzdæh dolar, dæh dolar, ye dolar; (see drill 20 of this lesson.)

b. Although the counting particles are commonly used in counting animate nouns, *dune* is more commonly omitted than not:

چند تا شاگرد؟

یه شاگرد، دو تا شاگرد، سه تا شاگرد، چار تا شاگرد

یه خواهر، یه برادر، دو تا معلم

"How many students? One student, two students, three students, four students;"

"one sister, one brother, two teachers..."

The only time you will really hear the plain numbers without counting words, other than the exception mentioned above, is when you are asked to count numbers in the abstract, such as, say, to count from one to ten, one to a hundred, or when you count to ten before you start a task, etc.

Later in the text, in section 8.9.4, you will learn the rules necessary for writing these phrases correctly in FWP.

Practice:

Spoken:

من هرروز دو تا سیب و یه دونه انار می خورم و بعد یه ساعت تو کتابخونه کار می کنم.

Written:

من هرروز دو سیب و یک انار می خورم و سپس یک ساعت در کتابخانه کار می کنم.

5.11.4 The Verb Phrase

dasht-dan "to have" "to have": Present Tense

The verb /dasht-dar/, "to have," does not take the usual present tense marker /mí-/. It is one of the two verbs in Persian that behave this way. The other, "to be," will be introduced at length in Lesson 6.

/næ-/: A Variant of the Negative Particle

The verbal prefix /mí-/, when negativized, is preceded by the negative particle in the form /né-/:

| mídunæm | "I know" | némidunæm | "I don't know" |
| dǽrs mìdæm | "I teach" | dǽrs némidæm | "I don't teach" |

When the verb has no /mí-/ prefix, as in the simple past, the imperative, or the present tense of *dasht-dar*, the negative particle form is /næ-/, added directly to the stem. Examples:

dáræm	"I have"	nædaræm	"I don't have"
fæhmídæm	"I understood"	næfæhmidæm	"I didn't understand"
tekrár konìd	"Repeat"	tekràr nækonid	"Don't repeat"

5.11.5 The Infinitive

The infinitive in Persian is formed by adding the infinitive marker /-æn/ to the past stem of the verb. You have seen the infinitive form in two words, *khundæn* and *neveshtæn*. The Persian infinitive form does not have the same use as the English infinitive. It is more like the English verbal noun that ends in "-ing" and is not as commonly used as the English infinitive:

| khundæn | "reading" | hærf zædæn | "speaking, speech" |
| neveshtæn | "writing" | dærs dadæn | "teaching" |

It has been a convention of Persian grammars and dictionaries to use the infinitive as the citation form of verbs. In Persian it is called the *mæsdær*. Verbs in dictionaries are listed in the infinitive form only. If you are looking up the word "to eat" in a dictionary, you will find: "خوردن." In this textbook, we have chosen to cite verbs by their two stems, present and

past, and to gloss them with the English infinitive as a means of helping the student to learn the two stems together. We list the above verb as follows:

to eat	khord-khor (roots)	خورد خور
to see		دید بین
to go		رفت رو
to say		گفت گو
to hear		شنید شنو

5.11.6 Verbs with Obligatory Objects

Certain verbs, for grammatical reasons, usually do not stand alone, and may only do so when their context is already spelled out very explicitly, such as having been mentioned in an immediately preceding sentence.

a. **míkhunæm/khund** You have learned that the verb *míkhunæm/khund* means "to study" or "to read." It also means "to sing." These three meanings are all connected. Studying usually involves reading, and in British English "reading" is often used where Americans would prefer "studying" (e.g., "My brother is reading Persian at Cambridge."). Moreover in the Middle East and many parts of Asia, studying entails reciting or chanting one's lessons aloud. To keep the three meanings distinct, modern Persian requires the verb *míkhunæm/khund* to be accompanied by an object that makes clear what is intended. The object can be dropped only when the context makes the meaning unambiguous:

shoma æræbi míkhunin?

næ, némikhunæm. (In the second sentence the object <u>æræbi</u> is assumed.)

Suppose you wish to employ the verbs "to read," "to study" or "to sing" in a general sense in Persian without specifying **what** you are reading, studying, or singing. In these cases a general noun is used to serve as an unspecified object: *dærs* "lesson," *ketab* "book," and *avaz* "song." The new combination becomes a compound verb:

mæn ziad dærs míkhunæm.   "I study a lot."

Lesson Five *MODERN PERSIAN* درس پنجم

    mæn ziad ketáb mìkhunæm. "I read a lot."

    mæn ziad aváz mìkhunæm. "I sing a lot."

This type of compound verb, such as *ketáb mìkhunæm* "I read," does not necessarily suggest that one's reading is restricted to books alone. In addition, the verb "to read" in general, without regard to what is read, is often expressed by a different vocabulary item, /motaleé mìkonæm/ "read, study":

    mæn ziad ketáb mìkhunæm. "I read a lot of books; I read (various things) a lot."

    mæn hæmishe shæba motaleé mìkonæm. "I always read at night; I always study at night."

b. **míkhoræm/khord** The verb *míkhoræm/khord* "to eat" also requires a direct object. When you wish to use the verb "to eat" without specifying an object, the noun *qæza* may be used as a generic object. Again, this combination yields a compound verb that should be translated simply as "eat":

    shoma koja qæza míkhorin? "Where do you eat?"

    mæn dær khabga qæza míkhoræm. "I eat at the dorm."

5.11.7 *to* — The Second Person Familiar

The second person singular form, /to/, the familiar form of the pronoun "you," was introduced in 3.11.2. Some of the forms that agree with this pronoun were also given there and in 2.11.4. Let us summarize these forms here:

1. The personal possessive ending attached to the noun is /-et/. You have seen this ending already in the expression:

    hálet chetór-e? How are you? (familiar form)

This ending is used on other nouns as well:

    pedǽro madǽret koja zendegí mìkonænd? Where do your parents live?

2. The verb form that agrees with /to/ is /-i/; as with other pronouns, *to* may be omitted:

Lesson Five MODERN PERSIAN درس پنجم

| farsi khub hærf mìzæni. | فارسی خوب حرف میزنی. | You speak Persian well. |
| chænd-ta sib dari? | چند تا سیب داری؟ | How many apples do you have? |

The Command Form

The second person imperative is formed from the present stem of the verb. In most cases, the prefix /bé-/ is added to that stem. In the compound verbs formed with /kærd-kon/ and /shod-sh/, the prefix is generally not used. The person of the verb is indicated by the ending /-id, -in/ for the plural and no ending (-Ø) for the singular (second person familiar). Examples:

	hærf bèzænid	حرف بزنید	Speak! (plural)
	hærf bèzæn	حرف بزن	Speak! (singular, familiar)
but:	tekrár konìd	تکرار کنید	Repeat! (plural)
	tekrár kòn	تکرار کن	Repeat! (singular, familiar)
and:	béporsid	بپرسید	Ask! (plural)
	bépors	بپرس	Ask! (singular, familiar)
but:	tærjomé konìd	ترجمه کنید	Translate! (plural)
	tærjomé kòn	ترجمه کن	Translate! (singular, familiar)

Lessons 11 and 12 contain exercises on all forms of the Imperative and there is a fuller description of their formation in sections 11.11.2 and 11.11.3.

5.11.8 Personal Endings

You have so far learned two sets of personal endings. One set is attached to verbs and indicates agreement with subject. We will call these endings **Set 1**. The other set — of which three new ones have been introduced in this lesson — is attached to nouns and indicates personal possession. We will call these endings **Set 2**. The forms of both Sets that you have learned are the forms they take when attached to noun and verb stems that end in consonants:

Lesson Five *MODERN PERSIAN* درس پنجم

Set 1	Set 2
-æm	-æm
-i	-et
(-e)	-esh
-im	-emun
-in/-id	-etun
-ænd	-eshun

There are several alternations in both Sets 1 and 2 depending on their context:

Set 1

1. As discussed in the writing section of 6.9.3-4, there are changes in the written forms of Set 1:

   a. /-e/, third person singular, is always written /-æd/ (except occasionally to indicate colloquial dialogue):

   zendegí mìkone =========> زندگی میکند

   b. the second person plural alternates between /-id/ and /-in/ in colloquial Persian. In written Persian, however, it should always be written /-id/ (except to indicate colloquial dialogue):

   mídunin? ==========> میدانید؟

2. The Set 1 endings given above are the forms they take when attached to verb stems ending in consonants — which includes almost all verbs. As you will see in the exercises of Lesson 6, however, Set 1 in colloquial speech changes slightly after a few present stems that end in /-a/ such as /-kha-/ "to want" and /-a-/ "to come." The following changes occur:

   a. the vowel /æ/ of the endings is dropped and the consonants of endings attach directly to the verb stem:

   mí + kha + (æ)m ====> mí-kha-m   "I want"

            + (æ)nd ====> mí-kha-nd   "they want"

216

Lesson Five   *MODERN PERSIAN*   درس پنجم

b. the third person singular form /-e/ changes to its literary (and older) form /-æd/, in which case the /æ/ is dropped as above:

     mí + kha + (æ)d   ====>   mí-kha-d   "he/she wants"

c. the other endings either remain as they are or become diphthongs:

míkhai	or	míkhay
míkhaim	or	míkhaym
míkhain	or	míkhayn

As you will see in Lesson 7 (section 7.9.2, Lengthened Verb Stems), in written Persian, rather than coalescing the endings with the stems, thus losing the /æ/ vowel in /-æm/, /-æd/ and /-ænd/ or forming a diphthong with /-i/, /-im/, /-id, -in/, there is a consonant — /h/ or /y/ — between the stem and the endings:

Colloquial   **Formal**

míkham   (= mí-kha-m)   میخواهم   read: míkha<u>æm</u>   "I want"

míam   (= mí-a-m)   میایم   read: <u>míayæm</u>   "I come"

Examples:

میرویم	میروم	میخواهیم	میخواهم	کار میکنیم	کار میکنم
میروید	میروی	میخواهید	میخواهی	کار میکنید	کار میکنی
میروند	میرود	میخواهند	میخواهد	کار میکنند	کار میکند
میخوریم	میخورم	میاییم	میایم	داریم	دارم
میخورید	میخوری	میایید	میایی	دارید	داری
میخورند	میخورد	میایند	میاید	دارند	دارد

Endings:

یم	م
ید	ی
د \ - ند	

217

Lesson Five   *MODERN PERSIAN*   درس پنجم

Set 2

1. As you will see in Lesson 6 (Drill 15), Set 2 also changes after nouns ending in vowels. The vowel of the ending is dropped and the consonant of the ending is attached directly to the vowel of the noun:

farsi + (æ)m	farsím	"my Persian"
farsi + (e)t	farsít	"your Persian"
farsi + (e)sh	farsísh	"his Persian"
farsi + (e)mun	farsímun	"our Persian"
farsi + (e)tun	farsítun	"your Persian"
farsi + (e)shun	farsíshun	"their Persian"

As you will see in Lesson 9 (Exercises 4 and 5), when a word ends in /-e/ and any of the Set 2 endings is attached to it, the /-e/ changes to /-æ/:

khuné + (æ)m	khunǽm	"my house"
khuné + (e)t	khunǽt	"your house"
khuné + (e)sh	khunǽsh	"his house"
khuné + (e)mun	khunǽmun	"our house"
khuné + (e)tun	khunǽtun	"your house"
khuné + (e)shun	khunǽshun	"their house"

2. In FWP, two changes occur in the Set 2 endings:

    a. Rather than attaching directly to the stem as in colloquial, the endings are kept separate from the stem. After stems ending in the vowel /-a/, a /-y-/ is placed between the stem and the ending:

سینمایم   (سینمای من)   (read: sinemáyæm)

روزهایم   (روزهای من)   (read: ruzháyæm)

In the case of other vowels, no consonant is used but the endings are still pronounced as separate syllables. To indicate this separation, the personal endings are written as independent words:

Lesson Five   MODERN PERSIAN   درس پنجم

	Written Form		Read
farsi + æm	فارسی ام	(فارسی من)	<u>farsíæm</u>
khané + et	خانه ات	(خانه تو)	<u>khanéæt</u>

    b.   the endings that begin with /-e-/ (all but the first person singular) change that vowel to /-æ-/ in all positions in formal Persian:

Colloquial	Written Form	Read
ketábet	کتابت	<u>ketábæt</u>
ketábesh	کتابش	<u>ketábæsh</u>

Examples:

کتابم	کتابمان		خودکارم	خودکارمان
کتابت	کتابتان		خودکارت	خودکارتان
کتابش	کتابشان		خودکارش	خودکارشان

Endings:

م	مان
ت	تان
ش	شان

The differences between Set 1 and Set 2 in colloquial Persian, as well as full examples of each of these sets, will be given in section 8.11.1. The colloquial and FWP differences in the Set 2 endings will be summarized in section 10.9.1.

5.12 Meals and Food: Part II: Kabab, Khoresh, Polow

Iranian food is varied, subtle in flavor, and delicious. It resembles the cuisines of Iran's neighbors in a number of ways, especially in the preparation and use of rice, but it is a distinctive cuisine unto itself — using neither the pungent spices of Indian food, nor the olive oil, tahini paste, garlic, and tomatoes of the eastern Mediterranean and Turkey. The flavors of Iranian food come from the use of herbs and spices and the long simmering of chunks of meat

Lesson Five   *MODERN PERSIAN*   درس پنجم

with fruits or vegetables.

The most popular meat used in Iranian cooking is lamb, although beef has gained a degree of acceptance in recent decades. Iranian sheep are of the fat-tailed variety, which means that the strong tasting sheep fat is concentrated in the tail, not in the meat. As a consequence, Iranian lamb has a much milder flavor than does the lamb available in the United States. Almost all meals are accompanied by چلو *chelow*, plain cooked white rice. In Iran rice is first soaked and parboiled, then drained, returned to the pot, laced with butter, and steamed. The result is a dry, fluffy rice quite unlike the soggy mass usually seen on some tables.

Although there is a great variety in Iranian cooking, most dishes can be classified into three basic types:

1. کباب *kæbab*. Iranians generally use lamb that they tenderize and marinate in onion juice for several days. Turmeric and/or yogurt are often added to the marinade. The *kæbab* may be made up of chunks of meat — کباب برگ *kæbáb-e bærg* — or ground meat — کباب کوبیده *kæbáb-e kubide*. In either case the meat is placed on a long, flat skewer, or سیخ *sikh*, and broiled over charcoal. Although tomatoes, green peppers, and onions are usually not added to the skewer of an Iranian kebab, tomatoes are often broiled separately and served as a side dish. There is another type of *kæbab*, named شیشلیک *shishlik*, of Caucasian origin; it is more like what one gets in American restaurants as "shish kebab." (The word *shish*, like سیخ *sikh*, means "skewer.") *kæbab* is usually served with bread, نان *nun*, or *chelow*, in which case it is known as چلو کباب *chelow kæbab*. The second most popular kind of *kæbab* is made with young chicken (جوجه *juje*) and is known as جوجه کباب *juje kæbab*.

2. خورش *khoresh*, or colloquially kh*oresht*. A *khoresh*, like a gumbo, has a consistency between a stew and a thick sauce. It is always served over *chelow* and is often called چلو خورش *chelow-khoresh*. There are many wonderful varieties of *chelow-khoresh* in Iranian cuisine; among the most popular are:

Lesson Five *MODERN PERSIAN* درس پنجم

Persian dinner spread (rice, stew, kabab, kofteh, and other dishes)

خورش بادمجان *khorésh-e bademjun* Lamb or chicken sautéed with onions, tomatoes and strips of eggplant (بادمجان *bademjan,* colloquial *bademjun*).

خورش فسنجان *khorésh-e fesenjun* Duck, chicken, or tiny meatballs seasoned with turmeric and stewed in a sauce made of ground walnuts, onions, and pomegranate syrup.

قرمه سبزی *qorme sæbzi* Chopped greens — flat leaf parsley, scallions, Iranian leeks (*tære* تره), leaf fenugreek (*shæmbælile* شنبلیله), and sometimes spinach — stewed with lamb, dried limes (*limu æmani*/لیموی عمانی), and black-eyed peas (*chéshm-e bolboli* چشم بلبلی, "nightingale eyes").

خورش آلو *khorésh-e alu* Lamb or chicken stewed with Iranian sour plums (*alu*) and onions, seasoned with cinnamon.

خورش قیمه *khorésh-e qeyme* Finely diced lamb seasoned with turmeric and stewed with lime juice or powdered lime peel, tomato paste, and yellow split peas (لپه *læppe*), to which home-fried potatoes are added just before serving.

خورش کرفس *khorésh-e kæræfs* Lamb, celery (کرفس *kæræfs*), and onions stewed with lime juice, mint, parsley, and saffron (زعفران *zæ:færun*).

221

Lesson Five　　　　　　　MODERN PERSIAN　　　　　　　درس پنجم

3. پلو　　*polow* This word has come into English, through Armenian, as "pilaff." It is *chelow* to which some combination of herbs, vegetables, fruit, or pieces of meat has been added before steaming. Some popular *polows* are:

باقالی پلو　　*baqali polow* Lamb, small fava beans (*baqali* or *baqala*), and lots of fresh dill (*shevid* شوید or, in colloquial Tehrani speech, *shivit*). In the United States, baby lima beans are often substituted for the fava beans. This is a very attractive dish with its shades of green, and is a favorite in late spring and early summer when the dill and beans are just coming into season.

اسلامبلی پلو　　*eslamboli polow* Diced lamb, cinnamon, tomato paste, and tomatoes.

لوبیا پلو　　*lubia polow* Diced lamb, green beans, turmeric, and tomatoes.

آلبالو پلو　　*albalu polow* Lamb and آلبالو "sour cherries." A very simple and delicious dish that comes out a spectacular pink.

سبزی پلو　　*sæbzi polow* Finely chopped greens (*sæbzi*) — scallions, dill, parsley, leaf fenugreek, and coriander (*geshniz/gæshniz* گشنیز). This *polow* is usually served with fried white fish and is a favorite at Now Ruz (see 9.12).

شیرین پلو　　*shirin polow* "Sweet Pilaff" is sauteed chicken served with *chelow* that is flavored with candied orange peel and julienned carrots, saffron, sugar, pistachios, and slivered almonds for decoration.

abgusht, kotlet, kuku, ash and shirini (some recipes at the end of lesson 7)

There are several other dishes that don't fit easily into any of these categories but without which any description of Iranian cuisine would be incomplete.

4. آبگوشت　　*abgusht*, also called *dizi* for the earthen pot in which it was once cooked, really is a stew. It is almost a category in itself since there are as many recipes for it as there are cooks who make it, but its principal ingredients are, as its name promises, آب *ab* "water" and گوشت *gusht* "meat." It also contains نخود *nokhod* "chickpeas" and سیب زمینی *síb(-e) zæmini* "potatoes" and can be flavored with زردچوبه *zærdcube* "turmeric" or with saffron.

Lesson Five MODERN PERSIAN درس پنجم

5. کتلت   *kotlet* or کتلت کوبیده *kotlét-e kubide* is a mixture of ground meat, bread, onions and spices that has been formed into patties and fried. It is served hot or cold.

6. کوکو   *kuku* is an egg dish that is often identified as an Iranian omelette. *kuku* is much more like a frittata since the ingredients are mixed into the eggs before being slowly fried until the eggs are firmly set. There are many variations on the kuku, of which کوکو سبزی *kuku sæbzi* is the most popular. It contains finely chopped lettuce and green herbs. Like the *kotlet, kuku* may be served hot or cold.

7. آش   *ash* This is a generic term that refers to soups made of vegetables, sometimes with meat, that are thickened by the addition of rice flour or legumes.

8. شیرینی   *shirini* "sweets" Desserts tend to be simple in Iranian cooking. There is شیر برنج *shirberenj* "rice pudding" made from برنج "rice" and "milk" and flavored with گلاب *golab* "rosewater," and حلوا *hælva* a mixture of cooked flour, shortening and sugar that is flavored with گلاب or زعفران. Western style ice cream and bakery goods are much admired but not widely available outside the capital.

دهنم آب افتاده !   *dæhænæm ab oftade!* "My mouth is watering!"

Food and Taarof

In Iran it is considered bad manners not to offer guests food or drink, even during a brief visit. It is also impolite to eat anything in public without offering to share it. In every social situation, there is, of course, both a correct way to offer food and drink, and a correct way to accept or decline it. For the most part, food is neither offered casually, nor declined in an offhand way, although the exchange may be quite simple. One fairly polite way to offer tea, for example, is to say:

áqa/khánum, chai míkhorin?

áqa/khánum, chai míkhorin?   (note difference in sentence stress)

The usual answer would simply be *mérsi* (*khahésh mìkonæm; mérsi, motshækér-æm*),

which is ambiguous, since it may mean either "yes" or "no," but more often than not, it will be interpreted as an acceptance. To decline you may say: *mérsi. némikhoræm.*

If you are a guest in someone's house, a refusal may be interpreted as shyness or mere politeness, and you will be asked again, possibly in different ways. Therefore, you should not be surprised if your host or hostess is fairly insistent and does not immediately take no for an answer.

It is worth noting that so long as you continue to clean your plate, your host or hostess may continue to insist that you eat more. Leaving a few bites on your plate indicates that you have eaten as much as it is humanly possible for you.

When offering food or drink the polite alternative to the usual verb meaning "to eat/drink," is *meyl kærd/kon.*

Lesson 5, Drill 23: Cued Question/Answer:
(Note that spoken and written forms are the same here.)

۱ - آقا/خانم، قهوه میخورید؟

۲ - مرسی، آقا/خانم. (میخورم.)

(چایی، چلو کباب، شکلات، کیک، چلو خورش، سیب، آب پرتقال،   کمپوت، غذا، پلو،   چلو، {قهوه})

Lesson 5, Drill 24:   Cued Question/Answer:

۱ - آقا/خانم، قهوه میخورید؟

۲ - مرسی.

۱ - بفرمائید، خواهش میکنم.

۲ - مرسی. نمیخورم.

(چایی، چلو کباب، شکلات، کیک، چلو خورش، سیب، آب پرتقال، غذا، کمپوت، پلو، چلو، {قهوه})

Repeat both exercises substituting *meyl kærd/kon.*

Drill 25   soálo jævab

ki qæzá-ye irani míkhore? bishtær chi míkhorin(?), qæzá-ye irani (?) ya qæzá-ye emrikai.

ki qæzá-ye irani doróst mìkone? chi doróst mìkonin? fæqæt qæzá-ye irani doróst mìkonin? qæzá-ye chini chetor?

shoma chetor? khoresh doróst mìkonin? khorésh-e chi? khoresh gusht dare?

qæzá-ye irani koja doróst mìkonin? dær khabgah?

shoma kæbab doróst mìkonin?

khorésh-e badmjun badmjun dare? máshallah! gusht chetor?

shoma sobane míkhorin? koja sobane míkhorin?

ba sobane qæhve míkhorin?soba áb-e portoqal míkhorin? áb-e sib chetor?

shoma soba qæhve míkhorin (?) ya chai. bishtær qæhve míkhorin (?) ya chai.

shoma kompot míkhorin? soba kompot míkhorin?

shoma sær-e kelas sandvich míkhorin? shokolat chetor? (chéra? rezhim darin?)

5.15 Phonology: The Vanishing /h/

While in formal Persian, the sound /h/ (represented by ح and ه) is pronounced as written, in colloquial Persian it is often elided. What follows in this and subsequent modules is a description of where /h/ is elided in the words it occurs in. The sociolinguistic constraints on when and how /h/ is elided have never been researched clearly and comprehensively. The pronunciation or elision of /h/ in colloquial speech is intimately connected with the issue of different spoken styles of the colloquial language that are discussed in more detail in the Module 7 (section 7.9.1).

By and large, /h/ is elided in the same phonetic environments that the glottal stop is and, like the glottal stop (see section 5.1), leaves a compensatory lengthening of the preceding vowel when dropped. However, the glottal stop will be elided most commonly except in the most formal contexts, whereas /h/ is for the most part retained but dropped more in very

Lesson Five   *MODERN PERSIAN*   درس پنجم

informal contexts. For example, /h/, like /:/, is elided when it follows a vowel and precedes a consonant (VhC). However, the usual pronunciation of معنی is /mæ:ni/, while the pronunciation of a word like مهناز varies between /mæ:naz/ and /mæhnaz/ quite freely. This can lead to occasional ambiguities.

Imitation of Vowel Length (Loss of /h/)

تهران	/te:ran/	بهتر	/be:tær/	صحبت	/so:bæt/	شهلا	/shæ:la/
احمد	/æ:mæd/	فهمید	/fæ:mid/	احساس	/e:sas/	مهری	/me:ri/
احتمال	/e:temal/	عهده	/o:de/	محمود /mæ:mud/	می فهمم	/mífæ:mæm/

5.16 Translation Practice: Read and translate

۱. سلام آقای صادقی. بفرمائید اینجا.

۲. خدا حافظ خانم صادقی. من خیلی خوشوقت شدم.

۳. لطفا خوب تلفظ کنید. لطفا بنویسید «آذربایجان».

۴. الآن پروین و رضا عربی یاد میگیرند.

۵. فریدون و محمود عربی و عبری یاد میگیرند.

۶. بله، آقای اصفهانیان «چیر» یعنی «صندلی.»

۷. من خوب مینویسم ولی یواش مینویسم.

۸. ما خیلی کم صبحانه میخوریم.

۹. این سئوال زیاد سخت نیست.

۱۰. چرا ویدا و حسین فقط مکالمه تمرین میکنند؟

Lesson Six   درس ششم

TOPICS COVERED IN THIS LESSON

- Asking and Giving Opinions about the Quality of Things: Do you think Washington is beautiful? expensive? It's relatively expensive. Is Tehran very far away? I think it's pretty far away.

- Places and Nationalities: Asking and talking about where you/other people are from. Other people's nationalities. Famous people and where they are from.

- The Countries, Languages, and Peoples of the World.

- Simple Questions about Occupations: I am a student. Dan Rather is a journalist. I am not a teacher, etc.

- Classroom Expressions: Blackboard, chalk. It depends. There's no difference. Good job! I'll tell you later, etc.

Listening Materials

    Tom and Hossein Run into Mr. Kazemi at the Movies (Part I)

RESOURCES AND BACKGROUND: INFORMATION AND ACCURACY

Phonology

    Gemination (Doubled Consonants)

    Final Consonant Clusters (B)

Grammar Patterns to Be Drilled

    Noun Phrase

        Nationalities and Inhabitants: *æhl-e*   *kojai -í*

        Possessive Endings after Words Ending in Vowels (except /-e/)

    Verb Phrase

        The Verb "to be" (Present):   /-æm/   /-i/   /-e/   /-im/   /-in/   /-ænd/

        The Variants of "to be":   *hæsti*   *hæstim*   *hæstin*

        Negative Form of "to be":   /nist-/

Lesson Six   *MODERN PERSIAN*   درس ششم

Sentence Pattern

   Complement Clauses: Verb + (ke) + Clause

      reza míge (ke); mæn fékr mìkonæm (ke)

   Noun/Adjective + "to be"

Word-Building

   Nationalities and Place Names

Spoken/Written Transformations, Part I

   Rules Affecting Phonology

      /un/, /um/ = <u>an</u>, <u>am</u>

      /-mb-/ ‍ـنب‍

   Rules Affecting Grammatical Categories

      -e/ = <u>-æd</u>, <u>æst</u>   (3rd singular present tense verb ending)

      -<u>id</u>/-in (2nd person plural ending, all tenses)

Grammar Discussion

   Noun Phrase

      Nationalities and Inhabitants: *æhl-e/mál-e   kojai -í*

   Verb Phrase

      The Verb "to be" (Present): General Introduction

      Grammar and Usage of the Verb "to be" in Colloquial Persian

      /i/ + Verb Endings /-i/, /-im/, and /-id ~ -in/

      Emphasis and Sentence Stress with "to be"

      "to be" of Existence

Cultural Materials

   Introductions

   Iranian Money

Lesson Six *MODERN PERSIAN* درس ششم

6.1 Phonology: Gemination (تَشدید)

As mentioned above under the discussion of تشدید (written ّ , see section 4.9.2), a distinction is made in Persian between a single consonant and a lengthened or doubled consonant. This doubling is called <u>gemination</u>. Gemination is more likely to occur in words of Arabic origin, although there are also words of pure Persian origin that contain doubled consonants.

In colloquial Persian, geminated consonants are generally reduced to single consonants, although gemination is not unusual even in quite informal speech. A geminated /q/ seems never to be reduced in this way. Geminated consonants are almost always pronounced when reading the more formal styles of written Persian aloud.

Pronunciation Drill 1

bænna	bæna	mola	molla	بنّا	بنا	ملا	ملاّ
amma	sæbat	sæmmi	sæmi	امّا	ثبات	سمّی	سمی
mællæ	mæli	makkeh	sæfa	ملّ	ملی	مکّه	صفا
lævash	naqqash	tæppe	tæpesh	لواش	نقّاش	تپّه	تپش
hæyat	khæyyat	khæta	khættat	خطّاط	خطا	خیّاط	حیات

Pronunciation Drill 2

bænna	næjjar	kæffash	کفّاش	نجّار	بنا
bærraq	jeddæn	næqqash	نقّاش	جدّاً	راق
tæppe	hætta	tæmævvol	تموّل	حتّی	تپّه
ærre	tævæssot	bæzzaz	بزّاز	توسّط	ارّه
tælæffoz	tæshækkor	tæhæmmol	تحمّل	تشکّر	تلفّظ
hoqqe	æmma	mellæt	ملّت	امّا	حقّه

Lesson Six   *MODERN PERSIAN*   درس ششم

| khæyyat | tebbi | jællad | | جلاد | طبی | خیاط |
| zæhhak | bæshshash | dokkan | | دکان | بشاش | ضحاک |

Bazaar

6.2 Vocabulary

In order to distinguish between forms that are solely acceptable in either spoken or written usage, on the one hand, and those that are acceptable in both, on the other, all items in this and subsequent vocabulary sections of the lessons will be marked in the following way: (1) the phonetic transcription of purely colloquial forms will be enclosed in parentheses, and the word in Persian script will be written in the right-hand middle column, also enclosed in parentheses; (2) the phonetic transcription of written forms will be underlined and the word in script will be written in the left-hand middle column; (3) forms acceptable in both spoken and written usage will be in a separate column between them. In addition, when two pronunciations or two spellings of a word are equally acceptable, they will both be given — separated by a (/) — and marked appropriately. A superscript number indicates that there is a note following. The relation of FWP forms to colloquial forms is described and analyzed

Lesson Six MODERN PERSIAN درس ششم

below in sections 6.9, 7.9, 8.9, 9.9, and 10.9.

The first three items in the vocabulary below are examples of (1) spoken usage, (2) written usage, and (3) pronunciation acceptable in both spoken and written usage. The two pronunciations for the word for "state," for example, are acceptable in both spoken and written usage. There are also two ways of spelling /kojai/, and both are also acceptable when representing either spoken or written language.

Vocabulary Segments for Lesson Six

گفتاری و نوشتاری

Vocabulary, Dialogue 6		مکالمه ۶
(mæ:zeræt mìkham)	(معذرت میخوام)	excuse me (also:/mæ:zæræt/)
mæ:zeræt mìkhahæm[1]	معذرت میخواهم	
kojai[2]	کجائی/کجایی	native of what place, where from?
bud/hæst[3]	بود/هست	to be
(hæstin)/hæstid	(هستین/هستید)	you are
hæstid	هستید	
æhl[2]	اهل	citizen, inhabitant
eyalæt/æyalæt	ایالت	state (of U.S., etc.), province
jaleb	جالب	interesting
khæbærnegar	خبرنگار	reporter; journalist
(qórban/qórbun)[4]	(قربان/قربون)	sir (polite form of address, lit.: "sacrifice," See section 14.3.1)
daneshju	دانشجو	student (university level)
Vocabulary, Drills Part I		تمرینات، قسمت ۱
ostad	استاد	professor
karmænd	کارمند	(white collar) worker, office worker

231

Lesson Six *MODERN PERSIAN* درس ششم

mohændes	مهندس	engineer (also used as a title like "Dr.")
doktor	دکتر	doctor
ketabdar	کتابدار	librarian
monshi	منشی	secretary (the word سکرتر /sekreter/ is also commonly heard)
sekreter	سکرتر	secretary (also commonly heard)
míbinæm	میبینم	I see
did/bin	دید/بین	to see (see also 6.3.2, A Polite Expression)
mésl-e ìnke	مثل اینکه	it seems that; it seems so, it seems that way; it looks like; I guess so (qualified affirmative)
nahar/næhar	ناهار/نهار	lunch
sham	شام	dinner
modern	مدرن	modern
qæshæng	قشنگ	pretty, beautiful; beautifully, well (see also 6.3.2, A Polite Expression)
motmæen	مطمئن	sure, certain (adj. only)
motmæen bud	مطمئن بود	to be sure, certain
(motmæén-in?)	مطمئنین/مطمئنید؟	Are you sure? (see 6.2.2)
motmæén-id?	مطمئنید	
motmæén-æm	مطمئنم	I'm sure
motmæen nístæm	مطمئن نیستم	I'm not sure
mízænæm	میزنم	I play (musical instrument, lit.: *I hit*)

| Lesson Six | MODERN PERSIAN | درس ششم |

zæd/zæn	زد/زن	to play (musical instrument)
bank	بانک	bank
hazer	حاضر	ready, present (in class, etc.)
qayeb	غایب	absent, not here

Iranian Personal Names

Women's First Names

شهین	shæhin	شهناز		shæhnaz
مهین	mæhin	مینا		mina

Family Names

جعفری	jæ:færi	نژاد		nezhad

Place Names

(Adjectives, Nouns, and Language Names — see Vocabulary Building, section 6.5)

The following words are only the required items introduced in section 6.5. Not all of these items will be used in Lesson 6, but they will occur in subsequent lessons, as well as very likely in the classroom discussion.

گفتاری و نوشتاری

alman	آلمان	Germany
almani	آلمانی	German
azærbayjan	آذربایجان	Azerbaijan
azærbayjani	آذربایجانی	Azerbaijani
æfqanestan	افغانستان	Afghanistan
æfqani (adj, person)	افغانی	Afghan
æfqan (person)[5]	افغان	Afghan
ærmænestan	ارمنستان	Armenia
ærmæni	ارمنی	Armenian
æræb (person)	عرب	Arab

Lesson Six	*MODERN PERSIAN*	درس ششم	
æræbi (adjective)	عربی		Arabic
chin	چین		China
chini	چینی		Chinese
englestan	انگلستان		England
englis/(inglis)	انگلیس/ (اینگلیس)		England
englisi/(inglisi) or	انگلیسی/ (اینگلیسی)		English (adjective, person language)
espania	اسپانیا		Spain
espaniai (adj, person)[6, 7]	اسپانیائی		Spanish
espanioli (language)[7]	اسپانیولی		Spanish
esrail[6]	اسرائیل		Israel
esraili[6]	اسرائیلی		Israeli
færanse (country, language)[7]	فرانسه		France, French (language)
færansævi (adj, person)[7]	فرانسوی		French (adjective or person)
hendustan	هندوستان		India
hendi	هندی		Indian, Hindi
holænd	هلند		The Netherlands, Holland
holændi	هلندی		Dutch
italia	ایتالیا		Italy
italiai[6]	ایتالیائی		Italian
kordestan	کردستان		Kurdistan
kord	کرد		Kurd
lobnan	لبنان		Lebanon
lobnani	لبنانی		Lebanese
mekzik (pron.: megzik)	مکزیک		Mexico

Lesson Six *MODERN PERSIAN* درس ششم

mekziki (pron.: megziki)	مکزیکی	Mexican
orupa (also /urupa/)	اروپا	Europe
orupai (also /urupai/)[6]	اروپائی	European
ozbækestan	ازبکستان	Uzbekistan
ozbæki/ozbæk (person)	ازبکی	Uzbek
ozbæki (adjective, language)	ازبک	Uzbek, Uzbeki
pakestan	پاکستان	Pakistan
pakestani	پاکستانی	Pakistani
rusie	روسیه	Russia
rus (person)	روس	Russian
rusi (adjective, language)	روسی	Russian
suis	سوئیس	Switzerland
suisi	سوئیسی	Swiss
tajikestan	تاجیکستان	Tajikistan
tajiki/tajik (person)	تاجیک	Tajik
tajiki (adjective, language)	تاجیکی	Tajik, Tajiki
torkie	ترکیه	Turkey
tork (person)	ترک	Turk
torki (adjective, language)	ترکی	Turkish
tork(æ)mænestan	ترکمنستان	Turkmenistan, Turkmenia
tork(æ)mæn (person)	ترکمن	Turkoman
tork(æ)mæni (adjective, language)	ترکمنی	Turkoman
yonan	یونان	Greece (after the Ionian islands of Greece)
yonani	یونانی	Greek
zhapon	ژاپن	Japan

Lesson Six MODERN PERSIAN درس ششم

zhaponi	ژاپنی	Japanese
Vocabulary, Situational and Practical Drills and Drills, Part II		تمرینات، قسمت ۲
mæriz (bimar)	مریض(بیمار)	sick
næzær	نظر	opinion; viewpoint
be næzær-e shoma	به نظر شما	in your opinion
be næzær-e mæn	به نظر من	in my opinion
tæqribæn	تقریباً	approximately, "sort/kind of"
nesbætæn[8]	نسبتاً	relatively, "pretty much so"
(gerun)	(گرون)	expensive
geran	گران	
(ærzun)	(ارزون)	inexpensive, cheap
ærzan	ارزان	
bozorg	بزرگ	big, large
(kuchik)	(کوچیک)	small, little; young
kuchek	کوچک	
zesht[9]	زشت	ugly
sækht	سخت	difficult, hard
næzdik	نزدیک	near
dur	دور	far, distant
dúst dàræm	دوست دارم	I like, love
dust dar/dasht	دوست داشت/دار	to like, to love
(johær)	جوهر	ink
jowhær	جوهر	ink
roman	رمان	novel
mæqaze	مغازه	store
forushgah	فروشگاه	store

Lesson Six   *MODERN PERSIAN*   درس ششم

dokkan	دکان	store
pulover	پولور	sweater, pullover
boluz/boliz	بلوز	blouse
keravat	کراوات	necktie, tie

Vocabulary Notes

1. There are two accepted ways to write the present tense forms of verbs: one with the {mí-} morpheme attached to the rest of the word, and one with the {mí-} morpheme written separately, as if it were an independent word:

معذرت می خواهم   معذرت میخواهم

می بینم   میبینم

The difference between these two alternates is merely a matter of style, but the preference these days is for the tense marker to be written separately. This stylistic choice is actually part of a larger, more general trend to write most meaning-bearing prefixes and suffixes separately.

2. *kojai — æhl* There are two ways to say that someone is "from" a city, country, or region. (See also section 6.11.1 for a fuller description of these structures.)

3. *bud/hæst* "to be." The verb "to be" is described at length below in sections 6.11.2, 6.11.3, and 7.11.1.

4. قربان/قربون This is a word used commonly in *taarof*. It means "sacrifice" and is a shortened form of a phrase that means "May I be your sacrifice," i.e., "Let disaster strike me in your place." (See section 14.3.1.) **Taarof**

5. Although you will hear most Iranians use the word *æfqani* to refer to a person from Afghanistan, it is incorrect and Afghans usually find the Iranian misuse of the word a little irritating, since the word *æfqani* refers to the unit of money of Afghanistan. The correct term is *æfqan*, on the pattern of *æræb, tork, kord,* etc.

6. Words that have the sequence /ai/ in them can be spelled in two ways: ælef - hæmze -

Lesson Six   *MODERN PERSIAN*   درس ششم

ye and ælef - ye- ye. Hence the following adjectives/nationalities from the above list have two accepted spellings:

espaniai	اسپانیائی	اسپانیایی
esrail	اسرائیل	اسراییل
esraili	اسرائیلی	اسراییلی
italiai	ایتالیائی	ایتالیایی
orupai (also /urupai/)	اروپائی	اروپایی

7. Although you will often hear people say *færansævi* to refer to the language (French) and *espanioli* to refer to a person (Spaniard) or as an adjective (Spanish), these usages are in fact incorrect. *færanse* فرانسه is used for the language and the country and *færansævi* فرانسوی is the adjective. By the same token, *espanioli* اسپانیولی is only the language and *espaniai* اسپانیائی is the person and the adjective.

Since *færanse* فرانسه refers to the language and *færansævi* فرانسوی is the adjective, there is a distinction in the following two phrases:

ketáb-e færanse	کتاب فرانسه	French book (i.e., a book about the French language)
ketáb-e færansævi	کتاب فرانسوی	French book (i.e., a book from France about any topic)

8. Be careful to pronounce the /s/ in the word نسبتاً as an /s/ and not a /z/ as speakers of English might tend to do.

9. The word زشت can also be used in certain contexts where it means "repulsive, indecent, obscene."

Lesson Six *MODERN PERSIAN* درس ششم

6.3 Classroom Expressions (Optional Material)

6.3.1 The following are additional possible answers that you may wish to use in class. This vocabulary will not be drilled, but you may find it helpful in daily class use.

	(گفتاری) و نوشتاری (هردو)	
(sia)	سیا	black
<u>siah</u>	سیاه	
tækhte sia(h)	تخته سیا(ه)	blackboard (see also section 4.3)
gæc	گچ	chalk
(bælé?)	بله؟	"Pardon me?" (lit: "yes?" with question intonation) Used to request a repetition.
(jan?)	جان؟	same as *bælé?* above, (see section 13.3, Vol. II) (lit.: "soul, dear")
(bæ:dæn mígæm)	(بعداً میگم)	I'll tell (you) later. (بعدا میگویم)
(hala <u>né</u>migæm)	(حالا نمیگم)	I won't say now. (حالا = اکنون نمیگویم)
(bishtær <u>né</u>migæm)	(بیشتر نمیگم)	I won't say any more. (بیشتر نمیگویم)
æz <u>ki</u> béporsæm?	از کی بپرسم؟	Who(m) should I ask? (از که بپرسم)
(<u>færq</u> mìkone)	(فرق میکنه)	There's a difference. It depends. (فرقی میکند)
(<u>færq né</u>mikone)	(فرق نمیکنه)	There's no difference. (فرقی نمیکند)
bébækhshid. ba mæn-in	(ببخشید. با منین؟)	Sorry, are you talking to me/asking me? (lit: "Are you with me?")

239

Lesson Six *MODERN PERSIAN* درس ششم

(ببخشید با من هستید؟)

bárikælla/barikællá   بارک الله   Wonderful! Good going!

(آفرین)

6.3.2 A Polite Expression

When someone compliments you, particularly on something you are wearing, you may respond with the following expression, which is roughly equivalent to "beauty is in the eye of the beholder."

(چشم شما قشنگ میبینه.)   (chéshm-e shoma qæshǽng míbine.)

6.4 Dialogue 6   ۶٫۴ مکالمه ۶

The dialogues of Lessons 6 and 7 take place in Iran with an American named Tom. He is a graduate student in ethnomusicology and is in Iran doing research for his doctoral dissertation on traditional Iranian music. At present he is taking private lessons on the *sæntur* (an ancient precursor to the hammer and dulcimer) with an *ostad*, a master of the instrument.

Tom has a good ear for music and, aside from playing many kinds of musical instruments well, has a natural talent for foreign languages. In fact, his Persian is fluent, and he speaks it like the proverbial nightingale. Iranians are fascinated with him because he speaks the language so well and yet obviously does not look Iranian. He is originally from a small town in the American West.

Tom likes living in Iran and has adapted fairly well to the culture. Even in so large and cosmopolitan a city as Tehran, he seeks out and makes friends with more traditional Iranians. He is especially close to one family who enjoy having Tom over to their house quite often. They find it interesting that he has adapted to Iranian culture to some extent, speaks Persian so well, and is enthusiastic about Iranian food. One of the family's sons, Hossein, is Tom's best friend in Iran. Hossein is about Tom's age and enjoys accompanying Tom on trips through the city. Tom relies on him for explanations of cultural phenomena that are unfamiliar to him.

These two dialogues show two different levels of speech. The first (Lesson 6) is

Lesson Six   *MODERN PERSIAN*   درس ششم

between Tom and a person to whom he has just been introduced. The style is slightly formal. The second dialogue (Lesson 7) is between Tom and Hossein and shows a more informal style, using the familiar forms between friends. The two dialogues will help you gain insight into the linguistic and cultural differences between formal and friendly verbal interactions and the behavioral patterns often accompanying these styles. These two dialogues show an interaction between men, whereas similar differences in friendly and formal speech between women are shown in Dialogues 13 and 14 respectively. Another example of friendly interaction between Tom and Hossein appears in Dialogue 15.

Transcription and Translation

mæ:zeræt mìkham (also: mæ:zæræt)	excuse me
kojai	where from (lit: an inhabitant of where)
hæstin	you are (variant after /-i/)
Acquanintance: áqa-ye tomas, mæ:zeræt mìkham. shoma kojai hæstin?	(Mr.) Thomas, excuse me for asking, but where are you from?
emrikai	American
Tom: mæn emrikaí-æm.	I'm (an) American.
æhl	inhabitant, person from
Acq: æhl-e nio yórk-in, shoma?	Are you from New York?
eyalæt/æyalæt	state (of U.S., etc.)
Tom: nækhe(y)r. æhl-e eyalæt-e vashængtón-æm.	No, I'm from Washington state.
jaleb	interesting
khæbærnegar	reporter (news writer); journalist
Acq: khéyli jaléb-e. khæbærnegár-e ruznamé-in?	That's very interesting. Are you a newspaper reporter?
qórban	sir (polite form of address)

241

Lesson Six MODERN PERSIAN درس ششم

	fe:læn	at present; for the time being
	daneshju	(university) student
Tom:	nækhe(y)r qórban. mæn fe:læn daneshjú-æm.	No, I'm a student for the time being.

Text and Transcription

Acq:	áqa-ye tomas, mæ'zeræt mìkham shoma kojai hæstin?	آقای توماس، معذرت میخوام. شما کجائی هستین؟	آشنا:
Tom:	mæn emrikaí-æm.	من امریکائی ام.	تام:
Acq:	æhl-e nio yórk-in, shoma?	اهل نیو یورکین شما؟	آشنا:
Tom:	nækheyr. æhl-e eyalæt-e vashængtón-æm.	نخیر. اهل ایالت واشنگتنم.	تام:
Acq:	khéyli jaléb-e. khæbærnegár-e ruzamé-in?	خیلی جالبه. خبرنگار روزنامه این؟	آشنا:
Tom:	nækheyr qórban. mæn fe:læn daneshjú-æm.	نخیر قربان. من فعلا دانشجوام.	تام:

6.5 Vocabulary Building: Nationalities and Place Names (Optional Material)

The following is a list of some of the countries of the world (and the adjectives and nouns for the inhabitants) derived from those names. The third list gives the Persian names of the language(s) spoken in those countries if they are not the same as those in Column 2. In the cases of countries with complex linguistic situations, Column 3 will be simply marked by dashes (— —). You will note from the list of countries that place names of the world have come into Persian largely through French. N.B.: remember to pronounce these names with stress on the final syllable:

Lesson Six　　　*MODERN PERSIAN*　　　درس ششم

Immediate or Relevant Neighbors

Country	Persian Name	Adjective, Inhabitant	Language
Asia	**asia** آسیا	**asiai**	
Afghanistan	æfqanestan [1]	æfqan (person)	dæri (farsi)/pæshtu
		æfqani (adj., pers.) [2]	
Pakistan	pakestan	pakestani	ordu/— —
Turkey	torkie	tork (pers.)	torki
Kurdistan	kordestan	kord	kordi
		kordi (adj.)	
Azerbaijan	azærbayjan	azærbayjani, tork	azærbayjani
Armenia	ærmænestan	ærmæni	ærmæni
Georgia	gorjestan	gorji	gorji
Turkmenistan/	torkæmænestan	tork(æ)mæn (pers.)	
Turkmenia	torkmænestan	tork(æ)mæni (adj., pers.)	tork(æ)mæni
Uzbekistan	ozbækestan	ozbæk (pers.)	
		ozbæki (adj., pers.)	ozbæki
Tajikistan	tajikestan	tajik (pers.)	
		tajiki (adj., pers.)	tajiki
Kazakhstan	kazakhestan	kazakh (pers.)	
		kazakhi (adj., pers.)	kazakhi
Kirghizstan	qerqizestan	qerqiz (pers.)	
		qerqizi (adj., pers.)	qerqizi
India	hendustan	hendi	hendi/— —
Israel	esrail	esraili	ebri/— —

1.　The Persian spelling for the country names will be given after each section. The adjective, inhabitant name, and the language name can be figured out from that spelling:

243

Lesson Six *MODERN PERSIAN* درس ششم

گرجستان افغانستان پاکستان ترکیه کردستان آذربایجان ارمنستان
ترکمنستان ازبکستان تاجیکستان قزاقستان قرقیزستان هندوستا اسرائیل

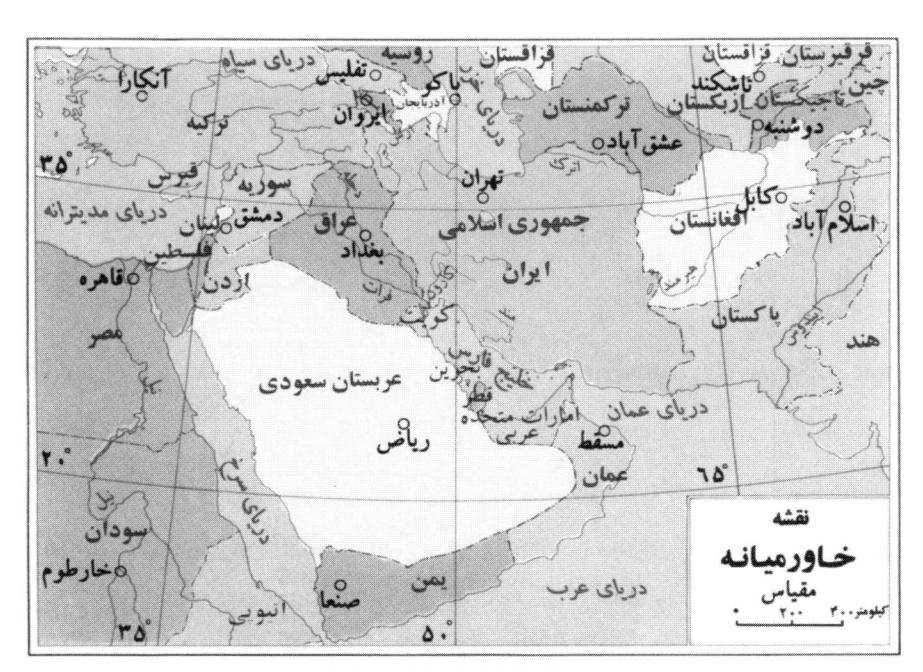

Map of the Middle East

2. See Note 5 in Vocabulary Notes at the end of section 6.2.3.

کشورهای عرب Arab World

Arab		æræb (person)	
Arabic		æræbi (adjective)	æræbi
Iraq	eraq/æraq	eraqi/æraqi	æræbi
Kuwait	koveyt	koveyti	æræbi
Saudi Arabia	æræbestán-e sæudi	sæudi	æræbi
Lebanon	lobnan	lobnani	æræbi
Syria	surie	suriei	æræbi
Jordan	ordon	ordoni	æræbi

244

Lesson Six   *MODERN PERSIAN*   درس ششم

Palestine	felestin	felestini	æræbi
Egypt	mesr	mesri	æræbi
Libya	libi	æhl-e libi	æræbi
Algeria	æljæzayer, æljæzire	æljæzayeri	æræbi/bærbæri
Tunisia	tunes	tunesi	æræbi/bærbæri
Morocco	mærakesh	mærakeshi	æræbi/bærbæri
Yemen	yæmæn	yæmæni	æræbi
Sudan	sudan	sudani	--------

فلسطین   اردن   سوریه   لبنان   عربستان سعودی   کویت   عراق
سودان   یمن   مراکش   تونس   الجزایر/الجزیره   لیبی   مصر

Europe	orupa	اروپا	orupai
Great Britain	beritaniá-ye kæbir	beritaniái	-------
England	eng(e)lis/inglis	inglisi	inglisi
	eng(e)lestan	inglisi	
Ireland	irlænd	irlændi	irlændi/inglisi
Scotland	eskotlænd	eskotlændi	eskotlændi/inglisi
France	færanse	færansævi	færanse
Holland	holænd	holændi	holændi
Belgium	belzhik	belzhiki	-------
Germany	alman	almani	almani
Austria	otrish	otrishi	almani
Switzerland	suis	suisi	-------
Italy	italia	italiai	italiai
Spain	espania	espaniai	espanioli
Portugal	portoqal/porteqal	portoqali	portoqali

Lesson Six *MODERN PERSIAN* درس ششم

Denmark	danmark	danmarki	danmarki
Norway	norvezh	norvezhi	norvezhi
Sweden	sued	suedi	suedi
Finland	fænland	fændlandi	fændlandi
Russia	rusie	rus (person)	
		rusi (adjective)	rusi
Estonia	estoni	estoni	estoni
Latvia	letoni/latvi	letoni/latvi	letoni/latvi
Lithuania	litvani	litvani	litvani
Belarus	belarus	belarusi	belarusi
Ukraine	okrain(ukrain)	okraini	okraini
Poland	læhestan/lehestan[1]	læhestani/lehestani	læhestani/lehestani
Czechoslovakia	cekoslovaki	cekoslovaki	-------
Hungary	mæjarestan[2]	mæjarestani/mæjari	mæjarestani/mæjari
Romania	rumani	rumani	rumani
(Yugoslavia	yugoslavi	yugoslavi	-------)
Croatia	kroati	kroat/kroati	kroati
Serbia	serbi/serbestan	serbi	serbi
Macedonia	mæqdunie	mæqduni	mæqduni
Greece	yonan	yonani	yonani
Bulgaria	bolqarestan	bolqari	bolqari
Albania	albani	albani	albani

Notes:

1. *Derived from the name of the legendary progenitor of the Polish nation, Lech /lekh/, also seen in Lech Walesa's name.*

2. *Derived from the Hungarian self-designation, /magyar/.*

Lesson Six *MODERN PERSIAN* درس ششم

فرانسه	اسکاتلند	انگلیس/انگلستان ایرلند	بریتانیای کبیر
سوئیس	اتریش	آلمان	بلژیک	هلند
نروژ	دانمارک	پرتقال	سپانیا	ایتالیا
لیتوانی	استونی	روسیه	فنلاند	سوئد
مجارستان	چکوسلواکی	لهستان	اوکرائین	بلاروس
بلغارستان	یونان	مقدونیه	یوگوسلاوی	رومانی
		سربی/سربستان		آلبانی

Asia

Burma	birme	birmei	birmei
Thailand	taylænd	taylændi	tay/taylændi
Cambodia	kamboj	kamboji	kamboji
Vietnam	vietnam	vietnami	vietnami
Indonesia	ændonezi	ændonezi	ændonezi
Philippines	filipin	filipini	filipini
China	chin	chini	chini
Japan	zhapon	zhaponi	zhaponi
Korea	kore	korei	korei
Mongolia	moqolestan	moqol (person)	
		moqoli (adj, pers)	moqoli

برمه تایلند کامبوج ویتنام اندونزی فیلیپین چین ژاپن کره مغلستان

North America   emriká-ye shomali   آمریکای شمالی

Canada	kanada	kanadai	— —
United States	emrika/amrika	emrikai/amrikai	inglisi/— —
Mexico	megzik	megziki	espanioli

مکزیک   امریکا/آمریکا   کانادا

Lesson Six   *MODERN PERSIAN*   درس ششم

South America	**emriká-ye junubi**	**آمریکای جنوبی**	
Venezuela	ven(e)zoela	ven(e)zoelai	espanioli
Brazil	berzil/berezil	berzili/berezili[1]	portoqali
Argentina	arzhantin	arzhantini	espanioli
Chile	shili	æhl-e shili	espanioli

شیلی   آرژانتین   برزیل   ونزوئلا

Africa	**efriqa**	**افریقا**	**efriqai**
Nigeria	nijerie	nijeriei	— —
Ethiopia	etiopi	etiopi	— —
Uganda	oganda	ogandai	— —

اوگاندا   اتیوپی   نیجریه

Other			
Australia	ostralia	ostraliai	inglisi/— —
New Zealand	zilænd-e no(w)		inglisi

زلاند نو   استرالیا

Note: Two words that you may find useful are /mottæhed(e)/ "united" and the corresponding noun form, /ettehad/, "union." These words show up in some familiar names:

Full Name

In this illustration the superscript letters refer to the specific order of specific components of a full name in Persian and English.

United[2] States[1] of America[3]   eyalát[1]-e mottæhedé[2]-ye amrika[3]

The (Organization[1] of) United[3] Nations[2]   saz(e)mán[1]-e mellæl[2] mottæhed[3]

Union[1] of Soviet[3] Socialist[4] Republics[2]   ettehád[1]-e jæmahír[2]-e sho(w)ræví[3]-e sosialisti[4]

ایالات متحده آمریکا   سازمان ملل متحد   اتحاد جماهیر شوروی سوسیالیستی

Short Name

United States; America   eyalát-e mottæhede; amrika

Lesson Six	MODERN PERSIAN	درس ششم

United Nations	saz(e)mán-e mellæl
Soviet Union	ettehád-e sho(w)rævi; sho(w)rævi
The former Soviet Union	sho(w)ræví-e sabeq

ایالات متحده   سازمان ملل   اتحاد شوروی   اتحاد شوروی سابق

6.6 Drills, Part I

درس ۶، تمرینات، قسمت ۱

Important Note: All drills in this section will be given in both transcription and Persian characters. Starting with Lesson 7, only Persian characters will be used to represent both the written formal Persian and the colloquial language used in drills and conversation. Iranians do not commonly write colloquial speech. They learn the spoken language informally and entirely by ear. Written Persian is exclusively the formal language of books. Occasionally colloquial speech is used in plays, short stories, and novels, where it is, of course, represented in Persian characters. A textbook for non-Persians such as this one requires that the spoken form of the language be represented in writing. The question is simply which alphabet to use, Latin or Arabic. We start with the former because it is more familiar to most of the students who take this course, and because it more accurately represents the sounds of the language. However, we don't wish students of Persian to learn to depend on phonetic transcription as a crutch, and so we are switching to the Persian writing system at this point. We would like you to get accustomed to reading Persian in its usual alphabet and to writing new words in Persian script as well. A word of caution, however: since the script is not used on a regular basis to represent colloquial Persian, we strongly encourage you **not to write colloquial Persian**. Whatever written work you do, whether in homework or in quizzes and examinations, will be in the written form of the language exclusively.

Lesson 6, Drill 1: Substitution

درس ۶، تمرین۱

a. mæn dúst-e *emrikai* daræm.

آ. من دوست امریکائی دارم.

(cues: iran, italia, yæzd, lobnan, alman, kerman, (ایران، ایتالیا، یزد، لبنان، آلمان، کرمان،

Lesson Six — MODERN PERSIAN — درس ششم

holænd, yonan, espania, (emrika))   هلند، یونان، اسپانیا، (امریکا))

[Before going on to the next exercise, we recommend that you go over the vocabulary section with the nationality names in this lesson, especially those that are formed irregularly.]

b. dústæm færansæví-e.   دوستم فرانسوی اه.

dústæm færansæví æst cues: دوستم فرانسوی است.

hendi	===>	hendustan	هندی	<===	هندوستان
tork	===>	torkie	ترک	<===	ترکیه
(inglisi)/englisi	===>	englestan	(اینگلیسی)/انگلیسی	<===	انگلستان
kord	===>	kordestan	کرد	<===	کردستان
æræb	===>	æræbestan	عرب	<===	عربستان
rus (also: rusi)	===>	rusie	روس (یا روسی)	<===	روسیه
tajiki (also: tajik)	===>	tajikestan	تاجیک (یا تاجیکی)	<===	تاجیکستان
ozbæki (also: ozbæk)	===>	ozbækestan	ازبک (ازبکی)	<===	ازبکستان
torkæmæn	===>	torkæmænestan	ترکمن	<===	ترکمنستان
ærmæni	===>	ærmænestan	ارمنی	<===	ارمنستان
færansævi)	===>	(færanse	فرانسوی)	<===	(فرانسه

Lesson 6, Drill 2: Substitution   درس ۶، تمرین ۲

a.   **S1:** dústetun kojaí-e?   دانشجو ۱: دوستتون کجائیه؟

       S2: iraní-e.   دانشجو ۲: ایرانیه

(cues: alman, englestan, tehran, hendustan, zhapon, spania, emrica, torkie, esfæhan, shiraz, færanse, chin, lobnan, (iran))

(آلمان، انگلستان، تهران، هندوستان، اسپانیا، امریکا، ترکیه، اصفهان، ژاپن، شیراز، فرانسه، چین، لبنان، (ایران))

b.   dústæm tórk-e. torki hærf mìzæne.   ب. دوستم ترکه. ترکی حرف میزنه.

(cues: espania, englestan, yonan, iran, lobnan, hendustan, færanse, esrail, ærmænestan, rusie, (torkie))

(اسپانیا، انگلستان، یونان، ایران، لبنان، هندوستان، فرانسه، اسرائیل، ارمنستان، روسیه، (ترکیه))

250

Lesson Six　　　*MODERN PERSIAN*　　　درس ششم

هندوستان، فرانسه، اسرائیل، ارمنستان، روسیه،(ترکیه))

c. Now turn to a partner and practice the nationalities and languages with the following pattern or your own version of it:

S1:	<u>dústetun</u> kojaí-e?	دانشجو ۱: دوستتون کجائیه؟
S2:	<u>tórk</u>-e.	دانشجو ۲: ترکه.
S1:	chi hærf mìzæne?	دانشجو ۱: چی حرف میزنه؟
S2:	<u>torki</u> (hærf mìzæne).	دانشجو ۲: ترکی (حرف میزنه).

Lesson 6, Drill 3: Substitution　　　درس ۶، تمرین ۳

a. shoma <u>daneshjú</u>-in?　　　آ. شما دانشجو این؟

(cues: ostad, khæ<u>bær</u>negár-e ruzname, moællém-e in mædrese, karmænd-e bimarestan, pesær-e khanúm-e nezhad, mohændes, shohær-e mæhnaz, madær-e vida, (daneshju))

(استاد، خبرنگار روزنامه، معلم این مدرسه کارمندِ بیمارستان پسرِ خانوم نژاد، مهندس، شوهر مهناز، مادر ویدا، (دانشجو))

b. <u>shoma</u> **daneshjú**-in? (una)　　　ب. / **شما** دانشجو این؟ (اونا)
　　<u>una</u> danesjú-ænd?　　　**اونا** دانشجو اند؟

(cues: ketabdar, **fereshte**, moællém-e bæradær-e hoseyn, <u>to</u>, dokhtær-e aqá-ye nezhad, <u>un</u>, karmænd-e bank, <u>mæn</u>, doktor, khæ<u>bær</u>negar, <u>una</u>, zæno shohær, mohændes, <u>ma</u>, ostád-e daneshgah, <u>shoma</u>, zæn-e mæhmud, (daneshju))

(کتابدار، **فرشته**، معلم برادر حسین، **تو**، دخترآقای نژاد، اون، کارمند بانک ، **من**، دکتر، خبرنگار، **اونا**، زن و شوهر، مهندس، ما، استاد دانشگاه، **شما**، زن محمود، (دانشجو))

Lesson Six — MODERN PERSIAN — درس ششم

Lesson 6, Drill 4: Substitution — درس ۶، تمرین ۴

a.   dústesh emrikaí-e. (iran)   دوستش امریکائیه. (ایران)
       dústesh iraní-e. (ma)   دوستش ایرانیه.(ما)
       dústemun iraní-e.   دوستمون ایرانیه.

(cues: færanse, **una**, espania, esfæhan,   اونا، اسپانیا، اصفهان، (فرانسه،
mæn, holænd, **ma**, englestan, mæshhæd,   من، هلند، ما، انگلستان، مشهد،
un, torkie, hendustan, **una**,   اون، ترکیه، هندوستان، اونا،
tehran, **un**, (emrika))   تهران، اون، (امریکا)

(N.B.: For /hæstin/, /hæsti/, /hæstim/ after words in /-i/, see section 6.11.3, Grammar and Usage of the Verbs "to be.")

b.   **shoma** emrikai hæstin?   ب. شما امریکائی هستین؟
(cues: iran, **ma**, færanse, hendustan, <u>to</u>,   (ایران، **ما**، فرانسه، هندوستان، <u>تو</u>،
tæbriz, zhapon, **shoma**, yonan, italia, **ma**,   تبریز، ژاپن، **شما**، یونان، ایتالیا، **ما**،
azærbayjan, alman, ærmænestan, <u>shoma</u>,   آذربایجان، آلمان، ارمنستان، **شما**،
(emrika))   (امریکا))

c.   Now break up into small groups and practice the "to be" and nationality patterns you have been drilling.

Lesson 6, Drill 5: Substitution — درس ۶، تمرین ۵

     <u>mæn daneshjú-æm</u>.   من دانشجو ام
(cues: **shoma**, karmænd-e bank, doktor, **un aqa**,   (**شما**، کارمند بانک، دکتر، **اون آقا**،
shohær-e mehri, irani, **ma**, moællem, **ælío reza**,   شوهر مهری، ایرانی، **ما**، معلم، **علی ورضا**،
mohændes, azærbayjani, **to**, bærædær-e hoseyn,   مهندس، آذربایجانی، **تو**، برادر حسین،
emrikai, **un zæn**, ostád-e zæbán-e farsi,   امریکائی، **اون زن**، استاد زبان فارسی،
ketabdar, **ma**, moællém-e fizíko shimi, **mæn**)   کتابدار، **ما**، معلم فیزیک شیمی،
     (**من**) (دانشجو)

Lesson Six — MODERN PERSIAN — درس ششم

Lesson 6, Drill 6   *Transformation* (Negative "to be")   درس ۶، تمرین ۶

mæn daneshjú-æm. ===> mæn daneshju nístam.   من دانشجو‌ام. ==> من دانشجو نیستم.

(Although only the affirmative forms will be given orally in this drill, the answers are all also written out for you as a reference so you may study the negative forms later.)

hálæm emruz behtær-e.	حالم امروز بهتر نیست.	<===	حالم امروز بهتره.
mæn motmæén-æm.	من مطمئن نیستم.	<===	من مطمئنم.
pæs, un zæn ketabdár-e.	پس، اون زن کتابدار نیست.	<===	پس، اون زن کتابداره.
tælæffózesh qæshæng-e.	تلفظش قشنگ نیست.	<===	تلفظش قشنگه.
ma færansævi hæstim.	ما فرانسوی نیستیم.	<===	ما فرانسوی هستیم.
in tæmrin bæd-e.	این تمرین بد نیست.	<===	این تمرین بده.
una khæbærnegár-ænd.	اونا خبرنگار نیستند.	<===	اونا خبرنگارند.
in mæjælle jaléb-e.	این مجله جالب نیست.	<===	این مجله جالبه.
to hala tænhá-i.	تو حالا تنها نیستی.	<===	تو حالا تنهائی.
mæn iraní-æm.	من ایرانی نیستم.	<===	من ایرانی ام.
jævábesh doróst-e.	جوابش درست نیست.	<===	جوابش درسته.
ma emshæb ba-hæm-im.	ما امشب باهم نیستیم.	<===	ما امشب باهم ایم.
in pul khéyli ziád-e.	این پول خیلی زیاد نیست.	<===	این پول خیلی زیاده.
shoma emrikai hæstid.	شما امریکائی نیستید.	<===	شما امریکائی هستید.

Lesson 6, Drill 7 *Cued Question/Answer* (negative "to be"   درس ۶، تمرین ۷ مکالمه

S1: khánum-e/áqa, mæ:zeræt mìkham,   دانشجو۱: خانوم/آقای (اسم دانشجو)، معذرت میخوام،

   shoma moællém-in?   شما معلمین؟

S2: nækher, khánum/áqa, mæn moællem   دانشجو۲: نخیر خانوم/آقا، من معلم
   nístæm mæn daneshjú-æm   نیستم. من دانشجوام
   (cues: daneshju/ketabdar, khæ bærnegar/monshi,   (دانشجو/کتابدار، خبرنگار/منشی،

253

Lesson Six	MODERN PERSIAN

tænha/ ba dústæm, karmænd-e ruzname/   تنها/ با دوستم، کارمند روزنامه/

karmænd-e bank, ostad/daneshju, irani/   کارمندِ بانک، استاد/دانشجو، ایرانی

emrikai, dúst-e hoseyn/ bæradær-e hoseyn,   امریکائی، دوستِ حسین/برادرحسین،

æhl-e eyalæt-e tegzas/ æhl-e eyalæt-e mishigan,   اهل ایالت تگزاس/اهل ایالت میشیگان،

(moællem/daneshju))   (معلم/دانشجو))

(Continue the conversation following the above model.)

Situational and Practical Drills

Lesson 6, Drill 8   Free Answer   درس ۶، تمرین ۸

be næzær-e shoma/be næzær-e mæn (Using props and pictures, practice adjectives + "to be.")

a. Full form   آ.

Teacher: be næzær-e shoma, in ___ gerún-e?   معلم: به نظر شما، این ـــــ گرونه؟

Student: bæle. be næzær-e mæn, gerún-e.   دانشجو: بله، به نظر من، گرونه.

b. Short form   ب.

Teacher: in___ gerún-e?   معلم: این ـــــ گرونه؟

Student: bæle. gerún-e.   دانشجو: بله، گرونه.

Other answers:

bæle. khéyli gerún-e.   بله. خیلی گرونه.

næ. gerun nist.   نه. گرون نیست.

khob. tæqribæn gerún-e.   خب. تقریباً گرونه.

bæle. nesbætæn gerún-e.   بله. نسبتاً گرونه.

Adjectives to use for sections a. and b.:

bozorg, kucik, qæshæng, sækht, asun,   بزرگ، کوچیک، قشنگ، سخت، آسون،

dorost, zesht, jaleb, næzdik, mæriz,   درست، زشت، جالب، نزدیک، مریض،

khub, shik, moshgel (sækht), modern (no, jadid)   خوب، شیک، مشکل (سخت)، مدرن

Lesson Six　　　*MODERN PERSIAN*　　　درس ششم

Full or short form

Teacher:	(be næzær-e shoma,) <u>tehran</u> <u>dúr</u>-e?	معلم: تهران دوره؟
Student:	bæle. (be næzær-e mæn,) tehran dúr-e.	دانشجو: بله. (به نظر من،) تهران دوره.

(**noun cues**: nio york, khuné-ye jæmshid, bimarestán-e daneshgah, apartemán-e ___, emteháneemun, in soal, læhjé-ye mehri, names of restaurants, theaters, etc. familiar to students)

(نیو یورک، خونه جمشید، بیمارستان دانشگاه، آپارتمان ـــــ ، امتحانمون، این سئوال، لهجهٔ مهری،

(**adjective cues**:

bozorg, kucik, qæshæng, zesht, sækht
asun, dorost, jaleb, næzdik, mæriz (bimar),
khub, shik, modern)

(بزرگ، کوچیک، قشنگ، زشت، سخت،
آسون، درست، جالب، نزدیک، مریض (بیمار)،
خوب، شیک، مدرن)

Lesson 6, Drill 9　　*Cued Question/Answer*　　درس ۶، تمرین ۹

S1:	un <u>ketab</u> chetór-e?	دانشجو ۱: اون **کتاب** چطوره؟
S2:	mígænd <u>khub</u>-e væli <u>gerún</u>-e.	دانشجو ۲: میگند **خوبه** ولی **گرونه**.

(cues: roman - jaleb/sækht, mashin - bæd/qæshæng, sinema - gerun/khub, restoran - kucik/ærzun, mæjælle - jaleb/gerun, mæqaze - ærzun/dur, saæt - qæshæng/gerun)

(رمان جالب/سخت، ماشین ـــــ
بد/قشنگ،ـــــ سینما ـــــ گرون/خوب،
رستوران کوچیک/ارزون، مجله ـــــ
جالب/گرون، مغازه ـــــ ارزون/دور،
ساعت قشنگ/گرون)

Lesson 6, Drill 10　　　　درس ۶، تمرین ۱۰

Using props and pictures practice asking nationalities:

Teacher:	in kojaí-e?	معلم: این کجاییه؟
Student:	un emrikaí-e.	دانشجو: اون امریکاییه.
Teacher:	ina kojaí-ænd?	معلم: اینا کجایی اند؟

255

Lesson Six *MODERN PERSIAN* درس ششم

Student: una iraní-ænd.   دانشجو: اونا ایرانی اند.

6.9 Reading and Writing Persian: Colloquial/FWP Transformations, Part I   ۶/۹

All languages evolve with the passage of time. You may have noticed how styles of speech change from one generation to the next or even within one generation. The changes are often not dramatic, but they are striking and give one a sense of language as an ever-changing entity. Written language, which codifies the formal style of language, is very slow to reflect the subtle changes of colloquial use and is, in general, far more conservative. We often say "gonna" instead of "going to," but rarely do we see "gonna" in written form. We can, and in fact do, still read the style of English spoken almost 400 years ago in the form of Shakespearean and Biblical English. While native speakers all understand a question such as "Whither goest thou?" no one actually still speaks this way, nor would they even try to.

The gap in styles between spoken Persian and the written version reflects almost the same level of difference as written Biblical English and spoken modern English. Imagine if the only written form of modern English were Biblical English except for occasional Tom Sawyer--like transcriptions reserved solely for trying to portray conversational speech. That is, suppose that "Whither goest thou?" were the only acceptable written form of spoken "Where are you going?" This would not be too far off from the situation that we find in Persian today. Fortunately, however, the differences in Persian for the most part are consistent. They are covered by a relatively small number of rules and can be learned systematically.

The written form of Persian uses many pronunciations, grammatical forms, and words that no one would actually use today in conversation. As an equivalent example, let us compare the archaic English sentence "Whither goest thou?" with the simple Persian sentence "He is going to school" written in standard FWP. The sentences are not exactly equal because we needed to make some changes in order to show those areas between the two written languages that are different: third person instead of the English second person and a question not a

statement. The Persian is written /او به مدرسه می رود/ = /u be mædrese míræværd/, but will be said /او ن می ره مدرسه/ = /un míre mædrese/ (non-deferential form). In this example, there are about four differences between the written forms and the spoken forms in both languages:

In section 9 of Lessons 6, 7, 8, 9, and 10, we will describe the major rules for transforming colloquial language into the written style. A number of these rules are of very general application and hold true in all cases. Others are more limited in scope, and a few apply only to individual words. All the rules, however, are necessary elements of a single formula for transforming spoken Persian into writing. Unless all the rules are applied uniformly, the result will be a hodge-podge of spoken and written forms that will be understandable but comic.

The commonly used Persian terms for the these two styles of language are گفتاری *goftari* "spoken" or عامیانه/(عامیونه) amiane/(amiune), "vernacular, popular, vulgar," and نوشتاری *neveshtari*, "written" or کتابی /ketabi/, "bookish, written." In this text we will use both the terms گفتاری and نوشتاری. All languages use different styles in different situations, and نوشتاری and گفتاری are general terms, each including a number of substyles. Within written language, for instance, one finds literary, bureaucratic, and journalistic styles, among others. In the same way, the spoken styles of a language include everything from semiliterate or regional usage to learned, polite discourse. Our intention in this book is to introduce the general features that distinguish the two broad categories of "colloquial" and "written" from each other. In subsequent lessons we will, from time to time, give illustrations both of more informal colloquial language, and of more formal written language.

In the following sections on the transformation of colloquial speech to its written representation, we will first discuss those changes that affect phonology, then those changes that involve grammar.

Lesson Six   *MODERN PERSIAN*   درس ششم

Spoken/Written Transformations, Part I

Rules Affecting Phonology (un, um) = <u>an</u> آن <u>am</u> آم

1. آم /am/ آن /an/ and اوم /um/ اون /un/ **Change to** /an/ /am/

One of the first differences students notice between colloquial and written Persian is that the sequence /un/ in many common words is written <u>an</u> آن. This change also applies to colloquial /um/, written <u>am</u> آم. (See section 5.2, Vocabulary Notes.)

Examples:

Spoken		Written	
اون	(un)	آن	<u>an</u>
خونه	(khune)	خانه	<u>khane</u>
عامیونه	(amiune)	عامیانه	<u>amiane</u>
برادرتون	(bæradæretun)	برادرتان	<u>bæradæretan</u>
آسون	(asun)	آسان	<u>asan</u>
حموم	(hæmum)	حمام	<u>hæmam</u>
کدوم	(kodum)	کدام	<u>kodam</u>

Note also that the verbs "read" and "know" are examples of this rule:

| میخونم | (míkhunæm) | میخوانم | <u>míkhanæm</u> |
| میدونم | (mídunæm) | میدانم | <u>mídanæm</u> |

2. **/un/ and /um/ Do Not Change**

Not all words are subject to this rule and the few that do not simply have to be memorized. For example, /fereydun/ is written <u>fereydun</u> فریدون and /yonan/ "Greece" is written yon<u>an</u> یونان. The contrast in the two types is seen in this pair:

	Spoken		Written	
"bread"	نون	(nun)	نان	**nan**
"nun" (the letter)	نون	(nun)	نون	**nun**

3. **The Reverse Process: Written to Colloquial**

This conversion process cannot automatically be reversed. Not all words in the written

Lesson Six *MODERN PERSIAN* درس ششم

language that have an -<u>an</u>- or -<u>am</u>- are converted to /un/ and /um/ in colloquial. European loan words, personal names, and words of an official, literary character do not usually change. Examples:

Spoken and Written

رمان	/roman/	دانشگاه	/daneshgah/
آپارتمان	/aparteman/	نظامی	/nezami/ (Personal Name)
اسلام	/eslam/	تهرانی	/tehrani/ (PN)
نامه	/name/	بهرامی	/bæhrami/ (PN)
رستوران	/resturan, restoran, ræsturan/		

Some words of this type, especially place names, alternate between both styles. That is, in a colloquial style that is considered more casual, they are pronounced with an /un/ or /um/. This style is called *khodemuni* خودمونی "casual, informal (literally 'our own,' implying 'spoken among ourselves only')" and is usually used among family and closer friends. A fuller discussion of this style is also presented in section 9.9. In the majority of other styles of **spoken** Persian, these words will be pronounced with the unchanged /an/ and /am/ as in the written style and yet will not sound "bookish." You have already seen this with the word Examples: صبانه/صبحانه/صبونه

khodemuni		Other Colloquials and Written	
تهرون	(tehrun)	تهران	<u>tehran</u>
تهرونی	(tehruni)	تهرانی	<u>tehrani</u>
ایرون	(irun)	ایران	<u>iran</u>
ایرونی	(iruni)	ایرانی	<u>irani</u>
زبون	(zæbun)	زبان	<u>zæban</u>
اومد	umæd)	آمد	<u>amæd</u>

Lesson Six   *MODERN PERSIAN*   درس ششم

Vocabulary Review: Here are all the words you have encountered in this text so far that are affected by this rule:

Spoken	Written	Spoken	Written	Spoken	Written
(صبحونه)	صبحانه	(شون)	شانه	(قربون)	قربان
(بادمجون)	بادمجان	(نون)	نان	(فسنجون)	فسنجان
(آسون)	آسان	(ارزون)	ارزان	(گرون)	گران
(عامیونه)	عامیانه	(حموم)	حمام	(کدوم)	کدام

اون، *"that" and derivative words*:

آن (اون)   آنها (اونا)   آنجا (اونجا)

The plural pronominal possessive endings:

برادرمان (برادرمون)   برادرتان (برادرتون)   دوستشان (دوستشون)

خونه *and its derivatives:*

خانه (خونه)   کتابخانه (کتابخونه)   کارخانه (کارخونه)

An industrial factory in Tehran

Lesson Six   *MODERN PERSIAN*   درس ششم

The following numbers:

پانزده (پونزده) شانزده (شونزده) پانصد (پونصد)

دونه the counter word for one (although it is usually omitted completely in writing FWP):

دانه (دونه)

The verb خون/خوند "study, read" and its derivatives:

بخوانید خوان/خواند (خون خوند) (بخونید) خواندن (خوندن)

All forms of the verbs "read" and "know":

دانست (دونست) میدانم (میدونم) میخوانم (میخونم)

6.9.1 ـنب /-mb-/

The sequence /-mb-/ is usually written ـنب /-nb-/, but words of European origin are often not affected by this rule. Examples:

شنبه	/shæmbe/	"Saturday"
انبار	/æmbar/	"store room"
استانبول	/estambol ~ -bul/	"Istanbul" (also: اسلامبول)
تنبل	/tæmbæl/	"lazy"

but:

تمبر	/tæmbr/*	"stamp" (from French "timbre")

* The writing of the French borrowing "timbre" as تمبر is more of a concession to the French pronunciation than a true reflection of the Persian pronunciation. Since Persian phonology does not generally allow for three consonants to occur at the end of a word (or syllable), the pronunciation /tæmbr/ is generally not possible. Most people pronounce this word /tæmr/, but there are of course many people who know French and may include the /-b-/ in their Persian pronunciation of this word.

More rules involving phonological changes between colloquial and FWP will be presented in sections 7.9, 8.9, 9.9, and 10.9.

Lesson Six   *MODERN PERSIAN*   درس ششم

Naqashi

Rules Affecting Grammatical Categories

6.9.2 -e/-æd ~ -æst   است َـد / ـه   (third person singular present tense verb ending)

One of the most consistent transformations in the area of grammar is in the third person singular ending of the present tense of all verbs (except "to be"). The rule is simply that the spoken ending /-e/ ـه . in verbs other than in "to be" is written -æd َـد :

Examples:

Spoken		Written	
زندگی میکنه	(zendegí mìkone)	زندگی میکند	zendegí mìkonæd
میفهمه	(mífæhme)	میفهمد	mífæhmæd
حرف میزنه	(hærf mìzæne)	حرف میزند	hærf mìzænæd
داره	(dare)	دارد	daræd
کار میکنه	(kar mikone)	کار میکند	kar mikonæd
راه میرم	(rah miram)	راه میروم	rah mirævám
میخوره	(mikhore)	میخورد	mikhorad

In the case of the verb "to be," the spoken third person verb ending /-e/ ـه is written æst (آست) as a separate word:

Lesson Six   *MODERN PERSIAN*   درس ششم

Examples:

Spoken		Written	
(خوبه)	(khub-e)	خوب است	khub-æst
(درسته)	(doróst-e)	درست است	dorost-æst
(اهل ایرانه)	(æhl-e irán-e)	اهل ایران است	æhl-e irán-æst

6.9.3 -id/-in اید/این (second-person plural ending, all tenses)

As you have known since Lesson 1, the second person plural ending of the verb in all tenses is often, although not always, این /-in/ in spoken Persian. In its written form, however, it is invariably written اید /-id/.

Spoken		Written	
یاد میگیرین	(yád mìgirin)	یاد میگیرید	yad mìgirid
میپرسین	(míporsin)	میپرسید	míporsid
دارین	(darin)	دارید	darid
فهمیدین	(fæhmídin)	فهمیدید	fæhmídid

Exercises that drill the transformations from colloquial Persian to FWP are presented in section 6.14.

6.10 Drills, Part II   درس ۶، تمرینات، قسمت ۲

Lesson 6, Drill 11   Substitution (Verbs + Clauses)   درس ۶، تمرین ۱۱

<u>mæn fék(r) mìkonæm</u> (ke) <u>færda jævab mìdænd</u>.	من فکر میکنم (که) فردا جواب میدند
in aqa æz apartemánesh telefón mìkone	این آقا از آپارتمانش تلفن میکنه
soál-e shoma jaléb-e	سئوال شما جالبه
reza míge (ke)	رضا میگه (که)
shoma ba-hæm futbal bazí mìkonin	شما با هم فوتبال بازی میکنین
æli bishtær sigár mìkeshe	علی بیشتر سیگار میکشه
dobare nobæt-e mæn-e	دوباره نوبت منه

263

Lesson Six MODERN PERSIAN درس ششم

mæn motmæén-æm (ke)	من مطمئنم (که)
to qæshæng piano mízæni	تو قشنگ پیانو میزنی
emshæb do-ta tæklíf-e shæb darim	امشب دوتا تکلیف شب داریم
ésm-e in shagerd ælí-e	اسم این شاگرد علیه
una mídunænd (ke)	اونا میدونند (که)
to farsi qæshæng mínevisi	تو فارسی قشنگ مینویسی
nahár-e in restoran behtær-e	ناهار این رستوران بهتره
ma míbinim (ke)	ما میبینیم (که)
shoma bæ:d-æz-zohra værzésh mìkonin	شما بعدازظهرا ورزش میکنین
háleshun hænuz khúb nist	حالشون هنوز خوب نیست
una mínevisænd (ke)	اونا مینویسند (که)
fæqæt æz ebri be inglisi tærjomé mìkonænd	فقط از عبری به اینگلیسی ترجمه میکنند
hichvæqt dærs némikhunænd	هیچوقت درس نمیخونند
dær khabgah míkhabænd	در خوابگاه میخوابند
mæn fék(r) mìkonæm (ke)	من فک(ر) میکنم (که)
sham doróst mìkonænd	شام درست میکنند
se-ta dokhtæro car-ta pesær daerænd	سه تا دختر و چارتا پسر دارند

Lesson 6, Drill 12   Substitution   درس ۶، تمرین ۱۲

(In this drill /ke/ should occasionally be omitted from the cues.)

<u>fék(r) mìkonæm (ke) bæ:d-æz-zohra kelas daerænd.</u>	فک(ر) میکنم (که) بعد از ظهرا کلاس دارند.
un mærd futbal bazí mìkone	اون مرد فوتبال بازی میکنه
khéyli kæm esterahæt mìkone	خیلی کم استراحت میکنه
un dokhtær fæqæt dærs mìkhune(v)o kár mìkone	اون دختر فقط درس میخونه و کار میکنه

264

Lesson Six *MODERN PERSIAN* درس ششم

míge (ke)	میگه (که)
naháro sham doróst mìkone	ناهار و شام درست میکنه
to bishtær værzésh mìkoni	تو بیشتر ورزش میکنی
míbinæm (ke)	میبینم (که)
shoma khéyli kæm væqt darin	شما خیلی کم وقت دارین
ziad qæzá mìkhore	زیاد غذا میخوره
mésl-e ìnke	مثل اینکه
soba ruzname míkhunænd	صبا روزنامه میخونند
shoma farsi behtær tærjomé mìkonin	شما فارسی بهتر ترجمه میکنین
shoma hænuz soal darin	شما هنوز سئوال دارین
ælbæte (ke)	البته (که)
tond hæmúm mìkonæm	تند حموم میگیرم
ba-hæm mokaleme tæmrín mìkonim	باهم مکالمه تمرین میکنیم
fék(r) mìkonæm	فک(ر) میکنم
una gitar mízænænd	اونا گیتار میزنند
un pesær fæqæt qæzá mìkhore(v)o míkhabe	اون پسر فقط غذا میخوره و میخوابه
(bæ:d-æz-zohra kelas darænd)	(بعد از ظهرا کلاس دارند)

265

Lesson Six — *MODERN PERSIAN* — درس ششم

Lesson 6, Drill 13   Expansion   درس ۶، تمرین ۱۳

Now expand the same cue with different clauses from the above two drills:

fék(r) mìkonæm ke <u>færda emtehan darim</u>.	فکر میکنم که فردا امتحان داریم.
ælbæte ke <u>færda emtehan darim</u>.	البته که فردا امتحان داریم.
reza míge ke <u>færda emtehan darim</u>.	رضا میگه که فردا امتحان داریم.
una mídunænd ke <u>færda emtehan darim</u>, etc.)	اونا میدونن که فردا امتحان داریم.
vida nun némikhore.	ویدا نون نمیخوره.
nobæt-e mæn-e.	نوبت منه.
mæn ziad sigár mìkeshæm.	من زیاد سیگار میکشم.
pedær-e dústæm dær chin inglisi dærs mìde.	پدر دوستم در چین اینگلیسی درس میده.
shoma hichvæqt be inglisi jævàb némidin.	شما هیچوقت (هیچگاه، هر گز) به اینگلیسی جواب نمیدین.
una hichvæqt ba-hæm nahar némikhorænd.	اونا هیچوقت باهم ناهار نمیخورند.
sæntur khéyli jaléb-e.	سنتور خیلی جالبه.
pedæresh chaío qæhve némikhore. (نمینوشه)	پدرش چائی و قهوه نمیخوره. (نمینوشه)
fæqæt áb mìkhore. (minusheh) (مینوشه)	فقط آب میخوره. (مینوشه)
mæn khéyli khub míbinæm.	من خیلی خوب می بینم.
vida ruza gitar mízæne.	ویدا روزا گیتار میزنه.
in park qæshæng-e.	این پارک قشنگه.
una khéyli ba-hæm taaróf mìkonænd.	اونا خیلی با هم تعارف میکنن.
un bilít-e otobús-e.	اون بیلیط اتوبوسه.
unja kebrit darænd.	اونجا کبریت دارند.
un zæn dær opera aváz mìkhune.	اون زن در اپرا آواز میخونه.
to emruz chelow kæbab doróst mìkoni.	تو امروز چلو کباب درست میکنی.

Lesson Six — MODERN PERSIAN — درس ششم

Lesson 6, Drill 14   *Cued Question and Answer*   درس ۶، تمرین ۱۴

آ.

Answer affirmative or negative as you prefer.

a.   S1:   in boluz qæshæng-e?   دانشجو ۱: این بلوز قشنگه

     S2:   bæle. in boluz (khéyli) qæshæng-e..   دانشجو ۲: بله. این بلوز (خیلی) قشنگه.

          næ. in boluz qæshæng nist.   نه. این بلوز قشنگ نیست.

          (cue: in kar/sækht)   (کار/سخت)

   S1:   in kar sækht-e?   دانشجو ۱: این کار سخته؟

   S2:   bæle. in kar (khéyli) sækht-e.   دانشجو ۲: بله. این کار (خیلی) سخته.

       næ. in kar sækht nist.   نه. کار سخت نیست.

(cues: shagerd/yonani, keravat/zesht, ab/khub, dochærkhe/zhaponi, doktor/mæriz, daneshju/khub, dærs/moshgel, johær/ærzun, hotel/gerun, emtehan/moshgel, saæt/suisi, tæklíf-e shæb sækht, khodkar/ærzun, (boluz/qæshæng))

(شاگرد/یونانی، کراوات/زشت، آب/خوب، دوچرخه/ژاپنی، دکتر/مریض، دانشجو/خوب، درس/مشکل، جوهر/ارزون، هتل/گرون، امتحان/مشکل، ساعت/سوئیسی، تکلیف شب/سخت، خودکار/ارزون، (بلوز/قشنگ))

ب.

Answer affirmative or negative as you prefer.

b.   S1:   rusie bozórg-e?   دانشجو ۱: روسیه بزرگه؟

     S2:   bæle. rusie (khéyli) bozórg-e.   دانشجو ۲: بله. روسیه (خیلی) بزرگه.

         næ. rusie bozorg nist.   نه. روسیه بزرگ نیست.

         (cue: æræbi/jaleb)   (عربی/جالب)

   S1:   æræbi jaléb-e?   دانشجو ۱: عربی جالبه

   S2:   bæle. æræbi (khéyli) jaléb-e.   دانشجو ۲: بله. عربی (خیلی) جالبه.

       næ. æræbi jaleb nist.   نه. عربی جالب نیست.

(cues: bank/dur, benzin/gerun, holænd/qæshæng, kæbab/khub, lobnan/kucik, moællem/motmæen,

(بانک/دور، بنزین/گرون، هلند/قشنگ، کباب/خوب، لبنان/کوچیک، معلم/مطمئن،

Lesson Six   *MODERN PERSIAN*   درس ششم

mædrese/næzdik, futbal/jaleb, næhar/ærzun,   مدرسه/نزدیک، فوتبال/جالب، نهار/ارزون،
ostad/hazer, SSS/qayeb, (æræbi/jaleb))   استاد/حاضر، (اسم/دانشجو)/غایب، (عربی/جالب))

Lesson 6, Drill 15   Substitution   درس ۶، تمرین ۱۵

    khætetun khub-e   (un)   خطتون خوبه. (اون)
    khætesh khub-e.   (farsi)   خطش خوبه. (فارسی)
    farsish khub-e   فارسیش خوبه.

(cues: mæn, shoma, fekr, ebri, ma, inglisi,   (من، شما، فکر، عبری، ما، اینگلیسی،
emtehan, mæn, sændæli, neveshtæn, saæt,   امتحان، من، صندلی، نوشتن، ساعت،
æræbi, un, khæt, una, (shoma)   عربی، اون، خط، اونا، (شما))

Lesson 6, Drill 16   Review   درس ۶، تمرین ۱۶

Why? — Because   دوره (چرا؟ برای اینکه)

(Notice that /chéra/ normally follows the subject of the sentence, but precedes other elements.)

(cue: fæqæt áb mìkhori)   (فقط آب میخوری)

  S1: chera fæqæt áb mìkhori?   دانشجو۱: چرا فقط آب میخوری؟

  S2: bæràye ínke chaío qæhve némikhoræm.

                    دانشجو: برای اینکه چائی و قهوه نمیخورم.

(cue: roman némikhunin)   (رمان ژید نمیخونین)

  S1: chera roman némikhunin?   دانشجو۱: چرا رمان ژید نمیخونین؟
  S2: bæràye ínke jaleb nist.   دانشجو۲: برای اینکه جالب نیست.
  S3: bæràye ínke dùst nædaræm, etc.   دانشجو۳: برای اینکه دوست ندارم.

(cue: S1-o S2 emshæb ziad dærs mìkhunænd)

           ((اسم ۲ دانشجو) امشب زیاد درس میخونند)

  S1: S1-o S2 chera emshæb ziad dærs mìkhunænd?

       دانشجو۱: (اسم ۲ دانشجو) چرا امشب زیاد درس میخونند؟

  S2: bæràye ínke færda emtehan daræn.

Lesson Six *MODERN PERSIAN* درس ششم

دانشجو۲: برای اینکه فردا امتحان دارن.

(cues: zæbán-e chini yàd némigiri	(زبان چینی یاد نمیگیری
name be farsi néminevisi	نامه به فارسی نمینویسی
vidáo shæhla inja nístæn	ویدا و شهلا اینجا نیستن
nahar dær in restoran némikhorim	ناهار در این رستوران نمیخوریم
shoma dær aparteman zendegí mìkonin	شما در آپارتمان زندگی میکنین
ziad soal míporsæm	زیاد سئوال میپرسم
fæqæt ruzname-ye farsi míkhunin	فقط روزنامه فارسی میخونین
shoma ba-hæm dærs mìkhunin	شما باهم درس میخونین
S1-o S2 hala esterahæt némikonænd	(اسم ۲ دانشجو) حالا استراحت نمیکنند
sib némikhorin	سیب نمیخورین
ba medad néminevisi	با مداد نمینویسی
sær-e kelas bæche némibinim	سر کلاس بچه نمیبینیم
un mærd læhjé-ye emrikai dare	اون مرد لهجه امریکائی داره
farsi yævash hærf mìzænæm	فارسی یواش حرف میزنم
SSS emruz qayéb-e	(اسم دانشجو) امروز غایبه.
inja sham némikhorim	اینجا شام نمیخوریم
inja piano némizænin)	اینجا پیانو نمیزنین)

(Now go on making up questions with *chera* on the model of these cues.)

Lesson Six   *MODERN PERSIAN*   درس ششم

6.11 Grammar Discussion

6.11.1 Noun Phrase

Where are you from?

kojai — æhl Nationalities and the inhabitants of cities and regions can be formed from the given place name in two quite different ways:

1. Add stressed /-í/ to the end of the word to form a new word. This new word is usually both a noun and an adjective.

iran	irani	"Iranian"	(noun and adjective)
emrika	emrikai	"American"	(noun and adjective)

    æli iraní-e.   (noun = person)

    tomas sæntúr-e irani dare.   (adjective)

    tomas emrikaí-e.   (noun = person)

    tomas læhjé-ye emrikai dare.   (adjective)

2. a. In polite speech, add /æhl-e/ "inhabitant of " as a separate word before the place name:

    æhl-e eyalæt-e vashængton

    æhl-e nio york

Lesson Six *MODERN PERSIAN* درس ششم

b. In more informal speech the word /mál-e/ "belonging to, property of" is used with the same function as /æhl-e/:

> mál-e kalifornia
>
> mál-e verjinia
>
> (see also section 9.9.1, part f.)

Note that the above three forms may also be used with the word /koja/:

> (1) shoma kojai hæstin?
>
> (2a) shoma æhl-e kojá-in? Where are you from?
>
> (2b) shoma mál-e kojá-in?

Although the two forms listed above mean the same thing, they are used slightly differently.

Form 1: /-í/ is used mostly for names familiar to Persian-speakers, that is, place names that are either (a) foreign countries or (b) provinces, cities, and towns in Iran or in nearby countries but not (usually) for provinces, states, or cities of other countries:

	Countries	Iranian Provinces	Iranian Cities	Nearby Cities
kojai?	irani	azærbayjani	mæshhædi	eslamboli
	suedi	khorasani	tehrani	bæqdadi
	lobnani	mazænderani	shirazi	kaboli
	ostraliai	khuzestani	esfæhani	yerevani

Form 2: /æhl-e, mál-e/ may be used in all cases but is especially preferred for cities, states, or provinces within countries other than Iran and neighboring countries:

	Foreign States, Cities	Also Possible
æhl-e koja?	æhl-e kalifornia	æhl-e iran
mál-e koja?	mál-e nio york	mál-e sued
	æhl-e paris	æhl-e azærbayjan
	mál-e tokio	mál-e yæzd

N.B.: Be careful to use either Form 1, /-í/, or Form 2, /æhl-e, mál-e/, and not to mix them. These forms are never combined.

271

Lesson Six   *MODERN PERSIAN*   درس ششم

tekrár konid   تکرار کنید

shoma koja͟i hæstin?   mæn iraní-æm.

shoma æhl-e kojá-in?   mæn æhl-e nio yórk-æm.

shoma mál-e kojá-in?   mæn mál-e tegzás-æm.

6.11.2 Verb Phrase

The Verbs "To Be" in Colloquial Persian

The verbs "to be" in Persian, as with many languages of the world, are grammatically different from other verbs in the language. The principal differences that distinguish "to be" within Persian (Colloquial and FWP, for the most part) are as follows:

1. It has more than one present root. You will encounter the following roots (in order of most common occurrence): /-Ø-/, /hæst-/ هست, and /bash-/ باش. The past root of all three is /bud-/ بود.

2. The first verb root listed above — /-Ø-/ — is a "zero morpheme." When a root is represented by a zero, in effect no root is perceived and "to be" then consists entirely of the personal endings. (See also 6.11.3.)

3. "To be" and "to have" are the only verbs in the language that do not take the tense/aspect marker /mí-/ that you have encountered with all other verbs so far.

4. The present indicative has a special form for the negative: /níst-/ نیست. /khub-e/ becomes /khub nist/ in the negative: خوبه ====> خوب نیست.

5. The written form of the third person singular ending /-e/ of "to be" is -æst است, as we brought to your attention in 6.9.3.

6. The third-person of the verb root /hæst-/ هست, has two different meanings: one indicates "to be" when emphasized (see below section 6.11.3, point 2), and the other meaning is that of existence in the sense of "there is, there are." (See below section 6.11.3, point 3.)

7. In the third person singular of the root /hæst-/ هست, and in the negative form /níst-/ نیست, in the existence sense mentioned in the previous point, no person ending is used. This

Lesson Six — *MODERN PERSIAN* — درس ششم

is the only verb in the language in which the present root is the same as the third person singular. Each of these points as well as the differences in the various roots of "to be" are discussed below.

The Colloquial Forms of "To Be": /-Ø-/ and /hæst-/

Form As you have already seen, "to be" occurs commonly with nouns and adjectives. It has two principal roots, /-Ø-/ and /hæst-/. In colloquial Persian the /-Ø-/ root is used most commonly but certainly not to the exclusion of the /hæst-/ root. We do not wish to give you the impression that in a regular unstressed sentence you will only hear the forms /mæn moællém-æm/, etc. It is also quite common, especially when speaking in polite contexts, to hear: /mæn moællem hæstæm/, etc., but we have not drilled these forms in these lessons. (See also the discussion of the forms under stress, 6.11.3, point 2 below.)

Since a "zero root," /Ø/, has no phonetic representation, the /Ø/ form of "to be" is manifested only in the personal endings. A zero root can never take sentence or word stress and can never occur independently of the noun, adjective, or other element it is attached to. For this reason we use a hyphen to indicate that the noun/adjective and the following verb ending are pronounced as a unit. Although sequences are pronounced *moællém-æm* "I am a teacher" and <u>khú</u>b-*æm*, "I am fine," there is an underlying zero morpheme that represents "to be" and these phrases can respectively be represented <u>grammatically</u> as /moællém-Ø-æm/ and /<u>khú</u>b-Ø-æm/, etc., to include the verb root.

Colloquial Forms:

Noun + "to be":

Normal Form	Also Possible	Normal Form	Also Possible
/-Ø-/	/hæst-/	/-Ø-/	/**هست**/
moællém-æm	moællem hæstæm	معلمم/معلم ام	معلم هستم
moællém-i	moællem hæsti	معلمی/معلم ای	معلم هستی
moællém-e	(no unstressed form)	معلمه/ معلم اس	معلم اس

273

Lesson Six *MODERN PERSIAN* درس ششم

moællém-im	moællem hæstim	معلمیم/معلم ایم	معلم هستیم
moællém-in	moællem hæstin	معلمید/معلم اید	معلم هستید
moællém-ænd	moællem hæstænd	معلمند/معلم اند	معلم هستند

Adjective + "to be":

/-Ø-/	/hæst-/	/-Ø-/	/هست-/
khúb-æm	khub hæstæm	خوبم/خوب ام	خوب هستم
khúb-i	khub hæsti	خوبی/خوب ای	خوب هستی
khub-e	(no unstressed form)	خوب است	خوبه/
khúb-im	khub hæstim	خوبیم/خوب ایم	خوب هستیم
khúb-in	khub hæstin	خوبید/خوب اید	خوب هستید
khúb-ænd	khub hæstænd	خوبند/خوب ان	خوب هستند

6.11.3 Grammar and Usage of the Verbs "To Be" in Colloquial Persian

The /-Ø-/ and هست /hæst-/ roots

It is safe to say that the usual root for "to be" in Persian is /-Ø-/ and that you can never go wrong using this root in either colloquial or written Persian. There is a general tendency, however, for the /-Ø-/ root to occur more commonly in colloquial. The /hæst-/ root is more common in written Persian, but not greatly so. However, /-Ø-/ and /hæst-/ roots are used slightly differently in spoken Persian in the following ways:

1. /i/ + Verb Endings /-i/, /-im/ and /-id ~ -in/

Words that end in the vowel /i/ generally do not combine with the verb endings /-i/, /-im/, and /-id ~ -in/ directly in colloquial Persian, which is the case when the /-Ø-/ root is used. Although this combination does at times occur, it is considered awkward to have a sequence of two /i/'s. In these cases, the verb "to be" generally switches to the alternate /hæst-/ root.

Examples:

Lesson Six   *MODERN PERSIAN*   درس ششم

Possible Form (Considered Awkward)		Colloquial Preferred Form
/shoma emrikaí-Ø-in?/ =	shoma emrikaí -in?	shoma emrikaí hæstin?
	شما امریکائی اید؟	شما امریکائی هستید؟
/ma iraní-Ø-im/ =	ma iraní-im	ma irani hæstim.
	ما ایرانی ایم	ما ایرانی هستیم.
/to kojaí-Ø-i/ =	to kojaí-i?	to kojai hæsti?
	تو کجائی ای؟	تو کجائی هستی؟

The other persons of the verb "to be" generally remain in the short form (/-Ø-/ stem) in the other persons. The full conjugation of "to be" following a word ending in /-i/ in general colloquial is as follows, but remember the long form (/hæst-/ stem) may always be used as well:

/hæst-/ /هست		/-Ø-/	
(more common)		(also heard, unstressed)	
iraní-æm	ایرانی ام	iraní hæstæm	ایرانی هستم
iraní hæsti	ایرانی هستی	iraní hæsti	ایرانی هستی
iraní-e	ایرانی اه	(no unstressed form)	
iraní hæstim	ایرانی هستیم	iraní hæstim	ایرانی هستیم
iraní hæstin	ایرانی هستین	iraní hæstin	ایرانی هستید
iraní-ænd	ایرانی اند	iraní hæstænd	ایرانی هستند

2. Emphasis and Sentence Stress:

As mentioned above, since a zero morpheme has no phonological representation, the /-Ø-/ root cannot take sentence stress for emphasis as other verbs can. If, however, you wish to place emphasis on the verb "to be," you must replace the /-Ø-/ root with the /hæst-/ root in both Colloquial and FWP:

275

Lesson Six *MODERN PERSIAN* درس ششم

Normal Stress		Emphasis on Verb	
"We're <u>students</u>." ma daneshj<u>ú</u>-im.	"We **are** students."	ma daneshju hæstim.

ما دانشجوایم. ما دانشجو هستیم.

"His Persian's <u>good</u>." farsish <u>khub-e</u>. "His Persian **is** good." farsish khub **hæst**.

فارسیش خوبه. فارسیش خوب هست.

3. Existence

The third persons of the root /hæst-/ indicate existence in the sense of "there is, there are":

Simple "To Be"		"To Be" of Existence	
Colloquial	**Written**	**Colloquial**	**Written**
کتابه.	کتاب است.	کتاب هست.	کتاب هست.
/ketáb-e/	<u>ketáb-æst</u>	ketab hæst	ketab hæst
"It is a book."		"There's a book (here)." *	

The FWP forms of the verbs "to be," and their contrasting colloquial forms as given here, will be presented in section 7.11.

Reading Text   متن خواندنی (نوشتاری)

by the name of = به اسمِ	spouse = همسر
elementary student = دانش آموز	physician = پزشک
high school = دبیرستان	young (javan) = جوان
literature = ادبیات	name = نام

سلام. نام من جمشید است. من در تهران زندگی می کنم و در دانشگاه تهران اَدَبیاتِ فارسی میخوانم. پدر و مادرِ من هم در تهران زندگی میکنند. من دو خواهر به اسمِ پوران و پَروین و دو برادر به اسم فَرزاد و فَرهاد دارَم. پوران دانش آموز دَبیرِستان است و پَروین هَنوز خیلی جَوان است و مَدرسه نمیرود. فرزاد در کتابخانه دانشگاه اصفهان کار می کند. نام هَمسَرِ او آرزو است. فرهاد پِزشک است و در یک بیمارستان کار می کند.

276

Lesson Six　　　*MODERN PERSIAN*　　　درس ششم

تمرین: سؤال و جواب
جمشید کجا زندگی میکنه؟
جمشید چند تا خواهر و برادر داره؟
آرزو زن کیه؟
فرزاد چکاره است؟
جمشید کار میکنه؟

6.12 Cultural Materials: Iranian Money پول ایرانی /pul-e irani/

Iranian money comes in both "bills" اسکناس *eskenas* and "coins" سکّه *sekke*. The smallest unit is the ریال *rial,* which is also the standard international unit of exchange for Iran. The value of the *rial* is very little — about one and a half cents — and this leads to some confusion. It is as though the cent had replaced the dollar as our international unit. "One million rials" sounds like a fabulous sum, but it equals only a few thousand dollars. Iran's is a decimal currency. There are coins worth 1, 2, 5, 10, and 20 rials; bills worth 20, 50, 100, 200, 500, 1,000, and 10,000 rials, as well as some larger denominations that rarely circulate. You may also write a "check" چک *chek* for any figure you wish. Ten rials equal one تومان *tuman* (colloquial تمن *tomæn*), and in practice the *tuman* is the standard unit. Prices are quoted in *tumans,* or *tumans* plus *rials* (colloquial *hezar*). What is written هزار ریال *hezar rial* is spoken of as صد تمن *sæd tomæn* and what is written پنجاه ریال *pænjah rial* is spoken of as پنج تمن *pænj tomæn*.

Rial derives from the Portuguese word *real,* a term spread by the Portuguese to many coastal Asian countries, Saudi Arabia and Cambodia, among others. The meaning of *hezar* (= *rial)* is "thousand" and *tuman* derives from a Mongol/Turkic word for "ten thousand". In rapid colloquial speech, *hezar* is reduced to زار /zar/ and زارا(هـ) *ezar* . (See the "Vanishing /h/," sections 5.15, 7.1, 8.1).

ye tomæn = hezar rial

Lesson Six *MODERN PERSIAN* درس ششم

۵۳/ 53 rials = pænj tomæn seezar ریال   ۶۵۰/ 605 rials = shæst tomæn pæñzar ریال

Coins and bills of whatever denomination are designated by adding a stressed final /-í/. A two-*rial* coin is called a دوهزاری *do hezarí* (colloquial: *do-zarí* or *do-ezarí*), a ten-*tuman* note is a ده تومانی *dæh-tumani* (colloquial: *dæ(h)-tomæni*) and so on. This rule applies to all currencies, so that a ten-dollar bill in Persian is a ده دلاری *dæh-dolari* . (Sometimes other options are preferred. Five- and ten-cent pieces are usually simply called *nikél* and *daym* by Iranians living in the United States, although *pænj-senti* and *dæh-senti* are also heard.)

Vocabulary

rial	ریال	rial
(qerun)	(قرون)	rial (used to be colloquial, for one rial unit only)
(tomæn)	(تمن)	tuman, (ten rials)
tuman	تومان	
dolar	دلار	dollar
(púl-e khurd)	(پول خورد)	change
púl-e khord	پول خرد	
(khurd)	(خورد)	fragmented, in pieces (sometimes "small")
khord	خرد	

The following drills are optional. Since the material presented here may not make sense out of an Iranian context, the teacher may decide to perform these drills by replacing American currency for the Iranian currency in order to make the drill more relevant to a context that the students might actually encounter.

Lesson Six *MODERN PERSIAN* درس ششم

6.12.1 Drill ۶/۱۲/۱

S1: mæn púl-e khurd nædaræm. shoma chetor?

دانشجو۱: من پول خرد ندارم. شما چطور؟

S2: mæn fæqæt <u>hæsæd o</u> nævæd tomæn daræm.

دانشجو۲: من فقط هفتصد و نود تمن دارم

(cues: yek/no, pænjah/se, chel/pænj, bist/
hæsht, si/hæft, (pænj/do))

(یک/نه، پنجاه/سه، چل/پنج، بیست/
هشت، سی/هفت، (پنج/دو))

6.12.2 Drill ۶/۱۲/۲

S1: áqa/khánum, in <u>ketab</u> chænd-e?

دانشجو۱: آقا/خانوم، این کتاب چنده؟

S2: <u>sÆdo bist</u> tomæn-e, áqa/khánum.

دانشجو۲: صد و بیست تمنه، آقا/خانم.

(cues: dæftær/yek, pulover/chélo do, albom/
sædo si, film/sío no, shokolat/do,
sandvich/char, boluz/divist, keravat/
punzdæh, (ketab/sædo bist))

(دفتر/یک، پولور/چل و دو، آلبوم/
صد و سی،فیلم/سی و نه، شکلات/دو،
ساندویچ/چار، بلوز/دیویست، کراوات/
پونزده، (کتاب/صد و بیست))

6.12.3 Drill ۶/۱۲/۳

S1: <u>dozari</u> darin?

دانشجو۱: دو (هـ)زاری دارین؟

S2: bæle, befærmaid.

دانشجو۲: بله، بفرمائید.

(cues: do/tomæn, pænj/tomæn, pænj/(e)zar,
dæh/dolar, sæd/tomæn, pænj/dolar,
dæh/sent, (optional:pænj/pund), (do/zar))

(دو/تمن، پنج/تمن، پنج/(هـ)زار،
ده/دلار،صد/تمن، بیست/دلار،
ده/سنت، (پنج/پوند،) (دو/(هـ)زار))

Lesson Six   *MODERN PERSIAN*   درس ششم

6.12.4 Drill (optional) — Review of Numbers

Numbers may be reviewed with the following game: Coins in different denominations are placed in a box (note the word *jæ:be*, "box") or simply held in the hand. Two students then guess the number of cents or rials (<u>chænd sent</u> or <u>cæn(d) ezar</u>). The coins are then counted by a third student to see which one's guess was closer.

a.	shoma fék(r) mìkonin mæn chænd sent (rial/tomæn) daræm tu in jæ:be	آ. شما فکر میکنین من چند سنت (ریال،تمن) تو این جعبه دارم؟
b.	shoma fék(r) mìkonin mæn chænd sent (rial/tomæn) daræm tu dæstæm?	ب. شما فکر میکنین من چند سنت (ریال،تمن) تو دستم دارم؟

6.12.5 An Expression

In Iranian cities various kinds of foods are sold from pushcarts. In winter, a thick meat and vegetable porridge /ash/ is one of the more popular foods sold. Customers step up to the cart, pay what they like, and receive a bowl filled to the measure of what they have paid. From this common practice comes the expression:

(hærce pul mídi, ash míkhori/)   هرچه پول میدی آش میخوری.

"You eat as much *ash* as you pay for," that is, "You get what you pay for." (to which the cynical reply: انشاالله!)

6.12.6 Yellow Pages Entries   فهرست مشاغل، خدمات، و نیازمندیها

Money, Currency Exchange	ارز (خدمات ارزی، صرافی)
Rate	نرخ
Beauty Salon	آرایش و زیبایی
Driving School	آموزش رانندگی
Language School	آموزش زبان
Persian Classes	آموزش فارسی
Travel Agency	آژانس مسافرتی

Lesson Six *MODERN PERSIAN*	درس ششم
Government Offices	اداره های دولتی
Publishing	انتشارات
Gardening	باغبانی
Insurance	بیمه
Physician	پزشک
Official Translation	ترجمه رسمی
Repair shop	تعمیرگاه
Entertainment	تفریحات
Jewelry	جواهری
Construction Services	خدمات ساختمانی

A building in East Azerbaijan

Dentist	دندانپزشک
Restaurant	رستوران
Psychologist	روانشناس
Social Organizations	سازمان های اجتماعی

Lesson Six *MODERN PERSIAN*	درس ششم
Photography and Filming	عکاسی و فیلمبرداری
Eye Glasses	عینک سازی
Clothing Shop	فروشگاه لباس
Food Store (Supermarket)	فروشگاه مواد غذایی
Butcher	قصابی
Confectionery	قنادی
Bookstore	کتاب فروشی
Fruit Store	میوه فروشی
Nursery and Kindergarten	مهد کودک
Lawyer	وکیل

Golfrushi

Lesson Six   *MODERN PERSIAN*   درس ششم

🔊 **6.13 Long Dialogue (Part 1)**   ۶/۱۳ مکالمه بلند

(to be continued in section 7.13)

Tom and his friend Hossein have gone to the movies together to see a foreign film that has been dubbed into Persian. Hossein sees himself as Tom's host — offering him pistachios, making sure that he is comfortable and can see the screen. He is also curious as to just how much of the film Tom can understand.

/teátr/ "theater"

(حسین و توماس در تآتر (سینما) فیلم تماشا می کنند و با هم حرف میزنند.)

حسین: توماس، فیلم چطوره؟
توماس: خیلی خوبه

/honærpishe/ "actress, actor"

حسین: میدونی اون *هنرپیشه کیه؟
توماس: نه، نمیدونم.
حسین: امریکائیه. نیست؟
توماس: نه. فکر نمیکنم. مثل اینکه سوئدیه.
حسین: چی؟
توماس: میگم فکر میکنم سوئدیه.

/de:/ (expression of surprise)

حسین: ده ه؟ ممکنه.
توماس: مطمئن نیستم. فردا از دوستم میپرسم.
حسین: خوب بازی میکنه. نه؟
توماس: بله. خیلی خوب بازی میکنه.
حسین: توماس، خوب میبینی؟
توماس: بله، من خوب میبینم. تو چطور؟
حسین: من خوب میبینم ولی صندلیم خوب نیست.
توماس: چرا؟ چیه؟
حسین: نمیدونم. راحت نیست

/bérim/ "let's go"

توماس: خب *بریم اونجا.

283

/èyb nædare/ "never mind"; /peste/ "pistachio nut"	نه. اینجا خوبه. *عیب نداره. پسته میخوری؟	حسین:
	مرسی	توماس:
	چرا؟	حسین:
	مرسی. نمیخوام. پسته کم میخورم. حسین جون، من نفهمیدم. چی میگند؟	توماس:
	میگند که فردا میرند بانک. مثل اینکه اونجا کار دارند.	حسین:
	آها. خب. میبینم.	توماس:
	وقتیکه فارسی حرف میزنند، تو میفهمی؟	حسین:
	بله. تقریبا خوب میفهمم.	توماس:
/dublé mìkonænd/ "they dub"	خوب *دوبله میکنند. نه؟	حسین:
/bæ:zi oqat/ "sometimes"	بله، ولی *بعضی اوقات تند حرف میزنند و من نمیفهمم.	توماس:

6.14 Writing Persian   ۶٫۱۴ نوشتن فارسی

6.14.1 Spoken/Written Transformations: Exercises   ۶٫۱۴٫۱ گفتاری به نوشتاری

(key after Lesson 16)

Examples - Note the contrast in the colloquial and FWP forms of the following sentences:

     Written   <====   **Spoken**

    مادرتان فارسی میداند.   madæretun farsi mídune.

Convert the following sentences in Colloquial Persian to their usual FWP counterpart:

1. ma mídunim ke shoma ziad kár mìkonin.
2. ælbæte ke pænjshæmbe emtehan nædarim. pænjshæmbe kelas nædarim.
3. mínevise ke khahær-e hoseyn dær karkhune kár mìkone.
4. bæradær-e fereydun unja zendegì némikone.
5. hæsæn nun némikhore. dust nædare.

Lesson Six   *MODERN PERSIAN*   درس ششم

6. be næzær-e mæn in aparteman khéyli gerún-e.

7. næ. ketáb-e bæradæretun unja nist.

8. mina-vo shæhla færæbi khub míkhunænd-o hærf mìzænænd.

9. un khæ<u>bæ</u>rnegár-e færansævi almani khub mífæhme.

10. pedæretun dær kodum bimarestan kár mìkone?Q

Qaza

6.14.2 soálo jævab   ۶٬۱۴٬۲ سئوال و جواب

لطفاً به سئوالهای زیر جواب بدهید.

۱. شما ایرانی هستید؟

۲. شما فارسی خوب حرف میزنید؟

۳. شما برادر دارید؟ برادرتان فارسی حرف میزند؟

۴. شما در دانشگاه عربی میخوانید؟

۵. من کتابدارم؟ دانشجو ام؟

۶. به نظر شما، این دانشگاه قشنگ است؟

۷. امروز استادتان حاضراست یا غایب است؟ چرا غایب است؟

Lesson Six MODERN PERSIAN درس ششم

۸. شما رمان میخوانید؟ چرا؟

۹. شما امروز نهار میخورید؟

۱۰. شما امروز مریض اید؟

۱۱. شما دکتر دارید؟ دکترتان امریکائی است؟

۱۲. دکترتان فارسی میداند؟

۱۳. ما در دانشگاه کتابخانه داریم؟ بزرگ است؟

۱۴. کتابخانه دانشگاه نزدیک است یا دور است؟

6.15 Phonology: Final Consonant Clusters

Lesson 6, Pronunciation Drill 3 درس ۶ تمرین تلفظ ۳

bækhsh	ræqs	rækhsh	bæhs	بحث	رخش	رقص	بخش
tækht	chærkh	tælkh	tebq	طبق	تلخ	چرخ	تخت
khælq	morq	sedq	læqv	لغو	صدق	مرغ	خلق
ræshk	næskh	tæht	væhsh	وحش	تحت	نسخ	رشک
derækht	sæqf	rezq	næql	نقل	رزق	سقف	درخت
pækhsh	moshk	mæshq	æhd	عهد	مشق	مشک	پخش
æqd	næhb	næhy	næjd	نجد	نهی	نهب	عقد
qehf	sæhv	sæhq	rejs	رجس	سحق	صحو	قحف
bælkh	mæqz	omq	lokht	لخت	عمق	مغز	بلخ
hæjb	mæhz	næhj	mæskh	مسخ	نهج	محض	حجب

Lesson 6, Pronunciation Drill 4 درس ۶ تمرین تلفظ ۴

bæbr	ebn	ræzm	bædr	بدر	رزم	ابن	ببر
sejn	ædn	ædl	æzl	عدن	سجن	عزل	عدل
hæzm	zæjr	ræqm	æjz	عجز	رقم	زجر	حزم
ejl	æmr	æbr	ozr	عذر	ابر	امر	عجل

Lesson Six   *MODERN PERSIAN*   درس ششم

jæzr	væzn	hæjm	noql	نقل	حجم	وزن	جزر
omr	æql	jæbr	sædr	صدر	جبر	عقل	عمر
qæbl	bæzm	æmn	fæzl	فضل	امن	بزم	قبل

🔊 *Reading Text:*   متن خواندنی (نوشتاری):

therefore = بَنابَراین	few = چَند	I know = میدانم
future, next = آینده	girlfriend = دوست دختر	more = بیشتَر
one of = یِکی از	holidays = تَعطیلات	boyfriend = دوست پسر
by the name of = بِنام	marriage = اِزدِواج	

من فارسی، انگلیسی، فرانسوی، و عربی حرف میزنم. کمی هَم آلمانی میدانم. برادرم فرهاد آلمانی خوب حرف می زند. او چَند دوست آلمانی دارد. ولی دوستهای من بیشتَر آمریکایی هستند و بَنابَراین من بیشتَر انگلیسی حرف میزنم. یِکی از دوستهای آمریکایی من آلمانی هم حرف می زند و او یک دوست دختر ایرانی بِنام ناهید دارد که فرانسوی خوب می فهمد. ناهید اکنون در امریکا زندگی می کند و ۲۱ سال دارد و سال آینده با دوست پسر آمریکاییش اِزدِواج می کند. فرهاد برای تَعطیلات نوروز (Persian New Year Holidays) به آمریکا سفر میکند.

تمرین: سوال و جواب
من چه زبانهایی حرف میزنم؟
دوست دختر برادرم کجاییه؟
دوست پسر ناهید اهل کجاست؟
فرهاد فرانسوی حرف میزنه؟

Lesson Seven   درس هفتم

TOPICS COVERED IN THIS LESSON

- Introducing Yourself. Introducing Other People to Each Other
- Starting to Tell Time. What time is it? What time do you eat dinner? etc.
- Where are you going? How are you getting there? By bus, on my bike, walking, etc?
- More on Where People are From: Where are you originally from?
- Asking First Names and Last Names.
- Colors: What color are your checks? What color is Iranian money? What color is a three-cent stamp? etc.
- More Opinion Questions and Statements: Do you think our Persian class is very big? How is your Persian handwriting? Do you think the Safeway is expensive? etc.
- Classroom Expressions: Oral/Written Exam. Let's review. Write a sentence. Should I write it on the blackboard or on paper? etc.
- Useful Expressions: What a shame! Me, too/Me neither. What are you going to do tonight/tomorrow/tomorrow morning? etc.

Listening Materials

    Using Persian in the Workplace

    Tom and Hossein Run into Mr. Kazemi at the Movies (Part II)

RESOURCES AND BACKGROUND: INFORMATION AND ACCURACY

Phonology

    /:/ ه and /h/ (continued)

Grammar Patterns to Be Drilled

    Verbs

        Destination after Verbs of Motion

        Variant Endings on Verbs: میره، میاد/میخواد

Lesson Seven   *MODERN PERSIAN*   درس هفتم

        Colors: چه رنگ است؟/(چه رنگیه؟)

Nouns

     Noun + ezafe + Adjective (+ Possessive) (Colors, Nationalities)

Prepositions

     in/at   *dær/sær-e*

     Means-by-which: *chetori? ba dochærkhe.*

Vocabulary Building

     Nationalities and Place Names

Colloquial/Formal Written Persian Transformations, Part II

     Rules Affecting Phonology

        Vanishing /h/

        Colloquial: /-æm/, FWP: /hæm/, "also,"

        The Plural Marker /-a/, FWP -ha

        Other Contexts

     Rules Affecting Grammatical Categories

        Lengthened Verb Stems: میروم/(میرم) ،میدهم/(میدم) etc.

     Rules Affecting Syntax

        Motion + Destination = Prep (به) + Destination + Verb

Grammar Discussion

     Verbs

        The Colloquial and FWP Forms of "To Be"

        Nouns with /-Ø-/ and /hæst-/:   moællém-æm   moællem hæstæm

               من معلمم   من معلم هستم

        Adjectives with /-Ø-/ and /hæst-/:   khúb-æm   khub hǽstæm

               خوبم   خوب هستم

        Destinations and Verbs of Motion: من میرم مدرسه

289

Lesson Seven *MODERN PERSIAN* درس هفتم

Cultural Materials

    Introductions

    Telling Time

    An Introduction to Iranian Names

Reading and Writing خواندن و نوشتن

    "Suzanne's Story"

    Exercises for Converting Colloquial to FWP

    Composition: Introduce Yourself

Lesson Seven *MODERN PERSIAN* درس هفتم

7.1 Phonology: /'/ and /h/ (continued)

In 4.1 and 5.15 we described the pronunciation of /:/ and /h/ both at the beginning of a word (/:V/, /hV/) and between a vowel and a consonant (/V:C/), /VhC/). Here you will see that when these consonants occur at the end of a word — either after a vowel (/V:/, /Vh/) or after a consonant (/VC:/, /VCh/) —they are dropped in most cases. The /h/ is often pronounced in more formal speech, but usually elided in informal, rapid colloquial discourse. Thus, in everyday speech, final /:/ or /h/ after a vowel in words, such as شروع and دانشگاه, are generally not pronounced, yet may at times be heard. The glottal stop is more often deleted than the final /h/ in this position. You will hear /shoru/, for example, much more commonly than /shoru:/, but /daneshga/ only somewhat more commonly than /daneshgah/. Similarly, /vozu/, /shey/, /owza/, etc. are much more common than /vozu:/, /shey:/, /owza:/ (اوضاع، وضوء ،شئ, respectively). But /no/, /kola/, and /ra/, etc. are only slightly more common than /noh/, /kolah/, and /rah/ (نه ، کلاه, and راه, respectively).

Final /:/ or /h/ after a consonant in words such as ربع and صبح are generally not pronounced, and are much less commonly heard than when they occur after a vowel. You will hear /rob/ and /sob/ most commonly, and almost never hear /rob:/ or /sobh/. The same holds true for the other words listed in drills 3 and 4 below: /qæt/, /mæn/, /joz/, and /sæt/, /tær/, /sol/, etc. They may also, but not usually, be pronounced /qæt:/, /mæn:/, /joz:/, or /sæth/, /tærh/, /solh/, (قطع، منع، جزء, and سطح، طرح، صلح, respectively).

Dropping these two final consonants is not obligatory and, depending on the style of speech and the context, they will sometimes be heard. Another factor that must be discussed is the *type* of word these consonants occur in. That is, common, everyday words such as صبح، قطع، نه, are more likely to be pronounced without the final /:/ or /h/ than would be the case of more erudite words or words of religious content, such as وضوء، منع or طرح. As you listen to your teacher pronounce the words below, you will find that he/she will generally

Lesson Seven — MODERN PERSIAN — درس هفتم

drop the final /:/ or /h/ in some cases, and in other cases will find it very difficult or awkward to do so, depending on the type of word the sounds occur in. Follow your teacher's example, and be prepared to hear the same word pronounced in different ways, at times even in the same contexts. We should also mention that /:/ or /h/ in final position after a consonant often exchange places with those consonants. Thus, a final /VC:/ or /CVh/ may become /V:C/ or /VhC/. If this exchange of positions takes place, they then behave like the examples given in 5.1 and 5.15. There you saw that when /:/ or /h/ occurs after a vowel and *before* a consonant, they can be dropped with a compensatory lengthening of the vowel. Words like وضع or طرح may be pronounced in three ways: /væz:/, /væz/, or /væ:z/ and /tærh/, /tær/, and /tæ:r/, depending on the speaker and the context.

Lesson 7, Pronunciation Drill 1: درس ۷ ، تلفظ ۱

Imitation of Final CV('): Common words with final /h/ or /:/ usually elided

(shoru) (vozu) (qane) (owza)   اوضاع   قانع   وضوء   شروع
(æ:za)   (shey) (now)   (vaze)   واضع   نوع   شئ   اعضا

Lesson 7, Pronunciation Drill 2: درس ۷ ، تلفظ ۲

Imitation of Final CV(h): Common words with final /h/ or /:/ usually elided

(ra) (tæ) (no) (kola)   کلاه   نه   ته   راه

Lesson 7, Pronunciation Drill 3: درس ۷ ، تلفظ ۳

Imitation of Final VC(:): Common words with final /h/ or /:/ usually elided

(jæm) (qæt) (joz) (shæm)   شمع   جزء   قطع   جمع

Lesson 7, Pronunciation Drill 4: درس ۷ ، تلفظ ۴

Imitation of Final VC(h): Common words with final /h/ or /:/ usually elided

(sæt) (væj) (sob) (sol)   صلح   صبح   وجه   سطح

Lesson Seven   MODERN PERSIAN   درس هفتم

Lesson 7, Pronunciation Drill 5:   درس ۷ ، تلفظ ۵

Imitation of Final V(h) V(:), VC(h) and VC(:): Words Often Pronounced with or without Final /h/ or /:/

shoru:	(shoru)	vozu:	(vozu)	(وضو)	وضوء	شروع
					(شرو)	
særi:	(særi)	shey:	(shey)	(شی)	شئ	سریع
					(سرى)	
kolah	(kola)	tæfrih	(tæfri)	(تفرى)	تفریح	کلاه
					(کلا)	

Erudite or Religious Words (Final /h/ or /:/ usually retained)

shebh	khæl:	rih	jæmi:	جمیع	ریح	خلع	شبه

Everyday Words — often heard in one of three ways (originally /h/ or /:/ after a consonant)

væz:	(væ:z)	(væz)	وضع
joz:	(jo:z)	(joz)	جزء
shærh	(shæ:r)	(shær)	شرح
tærh	(tæ:r)	(tær)	طرح

7.2 Vocabulary   نوشتاری (گفتاری)

Vocabulary, Dialogue 7   مکالمه ۷

	(jun)	(جون)	dear (lit: "soul, life" see section 13.1)
	jan	(جان) جان	
	æl:an	الآن	now, right now
	(míræm)	(میرم)	I go
	ræft/(r)	رفت/(ر)	to go
	míræværm[1]	میروم	
	ræft/<u>ræv</u>	رفت/رو	(see Lesson 7, drills 1-4 for the syntactic use of verbs of motion)

293

Lesson Seven	MODERN PERSIAN	درس هفتم

to	تو	you (familiar) - see Sections 3.11.2, 5.11.7, 5.11.8
sæntur	سنتور	the santur — an Iranian musical instrument
bæ:dæn	بعداً	afterward, later (on)
kár daræm	کار دارم	I am busy, have something to do
kar dasht/dar	کار داشت/دار	to be busy, have something to do, have things to do, have an errand to do/commitment to go to
hætmæn	حتماً	definitely, for sure, absolutely
(míam)	(میام)	I come
amæd/(a)	آمد/(آ)	to come
míayæm[1]	میایم	
amæd/<u>ay</u>	آمد/(آی)	(see Lesson 7, drills 1-4 for the syntactic use of verbs of motion)

Vocabulary, Drills Part I   تمرینات ، قسمت ۱

otaq	اطاق/اتاق	room (as in a part of a building, not in the sense of "space = جا") (note the two acceptable spellings of this word.)
dæftær (2)	دفتر	office (i.e., someone's office, not as a place where many people work)
færda sob	فردا صبح	tomorrow morning
færda bæ:d-æz-zohr	فردا بعدازظهر	tomorrow afternoon
færda shæb	فردا شب	tomorrow night, tomorrow evening

Lesson Seven *MODERN PERSIAN* درس هفتم

bæráye[2]	برای	for
sær-e zohr	سر ظهر	right at noon, noon sharp
key?	کی	when?
hær	هر	each, every
hær ruz	هر روز	every day
mæ:mulæn	معمولاً	usually
æks	عکس	picture, photograph
æks mìgiræm	عکس میگیرم	I take a picture, I photograph
æks gereft/gir	عکس گرفت/گیر	to take a picture, to photograph
(chetorí)[3]	(چطوری)	how? by what means?
chetor(í)	چطور(ی)	how? by what means?
hævapeyma	هواپیما	airplane
teren/teræn	ترن (قطار)	train
piade	پیاده	on foot, by walking
(piade míræm mædrese)	(پیاده میرم مدرسه)	I walk to school
æslæn	اصلاً	originally, at all
(míkham)	(میخوام)	I want
khast/(kha)	خواست/(خوا)	to want
míkhahæm[1]	میخواهم	
khast/khah	خواست/خواه	

Vocabulary, Situational and Practical Drills

ashna (ba)	آشنا (با)	familiar, acquainted (with)
(ashná mìshæm)	(آشنا میشم)	I become acquainted/ get acquainted
ashná mìshævæm	آشنا میشوم	
ashna shod/(sh-)	(آشنا شد/شا)	to become acquainted/ get acquainted

295

Lesson Seven *MODERN PERSIAN* درس هفتم

ashna shod/shæv	آشنا شد/شو	
(*ashná bèshid*)	(آشنا بشین)	"Get acquainted!" (polite imperative used in introductions)
ashná bèshævid	آشنا بشوید	

Useful Words and Phrases

hæmintor	همینطور	likewise, the same way, just like that
(*mæn-æm hæmintor*)	(منم همینطور)	"me, too (with affirmative)," "me neither (with negative)," the same for me
mæn hæm hæmintor	من هم همینطور	
ésm-e kucik	(اسم کوچیک)	first name
ésm-e kucek	اسم کوچک	
ésm-e famili	اسم فامیلی	last name
(*dige*)[4]	دیگه	else, other, more (see note 4 below for a range of uses of this word)
digær	دیگر	(see section 8.9.3)
do(w)re	دوره	review (noun)
do(w)ré mìkonæm	دوره میکنم	I review
do(w)re kærd/kon	دوره کرد/کن	to review
æmma	اما	but (common alternate to ولی; we have not used it in our drills.)
heyf!	حیف!	Too bad! It's a shame/pity.
khéyli héyf-e!	خیلی حیف است!	It's really a shame/pity.

Names of the European Months

The European calendar is used in Iran for some purposes. The French names of the months were the ones adopted and are known quite widely in Iran. Many people also know the English names, and as you might expect, these are generally used by Iranians living in the

Lesson Seven *MODERN PERSIAN* درس هفتم

United States and Great Britain. See section 9.12 for the Iranian calendar and the names of the Iranian months.

zhanvie	ژانویه	January
fevrie	فوریه	February
mars	مارس	March
avril	آوریل	April
me	مه	May
zhuæn	ژوئن	June
zhuie	ژوئیه	July
ut	اوت	August
septambr	سپتامبر	September
oktobr	اکتبر	October
novambr	نوامبر	November
desambr	دسامبر	December

Vocabulary for Drills, Part II		تمرینات، قسمت ۲
ræng	رنگ	color
rængí	رنگی	color (adj), in color
che ræng?[5]	چه رنگی	(of) what color?
qermez[6]	قرمز (سرخ)	red
sia(h)	سیاه (سیا/سیاه)	black
sefid	سفید	white
sæbz	سبز	green
abi	آبی	light blue (< آب "water")
sormei	سرمه ای	dark blue
qæhvei	قهوه ای	brown (< قهوه "coffee")
zærd	زرد	yellow
khaki	خاکی	khaki

297

Lesson Seven *MODERN PERSIAN* درس هفتم

Some Optional Color Words:

portoqali	پرتقالی	orange (< پرتقل "orange (fruit)")
narenji	نارنجی	orange (< نارنج "sour orange")
suræti	صورتی	pink (< صورت "face")
khakestæri	خاکستری	gray (< خاکستر "ash")
bænæfsh	بنفش	purple, violet
rængaræng	رنگارنگ	multicolored
khaki	خاکی	khaki

من رنگ آبی دوست دارم برای اینکه آسمان آبی است و دریا هم آبی است. من دوست دارم به آسمان و دریا نگاه کنم. شما چه رنگی دوست دارید؟

Vocabulary Notes

1 میروم /ræft/ræv/ (ræft/r), <u>amæd</u>/<u>ay</u> (amæd/a), <u>khast</u>/<u>khah</u> (khast/kha): The lengthened FWP forms of Colloquial stems in the present tense for a number of common verbs are described below in section 7.9.2 "Lengthened Verb Stems." Section 7.9.3 also presents a

Lesson Seven   *MODERN PERSIAN*   درس هفتم

description of how verbs of motion function differently in FWP from their colloquial counterparts.

2 برای/*bæráye* "for": This word may be used in various ways as it is in English:

برای من	for me
برای فردا چکار کنیم؟	What should we do for tomorrow?
وقت برای خواندن ندارم.	I don't have time for reading.

3 چطوری/*chetorí* "how": In colloqual Persian this word asks "how," implying the method or means by which something is accomplished. It is different from the *chetor* you already know, which implies description, i.e., what something is like or what state it it is in. The difference is seen in the following contrast:

(این ماشین چطوره؟)	(in mashin chetór-e?)	"How is this car?" i.e., What's it like?
(این ماشین چطوریه؟)	(in mashin chetorí-e?)	"How does this car work?"

چطوری is considered a colloquial word and is not written in FWP. See Note 5 below and section 8.9.6 for a discussion of how to write this word in FWP.

4 دیگر/*(dige)*: This word has quite a wide range of uses. Here are some important ones that you may find useful at this stage in your learning. They are listed here in their colloquial and FWP equivalents as with entries in regular vocabulary lists:

(dige chi?)	(دیگه چی)	What else?
digær che?	دیگر چه	(see 8.9.1 and 8.9.3)
(dige ki?)	(دیگه کی)	Who else?
digær ke/ki?	دیگر که/دیگر کی	(see 8.9.1 and 8.9.3)
(dige koja?)	(دیگه کجا)	Where else?
digær koja?	دیگر کجا	(see 8.9.3)
(dige némidunæm.)	(دیگه نمیدونم)	I don't know any more than that; other than that I don't know
(yéki dige)	(یکی دیگه)	one more, an additional one

Lesson Seven　　*MODERN PERSIAN*　　درس هفتم

yéki digær	یکی دیگر	
(ye loqæt-e dige)	(یه لغت دیگه)	one more [word, etc.]
yek loqæt-e digær	یک لغت دیگر (یک واژه دیگر)	

بیژن: من این نوشابه (نوشیدنی drink) رو دوست دارم.
هوشنگ: یکی دیگه هم میخوای؟
بیژن: من علی رو تو خیابون دیدم.
هوشنگ: دیگه کی و دیدی؟

Other meanings and uses of this word will be introduced in subsequent vocabulary lists

5   The expression /che rængí-e?/, generally considered colloquial, should be written چه رنگ است in FWP. See section 8.9.6 for further discussion of this rule in FWP.

6   All color words may optionally be said as a compound of the color names listed here and the word رنگ:

قرمز or قرمز رنگ ، زرد or زرد رنگ ، پرتقالی or پرتقالی رنگ، etc.

7.3 Classroom Expressions (Optional Material)   ۷/۳

7.3.1 Classroom Expressions   ۷/۳/۱

do(w)re konim	دوره کنیم	let's review
shæfahi	شفاهی	oral
emtehán-e shæfahi	امتحان شفاهی	oral examination
kætbi	کتبی	written
emtehán-e kætbi	امتحان کتبی	written examination
kætbæn	کتباً	in writing
(kætbæn jæváb bèdim?)	(کتباً جواب بدیم؟)	Shall we answer in writing?
hæme ba hæm	همه با هم	(everybody) all together (see also 1.3.2)

Lesson Seven　　　*MODERN PERSIAN*　　　درس هفتم

yeki-yeki	یکی یکی	one by one, singly
(dune-dune)	(دونه دونه)	one by one, singly
jomle	جمله	sentence
(ye jom*le* bénevisin.)	(یه جمله بنویسین)	Write a sentence.
yek jomle bénevisid.	یک جمله بنویسید	
(ru)	(رو)	on
tækhte sia(h)	تخته سیاه	blackboard
bénevisæm?	بنویسم؟	should I write it?
(ru tækhte si*ah* bénevisæm?)	(رو تخته سیاه بنویسم؟)	Should I write on the blackboard?
(ru kaqæz bénevisæm?)	(رو کاغذ بنویسم؟)	Should I write on paper?
(ru tækhte si*ah* bénevisæm ya ru kaqæz?)	(رو تخته سیاه بنویسم یا رو کاغذ؟)	Should I write on the blackboard or on paper?
ba medad, ba gæch	با مداد، با گچ	with a pencil (in pencil), in chalk
	با مداد (گچ /خودکار) بنویسم؟	Should I write with a pencil?
ba me*dad* (*gæch*/khod*kar*) bénevisæm?		(chalk/ ballpoint pen)?

7.3.2 Classroom Drill ۷/۳/۲

Students break up into pairs for two to three minutes for this drill:

آقا/خانوم، لطفاً یه جمله بنویسین.

آقای/خانوم (اسم دانشجو۲)، لطفاً بخونین و بگین جمله (اسم دانشجو۱) درسته یا نه؟

(بخونین و بگین/بخونید و بگید)

301

Lesson Seven   *MODERN PERSIAN*   درس هفتم

🔊 7.4 Dialogue 7   مكالمه ۷

The dialogue in Lesson 6 was between Tom and a person to whom he had just been introduced. The style was slightly formal. The dialogue in this lesson, by contrast, is between close friends, Tom and Hossein, and illustrates the very informal, affectionate style of speech in which the familiar forms of the verbs are appropriate.

Transcription and Translation

jun	dear
æl:an	now, right now
míri	you go (familiar)
to	you (familiar)

Hossein: tómas jun, æl:an koja míri to?   Tom, where are you going now?

Tom: mæn? æl:an míræm sær-e kelas.   Me? I'm going to class now.

Hossein: míri daneshgah (?) ya khuné-ye moællémet.   Are you going to the university or your teacher's house?

sæntur   the santur — an Iranian instrument

Tom: míræm khuné-ye moællémæm.   I'm going to my teacher's house.

dærs-e sæntur daræm.   I have a santur lesson.

bæ:dæn   afterward

kár dari?   Are you busy? Do you have something to do?

Hossein: bæ:dæn kár dari?   Are you busy afterward?

Tom: næ. to chekár míkoni?   No. What are you going to do?

bæcheha (often pronounced /bæca/)   "the guys" (refers not only to a group of males, as in English, but to any group of friends, classmates, etc.)

Lesson Seven *MODERN PERSIAN* درس هفتم

mírim	we are going
míay/míai?	will you come? (lit: "do you come?")

Hossein: emshæb mǽno bæcheha mírim sinema. fílm-e farsí-e. tó-æm míay/míai?
The guys and I are going to the movies tonight. There's a Persian film. Why don't you come too?

hætmæn — definitely, for sure
míam — I come, I'll come

Tom: mérsi. hætmæn míam.
Thanks. I'll come for sure.

Text and Transcription

Hossein: tómas jun. æl:an koja míri to?   توماس جون. الآن کجا میری تو؟

Tom: mæn? æl:an míræm sær-e kelas.   من؟ الآن میرم سر کلاس.

Hossein: míri daneshgah ya khuné-ye moællémet?   میری دانشگاه یا خونهٔ معلمت؟

Tom: míræm khuné-ye moællémæm. dærs-e sæntur daræm.   میرم خونهٔ معلم. درس سنتور دارم.

Hossein: bæ:dæn kár dari?   بعداً کار داری؟

Tom: næ. to chekár míkoni?   نه. تو چکار میکنی؟

Hossein: emshæb mæno bæcheha mírim sinema. film-e farsí-e. tó-æm míay/míai?   امشب من و بچه ها میریم سینما. فیلم فارسیه. تو هم میایی/میای؟

Tom: mérsi. hætmæn míam.   مرسی. حتماً میام.

Lesson Seven — MODERN PERSIAN — درس هفتم

7.6 Drills, Part I   درس ۷، تمرینات، قسمت ۱

درس ۷، تمرین ۱

آ.   فعلاً میرم **خونه**. (مدرسه)

فعلاً میرم مدرسه. (**ما**)

فعلاً میریم مدرسه.

(بانک، **تو**، بیمارستان، خوابگاه، **اونا**، آپارتمانشون، **شما**، کارخونه، **من**، فتوکپی، حموم، **اون**، رستوران، **اونا**، کتابخونه، **من**، مغازه، تو، هتل، **اون**، اطاق پمپ بنزین، **من**، (خونه))

ب.   الآن میرم سر کار. (کلاس)

الآن میرم **سر کلاس**. (اون)

الآن میره سر کلاس.

(ما، کار، کلاس زبان، شما، امتحان، اونا، کار، دفترِ استادم، ما، کلاسمون، کار، (من))

درس ۷، تمرین ۲

دانشجو۱: تو الآن کجا میری؟   دانشجو۲: الآن میرم **مدرسه**.

دانشجو۱: پس بعداً کجا میری؟   دانشجو۲: بعداً میرم **سر کار**.

(کتابخونه/سینما، دانشگاه/خوابگاه، مدرسه/کار، بیمارستان/خونه، بانک/آپارتمان، امتحان/کلاس سنتور، پمپ بنزین/هتل، بانک/کار، ویدا، کلاس/کتابخونه، (مدرسه/کار))

درس ۷، تمرین ۳

آ.   دانشجو۱: **ساعت دو کجا میرین**؟   دانشجو ۲: **ساعت دو میرم مغازه**.

(فردا/نیو یورک، امشب/کار، ساعت دوازده/ناهار، فردا صبح/حموم، بعداً/کارخونه فردا شب/بیمارستان، ساعت شیش/شام، فردا بعد از ظهر/کلاسِ استاد جعفری، امروز/کلاس، امشب/خونۀ دوستم، ساعت ده، دفترِ استادمون، (ساعت دو/مغازه))

ب.   سؤال و جواب آزاد

Lesson Seven *MODERN PERSIAN* درس هفتم

درس ۷، تمرین ۴

دانشجو۱: علی کی دوباره میاد اینجا؟
دانشجو۲: فکر میکنم فردا میاد. (شما/امشب)
دانشجو۱: شما کی دوباره میایید اینجا؟
دانشجو۲: فکر میکنم امشب میام.

(ما/ساعت ده، اونا/صبح، دوستتون/سر ظهر، اون آقا/امروز، خواهر شهلا/ تقریباً ساعت چار، تو/بعداً، ما/امشب ساعت نه، (علی/فردا))

درس ۷، تمرین ۵

آ.
دانشجو۱: تو چطوری میری ایران؟
دانشجو۲: با هواپیما میرم. (کار/پیاده)
دانشجو۱: تو چطوری میری سر کار؟
دانشجو۲: پیاده میرم.

(سینما/تاکسی، کلاس/دوچرخه، دانشگاه/هلیکپتر (چرخ بال) (!)، کار/ اتوبوس، کتابخونه/ماشین، ایتالیا/هواپیما، کلاس/تانک (!)، یونان/اتوبوس، مسکو/ ترن، استرالیا/ماشین (!)، نیو یورک/ترن، آرژانتین/ سه چرخه (ایران/هواپیما)

ب. جواب آزاد

شما کی دوباره میایید اینجا؟ چطوری میایید؟
(اسم دانشجو) کی میاد سر کلاس؟ چطوری میاد؟
(اسم دانشجو) کی دوباره میره خونه؟ (از اوبپرسید) چطوری میره؟
من کی دوباره میام سر کلاس؟ فکر میکنید چطوری میام؟
شما امروز میایید دفترم؟ (شما امروز میایید به دفترم؟)
شما ساعت دو کجا میرید؟ چطوری میرید؟
شما ساعت شیش کجا میرید؟ چطوری میرید؟
شما فردا صبح کجا میرید؟ چطوری میرید؟ (نزدیکه؟ دوره؟)

Lesson Seven　　　　　*MODERN PERSIAN*　　　　　درس هفتم

(اسم دانشجو) امشب کجا میره؟ چطوری میره؟

(اسم دانشجو) امروز بعد از ظهر کجا میره؟ چطور میره؟

شما چطوری میرید خونه؟

شما چطوری میرید (اونجا)؟ (other cities, hometown, downtown, stores, etc.)

درس ۷، تمرین ۶

دانشجو۱: شما چندتا سیب میخواین؟ **دانشجو۲:** سه تا میخوام.

ما – فیلم/دو، کامران - بچه/یه، تو - بیلیط/شیش، خانوم امامی - شاگرد/پونزده، مهری -روزنامه/ فقط یه، فرشته -عکس/پنج، ما - پرتقال/سیزده، شما - میز - هفت، شما - صندلی/هفت، شوهرتون - کراوات/یه، اونا - بچه/چار (دو پسر و دو دختر)، معلممون - فتوکپی/بیست و چار،(شما - سیب/سه)

درس ۷، تمرین ۷

آ.　**دانشجو۱:** شما کی درس میخونین؟

دانشجو۲: من شبا درس میخونم. (پیانو زد/هیچوقت)

دانشجو۱: شما کی پیانو میزنین؟

دانشجو۲: من هیچوقت پیانو نمیزنم.

(والیبال بازی کرد/بعد از ظهرا، آمد اینجا/امروز، امتحان داد/فردا سر ظهر، نامه نوشت/هیچوقت،عکس گرفت/روزا، سیگار کشید/خیلی کم،تنها بود/ هیچوقت، آواز خوند/صبا در حموم،کباب خورد/سر ظهر، حموم کرد/صبا، خوابید/ساعت یازده، (درس خوند/شبا))

ب.　جواب آزاد

دانشجو۱: شما کی پیانو میزنین؟

دانشجو۲: جواب آزاد

(مکالمه تمرین کرد، شام درست کرد، ناهار خورد، استراحت کرد، رفت سینما،

Lesson Seven　　　　*MODERN PERSIAN*　　　　درس هفتم

ورزش کرد، رمان خوند، آمد مدرسه، تعارف کرد، رفت کتابخونه، خط تمرین کرد، کار کرد، (پیانو زد))

درس ۷، تمرین ۸　جواب آزاد

دانشجو۱: شما کجایی هستین؟　　دانشجو۱: پدرتون کجایی اه؟

دانشجو۲: من اهل (مالِ) واشنگتنم.　دانشجو۲: پدرم امریکایی اه.

دانشجو۱: خب، اصلاً کجایی هستین؟　دانشجو۱: خب، اصلاً کجایی اه؟

دانشجو۲: اصلاً اهل (مالِ) نیویورکم　دانشجو۲: اصلاً ایتالیایی اه.

(Now ask the above questions about each other and about family, friends, other students, the professor and teaching assistant, people in the department, famous people, etc.)

7.8　Greetings and Telling Time

As mentioned in section 5.8, the expression *khéyli khoshvæqt shodæm* is in the past tense and is used when you are leaving someone you have just met. When you are first introduced to someone, use the present tense of the same expression—*khéyli khoshvæqt-æm*. The response will also be in the present tense—*mæn-æm khoshvæqt-æm*.

Phrase:　　　　　khéyli khoshvǽqt-æm.

Response 1:　　　mǽn-æm khoshvæqt-æm.

Response 2:　　　mǽn-æm hǽmintor./mæn-æm hǽmintor.

If you are in a conversation with two people who haven't met, you may introduce them simply by saying *ashná bèshid*, which means "Meet each other! Get acquainted!" Although it is a command, it is accepted as a polite way to introduce people. You may say the names of your friends as you do this, but usually those being introduced will introduce themselves, giving their last names only. First name informality is not so common in Iran, or among Iranians, as it is among Americans, although it is becoming more and more so, even in Iran. Of course it would seem a little strange for you to introduce yourself to a fellow Iranian student this way in the United States, especially in a student context, where a first name basis is more

permissible.

Also please note that while it is a common practice in the United States to refer to yourself as Mr., Miss, Ms., or Mrs. when introducing yourself over the telephone or other situations ("This is Mr. Cooper. I would like to speak to..."), in an Iranian context it will be thought a faux pas to use *aqa* or *khanum* in reference to yourself. You simply state your last name with no titles or honorifics attached.

درس ۷ ، تمرین ۹

a. Introducing oneself

    S1: bébækhshid, áqa/khánum. ésmetun chi-e?

    S2: ésmæm (jæ:færí)-e. or simply: (jæ:færi), qórban.

    S1: khéyli khoshvǽqt-æm.

    S2: mǽn-æm khoshvǽqt-æm.

    S1: áqa/khánum, mæ:zerǽt mìkham. ésm-e shoma chi-e?

    S2: ésmæm (jæ:færí)-e. ésm-e shoma chi-e?

    S1: ésmæm (nezhad)-e.

    S2: khéyli khoshvǽqt-æm.

    S1: mǽn-æm khoshvǽqt-æm.

    S1: áqa/khánum, bébækhshid. ésmetun chi-e?

    S2: ésm-e mæn (jæ:færí)-e, qórban.

    S1: khéyli khoshvǽqt-æm.

    S2: mǽn-æm khoshvǽqt-æm.

    S1: áqa/khánum, mæ:zerǽt mìkham. ésm-e shoma chi-e?

    S2: ésm-e mæn (jæ:færí)-e. ésm-e shoma chi-e?

    S1: ésmæm (nezhad)-e, qórban.

    S1: khéyli khoshvǽqt-æm.

Lesson Seven		*MODERN PERSIAN*		درس هفتم

S2:   mæn-æm hǽmintor.   (or: mǽn-æm hæmintor.)

b.   Being introduced

    S1:   (áqayon/khánuma) ashná bèshid.

          aqá-ye/khanúm-e jæ:færí.   aqá-ye/khanúm-e nezhad.

    S2:   khéyli khoshvǽqt-æm.

    S3:   mǽn-æm khoshvæqt-æm.

    S1:   (áqayon/khánuma) ashná bèshid.   (The two shake hands and say their names at approximately the same time)

        jæ:færí /nezhad: jæ:færi nezhad.

        jæ:færí: khéyli khoshvǽqt-æm.

        nezhad: mǽn-æm khoshvæqt-æm.

c.   Telling Time — Stage 1   درس ۷، تمرین ۱۰

In telling time, the hour comes first and the number follows connected by an *ezafe*. In normal speech, the *ezafe* is usually dropped in connecting *saæt* to the number, but *saæt-e chǽnd-e* and *saæt-e dó-e,* etc., are also possible.

    a.   **Teacher:**   bébækhshid. saǽt(-e) chǽnd-e?

          Student: saǽt(-e) yék-e.

(do, hæsht, char, noh, pænj, shish, dæh, hæft, (yek))

    b.   **Teacher:**   bébækhshid. saǽt-e yék-e?

          Student: næ. hænuz saǽt-e yek nist.

(do, hæsht, char, noh, pænj, shish, dæh, hæft, (yek))

    c.   **Teacher:**   hala saǽt(-e) chǽnd-e?

          Student: mésl-e ìnke saǽt-e dó-e.

(yek, hæsht, char, noh, pænj, shish, dæh, hæft, (do))

Lesson Seven *MODERN PERSIAN* درس هفتم

N.B.: Be careful not confuse this time-telling construction with the construction (see Lesson 5, Drill 20 and section 5.11.3, Counting Nouns) in which the number precedes the hour with no *ezafe* or counting particle, *chænd saæt?, do saæt,* which means "How many hours? Two hours."

Compare:

ساعت چند	saæt(-e) chænd?	What time?
چند ساعت	chænd saæt?	How many hours?
ساعت یک	saæt(-e) yek	one o'clock
یک ساعت	yek saæt	one hour
ساعت دو	saæt(-e) do	two o'clock
دو ساعت	do saæt	two hours
ساعت ده	saæt(-e) dæh	ten o'clock
ده ساعت	dæh saæt	ten hours

7.9 Reading and Writing Persian: Colloquial/FWP Transformations, Part II, Rules Affecting Phonology

7.9.1 Vanishing /h/ ه ح

There are a number of phonetic contexts in which FWP /h/ (ح and ه) is elided in Colloquial Persian. These contexts are described in the phonology sections of Lessons 5, 7, and 8 (sections 5.15, 7.1, and 8.1). Those descriptions are not repeated here, but we simply point out that to convert colloquial speech into its FWP form, you will sometimes need to insert an /h/-sound in places you did not realize it existed.

1. **Colloquial /-æm/, FWP hæm** هم , "also"

A common word you have seen that requires the insertion of ه is the word /-æm/ "also," written هم. That is, /farsí-æm yád mìgirænd/ is written فارسی هم یاد میگیرند.

Examples:

	Colloquial		FWP
منم	(mæn-æm)	من هم	mæn hæm
مام	(ma-m)	ماهم	ma hæm
بچه م	(bæcæ-m)*	بچه هم	bæche hæm
پیانوام	(pianó-æm)	پیانوهم	piano hæm
لیموام	(limú-æm)	لیموهم	limu hæm
فارسی ام	(farsí-æm)	فارسی هم	farsi hæm

* On the change of final /-e/ to /-æ/, see section 8.11.1 below. A fuller discussion and more examples of hæm are also given in 8.11.1.

2. The Plural Marker /-a/, FWP -ha ها

The pronoun اونا una "they" is affected by both rules discussed above. It is written آنها anha. The -h- in this word is part of the plural marker which you have seen in words such as *ruza*, *shæba*, written روزها ruzha, شبها shæbha, etc. Further discussion of this ending and its FWP form is introduced in section 8.11.2 where there is also a fuller description of Persian and Arabic plurals.

3. /h/ Dropped from Other Contexts

Colloquial Persian, especially rapid speech, drops /h/ in many words:

	Colloquial		FWP
صب	(sob)	صبح	sobh
ممّد	(mæmmæd)	محمّد	mohæmmæd

See also 8.1 for further examples of /h/ dropped in various words.

Rules Affecting Grammatical Categories

7.9.2 Lengthened Verb Stems

The colloquial forms of many verb roots that you have already learned are shorter forms of the FWP verb roots. Since you have learned the shorter forms, you will have to add something to certain roots you now know in order to write them. What is added usually

311

Lesson Seven MODERN PERSIAN درس هفتم

consists of one vowel and an h, v or y, thus giving the FWP form one syllable more than the colloquial. The problem is that since any one of three different consonants (v, h, or y, depending on the root) is inserted, the FWP forms simply have to be memorized. Examples:

Colloquial Root	Present Tense		FWP Root	Present Tense
/d/	میدم	and its compounds	deh	میدهم
/kha/	میخوا	and its compounds	khah	میخواهم
/r/	میرم		ræv	میروم
/sh/	میشم	and its compounds	shæv	میشوم
/g/	میگم	and its compounds	gu(y)*	میگویم
/a/	میام		a(y)*	میایم

You have also seen almost all of these verbs as the verbal element in compound verbs:

Colloquial Form		FWP Form	
جواب میدم	(jæváb mìdæm)	جواب میدهم	jæváb mìdehæm
معذرت میخوام	(mæ:zeræt mìkham)	معذرت میخواهم	mæ:zeræt mìkhahæm
آشنا بشید/آشنا شید	(ashná (bè)shid)	آشنا بشوید/آشنا شوید	ashná (bè)shævid
راست میگید	(rást mìgid)	راست میگویید	rást mìguid

* As you will see when we come to a fuller presentation of the singular command forms of the verb (beginning in sections 2.11.3 and 5.11.7), -y- is not really a part of the verb root but only serves as a transition between a verb root ending in a vowel and the person ending beginning with a vowel:

mí + gu + (y) + æm = míguyæm (colloq: /mígæm/)

mí + a + (y) + æm = míayæm (colloq: /míam/)

An important maxim to keep in mind:

In Colloquial Persian there is a tendency to merge roots and endings (usually by losing a vowel);

Formal Written Persian has a tendency to separate roots and endings (usually by

inserting a consonant between them).

In later lessons you will learn other types of changes in verb roots from colloquial to FWP. The general rules for converting colloquial Persian to FWP continue in section 9 of Lessons 8 through 10. After that any new verbs that have different colloquial and formal forms will simply be listed as such in the vocabulary list.

As mentioned in Vocabulary Note 1 in the vocabulary of Lesson 6, the written form the prefix is often separated from the root:

mishævæm	می شوم	mídehæm	می دهم
míguyæm	می گویم	míkhahæm	می خواهم
míayæm	می آیم	mírævæm	می روم

Rules Affecting Syntax

7.9.3 Destinations and Verbs of Motion

As you have seen in this lesson, the noun generally comes **after** the verb when it is a destination of a verb of motion. The noun is also characteristically unmarked by a preposition:

من فردا نميرم مدرسه.   "I'm not going to school tomorrow."

This construction is considered colloquial and in FWP, both of these characteristics change. That is, the destination is brought **before** the verb and the preposition به "to" always accompanies the noun:

FWP:	**Colloquial:**
من فردا به مدرسه نميروم.	من فردا نميرم مدرسه.
من ساعت دو به خانه ميايم.	من ساعت دو ميام خونه.

There is a fuller discussion of this construction in colloquial Persian in section 7.11.2. There are also written drills that include this material in section 7.15.

Lesson Seven — *MODERN PERSIAN* — درس هفتم

7.10 Drills, Part II — درس ۷، تمرینات، قسمت ۲

درس ۷، تمرین ۱۱

آ. معلم: ماشینتون چه رنگیه؟ دانشجو: ماشینم **سفیده**.

(قرمز، سبز، آبی، قهوه ای، سیاه و سفید، زرد، سرمه ای،(سفید))

ب. معلم: **ماشینتون** چه رنگیه؟ دانشجو: جواب آزاد.

معلم: **کراواتم** چه رنگیه؟ دانشجو: جواب آزاد.

(سیب، ساک، بلوز، دفتر، صندلی، پلوور، کاغذ، خودکار، (و غیره))

درس ۷، تمرین ۱۲

آ. شما خودکار قرمز دارین؟

(اطاق/ارزون، پاکت/کوچیک، ساک/بزرگ، نون/افغانی، عکس/سیاه و سفید، مداد/سبز، بچه/مریض، بچه/بیمار، لهجه/عربی، جواب/درست، موزیک/ مدرن، اسم/ کوچیک ، کاغذ/آبی، ماشین/قهوه ای، مجله/سوئیسی ،کتاب/ آلمانی، دفتر/سیاه، قهوه/ترک، گچ/رنگی، کاغذ/کوچیک، نوشابه/خنک (خودکار/قرمز))

ب. **معلم**: شما خودکار قرمز دارین؟ **دانشجو**: جواب آزاد.

(جوهر/آبی، پول/خورد، کاغذ/سفید، ساعت/سوئیسی، جوهر/قرمز، لهجه/ امریکایی، ماشین/بزرگ، آپارتمان/مدرن، ماشین/ژاپنی، چایی/سبز، فیلم/ رنگی، سیب/زرد، دکتر/ایرانی، پاسپورت/امریکایی، رمان/اینگلیسی)

ج. دانشجو: کامران کتاب سیاه داره.

(Students describe each other's possessions using this pattern)

درس ۷، تمرین ۱۳

آ. کلاس زبانتون بزرگه. (اون)

کلاس زبانش بزرگه.

(جالب، (شما)، کلاس اینگلیسی، نزدیک، (اونا)، سخت، اسم کوچیک، امتحان

Lesson Seven *MODERN PERSIAN* درس هفتم

آلمانی، آسون، (شما)، کار شیمی، جالب، (ما)، کتاب فارسی، بزرگ، (اون)، ساک، عکس مادر، سیاه و سفید، (شما)، ماشین آمریکایی، کوچیک، (اونا)، دفتر شیمی، برادر، مریض، (شما)، دوست هندی، قشنگ، خط فارسی، زشت، (ما)، لهجه اینگلیسی، درست، خوب، کلاس زبان، (اون)، (بزرگ))

ب. **معلم:** کلاس فارسیتون بزرگه؟ **دانشجو:** جواب آزاد.

(کلاس اینگلیسی/جالب، خط فارسی/قشنگ، تکلیف شب فارسی/سخت، ساک بزرگ/زرد، امتحان آلمانی (وغیره)/آسون، کار شیمی/جالب، کلاس اینگلیسی/نزدیک، دفتر فارسی/بزرگ، ماشین آمریکایی/کوچیک، برادر کوچیک/مریض، تلفظ فارسی/درست، دوست هندی/جالب، وغیره)

ج. **معلم:** سالاد فصل گرونه؟ **دانشجو:** جواب آزاد.

(زبان فارسی/قشنگ، تلفظ فارسی/سخت، کلاس زبان/جالب (چرا؟)، فیلم رنگی/گرون، قهوه ترک/خوب، لهجۀ شیرازی/جالب، تلفظ عربی/مشکل (چرا؟)، خط فارسی/آسون، تکلیف شب فارسی/جالب، وغیره)

درس ۷، تمرین ۱۴

آ. کتاب فارسیتون چه رنگیه؟ ب. شما دوچرخه دارین؟ چه رنگیه؟
تلفنتون چه رنگیه؟ شما ماشین دارین؟ چه رنگیه؟
دفترتون چه رنگیه؟ شما خونه دارین؟ چه رنگیه؟
خودکارتون چه رنگیه؟ شما کتاب عربی دارین؟ چه رنگیه؟
این گچ چه رنگیه؟ شما کاغذ دارین؟ چه رنگیه؟
جوهرتون چه رنگیه؟ شما کراوات سرمه ای دارین؟ چه رنگیه؟
  دیگه چه رنگی دارین؟
مدادتون چه رنگیه؟ شما مجله دارین؟ چه رنگیه؟
آپارتمانتون چه رنگیه؟ شما شونه دارین؟ چه رنگیه؟
کتابتون چه رنگیه؟ شما پیانو دارین؟ چه رنگیه؟

Lesson Seven *MODERN PERSIAN* درس هفتم

شما چک دارین؟ چه رنگیه؟	صندلیتون چه رنگیه؟
شما پولوور دارین؟ چه رنگیه؟	شامپوتون چه رنگیه؟
شما بلوز آبی دارین؟ دیگه چه رنگی دارین؟	اطاقتون چه رنگیه؟

ج. سیب چه رنگیه؟   د. پول ایرانی چه رنگیه؟
تاکسی چه رنگیه؟   سالاد چه رنگیه؟
قهوه (!) چه رنگیه؟   شکولات (!) چه رنگیه؟
گچ چه رنگیه؟   تخته سیامون (!) چه رنگیه؟
نون چه رنگیه؟   آسپیرین چه رنگیه؟
سیگار چه رنگیه؟   پاسپورت امریکایی چه رنگیه؟
پول امریکایی چه رنگیه؟   تمبر سی و نه چهارسنتی چه رنگیه؟ (وغیره)
پول کانادایی چه رنگیه؟   تمبر بیست و پنج سنتی چه رنگیه؟
(کانادایی: پنج دلاری چه رنگیه؟   تمبر یک سنتی چه رنگیه؟
پنج دلاری؟ ده دلاری؟)   تمبر پنج سنتی چه رنگیه؟

درس ۷، تمرین ۱۵ سؤال و جواب

به نظر شما، پاریس قشنگه؟
به نظر شما، خط فارسی سخته؟
به نظر شما، فروشگاه (آ) گرونه؟ پس فروشگاه (ب) چطور؟
ایالت آریزونا نسبتاً دوره؟ (خیلی دوره؟/نزدیکه؟)
(حالا نوبت کیه؟) (مطمئنین؟)
شما فکر میکنین که تکلیف شب این کلاس زیاده؟
به نظر شما، زبان فارسی قشنگه؟ زبان روسی چطور؟
به نظر شما، شکولات هلندی بهتره، یا شکولات سوئیسی؟
شما درس میدین، یا درس میخونین؟
(اسم دانشجو)، معذرت میخوام، زبان آلمانی سخته یا آسونه؟

Lesson Seven — درس هفتم

(اسم دانشجو۲)، شما چی فکر میکنین؟
(دانشجوا) امروز مریضه؟
شما اینجا پیانو میزنین؟ گیتار چطور؟ (چرا؟)
شما خبرنگار روزنامه این؟
شما با (اسم هنرپیشه) آشنائین؟ چرا؟
شما شبا در آپارتمانتون شام درست میکنین؟
شما صبح ساعت چند میائین دانشگاه؟
شما فردا ظهر چکار میکنین؟
کی غذای هندی درست میکنه؟ شما چرا غذای هندی درست میکنین؟
من چطور؟
من از شما زیاد میپرسم؟
من چرا از شما زیاد میپرسم؟

Lesson Seven   *MODERN PERSIAN*   درس هفتم

7.11 Grammar Discussion

7.11.1 The Colloquial and FWP Forms of "To Be": /-Ø-/ and /hæst-/

Form As you have already seen quite often, "to be" occurs commonly with nouns and adjectives. It has two principal roots, /-Ø-/ and /hæst-/, and both are used in colloquial as well as FWP. The /hæst-/ root occurs more frequently in FWP than it does in colloquial. In colloquial Persian the /-Ø-/ root is used most commonly but certainly not to the exclusion of the /hæst-/ root.

Colloquial Forms: **FWP Forms:**

Noun + "to be":

Normal Form	Stressed Form	Normal Form	Stressed Form
/-Ø-/	/hæst-/	/-Ø-/	/هست/
moællém-æm [1]	moællem hǽstæm	معلمم	معلم هستم [1]
moællém-i	moællem hǽsti	معلمی	معلم هستی
moællém-e	moællem hǽst [2]	معلمه معلم هست [2]	معلم است
	moællem hǽst [3]		معلم هست [3]
moællém-im [4]	moællem hǽstim	معلم هستیم [4]	معلمیم
moællém-in	moællem hǽstin	معلم هستید	معلمین
moællém-ænd	moællem hǽstænd	معلم هستند	معلمند

Adjective + "to be":

/-Ø-/	/hæst-/	/-Ø-/	/هست/
khúb-æm [1]	khub hǽstæm	خوبم [1]	خوب هستم
khúb-i	khub hǽsti	خوبی	خوب هستی
khub-e	khub hǽst [2]	خوب است [2]	خوب هست
	khub hǽst [3]		خوب هست [3]
			خوبست، خوبه
khúb-im [4]	khub hǽstim	خوبیم	خوب هستیم

318

Lesson Seven *MODERAN PERSIAN* درس هفتم

khúb-in	khub hǽstin	خوبید	خوب هستید
khúb-ænd	khub hǽstænd	خوبند	خوب هستند

we are	ماییم	I am	منم
you are	شمایید (ین)	you are	تویی
they/those are اند	آنها (ایشان، ایشون، اونا)	he/she/it is	اوست (اونه)

Translate into Persian:

It is good.

I am sick.

It is beautiful.

Where are you?

Unscramble the following groups of words to form correct sentences:

=	است	امروز	او	کجا
=		است	کی	قشنگ
= حرف	میزنی	کمی		تند
=		هستند	سیب ها	قرمز

1. See also the discussion in 6.11.2-3.

2. Of the two meanings/usages of *hæst* mentioned (6.11.2-3), this is the one indicating emphasis and sentence stress, i.e., "He/she **is** a teacher" and "He/she/it **is** good."

3. Of the two meanings/usages of *hæst* mentioned (6.11.2-3), this is the one indicating existence and does not necessarily take sentence stress. This usage occurs only with nouns, thus giving this sentence the meaning "There is a teacher/There are teachers." Adjectives, when combining with this use of *hæst* as existence, must function as nouns as well, giving a sentence such as *khub hæst?* the meaning of "Are there any good ones?"

4. Note that the number of the noun remains singular although the ending is plural.

Lesson Seven MODERN PERSIAN درس هفتم

7.11.2 Destinations and Verbs of Motion

As you have seen in the dialogue and drills of this lesson, the noun generally comes **after** the verb when it is a destination of a verb of motion. The noun is also characteristically unmarked by a preposition except for a few nouns that require *sær-e*. This structure is colloquial only and, as discussed in section 7.9.3, it must be converted to a different structure for FWP. The following examples of the colloquial variant of this structure and its word order are taken from Dialogue 7. The destinations (double underline) appear after the verb (single underline)

حسین: توماس جون. الآن کجا میری تو؟
تام: من؟ الآن میرم سر کلاس.
حسین: میری دانشگاه یا خونه معلمت؟
تام: میرم خونه معلمم.
حسین: امشب من و بچه ها میریم سینما.

You will note the following from these examples:

1. The destination word always appears **after** the verb of motion.
2. Generally, no preposition is used (the word order is sufficient).
3. The preposition *sær-e*, however, is used with those words that generally require it (*kelas, kar, emtehan*, etc.).
4. The word order of destination after the verb is not observed with the question word *koja*.

Other information not found in the above examples but related to this construction includes the following points:

1. The construction remains the same for most other verbs of motion:
   What time are you coming home?   ساعت چند میایی خونه؟
2. Expression of destination and expression of location differ significantly in word order:
   I am going to Tehran (destination) tomorrow.   من فردا میرم تهران.

320

Lesson Seven *MODERN PERSIAN* درس هفتم

I work in Tehran (location).   من در تهران کار میکنم.

3. In colloquial Persian the preposition of location — در — may also be omitted in many sentences. In this case, it really is only word order that distinguishes destination from location:

I am going to Tehran (destination).   من میرم تهران.

I work in Tehran (location).   من تهران کار میکنم.

4. Even the destination word may be brought before the verb in cases of emphasis:

I am going to <u>Tehran</u> (not Esfahan or somewhere else).   من تهران میرم

Further information on destination and verbs of motion is given in sections 12.11.3 and 15.11.1.

7.12 Cultural Materials: An Introduction to Iranian Names

If you know how to read them, names tell interesting stories. They are not simply labels, but keys to the identity of the people who bear them and to the history and values of their culture. American names are often difficult to decipher. We are such a diverse and heterogeneous community. Our names are drawn from all the languages of Europe and Asia and they reflect the religions, mythologies, and histories of many cultures. Iranian names seem quite accessible by comparison since the vast majority of Iranians share a common religious and cultural heritage. What is required to understand most names is a modest familiarity with Islam and the Qur:ân, and some knowledge of Iranian history and literature. The introduction that follows will provide you with an introduction to these various elements, and to how they are combined into names.

The simple and neat scheme of names and surnames that we use in the West is a recent phenomenon in Iran, one of the modernizing or westernizing innovations of Reza Shah Pahlavi, who also forbade women to wear chadors and insisted that all Iranians adopt western dress. Prior to his reign, names in Islamic Iranian culture were a complicated and highly personal affair. Everyone was given a name at birth, such as Mohammad or Fâteme, which

Lesson Seven *MODERN PERSIAN* درس هفتم

gave adequate identification around the home and neighborhood, and could be abbreviated or converted into a nickname used by intimates. When more precision was necessary it was provided by adding the name of one's father—Mohammad the son of Ja'far, or Fâteme the daughter of Abdollah. When sons and daughters became parents themselves, they were known as the father, or mother, of their first child—Mohammad the father of Rostam or Maryam, Fâteme the mother of Qolâmali or Shirin. In addition to the given name and terms of relation, a person might become known for some distinguishing physical feature or personal trait (popeyes, red hair, great height), professional identity (cobbler, tinsmith, philosopher, calligrapher), ethnicity (Turk, Baluchi, Kurd), title (chief steward, palace guard), or place of origin. So the same Mohammad the son of Ja'far, the father of Rostam, could also be known as "the Kurd *(kordi)*," "the watchmaker *(sætchi)*," "the tall one *(derazi)*," "the man from Ardestân *(ærdestani)*," and "the pilgrim to Mecca *(hâji)*." In fact the same man was probably known to various groups in the community by different names made up of these different elements. It all depended on how well and in what context they knew him. Other watchmakers would hardly call him Sâatchi, and similarly the name Kordi would be appropriate only where Kurds were uncommon. Hâji is a title that he would have acquired only after making the pilgrimage, probably late in his life. It would also take immediate precedence over virtually every other "name."

Modern Iranian names and surnames reflect traditional naming practices but now conform to the western pattern. The sources for names and surnames are several. Since surnames often derive from names, we will start there.

Names

The first choice to be made in selecting a name is between Muslim or non-Muslim (as well as pre-Islamic or secular) —between Ahmad or Rostam, Mândânâ or Fâteme. However, since Iranians are usually given two personal names—one for use by the family, one for those outside it—the custom has been to make one of these Muslim and the other not. The choice is really whether a child will be Ahmad or Fâteme to the family and Rostam or Mândânâ to the

Lesson Seven   *MODERN PERSIAN*   درس هفتم

world, or vice versa. It should also be noted that given names are often abbreviated into nicknames (Manuch for Manuchehr, Fâti for Fâteme, Dâri for Dâryush, etc.).

In addition, all adults address children in terms of their own relationship to the child. Mothers and fathers will call their child *mâmân jun* or *bâbâ jun*, respectively, the paternal uncle of the same child will call him or her *æmu jun* "Dear Uncle," and so on. The reason for this seems to be that this is how they teach a small child the term it should use to address them. (Iranian kinship terms are dealt with extensively in Lesson 10, section 10.5.)

The names chosen for each gender reflect very different aspirations. Male names, especially the traditional Iranian ones, are often taken from royal and heroic figures, and suggest strength, authority, martial prowess, and manliness. Islamic names include a far wider range of attributes. The name of the Prophet is far and away the most popular masculine name both in Iran and throughout the Muslim world. In addition, other names from the same Arabic roots as Mohammad—Ahmad, Hamid, Mahmoud—are great favorites. In Shi'ite Iran the names of the emâms are next in popularity, beginning with Ali, the first emâm, the Prophet's son-in-law, and a man of exceptional virtues. Ali occupies a position of respect in Shi'ite Iran hardly less than that of Mohammad himself. After Ali come his two sons Hasan and Hossein, and then the other nine emâms. The eighth emâm, Reza, whose tomb is in Mashhad, is especially popular. In fact, all of the male names mentioned so far are so common that parents will often add a second name to help avoid confusion—Alirezâ, Hasanali, Mohammadhoseyn.

Next in the Islamic category are names derived from the attributes of God, such as Rahim, "merciful," Karim, "munificent," Nâser, "defender (of the Faith)," Sâdeq, "truthful, loyal (an epithet of the emâm Ja'far)," and so on. These names are, of course, all Arabic in origin, and in pious families, *abd*, "servant/slave," may be added to these names using an Arabic construction that is like the *ezafe* in Persian: Abdorrahim, "slave of the Merciful," Abdolkarim, "slave of the Munificent," Abdonnâser, "slave of the Defender." The basic form of this name is seen in its most common exemplar, Abdollâh, "slave of God."

Masculine names that contain the word *qolam*, another word for "slave," and have the

Lesson Seven *MODERN PERSIAN* درس هفتم

form Qolâmali, Qolâmhoseyn, are not simply further examples of this. They tell a different story. Male children are much desired, and parents will sometimes vow that if God will send them an heir, they will make him the servant of one of the emâms. Also, when a child is born who is exceptionally beautiful, he may be given the name "Qolâm" to deflect the envy of malignant spirits, who are believed to be powerful but stupid.

The range of Muslim names open to women is somewhat different than that for men. The names of the Prophet and the emâms are rarely if ever given to women, for example. However, those derived from God's attributes are, and the simple addition of the Arabic feminine ending changes masculine Rahim, Karim, Nâser, and Sâdeq to Rahime, Karime, Nâsere, and Sâdeqe. Women are more likely to be named for those of God's attributes that seem more appropriate to their sex, such as Tâhere, "pure," Atefe "kindly," Amine, "trustworthy," Nâdere, "rare, precious." Women are also given the names of the Prophet's wives—Khadije, his first wife, and Ayeshe, his favorite among his later wives, are the most popular—or his daughters, especially Fâteme who was also the wife of the first emâm, Ali. Furthermore, women's names are chosen to suggest beauty, elegance, richness, rarity, or the domestic and personal virtues. Thus, Zahrâ, "fair, bright faced (epithet of Fâteme)," Najibe, "chaste," Zohre, "Venus," Sorayyâ, "a bright constellation (the Pleiades)," Batul, "a virgin or a nun," Shahlâ, "a beautiful dark blue color that is tinged with red."

The study of the pre-Islamic history of Iran was encouraged under the Pahlavis and the names of the great Iranian emperors gained a considerable vogue. Many Iranian men are named Sirus, Dâryush, and Kâmbiz — royal names that are well known in the West in the Greek forms Cyrus, Darius, and Cambyses — and also Shahpur and Ardeshir — names that come from the last Iranian dynasty to rule before the Islamic conquest of Iran. However, the principal source of pre-Islamic Iranian names is the Iranian national epic, the *Shâhnâme* or Book of Kings. Chief among these are the names of its principal heroes—Rostam, Sohrâb, Siâvosh, and Esfandiâr. Also popular are the names of the legendary Iranian emperors and heroes—Jamshid, Manuchehr, Iraj, Fereydun, Hushang, Parviz, and Khosrow.

Lesson Seven   *MODERN PERSIAN*   درس هفتم

There are fewer women's names to choose from in the *Shâhnâme*, and often, as with the Islamic names, their importance stems principally from the fame of the men with whom they are associated. Mândânâ, for instance, was the mother of Cyrus, Tahmine, the mother of Sohrâb, Rudâbe, the mother of Rostam, and so on. As mentioned above, Iranian women's names emphasize beauty, rarity, and the feminine virtues: Zibâ, "beautiful," Marjân, "coral," Zhâle, "dew," Narges, "narcissus," Shirin, "sweet," Hâle, "halo," Mahshid, "moonlight," Nâhid, "Venus (Anahita)." It goes without saying that this issue, like many other cultural aspects, is constantly in flux as the sociopolitical situation changes.

Surnames

A surname may be a single word but usually consists of two parts: A name and a suffix which marks that name as a surname. Masculine names are the most common source of such names, but there are many others as well. The village, town, or region of one's origin, a father's title or occupation, or his tribal affiliation are also common. Finally, many surnames are taken from the names of virtues like bravery, piety, manliness, loyalty. One of the most influential figures in the history of modern Iranian prose is Sâdeq Hedâyat, whose name, when translated, sounds like that of one of the pilgrim fathers of the Iranian people, "Truthful Guidance."

The following suffixes convert names into family names:

/í/ Final stressed /í/: Mohammad becomes Mohammadi, Esfandiâr becomes Esfandiâri, Rahim becomes Rahimi, and so on. /nezhad/ This suffix means something like "race," or "nation." It may be added directly to a word, Paknezhâd, or as a second item after the stressed /í/—Mohammadínezhâd, Iraninezhâd. /zade/. "Born of" behaves exactly like *nezhad*-- Hasanzâde, Hasanizâde. /pur/ "son of". It, too, may be added either directly to a name or to the stressed /í/ It may also precede as well as follow a name--Purmohammadi, Mohammadipur. /iân/. This is thought of exclusively as an Armenian suffix in the West, but it is Iranian as well, although its etymology is different. The /-iân/ suffix is attached to a wide variety of names-- Rahimiân, Sâdeqiân, Mohammadiân, Tehrâniân.

Lesson Seven *MODERN PERSIAN* درس هفتم

Here are a few more examples of categories of surnames:

Place names: The names Khomeini, Rafsanjâni, and Khâmenei are formed from the names of small towns in the provinces of Esfahan, Fars, and Azerbaijan, respectively. Khorasani is itself the name of a province. Tehrâniân and Esfahâniân are taken from well known cities.

Titles

Mohammad Mosaddeq's name was originally his title Mosaddeq od-Dowle, which he was given as the Qajar governor of Shiraz. The ancestor of all those presently named Farmânfarmâiân was named Firuz. He was a minister of great authority in the Qajar court with the title Farmânfarmâ, which means roughly "the one who issues edicts." Sheikholeslâm, a high religious authority, yields the name Sheikholeslâmi, and so on.

Professions

Crafts and professions are a common source of surnames. For example, the professions of attorney, *vækil*, physician, *tæbib*, merchant, *bazærgan*, and engineer, *mohændes* yield the names Vakili, Tabibzâdeh or Tabibi, Bâzârgân and Mohandesi.

Virtues

Again, here is a small sample of a large category: Matini "firmness, resolve," Vafâ, "faithfulness," Javânmardi, "manliness, bravery," Sâdeqi, "truthfulness," Mo'men, "a pious man," Arjomand, "worthy, valuable," Tavakkoli, "trusting in God," E'temâd, "confidence."

There are many other possibilities. Some names are associated with particular religious groups and tribes, others have regional associations. In addition, there are many Turkish names and Turkish elements common in Iran, since more than a third of the population is Turkish speaking. There are also Armenian, Jewish, and Zoroastrian names that reveal the religious affiliation of their bearers to anyone who knows how to read them. However, to pursue all those possibilities would take us well beyond the scope of this introduction. Here are the Persian forms of the Iranian names given above, in addition to a few others:

Lesson Seven   *MODERN PERSIAN*   درس هفتم

اسمهای ایرانی

نام آقایان:

سیروس، داریوش، کامبیز، شاپور، اردشیر

محمد، محمود، علی، حسن، حسین، رضا، علیرضا، کریم، ناصر، غلام، غلامعلی

نام خانمها:

پروانه، پروین، پوران، پریچهر، نیلوفر، هاله، پانته آ، آذر، مهین، پوران دخت، پروین دخت، سارا، عاطفه، نادره، خدیجه، فاطمه، زهرا، زُهره، ثُریّا، شهلا

نام هایی از *شاهنامه*:

مرد: رستم، سهراب، سیاوش، اسفندیار جمشید، فریدون، هوشنگ، پرویز، خسرو

زن: ماندانا، تهمینه، رودابه، زیبا، ژاله، نرگس، شیرین، هاله، مهشید، ناهید (اناهیتا)

نام خانوادگی:

یگانه، مینوی، شیرازی، کرمانی، کریمی، کامرانی، محمدی، اسفندیاری، رحیمی، زنگنه، پاکنژاد، محمدی نژاد، ایرانی نژاد، حسینزاده، پورمحمدی، محمدی پور، صادقیان، محمدیان، تهرانیان، رفسنجانی، خامنه ای، خراسانی، مصدق، ساعتچی، وکیلی، طبیب زاده، پزشک زاده، بازرگان، متینی، صادقی، مؤمن، ارجمند، سروش

For additional information on Iranian/Islamic names, we refer you to the following sources:

    The articles *ism, kunya, laqab* in <u>The Encyclopedia of Islam</u>, 2nd edition.

    Schimmel, Annemarie, <u>Islamic Names</u>, Edinburgh University Press, 1989, Edinburgh.

Lesson Seven *MODERN PERSIAN* درس هفتم

Painting from the Shahnameh

7.13 Long Dialogue ۷/۱۳۰ مکالمه بلند

This is the conclusion of the dialogue begun in 6.13.

(بعداً در آنتراکت حسین و توماس بیرون میروند. "/anterákt/ "entr'acte, intermission
حسین سیگار میکشد و توماس کانادا میخورد. امشب آقای کاظمی هم در تآتر است.
آقای کاظمی با حسین کار میکند. الان میاید و با حسین حرف میزند.)

Lesson Seven — درس هفتم

کاظمی:	آقای جعفری، سلام! حال شما چطوره؟
حسین:	آقای کاظمی، سلام! حال شما؟ من خوبم. حال شما چطوره؟
کاظمی:	مرسی. متشکرم.
حسین:	آقایون، شما آشنا هستین؟
توماس:	توماس.
کاظمی:	کاظمی قربان.
توماس:	خیلی خوشوقتم.
کاظمی:	منم خوشوقتم. شما امریکایی هستین؟
توماس:	بله قربان. من امریکایی ام.
کاظمی:	ماشا لله. خیلی قشنگ فارسی حرف میزنین.
توماس:	خواهش میکنم.
کاظمی:	نه. والله. تعارف نمیکنم.
توماس:	به نظر شما، این فیلم چطوره؟
کاظمی:	به نظر من، خیلی جالبه.
توماس:	منم فکر میکنم جالبه.
حسین:	بله. آقای کاظمی. آقای توماس میگند که بعضی اوقات در فیلم فارسی حرف میزنند و ایشون نمیفهمند.
کاظمی:	بله، راست میگند، خوب ترجمه نمیکنند.
توماس:	نه، آقا. خوب ترجمه میکنند. خوبم دوبله میکنند. فقط بعضی اوقات تند حرف میزنند و من نمیفهمم.
کاظمی:	آقای توماس، معذرت میخوام، سینما در امریکا چنده؟
توماس:	خیلی گرونه. حتماً هفت - هشت دلاره.
حسین:	راست میگین؟
توماس:	بله. گرونه.
کاظمی:	آقای جعفری، دوستتون خیلی قشنگ فارسی حرف میزنند!
حسین:	بله. مثل بلبل حرف میزنند.

329

توماس: خواهش میکنم. من هنوز خیلی کم میدونم. مثلاً میام سینما، نمیفهمم.

کاظمی: ولی لهجهٔ فارسیتون خیلی خوبه.

توماس: خواهش میکنم.

۷/۱۳/۱ خواندن و نوشتن

اسم من سوزان است. من آمریکایی هستم و حالا در ایالت واشنگتن زندگی میکنم. اصلاً اهل پنسیلوانیا هستم و پدر و مادرم هنوز در فیلادلفیا زندگی میکنند. من در کتابخانهٔ دانشگاه واشنگتن کار میکنم. یعنی من کتابدار هستم و با کتابهای عربی و فارسی کار میکنم. من از عربی بهتر حرف میزنم ولی حالا سر کلاس فارسی هم یاد میگیرم. من فوق لیسانسِ کتابداری دارم ولی حالا برای دکترای زبانهای خاورِ میانه[1] درس میخوانم.

الآن ماهِ ژانویه[2] است و من در ماهِ ژوئن[3] برای دکترایم امتحان های عربی و فارسی دارم ولی هنوز حاضر نیستم برای اینکه هنوز فارسی خوب نمیدانم. البته من در کتابخانه بیشتر با کتابهای عربی کار میکنم. برای کار کتابخانهٔ ما، زبان عربی خیلی مهم[4] است ولی زبان فارسی برای من شخصاً[5] بسیار مهم است.

من شب های دوشنبه و پنجشنبه[6] در یکی از بیمارستانهای شهرِ[7] سیاتل داوطلبانه[8] کار میکنم و در بیمارستان خیلی ایرانی می بینم. بعضی اوقات از جامعهٔ[9] ایرانی، بیمارانی[10] به بیمارستان می‌آیند که انگلیسی نمیدانند. من از آنها به فارسی سؤال میکنم و برای دکترها ترجمه میکنم. البته فارسیِ من صد در صد[11] درست نیست ولی کارها همیشه درست میشود[12]. هر هفته در بیمارستان کمی بیشتر فارسی یاد میگیرم. به طورِ کلی،[13] این کارِ داوطلبانه برای من بسیار رضایت بخش[14] است.

1. Middle East (khavær-e miane) 2. January (zhanvie) 3. June (zhuæn) 4. important (mohemm) 5. personally (shækhsæn) 6. Monday and Thursday 7. city (shæhr) 8. as a volunteer (davtælæbane) 9. community (jamee) 10. (some) patients (bimaráni) 11. 100% /sæd dær sæd/

Lesson Seven   *MODERN PERSIAN*   درس هفتم

12. things always work out /karha hæmishe dorost míshævæd. /(kara hæmishe doróst mìshe.)

13. in general /be tór-e kolli/   14. rewarding, satisfying /rezayætbækhsh/

۷/۱۳/۲ پرسش

۱. سوزان در کدام ایالت زندگی میکند؟

۲. در کتابخانه چکار میکند؟

۳. در بیمارستان چکار میکند؟

۴. در دانشگاه چکار میکند؟

۵. سوزان فوق لیسانسِ زبان عربی دارد؟

۶. شما فوق لیسانس دارید؟

۷. زبان عربی برای شما مهم است؟ چرا/چرا نه؟

۸. سوزان چرا فارسی یاد میگیرد؟

۹. شما چرا فارسی یاد میگیرید؟

۱۰. شما فکر میکنید سوزان سه شنبه شب چکار میکند؟

۱۱. شما هم مثل سوزان جایی* کار داوطلبانه میکنید؟   */jái/ "somewhere"

7.15 Writing Persian   ۷/۱۵ نوشتن فارسی

7.15.1 Spoken/Written Transformations: Exercises ۷/۱۵/۱ گفتاری به نوشتاری

(key after Lesson 16)

Examples --Note the contrast in the colloquial and FWP forms of the following sentences:

FWP	Colloquial
دوستهای پدرتان نان میخواهند.	دوستای پدرتون نون میخواند.

Convert the following sentences in Colloquial Persian to their usual FWP counterpart:

۱ - رضا میگه که فرشته امروز میاد سینما.

۲ - استادمون میگه که درس دوازده حاضره.

۳ - معذرت میخوام، شما ساعت دارین؟

۴ - معلمتون کجا درس میده؟

۵ - لطفاً بگید کدوم شاگردا فارسی میخونند.

Lesson Seven *MODERN PERSIAN* درس هفتم

۶ – اونا با شما میرند مازندران؟
۷ – دوستشون نون میخواد ولی نمیره مغازه.
۸ – کامران روزا کار میکنه و شبا درس میخونه.
۹ – استاد محمدی حتماً قهوه میخواد.
۱۰ – تو میدونی که اونا بعد از ظهرا در کتابخونه درس میخونند؟

7.16 Composition ۷٫۱۶ انشا

Write a brief composition about yourself, similar to "Suzanne's Story." Try to stay within the limits of the grammatical patterns that you know up to this point.

Some common spices used in Persian dishes

Optional Reading: Recipes for Rice and Eggplant Sauce

To read the following recipes, you should know the imperative form (these are in written form). To make an imperative form, add a ب to the present stem. For plural, add the plural ending as well.

Glossary	Imperative, plural	Imperative, singular	Infinitive
	بروید	برو	رفتن (to go)
	بشویید	بشوی	شستن (to wash)
	بخیسانید	بخیسان	خیساندن (to soak)
	اضافه کنید	اضافه کن	اضافه کردن (to add)
	بهم بزنید	بهم بزن	بهم زدن (to mix)

Lesson Seven — *MODERN PERSIAN* — درس هفتم

ریختن (to pour)	بریز	بریزید
آوردن (to bring)	بیاور	بیاورید
کنار گذاشتن (to set aside)	کنار بگذار	کنار بگذارید
بریدن (to cut)	بر	ببرید
سرخ کردن (to fry)	سرخ کن	سرخ کنید
کم کردن (to decrease)	کم کن	کم کنید
پختن (to cook)	پز	بپزید

طرز تهیه چلو ساده برای چهار نفر
(plain rice recipe, for four)

مواد لازم (ingredients)

برنج: ۲/۵ فنجان   کره یا روغن: نیم فنجان

نمک: ۴ قاشق سوپ خوری

برنج (uncooked rice) را بشویید و بعد آن را در آب با دو قاشق سوپ خوری نمک برای یک ساعت بخیسانید (soak). بعد آب آن را دور بریزید. دو لیتر آب بجوشانید و دو قاشق سوپ خوری نمک به آن اضافه کنید. بعد برنج خیس را به آب جوش اضافه کنید و برای پانزده تا بیست دقیقه آن را بپزید. در این مدت چند بار برنج را بهم بزنید (mix). دیگ را از روی اجاق (stove) بردارید و برنج را در یک آبکش (colander, صافی) بریزید و آن را با آب سرد آبکش (strain it) کنید (بشویید). مقداری کره آب شده یا روغن در ته دیگ (pot) بریزید و سه قاشق آب به آن اضافه کنید. برنج پخته شده و آب کشیده را (که حالا چلو می باشد) بشکل یک گنبد (dome) روی آب و روغن بریزید و مقداری کره یا روغن روی آن بریزید. در دیگ را بگذارید و برای مدت پانزده دقیقه چلو را بپزید و سپس حرارت اجاق را کم کنید و با حرارت ملایم (low heat) آن را برای ۳۵ دقیقه دیگر بپزید. در این ۳۵ دقیقه چلو دم می کشد (will be steamed).

طرز تهیه خورش بادنجان برای چهار نفر
(eggplant sauce for four)

Lesson Seven — *MODERN PERSIAN* — درس هفتم

مواد لازم (ingredients)

بادنجان (eggplant): سه عدد — گوشت تکه شده: نیم کیلو

پیاز (onion): یک عدد — رب گوجه فرنگی (tomato paste): یک و نیم فنجان

نمک: یک قاشق چایخوری — فلفل: نیم قاشق چایخوری

روغن: شش قاشق سوپخوری — کره: دو قاشق سوپخوری

گوجه فرنگی: یک دانه — عصاره لیمو ترش (lemon essence): سه قاشق سوپخوری

آب: یک فنجان — دارچین کوبیده و زرد چوبه: هرکدام نیم قاشق چایخوری

بادنجان ها را پوست بگیرید (peel) و آنها را از درازا (from their length) ببرید. کمی نمک روی آنها بپاشید و برای ۲۰ دقیقه کنار بگذارید (put them aside). کره را در دیگ آب کنید (melt) و پیاز را در آن سرخ کنید (fry) و سپس گوشت را همراه با ادویه ها در آن بریزید و کمی سرخ کنید. سپس رب گوجه فرنگی و آب را اضافه کنید و همه را برای ۴۰ دقیقه با حرارت کم بپزید. بادنجانها را بشویید و با دستمال خشک کنید (dry) و سپس آنها را جداگانه (separately) در روغن سرخ کنید. حدود پانزده دقیقه پیش از صرف غذا، بادنجان سرخ شده (fried eggplants) و قطعه های گوجه فرنگی (cut tomatoes) را به گوشت اضافه کنید و با گرمای ملایم بپزید.

| Lesson Eight | درس هشتم |

TOPICS COVERED IN THIS LESSON

- Fields of Study: What are you studying? Medicine, history, art, political science, archeology, anthropology, mathematics, linguistics, etc.

- Do you know how to? Do you like to: Paint, sew, cook, do carpentry work, do photography, drive, dance the polka, play the piano, type, ski, work with computers, tinker with cars, read music, etc.

- Classroom Expressions: Affirmative, Negative, Singular, Plural, Sentence, Word, Example. Write it together (as one word), separately, etc.

- Identification of Places: Where are we? In a university, in a classroom, etc.

- Work with Pictures: Where is this? It's the Sears Tower in Chicago. It's Tehran. It's the former Soviet Union. etc.

RESOURCES AND BACKGROUND: INFORMATION AND ACCURACY

Phonology

/:/ and /h/ continued and concluded

Grammar Patterns to Be Drilled

Verbs

"to know" — forms and usage of: شناخت/شناس، بلد بود، دانست/دان

The variants of "to be" (Present):

/-st/ after words ending in /-a/: کجاست؟

Noun Phrase

Plural of Nouns

Extended *ezafe* Constructions

N + N + N (+N): برادرِ شوهرِ دوستِ (استادِ) من

N + adjective + possessive ending (continued): کتابِ قرمزم

endings in Combination with Nouns/Adjectives: دانشجوشون، دانشجواند

Lesson Eight *MODERN PERSIAN* درس هشتم

    Sentence Patterns

        both ___ and ___   هم ___ هم ___

    Word-Building

        Professions and Professionals

Spoken Written Transformations, Part III

    Rules Affecting Phonology

        /i/ = /e/

        /o/ = /ow/

    Changes for Individual Words

    Rules Affecting Grammatical Categories

    Counting People and Objects

Grammar Discussion

    Verb Phrase and Noun Phrase

        Endings in Combination with Roots Ending in Vowels

    Noun Phrase

        Plural of nouns: Persian and Arabic Plurals

Cultural Materials

    Poetry and Proverbs

    Shi'ite Islam

Lesson Eight   *MODERN PERSIAN*   درس هشتم

8.1 Phonology: (:) and (h) (concluded)

In this final lesson on the glottal stop /:/ and /h/, we will describe what happens when they occur between two vowels or a consonant and a vowel.

When /:/ occurs between two vowels it is elided in most styles of both colloquial and FWP usage. When /h/ occurs between two vowels, it is pronounced in FWP usage and careful colloquial, but often elided in rapid colloquial. /:/ is also occasionally pronounced in this position in some very careful colloquial and FWP usages, but much less so than /h/.

Lesson 8, Pronunciation Drill 1: Imitation of (V:V => VV)

Colloquial   **FWP**

moællem	saæt	shaer	bæid	بعید	شاعر	ساعت	معلم
sæid	shour	soal	motmæen	شعور	معین	مطمئن	سؤال

The tomb of Hafez, a poet of Shiraz

Lesson Eight　　　　　　　　MODERN PERSIAN　　　　　　　درس هشتم

Lesson 8, Pronunciation Drill 2: Imitation of VhV　　　درس ۸ تمرین تلفظ ۲

(in fairly rapid and slightly more careful colloquial speech)

	Colloquial				FWP	
moændes	no-o nim	tæ-e del		ته دل	نه و نیم	مهندس
mohændes	noh-o nim	tæh-e del				
rái	bæchea	fokai		فکاهی	بچه ها	راهی
ráhi	bæcheha	fokahi				

When /:/ and /h/ occur between a consonant and a vowel they are pronounced in FWP, and in colloquial they are either pronounced or elided depending, again, on the rapidity of speech and the frequency of occurence of the word being used. There is another factor to consider here, as well: the preceding consonant. When /:/ and /h/ occur after stops /p, t, k, b, d, g, q/ and affricates /c, j/, they are dropped in colloquial usage, and there is no phonetic compensation. This combination is more common with /h/ than with /:/.

When /:/ and /h/ occur after other consonants — /f, v, s, z, sh, zh, kh, m, n, l, r, y, h/ — they may or may not be pronounced depending on the factors already mentioned.

Lesson 8, Pronunciation Drill 3: Imitation of C'V　　　درس ۸ تمرین تلفظ ۳

	Colloquial					FWP	
tæbi	qæti	khode	væqe	وقعه	خدعه	قطعی	طبعی
tæb:i	qæt:i	khod:e	væq:e				
ælan	jome	ænam	soræt	سرعت	انعام	جمعه	الآن
æl:an	jom:e	æn:am	sor:æt				
qoran	æsæd	jæmæn	shéyi	شیئی/شی‌ءای	جمعاً	اسعد	قرآن
qor:an	æs:æd	jæm:æn	shéy:i				

338

Lesson Eight   *MODERN PERSIAN*   درس هشتم

Lesson 8, Pronunciation Drill 4: Imitation of Ch. V   درس ۸ تمرین تلفظ ۴
Colloquial* FWP

| mæshæd sæfe | shæri | solamiz | صلح آمیز | شرحی | صفحه | مشهد |
| mæshhæd | shærhi | solamiz |

* Many of these words are not heard in everyday conversation and will therefore not necessarily conform to colloquial pronunciation.

Note: The /h/ in هم "too, also" and in the ها plural marker is inevitably elided in normal speech. These two occurrences are of such common usage that to pronounce the /h/ except when reading aloud sounds artificial. Of course, when /hæm/ in initial position, as it is when it means "both...and..." *(hæm farsi bælæd-e hæm torki)*, the /h/ is pronounced. See Sections 7.9.1, 8.11.1 for fuller information on the pronunciation of these two particles.

8.2 Vocabulary ۸/۲

(گفتاری) و نوشتاری

Vocabulary, Dialogue 8   مکالمه ۸

yéki æz (+ plural noun)	یکی از	one of
reshte	رشته	field (of study)
ce___´-ì (unstressed /i/)	چه ــ ی	what (noun)? which (noun)?
bastanshenasi	باستانشناسی	archaeology
ælaqe	علاقه	interest, liking, affection
ælaqé dáræm	علاقه دارم	I am interested (in), I like, I'm fond (of)
ælaqe dasht/dar (be)	علاقه داشت/ دار (به)	to be interested (in), to like, be fond (of)
hæm___hæm___	هم ــ هم ــ	both___and___

339

Lesson Eight *MODERN PERSIAN* درس هشتم

bælǽd-æm [1]	بلدم	I know, I know how (to) (See note)
bælæd bud/Ø	بلد بود	

Vocabulary, Drills Part I تمرینات، قسمت ۱

hæme (requires a plural verb)	همه	everyone, all
hæmé-ye ___ [2]	همهٔ ___	all ___s, all the ___s (followed by a plural noun, generally **animate**)
tæmám-e ___ [2]	تمامِ ___	the whole ___ (sg), all (of) the ___ (pl) (followed by any noun)
khareji	خارجی	foreign (adj), foreigner (n)
bæ:zi oqat	بعضی اوقات	sometimes
hæmishe	همیشه	always
ja	جا	place, room, space; seat
hæfte	هفته	week
(yeshæmbe)	(یه شنبه)	Sunday
<u>yekshæmbe</u>	یکشنبه	
tarikh	تاریخ	history
she:r	شعر	poetry, poem, song, lyric
ædæbiat	ادبیات	literature
mærdomshenas	مردمشناس	anthropologist
mohændes	مهندس	engineer
næqqash	نقاش	painter
khæyyat	خیاط	seamstress, tailor
næjjar	نجار	carpenter
pezeshk	پزشک	physician
tækhæssos	تخصص	specialty

340

Lesson Eight *MODERN PERSIAN* درس هشتم

| motækhæsses | متخصص | specialist |
| æslæn (2) (negative) | اصلاً | (not) at all (with negative verb) |

Iranian Personal Names

Men's Names (see also section 7.12, Iranian Names)

جلال	jælal	سیروس	sirus	قاسم	qasem
بیژن	bizhæn	غلامحسین	qolamhoseyn	عبدالله	æbdollah
جعفر	jæ:fær	مرتضی³	morteza	هوشنگ	hushæng

Women's Names (see also section 7.12, Iranian Names)

فریده	færide	مینا	mina	ثریا	soræyya
ژاله	zhale	منیژه	mænizhe	زهرا	zæhra
فریبا	færiba	سهیلا	soheyla	سیما	sima

Family Names (see also section 7.12, Iranian Names)

| نوری | nuri | علیزاده | ælizade | پارسا | parsa |
| صبا | sæba | محمدی | mohæmmædi | نوربخش | nurbækhsh |

Vocabulary Field: Specialists and Specialties for Drills, Part I, Practical
Drills and Drills, Part II (See Vocabulary Building, section 8.5)

متخصص   تخصص

جامعه شناس	jame:eshenas	sociologist	جامعه شناسی	jame:eshenasi	sociology
مردمشناس	mærdomshenas	anthropologist	مردمشناسی	mærdomshenasi	anthropology
روانشناس	rævanshenas	psychologist	روانشناسی	rævanshenasi	psychology
باستانشناس	bastanshenas	archaeologist	باستانشناسی	bastanshenasi	archaeology
ایرانشناس	iranshenas	Iranist	ایرانشناسی	iranshenasi	Iranian studies
موسیقی شناس	musiqishenas	musicologist	زیست شناسی	zist shenashi	biology
(موسیقی دون)	(musiqidun)		موسیقی	musiqi	music
موسیقی دان	*musiqidan*	musician	زبانشناس	zæbanshenas	linguist

341

Lesson Eight   *MODERN PERSIAN*   درس هشتم

zæbanshenasi	linguistics	زبانشناسی	joqrafi	geography	جغرافی
joqrafia	geography	جغرافیا	eqtesad	economics	اقتصاد
riazi/riaziat	mathematics	ریاضی/ریاضیات			

متخصص   تخصص

mohændes	engineer	مهندس	mohændesi	engineering	مهندسی
ketabdar	librarian	کتابدار	ketabdari	library science	کتابداری
næqqash	painter	نقاش	næqqashi	painting	نقاشی
khæyyat	seamstress, tailor	خیاط	khæyyati	sewing	خیاطی
næjjar	carpenter	نجار	næjjari	carpentry	نجاری
ashpæz	cook, chef	آشپز	ashpæzi	cooking	آشپزی
ækkas	photographer	عکاس	ækkasi	photography	عکاسی
pezeshk	physician	پزشک	pezeshki	medicine(field)	پزشکی
(dændunpezeshk)		(دندون پزشک)	(dændunpezeshki)		(دندون پزشکی)
dændanpezeshk dentist		ندان پزشک	*dændanpezeshki* dentistry		دندان پزشکی

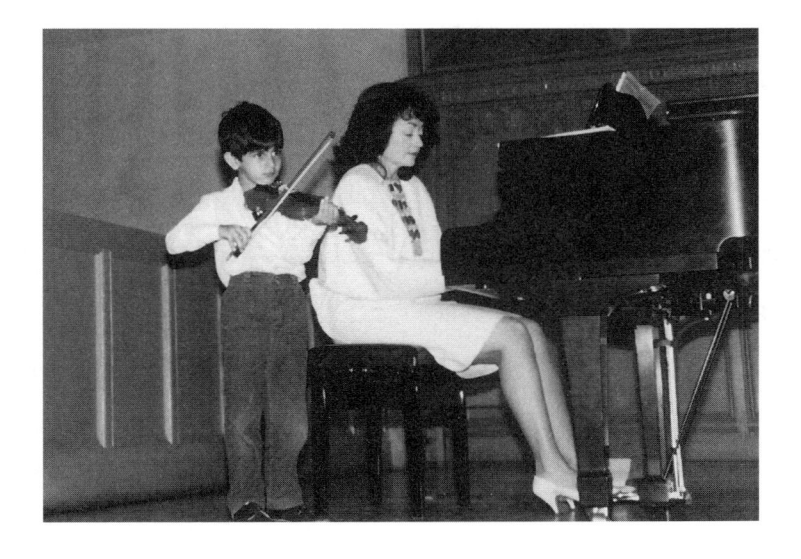

Musiqidan

Lesson Eight *MODERN PERSIAN* درس هشتم

Other Fields of Study and Related Words

honær	هنر	art
taríkh-e honær	تاریخ هنر	art history
olúm-e siasi	علوم سیاسی	political science
hoquq	حقوق	law (other than Qur:anic)
qor:an	قرآن	Koran/Qur'an
din	دین	religion
fælsæfe	فلسفه	philosophy
amuzésh-o pærværesh	آموزش و پرورش	education (as a field of study)
næqqashi kærd/kon	نقاشی کرد/کن	to paint
khæyyati kærd/kon	خیاطی کرد/کن	to sew, to work as a tailor, seamstress
ashpæzi kærd/kon	آشپزی کرد/کن	to cook (intr, does not take object)
ækkasi kærd/kon	عکاسی کرد/کن	to do photography, to be in photography
tæhqiq kærd/kon	تحقیق کرد/کن	to do research

Vocabulary, Drills Part II تمرینات، قسمت ۲

folut	فلوت	flute
mæhæl(l)	محل (جا)	place, locale
mæhæll-e kar	محلِّ کار	place of work
(aqayon)	(آقایون)	sirs, gentlemen
<u>aqayan</u>	آقایان	
shæhr	شهر	city
ranænde	راننده	driver
ranændegi	رانندگی	driving

343

Lesson Eight *MODERN PERSIAN* درس هشتم

bazar	بازار	market, bazaar
zist shenasi	زیست شناسی	biology

Classroom Expressions: Vocabulary for Drills and Grammar

mænfi	منفی	negative
mosbæt	مثبت	affirmative, positive
væ qeyre	و غیره	and so on, et cetera (Arab: "and others")
mofræd	مفرد	singular
jæm(:)	جمع	plural
jomle	جمله	sentence
loqæt (vazhe)	لغت (واژه)	word
nemune	نمونه	example
qesmæt	قسمت	section, part
hæst [4]	هست	there is, there are
sær-e hæm	سر هم	joined, together, connected
sær-e hæm bénevisid	سر هم بنویسید	Write (it/them) all together/connected.
joda/joda-joda	جدا/جدا جدا	separate, separately
joda(-joda) bénevisid	جدا (جدا) بنویسید	Write (it/them) separately
joda kærd/kon	جدا کرد/کن	to separate

Vocabulary Notes:

1. **to know** There are three verbs in Persian that are equivalent to English "to know." (1) دانست/دان, which you already know, is used for knowing facts, languages, and other general items.

من فارسی میدانم.(من فارسی میدونم.)   I know Persian.

Lesson Eight   MODERN PERSIAN   درس هشتم

Ali knows where it is. (fact)   علی میدونه کجاست.(علی میداند کجاست.)

a. بلد بود, introduced in this lesson, is a compound verb consisting of an adjective and the verb "to be." It is used to indicate knowledge of trades, skills — including language skills — games and for knowing how to do something in general. This verb is also used for knowing one's way around in a place, or one's way to a place.

I don't know how to sew/cook.   من خیاطی/آشپزی بلد نیستم.

You know Persian well. (i.e. "You know how to speak it well.")   شما فارسی خوب بلدید.

Do you know how to get to Ali's house?   خانه علی را* بلدید؟

In sum, you will use this verb to talk about knowing how to play a sport, how to drive, how to sew, how to play chess, how to speak French, etc. (Note: چطور is never used with this verb in the sense of "know **how** to.")

b. شناخت/شناس, which will be introduced as a verb in Lesson 10, is used (a) when speaking of knowing people, and (b) to express an intimate personal knowledge of something inanimate, as a building, city, neighborhood, or country. This latter usage is more common in colloquial Persian, and is interchangeable with بلد بود. As you can see from the vocabulary for this lesson, the present stem شناس, is also used in many compound nouns that describe specialists and specializations.

It should be stressed that شناخت/شناس is almost always used with people, and بلد بود and دانست/دان **must not be**.

I know Persian.   من فارسی میدانم./من فارسی بلد هستم.

I know Ahmad.   من احمد را* میشناسم.

* Some direct objects in Persian are marked by the suffix را /ra/. On the use of the را /ra/ with direct objects, see section 10.11. The contrast between شناخت/شناس and بلد بود-دانست/دان will be drilled in Lesson 10 (Drills 14-18).

2. **all (of):** There are two important words given in the vocabulary that translate as "all" in

Lesson Eight *MODERN PERSIAN* درس هشتم

English:

   a. hæmé-ye ____/____ همهٔ, as indicated, is followed by a plural, generally **animate**, noun. It implies plurality.

   b. tæmám-e ____/____ تمام can be followed by singular or plural, animate or inanimate nouns. English, of course, uses different words depending on whether the noun that follows is singular ("the whole __") or plural ("all of __") and one phrase for both ("all of the __ sg/pl"). These translations are a problem of English phraseology. The following examples should help you sort out the usage of the two Persian words:

(همهٔ بچه ها اینجاند.)	All the children are here.
(تمامِ بچه ها اینجاند.)	" " " " "
(تمامِ امتحانا سخته.)	All tests are hard./All of the tests are hard.
(تمامِ امتحان سخته.)	The whole test is hard./All of the test is hard.
(تمامِ دانشجوا/همهٔ دانشجوا)	all the students/all of the students/all students
(تمامِ کلاسا/همهٔ کلاسا)	all the classes/all of the classes/all classes
(تمامِ کلاس)	the whole class/all the class/all of the classes/all classes
(تمامِ هفته)	the whole week

3. مرتضی *morteza* There are a few words in Persian, mostly names, that are written with a final ی but pronounced /a/: موسی /musa/, عیسی /isa/, مجتبی /mojtæba/, مصطفی /mostafa/, یحیی /yæhya/.

4. **there is/there are:** Here we give some useful sentences with this verb:

(چند تا لغت رو تخته سیاه هست؟)	How many words are there on the blackboard?
(چند تا سیب رو میز هست؟)	How many apples are on the table?
(چند تا دانشجو سر کلاسمون هست؟)	How many students are there in our class?

Lesson Eight *MODERN PERSIAN* درس هشتم

8.3 Poetry and Proverbs ۸/۳ شعر و مثل

These proverbs and lines of poetry have been chosen to illustrate the grammar or vocabulary taught elsewhere in this lesson.

دیوار موش دارد. موش گوش دارد. *divar mush dare. mush gush dare.*
"The walls have mice. The mice have ears."
("The walls have ears").

سوار از پیاده خبر ندارد. *sævar æz piade khæbær nædare.*
"A man on horseback doesn't understand a man on foot."

سیر از گرسنه خبر ندارد. *sir æz gorosne khæbær nædare.*
"Full doesn't understand hungry."
(An alternate form of the preceding a proverb.)

سگ زرد برادر شغال است. *sæg-e zærd bæradær-e shoqal-e.*
"The yellow dog is brother to the jackal."
("One is as bad as the other." "It's six of one, half dozen of the other").

🔊 8.4 Dialogue 8 مکالمه ۸

The dialogues of Lessons 8 and 9 are presented as two variations on the same form and theme. In this dialogue, Hossein asks Tom about a student whom Tom waves to on their way to the movie. Note that Hossein refers to him as پسر . It is common in informal Persian to use the terms for "boy," "girl," and "kid" to refer to people who are long past their childhood, somewhat as we use "the girls" and "the boys" or "the guys." Thus a person will refer to his/her group of friends/students, and so on as بچه ها . (See 7.4, dialogue).

Lesson Eight *MODERN PERSIAN* درس هشتم

Text and Translation

Hossein:	Who is that guy?	حسین: اون پسر کیه؟
	-á (plural marker)	ا
	one of	یکی از
Tom:	One of Vida's friends.	تام: یکی از دوستای ویداست.
	His name's Jean-Luc.	اسمش ژان لوکه.
Hossein:	Where's he from?	حسین: اهل کجاست؟
Tom:	He's from Canada.	تام: اهل کاناداست.
	what (noun)	چه -- ای
	field (of study)	رشته
Hossein:	Do you know what (field) he's studying?	حسین: تو میدونی چه رشته ای میخونه؟
	archaeology	باستانشناسی
	he's interested in __	به ___ علاقه داره.
Tom:	Yes. He's studying archaeology. And he's very interested in the archaeology of Iran.	تام: بله. باستانشناسی میخونه. به باستانشناسیِ ایرانم خیلی علاقه داره.
	he knows	بلده؟
Hossein:	Does he know Persian well?	حسین: فارسی خوب بلده؟
	both __ and __ (as well as __)	هم ___ هم ___
Tom:	Of course. He knows both Persian as well as English and French.	تام: البته. هم فارسی قشنگ بلده، هم اینگلیسی و هم فرانسه.
Hossein:	Oh, he must be from Montreal.	حسین: خوب، حتما اهل منراله (منتراله).

Text and Transcription

Hossein:	un pesær <u>kí</u>-e?	حسین: اون پسر کیه؟
Tom:	yéki æz dustá-ye vi<u>dast</u>.	تام: یکی از دوستای ویداست.

Lesson Eight   *MODERN PERSIAN*   درس هشتم

	ésmesh zhan<u>lúk</u>-e.	اسمش ژان لوکه.
Hossein:	æhl-e ko<u>jast</u>?	حسین: اهل کجاست؟
Tom:	æhl-e kana<u>dast</u>.	تام: اهل کاناداست.
Hossein:	to <u>mí</u>duni che reshtéi <u>mí</u>une?	حسین: تو میدونی چه رشته ای میخونه؟
Tom:	<u>bæ</u>le. bastanshena<u>si</u> míkhune.	تام: بله. باستانشناسی میخونه.
	irán-æm khéyli æla<u>qé</u> dare.	به باستانشناسیِ ایرانم خیلی علاقه داره.
Hoseyn:	farsi <u>khub</u> bælǽd-e?	حسین: فارسی خوب بلده؟
Tom:	<u>æl</u>bæte. hæm farsi qæ<u>shæng</u> bælǽd-e,	تام: البته. هم فارسی قشنگ بلده،
	hæm inglisío færan<u>se</u>.	هم اینگلیسی و هم فرانسه.
Hoseyn:	khob. hǽtmæn æhl-e	حسین: خب، حتماً اهل منرآله./منترآله.
	monreál-e./montreál-e.	

8.5 Word-Building: Professions and Professionals (All obligatory vocabulary items from this list have been listed in section 8.2)

Professions and Professionals, Specializations and Specialists

The principal way of forming terms in Persian for professionals and specialists of various kinds is to use a compound noun in which the second element is the present stem of one of the verbs meaning "to know" — شناس- /-shenas/ and دان- /-dan/, colloquial (dun). Words formed with شناس- /-shenas/ and دان- /-dan/ refer to those who practice a profession, are masters of a complex set of skills, or specialize in an academic discipline—categories for which English uses the nominal suffixes "-ist," "-ian," and "-ologist." Usually either one stem or the other is used with any given noun, but occasionally two terms are formed in order to make distinction between two similar or closely allied fields.

| زبان دان | *zæbandan* | polyglot | زبانشناس | *zæbanshenas* | linguist |
| موسیقیدان* | *musiqidan* | musician | موسیقی شناس | *musiqishenas* | musicologist |

349

Lesson Eight   *MODERN PERSIAN*   درس هشتم

*You will also encounter the French loan words موزیک /muzik/ "music" and موزیسین /muzisiæn/ "musician."

While the following list is not exhaustive, we have included the names of most of the professions and professionals, special fields and specialists whom you are likely to encounter.

		Specialization	Specialist "-ologist" –شناس		
زبان	zæban	language	زبانشناس	zæbanshenas	linguist
جامعه	jame'e	society	جامعه شناس	jame'eshenas	sociologist
مردم	mærdom	people	مردمشناس	mærdomshenas	anthropologist
روان	rævan	psyche, spirit	روانشناس	rævanshenas	psychologist
باستان	bastan	ancient times	باستانشناس	bastanshenas	archaeologist
ایران	iran	Iran	ایرانشناس	iranshenas	Iranist
زیست	zist	life, living	زیست شناس	zistshenas	biologist

		Specialization	Specialist "-ologist" (–دون) –دان		
جغرافی[1]	joqrafi	geography	جغرافی دان	joqrafidan[2]	geographer
تاریخ	tarikh	history	تاریخ دان	tarikhdan	historian
ریاضی	riazi	mathematics	ریاضی دان	riazidan	mathematician

Notes:

1 also جغرافیا.

2 We have given the FWP pronunciation along with the written forms of the terms for specialists. In colloquial usage the ‐دان /-dan/ generally becomes (‐دون) /-dun/, but not always. You will hear these terms pronounced both ways in colloquial Persian. The choice of which pronunciation depends on the person, their education, and the context in which they are using the word. (See section 6.9.1).

Lesson Eight MODERN PERSIAN درس هشتم

Names of Professions and Specialties

The names of professions, specialties, and crafts in Persian are often derived from the name of the person in that profession by the addition of stressed /-i/ ("-ology" /-shenasi/):

مردمشناس *mardomshenas* anthropologist مردمشناسی *mardomshenasi* anthropology

A list of professionals and the professions derived from them are:

	Specialist "-ologist" شناس			Specialization	
زبانشناس	*zæbanshenas*	linguist	زبانشناسی	*zæbanshenasi*	linguistics
جامعه شناس	*jame'eshenas*	sociologist	جامعه شناسی	*jame'eshenasi*	sociology
روانشناس	*rævanshenas*	psychologist	روانشناسی	*rævanshenasi*	psychology
باستانشناس	*bastanshenas*	archaeologist	باستانشناسی	*bastanshenasi*	archaeology

Not all such terms end in شناسی– or دان–. However for many of those which don't, the term for the person who practices the skill or profession is formed by dropping the stressed /-í/:

	Specialist			Specialization	
مهندس	mohændes	engineer	مهندسی	mohændesi	engineering
کتابدار	ketabdar	librarian	کتابداری	ketabdari	library science
خبرنگار	khæbærnegar	reporter, journalist	خبرنگاری	khæbærnegari	journalism
آشپز	ashpæz	cook, chef	آشپزی	ashpæzi	cooking, cuisine
پزشک	pezeshk	physician	پزشکی	pezeshki	medicine (field)
دندان پزشک	dændanpezeshk	dentist	دندان پزشکی	dændanpezeshki	dentistry

The following are some other fields of study and associated words you should learn:

تخصص	tækhæssos	specialty	متخصص	motækhæsses	specialist
هنر	honær	art	تاریخ هنر	taríkh-e honær	art history
علوم سیاسی	olúm-e siasi	political science	حقوق	hoquq	law (as a field)
قرآن	qor:an	Qur'an	دین	din	religion
آموزش و پرورش	amuzésh-o pærværesh	education	تعلیم و تربیت	tæ:lim-o tærbiæt	education

351

Lesson Eight *MODERN PERSIAN* درس هشتم

Both آموزش و پرورش *amuzésh-o pærværesh* and تعلیم و تربیت *tæ:lim-o tærbiæt* are used to describe education as an academic field. There are also two other important words:

کارشناس *karshenas* specialist   تحقیق/تحقیقات *tæhqiq(at)* research

Memorize the following verbs which are formed from nouns you met in the previous sections:

نقاشی کرد/کن	*næqqashi kærd/kon*	to paint
خیاطی کرد/کن	*khæyyati kærd/kon*	to sew
آشپزی کرد/کن	*ashpæzi kærd/kon*	to cook
عکاسی کرد/کن	*ækkasi kærd/kon*	to do photography, to be in photography
تحقیق کرد/کن	*tæhqiq kærd/kon*	to do research

(Note: as a noun the plural form (تحقیقات) is preferred, but in the compound verb, the singular form of the noun (تحقیق کرد/کن) is preferred.

8.6 Drills, Part 1   درس ۸، تمرینات، قسمت ۱

Substitution: The verb "to be"/affirmative and negative 1   درس ۸، تمرین ۱

آ. دوستم اهل **آمریکا**ست. (منفی)
    دوستم اهل آمریکا **نیست**.

(کانادا، (مثبت)، کالیفرنیا، اینجا، (منفی)، آریزونا، (مثبت)، ایتالیا، نبراسکا، فیلادلفیا، استرالیا، (منفی)، اوساکا (Osaka)، آمریکا، (مثبت)

ب. **من** اهل آمریکام. (تو)
    تو اهل آمریکایی.

(دوست پدرتون، پدر و مادرتون، تام، ما، کی، شما، پروین، پروین و ویدا، غلامحسین، من و تو، خانوم صبا، (من))

ج. شما اهل چه ایالتی هستید؟ (دانشجو ۱)
    (دانشجو ۱) اهل چه ایالتیه؟

(Continue asking questions about each other, and about other people known to the class.)

Lesson Eight   *MODERN PERSIAN*   درس هشتم

Substitution: The verb "to be"/affirmative and negative   **درس ۸، تمرین ۲**

آ.   جُرج اهل آمریکاست. (من)

من اهل آمریکا**م**. (منفی)

من اهل آمریکا **نیستم**.

(کانادا، شما، (مثبت)، من و برادرم، فیلادلفیا، ایالت واشنگتن، (منفی)، دوستم، ایتالیا، (مثبت)، ایران، اونا، (منفی)، ما، استرالیا، (مثبت)، آریزونا، (منفی)، حسین و رضا، ژاپن، (مثبت)، آمریکا، (جرج))

ب.   **Substitution (Optional)**

من اهل **بلژیک**م. (ایوان/مسکو)

ایوان اهل **مسکو**ه.

(غلامحسین/یزد، ژاله و منیژه/آذربایجان، ادوارد/یوتا، پدر و مادر ماری/کانادا، آقای محمدی/خوزستان، خانوم علیزاده/اینجا، آقای نوربخش/گیلان، زن حمید/عربستان سعودی، خانوم نوری و شوهرش/افغانستان، پانچو/ونزوئلا، آقا و خانم فیلیپس/آلاباما، خانوم جونز/کُلُرادو، آقای جونز/ایندینا، ماریا/پرو، آقای پتروویچ/یوگوسلاوی، (من/بلژیک))

درس ۸، تمرین ۳

آ.   **علی** چرا **تنها**ست؟ (شما/اینجا)

شما چرا **اینجا**یین؟

(ما/تنها، من/اینجا، بچه ها/تنها، مداد/اونجا، این آقایون/اینجا، نون/سیا، دخترا/اونجا، (علی/تنها))

ب.   اسم دوست ایرانیم **رضا**ست. (پروین)

اسم دوست ایرانیم **پروین**ه.

(سیما، کامران، ارژنگ، هوشنگ، غلامحسین، سهیلا، فریبا، جعفر، زهرا، ثریا، پانته آ، مرتضی، مینا، بیژن، عبدالله، قاسم، (رضا))

ج.   **دانشجو** ۱: اسم دوست ایرانیون چیه؟   **دانشجو** ۲: جواب آزاد

(Continue to ask each other questions about Iranians you know.)

Lesson Eight   *MODERN PERSIAN*   درس هشتم

Imitation   درس ۸، تمرین ۴

آ.   دوست   ======   دوستا   ======   دوستاتون

     استاد   استادا   استاداشون

     پسر   پسرا   این پسرا

     خواهر   خواهرا   خواهراش

     بچه   بچه ها   بچه هامون

     ایرانی   ایرانیا   اون ایرانیا

     معلم   معلما   معلمات

     عکس   اون عکسا   اون عکساشون

     زن   اون زنا   زن

     جا   جاها   جاهاتون

     کتاب   کتابا   کتابارو ببندید

ب.   دوستاتون کجا زندگی میکنند؟   بچه هاشون شب و روز درس میخونند.

     شاگردامون چرا بلند حرف میزنند؟   اون مردا همه اهل واشنگتنند.

     اون زنا باهم میرند سر کار.   این خارجیا فارسی یاد میگیرند.

     دوستاتون کی میرند ایران؟   استاداشون اصلاً (هیچی) وقت ندارند.

     این بچه ها دوباره مریضند.   دکترا الآن مطمئنند؟

     خواهرام گیلکی* حرف میزنند   بچه هام دوچرخهء سرمه ای دارند.

     *(گیلکی/gilæki/)   یکی از زبانهای ایرانی است.)

Transformation: Singular to Plural   درس ۸، تمرین ۵   مُفْرَد به جَمْع

دوستتون کجا زندگی میکنه؟   ======   دوستاتون کجا زندگی میکنند؟

معلمتون فارسی حرف میزنه؟   پس این دانشجو تاریخ میخونه؟

اون نجار خیلی تند کار میکنه.   برادرتون هنوز مریضه؟

اون مرد امشب شام نمیخوره.   استادشون کجائیه؟

دوستم این هفته غذا درست میکنه.   دخترش فعلاً ریاضی میخونه؟

Lesson Eight   *MODERN PERSIAN*   درس هشتم

اون زن عبری میدونه؟	برادر منیژه یکشنبه ساعت چار میاد؟
این زن از اینجا نسبتاً دور زندگی میکنه.	شاگردش بعضی اوقات شعر فارسی مینویسه.
اون خانوم اهل این ایالت نیست.	این خارجی فارسی خوب حرف میزنه.
نقاش چی میخواد؟	دوست ایرانیم بعد از ظهرا استراحت میکنه.

درس ۸، تمرین ۶   *Cued Question/Answer*

آ. دانشجو ۱: این پسر دانشجواه؟   دانشجو ۲: بله، همهء این **پسرا دانشجو** اند.

(Alternate:)

(دانشجو ۱: این پسر دانشجواه؟   دانشجو ۲: بله، تمامِ این پسرا دانشجو اند.)

(مرد/روانشناس، بچه/مریض، مهندس/ایرانی، زن/خیاط، مرد/نجار، آقا/تنها،
دانشجو/باستانشناس، دکتر/متخصص، استاد/اروپایی، (پسر/دانشجو))

ب. جواب آزاد   (Continue to ask each other questions using the above pattern.)

درس ۸، تمرین ۷   *Expansion*

آقای نوری استاد نیست. (فلسفۀ اروپایی)   ==>   آقای نوری استاد فلسفه اروپایی نیست.

ما دانشجو نیستیم. (رشتۀ تاریخ هنر)	من دانشجو نیستم. (رشتۀ ادبیات)
خانم امامی روانشناس نیست. (بیمارستان دانشگاه)	من متخصص نیستم. (هنر اروپایی)
شما متخصص نیستید. (جامعه شناسی ایران)	این محل کار نیست. (دوست ارمنیم)
پدر و مادرم استاد نیستند. (دانشگاه تبریز)	این دفتر چک نیست. (خانم علیزاده)
این عکس نیست. (دوست حمید)	من کتابدار نیستم. (کتابخانه دانشگاه)
شما کارمند نیستید (بانک ملی*)	

*(ملی/ melli/ = national)

Lesson Eight   *MODERN PERSIAN*   درس هشتم

8.8 Situational and Practical Drills ۸/۸

Cued Question/Answer   درس ۸، تمرین ۸

دانشجو ۱:   شما چه رشته ای میخونید؟

دانشجو ۲:   من **مهندسی** میخونم. شما چطور؟

دانشجو ۱:   من **تاریخ** میخونم.

(پزشکی/روانشناسی، فلسفه/هنر، کتابداری/علوم سیاسی، مردمشناسی/ریاضی، فیزیک/زبانشناسی، تاریخ هنر/جغرافیا، آموزش و پرورش/دین، ایرانشناسی/حقوق، اقتصاد/موسیقی شناسی، جامعه شناسی/باستانشناسی، هنر/ادبیات، (مهندسی/تاریخ))

درس ۸، تمرین ۹   جواب آزاد

دانشجو ۱:   شما چه رشته ای میخونید؟

دانشجو ۲:   من ــــــ میخونم. شما چطور؟

دانشجو ۱:   من ــــــ میخونم.

درس ۸، تمرین ۱۰   جواب آزاد

(This drill is conducted using a variety of pictures indicating various places in the United States, Iran, and the world that students will recognize.)

آ.   معلم/دانشجو ۱:   اینجا کجاست؟

     دانشجو ۲:   اونجا **تهرانه**. (**اسپانیاست**، و غیره)

ب.   معلم/دانشجو ۱:   لندن کجاست؟ (لس آنجلس و غیره)

     دانشجو ۲:   در اینگلیسه.

Lesson Eight　　　　　　*MODERN PERSIAN*　　　　　درس هشتم

8.9 Reading and Writing Persian: Colloquial/FWP Transformations, Part III ۸/۹

Rules Affecting Phonology

8.9.1 /i/ = e　　　　　　　　　　　　　　　　　　　　　　　۸/۹/۱

There is a small but commonly used group of words in which colloquial /i/ in the beginning or middle of a word is /e/ in FWP. There is no rule for determining which words will be affected by this rule. You must memorize them as they occur. Examples:

Colloquial		FWP		
اینگلیسی	/inglisi/	انگلیسی	englisi	"English"
کوچیک	/kucik/	کوچک	kucek	"small, little"
چی	/chi/	چه	che	"what?"
کی	/ki/	که	ke	"who?"
شیش	/shish/	شش	shesh	"six"
شیشصد	/shishsæd/	ششصد	sheshsæd	"six hundred"
بیلیت	/bilit/	بلیت	belit	"ticket"
هیفده	/hivdæh/	هفده	hefdæh	"seventeen"
هیژده	/hizhdæh/	هجده	hejdæh	"eighteen"
دویست	/divist/	دویست	devist	"two hundred"

Note also that the first two question words in writing are generally joined directly to the present tense of the verb "to be" (third person):

Colloquial		FWP		
چیه؟	/chi-e/	چیست؟	chist	"what is it?"
کیه؟	/kí-e/	کیست؟	kist	"who is it?"

See also section 8.9.5 below for the writing of the accompanying pronouns.

Lesson Eight   *MODERN PERSIAN*   درس هشتم

8.9.2 /o/ = ow

A number of Colloquial words that you have learned with an /o/ vowel are represented in FWP with an /ow/ glide:

Colloquial			FWP	
شوهر	/shohær/	شوهر	showhær	"husband"
چطور	/chetor/	چطور	chetowr	"how?"
دوره	/dore/	دوره	dowre	"review"
نوبت	/nobæt/	نوبت	nowbæt	"turn"
چلو	/chelo/	چلو	chelow	"rice (cooked, plain)"
پلو	/polo/	پلو	polow	"rice (cooked, mixed)"
نو روز	/no ruz/	نو روز	now ruz	"Now Ruz"
فوق ليسانس	/foq-e lisans/	فوق ليسانس	fowq-e lisans	"master's degree"
بعضی اوقات	/bæ:zi oqat/	بعضی اوقات	bæ:zi owqat	"sometimes"
برو	/bóro/	برو	bérow	"go!" (singular/familiar imperative)

Note, however, that not all words with /o/ are represented by a glide in FWP:

Colloquial			FWP	
تو	/to/	تو	to	"you (singular)"
پیانو	/piano/	پیانو	piano	"piano"
پالتو	/palto/	پالتو	palto	"(over)coat"

8.9.3 Individual Changes/Isolated Cases

The following individual words are isolated cases of Colloquial/FWP differences. Sometimes the difference is a matter of pronunciation, as colloquial /chai/ (two syllables) is FWP *chay* (one syllable), but it can also be a matter of the whole word. That is, some words are acceptable in colloquial, but not in many styles of FWP. One important example of this is the word /khéyli/ which is replaced in some styles of FWP usage by /besiar/ or /ziad/. In a

Lesson Eight *MODERN PERSIAN* درس هشتم

parallel case, an English equivalent of خیلی, "a lot of," is also not acceptable in many forms of written English. The following examples of isolated words that have special pronunciation in FWP must simply be memorized:

	Colloquial		FWP	
چائی چایی	/chai/ (two syllables)	چای	chay (one syllable)	"tea"
خانوم	/khanum/	خانم	khanum	"Mrs., madam"
یه	/ye(k)/	یک	yek	"one, a"
یه شنبه	/ye(k)shæmbe/	یک شنبه	yekshæmbe	"Sunday"
چار	/char/	چهار	chæhar	"four"
چار صد	/charsæd/	چهار صد	chæharsæd	"four hundred"
چار شنبه	/charshæmbe/	چهار شنبه	chæharshæmbe	"Wednesday"
چل	/chel/	چهل	chehel	"forty"
دیگه	/dige/	دیگر	digær	"other, else"
خورشت	/khoresht/	خورش	khoresh	"khoresh, stew"
دئیقه/دقه	/dæiqe/, /dæqqe/	دقیقه	dæqiqe	"minute"
مشگل	/moshgel/	مشکل	moshgel	"difficult"

(note that this word is pronounced the same in both styles but written differently) and in some styles:

خیلی	/khéyli/	بسیار، زیاد	besiar, ziad	"very, very much"

Rules Affecting Grammatical Categories

8.9.4 Counting People and Objects

You have learned to use the counters *dune*/*ta* for counting people and objects in colloquial Persian, as in:

    Q: chænd-ta ketab darid?   A: ye dune

    Q: chænd-ta moællem darid?   A: do-ta

In some styles of FWP, both of these counters are generally omitted:

Lesson Eight   *MODERN PERSIAN*   درس هشتم

دو شاگرد/دو کتاب   do shagerd/do ketab

You need not assume that this rule takes place across the board in FWP. It occurs only in certain styles. It is often the case, however, even in colloquial Persian, that in counting animate nouns, the counter *dune* is not used with one, but *ta* is used with more than one:

ye moællem, do-ta moællem, se-ta moællem

ye bæradær, do-ta bæradær, se-ta bæradær, etc.

8.9.5 Third Person Singular Pronouns

You saw above in 8.9.1 that

Colloquial		are written	**FWP**	
چیه؟	/chi-e/	چیست؟	<u>cist</u>	"what is it?"
کیه؟	/kí-e/	کیست؟	<u>kist</u>	"who is it?"

You will also remember that the colloquial pronouns change in FWP (see section 3.11.2 The Pronouns of Persian). /un/, aside from its social constraints, changes to او for animates ("he, she") and, according to the regular change of /un/ to /an/, آن for inanimates ("it"). Thus the two colloquial phrases change in two ways in FWP:

Colloquial	**FWP**	
(اون چیه؟)	آن چیست؟	"what is it/that?"
(اون کیه؟)	او کیست؟	"who is he/she?"

For more on the social constraints related to the pronoun /un/, see 9.3.1.

8.9.6 A Colloquial Ending

A stressed /-í/ ending is used in the words چطوری /chetorí/ "how (of means)," and چه رنگی /che rængí/ "(of) what color." This ending in both words is considered colloquial and is generally not written in FWP. Instead, it is simply dropped and these words are written چه رنگ and چطور respectively.

Lesson Eight *MODERN PERSIAN* درس هشتم

Colloquial	FWP
shoma chetori mírin?	شما چطور می روید؟
mashínetun che rængí-e?	ماشینتان چه رنگی است؟

In some styles of written Persian, you may see people write چه رنگی. It is not an expression that often occurs in literary written contexts.

8.10 Drills, Part II   درس ۸ تمرینات، قسمت ۲

درس ۸، تمرین ۱۱

رمان آلمانیم کجاست؟

(کت/قهوه ای، روزنامه/روسی، (ما)، مجله/ایرانی، (تو)، بلوز/آبی، پولوور/سرمه ای، ساعت/ژاپنی، (اون)، (شما)، غذا/ترکی، دفتر/سبز، (اونا)، معلم/فارسی، (من)،گچ /رنگی، (رمان/آلمانی))

Cued Question/Answer   درس ۸، تمرین ۱۲

آ.   **دانشجو ۱:** چرا **زیست شناسی** نمیخونی؟/نمیخونید؟

    دانشجو ۲: برای اینکه اصلاً به **زیست شناسی** علاقه ندارم.

(فلسفه، مردمشناسی، ریاضی، تاریخ، ادبیات، جامعه شناسی، حقوق، اقتصاد، علوم سیاسی، باستانشناسی، کتابداری، جغرافیا، هنر، موسیقی، نقاشی، (زیست شناسی))

ب.   **دانشجو ۱:** شما به ـــــــــ علاقه دارید؟

    دانشجو ۲: جواب آزاد.

(فلسفه، مردمشناسی، ریاضی، تاریخ، ادبیات، جامعه شناسی، حقوق، اقتصاد، علوم سیاسی، باستانشناسی، کتابداری، جغرافیا، هنر، موسیقی، نقاشی، (و غیره))

Transformation   درس ۸، تمرین ۱۳

<u>خانومتون</u> فارسی بلده؟ (منفی)

خانومتون فارسی بلد نیست؟ (دوستا)

Lesson Eight *MODERN PERSIAN* درس هشتم

دوستاتون فارسی بلد نیستند؟
(دوستاش، پسرت، رانندگی، (مثبت)، پیانو، شما، نقاشی، دخترش، نجاری، (منفی)، ما، عکاسی، انگلیسی، تو، (مثبت)، دوستای هندیشون، فارسی، (خانومتون))

درس ۸، تمرین ۱۴   سؤال و جواب

(The class breaks up into small groups or pairs and asks each other questions about their likes and abilities. The examples given here are not patterns for drills but sample dialogues.)

نمونه ۱:   نمونه ۲:

دانشجو ۱: تو **نقاشی** بلدی؟   **دانشجو ۱**: تو به **نقاشی** علاقه داری؟

دانشجو ۲: بله، بلدم.   **دانشجو ۲**: نه زیاد.

دانشجو ۱: خوب بلدی؟   **دانشجو ۱**: چرا نه؟

دانشجو ۲: کم و بیش. تو چطور؟   **دانشجو ۲**: (جواب آزاد)

(خیاطی، آشپزی، فرانسه، عکاسی، نجاری، رانندگی، روسی، شعر، موسیقی، پیانو، آلمانی، گیتار، فلوت، هندی، والی بال، فوتبال امریکایی، فوتبال ایرانی، یونانی، خط عبری، والس، دیسکو، نت موسیقی، آواز، مکانیکی، ویولن، کامپیوتر (رایانه)، سخت افزار (hardware) و نرم افزار (software)، اسکی (اسکی بازی)، ماشین نویسی

362

Lesson Eight　　　MODERN PERSIAN　　　درس هشتم

Cued Question/Answer (Map Work) 1　　　درس ۸، تمرین ۵

در یک ایستگاه اتوبوس در تهران.

مسافر: معذرت میخوام آقا. این اتوبوس میره **یزد**؟

راننده: نخیر خانوم/قربون. این میره **اصفهان**. اون یکی میره **یزد**.

(تبریز/همدان، مشهد/قم، شیراز/یزد و کرمان، شمرون/پارک شهر۲، بازار/ دانشگاه، کرج و قزوین/آمل و بابلسر، شهر/شمرون، (یزد/اصفهان))

۱　مسافر /mosafer/ "traveller" (here: "passenger") Note that the driver changes /an/ to /un/ in words that would not be changed by people speaking more formally.

۲　Your teacher can show you on the map where the various cities mentioned here are located, and also where شمیران /shemiran/ (colloquial: شمرون /shemrun/) and پارک شهر /park-e shæhr/ are to be found in Tehran.

Antonyms　　　درس ۸، تمرین ۱۶

هوشنگ و ایرج در فروشگاه هستند. هوشنگ کفش می خرد.

هوشنگ: این یکی خوبه؟

ایرج: بله این یکی خوبه ولی اون یکی **بده**.

(گرون، بزرگ، خوش رنگ، بد رنگ، رنگی، قشنگ، کوچیک، خیلی کوچیک، (خوب))

8.11 Grammar Discussion　　　۸/۱۱

8.11.1 Endings in Combination with Roots and Ending in Vowels (Colloquial Persian)

When roots or stems of words ending in vowels are combined with endings beginning with vowels, the result is two vowels in sequence (e.g. /daneshju-æm/). Colloquial Persian tolerates some of these sequences and not others. That is, one of the vowels in some sequences is dropped. You have already encountered most of these combinations in the drills of various lessons, and have a sense of which ones remain unchanged and which drop a vowel, but we summarize them for you here in schematic form. These rules apply particularly to

Lesson Eight　　　　　*MODERN PERSIAN*　　　　　درس هشتم

Colloquial Persian but certain ones also apply to FWP as it is <u>read aloud</u>. The FWP representation of these same combinations are summarized for you in section 10.9.

The following endings (3 sets + 1 single) begin with vowels in colloquial Persian:

	-(h)æm	Present Tense	
To Be	Also	Verb Endings	Possessive
-æm	-(h)æm	-æm	-æm
-i		-i	-et
-e/-st		-e/-d	-esh
-im		-im	-emun
-in		-in/-id	-etun
-ænd		-ænd	-eshun

When the above endings are attached to roots ending in the vowels /i/, /u/ or /o/, the endings split into two types: those which retain the initial vowel of the ending (e.g. /daneshju-æm/ "I am a student") and those that lose it (e.g. /daneshju-m/ "my student"). With roots ending in the vowels /a/, /e/, or possibly /æ/ (see below), all of the above endings lose their initial vowel and connect the remaining consonant directly to the root. Remember the maxim presented in 7.9.2:

-Colloquial Persian has a tendency to <u>merge</u> roots and endings (usually by losing a vowel);

-Formal Written Persian has a tendency to <u>separate</u> roots and endings (usually by inserting a consonant between them).

Lesson Eight *MODERN PERSIAN* درس هشتم

Examples in paradigm form:

Final Vowel

	of Root			Endings
	To Be	-(h)æm Also	Verb Root + Verb Ending	Possessive
	Endings Don't Lose Initial Vowel			Endings Lose Vowel
u = daneshju	daneshju	daneshjú-æm	none[1]	daneshju-m
	daneshjú-i		none	daneshju-t
	daneshjú-e		none	daneshju-sh
	daneshjú-im		none	daneshjú-mun
	daneshjú-in		none	daneshjú-tun
	daneshjú-ænd		none	daneshjú-shun
	"I am a student"	"the student also"		"my student"
	etc.			etc.
o = piano	pianó-æm [2]	pianó-æm	none	piano-m
	pianó-i		none	piano-t
	pianó-e		none	piano-sh
	pianó-im		none	pianó-mun
	pianó-in		none	pianó-tun
	pianó-ænd		none	pianó-shun
i = almani	almaní-æm	almaní-æm	none[1]	almani-m
	*(see 6.11.3)		none	almani-t
	almaní-e		none	almani-sh
	*(see 6.11.3)		none	almaní-mun
	*(see 6.11.3)		none	almaní-tun
	almaní-ænd		none	almaní-shun

Lesson Eight   *MODERN PERSIAN*   درس هشتم

Ending Loses Initial V

a = koja	koja-m	koja-m	míkha-m	koja-m
	kojá-i		míkha-y	koja-t
	koja-st [3]		míkha-d [4]	koja-sh
	kojá-im		míkha-ym	kojá-mun
	kojá-in		míkha-yn	kojá-tun
	kojá-nd		míkha-nd	kojá-shun

Roots Ending in /-e/

When a root ending in the vowel /-e/ is combined with the /-e/ or /-æ/ of an ending (-et, -esh, -emun, -etun, -eshun, or -æm), the /-e/ of the root changes to /æ/ and the initial vowel of the ending is dropped. The final /-e/ does not change with endings beginning with /-i/:

Final Vowel

of Root				**endings**
		-(h)æm	Verb	
	To Be	Also	Ending	Possessive
	Ending Loses Initial V			
e = bæche	e.g., /bæche + æm/ yields /bæcæ + (æ)m/ resulting in /bæcæ-m/:			
	bæchæ-m [5]	bæcæ-m	none	bæcæ-m [5]
	bæché-i	none		bæcæ-t
	bæchæ-st [3]	none		bæcæ-sh
	bæché-im	none		bæchæ-mun
	bæche-in	none		bæchæ-tun
	bæchæ-nd [6]	none		bæchæ-shun

Notes on Grammar and Phonology:

1   Although there are certain verbs whose present roots end in /-i/ or /-u/ (/zi-/ "to exist," /ru-/ "to grow (of plants)," they are not commonly used in colloquial Persian and for all practical purposes will never be heard.

2   Some of these phrases are used here for the sake of illustration — such as /piano/ + suffixed "to be" as in /piano-æm/, which means "I am a piano" — and obviously do not make very much sense as such. The sequence, however, may well occur in a fuller phrase such as /mæn næzdik-e piano-æm/ "I am near the piano" and so on. The goal here is to give you examples of the endings attached to any word to represent all the words that end in that vowel. You may indeed never hear /piano/ connect with /-æm/, but you will definitely hear other possible combinations with words ending in /-o/: /mæn æhl-e poló-æm/ "I adore pilaff, I'm 'into' rice."

3   For the third person singular present tense verb ending see 6.9.3. This form is drilled in 9.6, Drills 1-3.

4   See discussion of /míad/, /míkhad/ in 7.9.2 Reduced Verb Roots.

5   Note that even though the final (stressed) vowel changes from /-e/ to /-æ/ and the initial vowel of the ending is dropped, the stress pattern does not change. That is, a word ending in a stressed /-e/ retains the stress in its original place:

> bæché + æm ____> [bæchǽ-m] ____> /bæchǽm/

It may seem that you are placing the stress on the ending but such is not the case, since the ending loses its vowel. Thus, /bæchǽm/ is analyzed as [bæchǽ-m], not [bæch-ǽm]. The retention of the stress pattern leads to an important distinction in pronunciation:

khuné "house" *khunǽm* "my house"   *khun* "blood"   *khúnæm* "my blood"
= *[khunǽ-m]*   = *[khún-æm]*

gushé "corner" *gushǽm* "my corner" *gush* "ear"   *gúshæm* "my ear"
= *[gushǽ-m]*   = *[gúsh-æm]*

6   Remember that all of the short forms of "to be" you see here are the most common forms in colloquial Persian but are not the exclusive forms. You will also find the full form of to be used quite commonly, especially in more polite contexts:

Lesson Eight *MODERN PERSIAN* درس هشتم

Short Form	**Long Form**
mæn daneshjú-æm	mæn daneshju hæstæm
mæn almaní-æm	mæn almani hæstæm
shoma kojá-in?	shoma koja hæstin?
mæn bæcæ-m	mæn bæche hæstæm

Bache va ketabhayash

8.11.2 Formation of Noun Plurals

There are essentially two ways of forming plurals in Persian, by adding a <u>suffix</u> or, in some words of Arabic origin, by changing the <u>internal structure</u> of the word.

Suffixes

Suffixes of Persian Origin

a.   The common plural suffix in Persian is the stressed (ها/ا)/ ها. It may be added to most nouns. It has only one form in FWP, but in Colloquial the /h/ is retained only after /a/ and /e/ and generally drops out in all other positions. (See sections 7.9.1 and 8.1)

Lesson Eight *MODERN PERSIAN* درس هشتم

	Colloquial		**FWP**
کتابا	/ketaba/	کتابها	ketabha
لیموا	/limua/	لیموها	limuha
ایرانیا	/irania/	ایرانیها	iraniha

but:

مدرسه ها	/mædreseha/	مدرسه ها	mædreseha
بچه ها	/bæcheha/	بچه ها	bæcheha
ملاها	/mollaha/	ملاها	mollaha
			"mullahs,"*

Note: The plural formations in Persian other than stressed ها /(a)/ are used far more in writing than in speech. In these lessons you will be expected to recognize these alternate plurals, but not to employ them in speech or writing.

b. ان/–یان/–گان /-an/, /yan/, /gan/ — A second suffix that is, like the preceding, of Persian origin is ان– /-an/ and its variants. With certain exceptions, this plural suffix is usually added only to <u>animate</u> nouns — that is, people, animals, certain body parts, and sometimes plants.

The base form of this suffix is a stressed ان– /-an/, but after the letters و and ا، ی– is inserted, and after the final vowel ه– /e/,a/ گ–/ is inserted and the ه– drops.

Singular		**Plural**
پسر، دختر	پسران، دختران	/pesæran/, /dokhtæran/
خدا، آقا	خدایان، آقایان *	/khodayan/, /aqayan/
دانشجو	دانشجویان	/daneshjuyan/
بچه	بچگان	/bæchegan/
مورچه	مورچگان	/murchegan/
فرشته	فرشتگان	/fereshtegan/ "angels"

* Note the colloquial form of this word (آقایون /aqayon/) "sirs, gentlemen" as in (/áqayon væ khánumha/ «آقایون و خانوما») "ladies and gentlemen!"

369

Lesson Eight   *MODERN PERSIAN*   درس هشتم

Suffixes of Arabic Origin

c.   -at/-in/, ات/ين–   These two suffixes are of Arabic origin. They are respectively the feminine plural and one of the masculine plural forms (used for animates). They usually appear in words of Arabic origin only, but are sometimes used with Persian words, as well. Although there is no difference between Colloquial and FWP for these alternate plural forms, they are more common in writing than in speech.

Singular	Plural	
معلم	معلمين	/moællemin/
تمرين	تمرينات	/tæmrinat/
امتحان	امتحانات	/emtehanat/

Note also the feminine plural found in section 8.12 on Shi'ite Islam:

آيه/آيات   aye/ayat "A verse of the Qor'an"

Internal Changes

d.   Arabic also forms plurals in masculine nouns and adjectives by altering their form rather than by adding suffixes. Such plurals are known as "broken" plurals. Thus خبر /khæbær/, "news, news item," has the plural اخبار /ækhbar/, "news, news program," and عالم /alem/, "religious scholar, Muslim clergyman," has the plural علما /olæma/, "Muslim clergy, Ulema." There are many different singular-to-plural patterns in Arabic and virtually all of them occur in Persian. We illustrate a few of these patterns below. There is a fuller discussion of Arabic word formation in 14.5, and of Arabic plurals in particular, in 15.5.

Singular		Plural		
مسجد	/mæsjed/	مساجد	/mæsajed/	"mosques"
علم	/elm/	علوم	/olum/	"science(s)"
وقت	/væqt/	اوقات	/o(w)qat/	"times"
كتاب	/ketab/	كتب	/kotob/	"books"
خبر	/khæbær/	اخبار	/ækhbar/	"news, news program"
عالم	/alem/	علما	/olæma/	"religious scholars,

Lesson Eight   *MODERN PERSIAN*   درس هشتم

Muslim clergymen"

Note also the broken plural found in section 8.12 on Shi'ite Islam:

رکن/ارکان   rokn/ærkan "Pillar(s)."

A fuller description of Arabic broken plurals with further examples for each type are given in Lesson 14 (section 14.5).

Inside a Mosque

Summary

The plural suffix that may be used with all nouns — animate, inanimate, Arabic or Persian — is -ha/ها-. The other suffixes, and "broken" Arabic plurals are additional plural forms, occurring in various types of words. They turn up more frequently in writing than in speech, but some, such as علما /olæma/, are quite common in all forms of the language. For the present, you are responsible only for recognizing these alternate forms, except as indicated in the vocabulary sections of each lesson.

Lesson Eight *MODERN PERSIAN* درس هشتم

(Arabic) Occasional FWP	(Persian) Occasional FWP	(Persian) Usual FWP	(Persian) Usual Colloquial	Singular
\multicolumn{5}{c}{**Animate Nouns (Arabic)**}
مهندسین	مهندسان	مهندسها	مهندسا	مهندس
معلمین	معلمان	معلمها	معلما	معلم
\multicolumn{5}{c}{**Inanimate Nouns (Arabic)**}
اخبار		خبرها	خبرا	خبر
اوقات		وقتها	وقتا	وقت
کتب		کتابها	کتابا	کتاب
مساجد		مسجدها	مسجد	مسجد

	(Persian) Occasional FWP	(Persian) Usual FWP	(Persian) Usual Colloquial	Singular
\multicolumn{5}{c}{**Animate Nouns (Persian)**}
	پسران	پسرها	پسرا	پسر
"horse" /æsb/	اسبان	اسبها	اسبا	اسب

Other Words

	آقایان/(آقاها)	آقاها/آقایون	آقا
	بچه ها	بچه ها/(بچا)	بچه

Inanimate Nouns (Persian)*

	نامه ها	نامه ها	نامه
	شهرها	شهرا	شهر
	ماشینها	ماشینا	ماشین

* All non-Arabic words of whatever origin follow the Persian model as well.

Lesson Eight MODERN PERSIAN درس هشتم

Yek pesar va asbash

8.12 Shi'ite Islam

Well over 90 percent of the population of Iran belongs to the community of Shi'ite Muslims. Another 2 or 3 percent — principally Kurds, Turkomans, and Arabs — are Sunni Muslims. The remainder of the population is divided among several Christian sects — primarily Armenian Gregorians, Nestorians, Presbyterians, Episcopalians — and Jews, Zoroastrians, and Baha'is. There are a number of good brief introductions to the religion of Islam available, most of which contain helpful chapters on Shi'ite Islam. What follows here are some brief definitions of various terms used in Persian to describe Islamic beliefs and practices. Most of these terms are, as one would expect, Arabic in origin. Terms of Persian origin are marked with an asterisk. A slash is used where both the singular and the plural of a term are given.

*دین/آیین   din - a'in. "Religion"

اسلام   eslam. "Submission" to (the will of God), the religion of Islam, the community of Muslims.

Lesson Eight *MODERN PERSIAN* درس هشتم

مسلم/مسلمان **moslem - mosælman**. Literally "one who submits," both terms are used interchangeably in Persian to designate a member of the Islamic faith.

مذهب **mæzhæb**. "Religion" and also "sect." Both دین *din* and مذهب *mæzhæb* are used with اسلام *eslam*, but only مذهب *mæzhæb* with شیعه *si:e* "Shi'ite."

شیعه **shi'e**. Originally this term, which means "faction," was used to designate those who supported the candidacy of Ali ebn abi Taleb, علی بن ابی طالب son-in-law of the Prophet Mohammad, as his successor and leader of the community. (see خلیفه **khælife** below)

رکن/ارکان **rokn/ærkan**. "Pillar(s)." There are five practices that are obligatory for all Muslims. They are known collectively as the "five pillars of Islam." They are:

I   شهادت **shæhadæt**. First, the profession of faith ("Testimony"). It is uttered in Arabic and has the form:

II   نماز* **næmaz**. Second, ritual "prayer." Muslims are enjoined both to perform individual prayers at specified times during the day and to participate in communal prayer on Friday. (see جمعه **jom'e** below)

III   روزه* **ruze**. Third, "fasting" from sunrise to sunset during the month of Ramadan (رمضان).

IV   زکات **zækat**. Fourth, the giving of "alms" to the needy.

V   حج **hæjj**. Fifth, the "pilgrimage" to Mekka. One who has completed the pilgrimage is known as a حاجی **hajji**.

جهاد **jehad**. "Holy War." The obligation to defend Islam from its enemies is often spoken of as the "sixth pillar."

محمد **Mohammad (mohæmmæd)** is the last of the prophets of God, and the one to receive the final, perfect revelation from Him. Mention of the name of the Prophet, whether in speech or in writing, should be followed by the Arabic phrase صلی الله علیه و آله و سلم *sælæ ællaho 'ælæyhi væ alihi væ sællæm* "May God pray for him and his family and give him

Lesson Eight   *MODERN PERSIAN*   درس هشتم

peace." In writing this phrase is abbreviated to (ص) or (صلم).

رسول اللّه   **ræsulollah.** Prophet/Messenger of God.

پیغمبر خدا*   **peyqæmbær-e khoda.** Prophet/Messenger of God.

قرآن   **qor'an.** The revelations that Mohammad received throughout the latter part of his life. The canonical text of the Qor'an was established roughly in the second decade after the death of Mohammad. One usually speaks of the Qor'an as کریم *kærim* "the noble" or مجید *mæjid* "the glorious."

سوره   **sure.** A chapter of the Qor'an.

آیه/آیات   **aye/ayat.** A verse of the Qor'an.

بسم اللّه الرحمن الرحیم **besme-llahe-rræhmane-rræhim.** "In the name of God, the Merciful, the Munificent" This invocation appears at the beginning of each Surah of the Qor'an, except number IX. It is also used by Muslims at the beginning of any book or other writing and is spoken at the beginning of any public utterance.

مکه   **mække,** commonly spelled Mekka or Mecca. The city of Mohammad's birth and the site of the Ka'ba (کعبه *kæ:be*) — a square stone building with a meteorite set in one corner. The کعبه, which was sacred to the Arabs before Islam, is the shrine that is the focus of the حج *hæjj* for all Muslims.

مدینه   **mædine.** Medina. The city to which Mohammad and his fledgling community fled when their continued existence in Mekka was made impossible by the opposition of the city's leaders.

هجرت   **hejræt.** Flight, hegira. Mohammad's flight from Mekka took place, probably, in the early fall of the year 622 in the Julian calendar. The Islamic calendar dates from the first day of the first month of that year, which fell on July 16, and is known as the هجری *hejri* calendar. The Islamic calendar is a lunar calendar, and so the months shift gradually from season to season over the years. The lunar calendar is impractical for regulating commercial and administrative affairs, and as a consequence there is usually a solar calendar in use in Islamic countries as well. The religious calendar, the lunar, is known in Iran

375

Lesson Eight   *MODERN PERSIAN*   درس هشتم

as هجری قمری *hejrí-e qæmæri*, the solar, administrative calendar is designated هجری شمسی *hejrí-e shæmsi* (*qæmær* and *shæms* are Arabic for, respectively, "moon" and "sun"). In Iran the year 1980 by our reckoning was the year 1400 *hejrí-e qæmæri*, and the year 1359 *hejri-e shæmsi*. (On the Iranian solar calendar see Lesson 9, section 12.)

خليفه   **khælife**. "Caliph" On the death of Mohammad in 10/632, leadership of the community fell to men who could lay no claim to his prophetic office. They first called themselves "the vicar of the prophet of God" or خليفه رسول الله *khælifætu ræsulellah*, but this was soon shortened simply to خليفه *khælife*.

محرم   **mohærræm**. The first month of the Islamic calendar, and one with a special significance for Shi'ites. In the year 80 A.H., Hossein, the younger son of Ali and the grandson of the Prophet, had gone to Iraq to mount a campaign to regain the caliphate for himself and his line. He was intercepted by the caliph's troops and on the tenth day (عاشورا *cashura*) of the month, he and all his followers were brutally slain at کربلا Karbala. This event, or series of events, is commemorated annually by acts of public, communal mourning and passion plays known as تعزیه *tæ:zie*.

امام   **emam**. (Also commonly spelled *Imam*) This is the other common term for the "caliph." It simply means leader, and was used to designate the one who stood before the community and led it in prayer. The same term came to be applied to the descendants of Mohammad through his son-in-law, Ali ebn abi Taleb, whom Shi'ites believed were the only legitimate leaders of the Islamic community. The majority of Shi'ites believe that there were twelve such Emams. Hence the name "Twelver Shi'ites." Others set the number at five or seven. Shi'ites believe that the Twelfth Emam, Abol Qasem Mohammad, removed himself from direct contact with the world in 260 A.H./874 C.E.

Lesson Eight *MODERN PERSIAN* درس هشتم

The Gold Dome, Khurasan

الراشدون   ær rashedun The first four caliphs are known collectively as the "Rightly Guided."

ابو بکر   **Abu Bakr** 10 - 12/632 - 634.

عمر   **Omar** ('Umar) 12 - 23/634 - 644.

عثمان   **Osman** ('Uthman) 23 - 35/644 - 655.

علی   **:ali** 36 - 40/656 - 661.

علیه السلام   æleyhi-s-sælam "Upon him peace." A phrase repeated after the mention of the name of a prophet or Imam.

مسجد   mæsjed Mosque. The term مسجد means literally a place of prostration and prayer.

قبله   qeble The marker placed in the appropriate wall of a mosque or other room to indicate the direction of prayer—always toward Mekka and the Ka'ba.

Lesson Eight *MODERN PERSIAN* درس هشتم

جمعه   **jom'e** "congregation." The name of the day, Friday, when the Muslim community takes its day of rest and gathers in the principal mosque of the community at noon for communal prayers, نماز جمعه *næmáz-e jom:e*.

منبر   **membær** The pulpit from which the Friday sermon is delivered. The terms used to designate religious leaders appear in the description of the Iranian educational system in Lesson 10, Volume II.

🔊 Optional Reading: Islam

اسلام:

اسلام دینی است که حضرت محمد در قرن هفتم میلادی (seventh century) آورد. معنی اسلام یعنی صلح (peace) و ایمنی (security) و رهایی (freedom) و همچنین (also) یعنی اطاعت از خدا. اسلام یک دین عمده (major) در جهان است و مانند مسیحیت (Christianity) و یهودیت (Judaism) یک آیین ابراهیمی است. نام کتاب مقدس (holy book) مسلمانان قرآن است. به نظر مسلمانان (according to the Muslims) محمد آخرین پیامبر است ولی البته مسلمانان به پیامبران پیشین (previous messengers) مانند آدم، نوح، موسی، و عیسی نیز باور دارند. دین اسلام دو گروه عمده دارد (has two major groups): سنی و شیعه و هرکدام از این دو مذهب خود به شعبه های مختلفی تقسیم می گردند (are divided into diverse groups).

مسلمانان به پنج اصل یا عقیده اساسی باور دارند (believe in) و به آنها عمل می کنند (exercise): عقیده به خدا و محمد، نماز، پرداخت خمس و ذکات، روزه، و حج. از نظر سیاسی (from a political point of view)، دو نوع نظر وجود دارد. یکی بنیاد گرایی (fundamentalism) است و یکی اسلام نوگرایانه (Modernist) است یا آزادیخواهانه (Islamic liberalism) است.

Lesson Eight   *MODERN PERSIAN*   درس هشتم

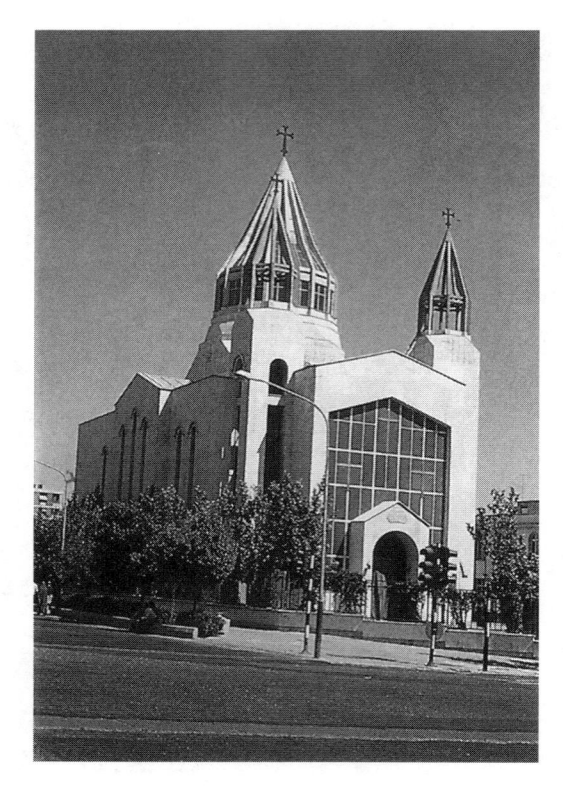

A church in Tehran

Further Reading:

There are a number of good short introductions to Islam, among them those by H. A. R. Gibb, *Mohammedanism: An Historical Survey,* 2nd edition (New York: Oxford University Press, 1962); John L. Esposito, *Islam the Straight Path,* (New York: Oxford University Press, 1988). Both books contain chapters on Shi'ite Islam. Moojan Momen's, *An Introduction to Shi'i Islam: The History and Doctrines of Twelver Shi'ism* (New Haven: Yale University Press, 1985), is the best available one volume survey of Shi'ism, and includes an extensive bibliography. And Mansoor Moaddel and Kamran Talattof, ed., *Contemporary Debates In Islam: An Anthology Of Modernist And Fundamentalist Thought.*, (New York : St. Martin's Press, 2000).

Lesson Eight   *MODERN PERSIAN*   درس هشتم

8.15 Colloquial to FWP Transformations: Exercises

8.15.1 Spoken/Written Transformations: Exercises   ۸/۱۵/۱ گفتاری به نوشتاری

Convert the following sentences in Colloquial Persian to their usual FWP counterpart. Please read section 8.9 before doing this drill. See section 6.14 for an example of the type of conversion requested here:

۱. من جامعه شناسی و تعلیم و تربیت (آموزش و پرورش) میخونم.

۲. شما اونجا با کی درس میخونید؟

۳. حال شما چطوره؟

۴. برادر فریدون هنوز کوچیکه؟

۵. علی اونجا انگلیسی میخونه.

۶. شوهر منیژه چل تا بیلیت میخواد.

۷. دختر اون خانوم چایی میخوره.

۸. شما خیلی خوب شعر میخونین.

۹. نُبت (نوبت) کیه؟

۱۰. من صبا ساعت شیش حموم میکنم.

8.15.2 Questions and Answers   ۸/۱۵/۲ سوال و جواب

۱. شما در نیو یورک زندگی میکنید؟

۲. استاد شما یکشنبه درس میدهد؟

۳. شما کراوات سرمه ای دارید؟

۴. شما کجا فارسی تمرین میکنید؟ با که تمرین میکنید؟

۵. خط فارسی شما چطور است؟

Glossary   واژه نامه

English to Persian   انگلیسی به فارسی
and   و
Persian to English   فارسی به انگلیسی

Glossary MODERN PERSIAN واژه نامه

English to Persian

Introduction

How to use the glossary

The English words that appear in the glossary are taken from those used to define the Persian words that appear in the other half of the glossary. Where several words have been used, each will appear here as a separate entry. Choosing any one of the following English words, for example, will lead you to *akhær*:

"But..., Well..." (interjection)	akhær (akhe)	آخر (آخه)
end, last, final	akhær (akhe)	آخر (آخه)
final, end last	akhær (akhe)	آخر (آخه)
last, final, end	akhær (akhe)	آخر (آخه)
"Well..., But..." (interjection)	akhær (akhe)	آخر (آخه)

Phrases are listed by the central element of the phrase:

"Get ACQUAINTED!"	آشنا بشوید (آشنا بشید)	Ashna beshævid (ashna beshid)
"It SEEMS that... It appears that..."	مثل اینکه	mesl-e inke
"Don't be UPSET!"	ناراحت نشو	narahæt næsho(w)

Words appear in full capitals when the word alphabetized is not on the left margin, as in the preceding examples. In this half of the glossary adjectives of places that refer to Iranian towns or regions will have the same form they have in Persian—place name + stressed /i/ suffix. Thus "Abadani," not "of or from Abadan."

Primary verbs are often listed on two lines: the infinitive is on the first line and the present and past roots are on the second line. Both lines will be marked to show you that the lines belong together. There is no English gloss for the second line. Compound verbs formed from these primary verbs will only be listed by their infinitives. Their present and past roots will not be given and they will not be highlighted.

to STUDY (with object); read, to sing 4	خواندن (خوندن)	khandæn (khundæn)
	خواند خوان (خوند خون)	khand/khan (khund/khun)
to STUDY (general) 4	درس خواندن (خوندن)	dærs khandæn (khundæn)

Some personal names have appeared in the list and they are marked by P.N. The number after a word indicates the lesson in which it first appears. Only the words from the first nine lessons have been marked in this way.

a, one 2	یک (یه)	yek (ye)

A listing of the first person singular present form of most of the verbs that appear in the textbook in Appendix A is located between the two sections of the glossary.

Glossary   *MODERN PERSIAN*   واژه نامه

A

English	Transliteration	Persian
a, one 2	yek (ye)	یک (یه)
abadan 1	abadan	آبادان
Abadani	abadani	آبادانی
to be ABLE, can	tævanestæn (tunestæn)	توانستن (تونستن)
about, approximately	tæqribæn; dær hodud-e	تقریباً، در حدود
about, concerning, regarding	dær bare-ye	در باره
about, concerning, regarding	raje be	راجع به
above, up	bala	بالا
absent 6	qayeb	غایب
accent; dialect 5	læhje (læ:je)	لهجه
to ACCEPT	qæbul kærdæn	قبول کردن
to be ACCEPTed	qæbul shodæn	قبول شدن
to have ACCESS to ___	be___rah dashtæn	به ـــ راه داشتن
across from, face to face, opposite	ruberu	رو برو
to be ACCUSTOMED to, in the habit of	adæt dashtæn	عادت داشتن
acquainted, familiar (with) 7	ashna, ashena (ba)	آشنا (با)
to become ACQUAINTED 7	ash(e)na shodæn	آشنا شدن
"Get acquainted!" (polite imperative) 7	ash(e)na beshævid (ashna beshid)	آشنا بشوید (آشنا بشید)
to ACQUIRE	bedæst aværdæn (ovordæn)	به دست آوردن (اوردن)
to ADD to	ezafe kærdæn (be)	اضافه کردن (به)
address	neshani; adres	نشانی؛ آدرس (نشونی)
administrative division	modiriyæt	مدیریت
advantage, benefit, use	estefade	استفاده
affectionate, kind	mehreban (mehrebun)	مهربان (مهربون)
affirmative, positive 8	mosbæt	مثبت
Afghan (person) 6	æfqan, æfqani	افغان، افغانی
Afghanistan 6	æfghanestan	افغانستان
to be AFRAID of, fear	tærsidæn (æz)	ترسیدن (از)
after (preposition)	bæ:d æz	بعد از
after, then (adverb)	bæ:d	بعد
afternoon 5	bæ:d-æz-zo(h)r	بعد از ظهر
this AFTERNOON	emruz bæ:d-æz-zo(h)r	امروز بعد از ظهر

G3

Glossary — MODERN PERSIAN — واژه نامه

English	Transliteration	Persian
afternoons, in the afternoon 5	bæ:d-æz-zo(h)ra	(بعدازظهرا)
afterward 7	bæ:dæn	بعداً
again 1	dobare	دوباره
ago; last	pish	پیش
ago, previous to	qæbl	قبل
AGREE: in agreement, concurring	movafeq	موافق
I agree with you.	mæn ba shoma movafeq-æm	من با شما موافقم
to AGREE upon, make arrangements	qærar gozashtæn	قرار گذاشتن
agreeable, pleasant, nice	khoshækhlag	خوش اخلاق
agriculture	keshavarzi	کشاورزی
Ahwaz	æhvaz	اهواز
to AID, help, assist	komæk kærdæn (be)	کمک کردن (به)
air, weather	hæva	هوا
airplane 7	hævapeyma	هواپیما
airport	forudgah	فرودگاه
Alabama	alabama	آلاباما
Alabamian	alabamai	آلابامایی
album	albom	آلبوم
alhamdollah "Praise (be) to God." (3.3.4)	ælhæmdolellah or ælhæmdollah	الحمدلله
Ali	æli	علی
alike, resembling each other	mesl-e hæm	مثل هم
Alizade 8	ælizade	علیزاده
all, every 7	hæme	همه
all___s, all the___s	hæme-ye	همه
all of, the whole (noun) 8	tæmam-e (tæmum-e)	تمام (تموم)
all of it 8	hæmeæsh (hæmæsh)	همه اش
allow, to put, place (colloquial roots only prefixes)	gozashtæn gozasht/gozar (-zasht/-zar)	گذاشتن گذاشت / گذار (ذاشت / ذار)
alone; only; lonely 5	tænha	تنها
also (literary)	niz	نیز
also; same (in compounds)	hæm (æm/hæm)	هم
although	bainke	با اینکه
aluminum	aluminiom	آلومینیوم
always 8	hæmishe	همیشه
a.m.	pish-æz-zo(h)r	پیش از ظهر
America, U.S.A. 2	emrika	امریکا

Glossary   *MODERN PERSIAN*   واژه نامه

English	Transliteration	Persian
America, U.S.A. 2	amrika	آمریکا
American 6	emrikai	امریکایی
American 6	amrikai	آمریکایی
Amman 2	æmman	عمان
a small AMOUNT	kæmi	کمی
small AMOUNT	kæm	کم
ancient, old; out of date	qædimi	قدیمی
ancient times, antiquity	bastan	باستان
and 3	væ (o, vo)	و
angry, unhappy, upset	narahæt	ناراحت
angry; impatient	æsæbani (æsæbuni)	عصبانی (عصبونی)
to get ANGRY	æsæbani shodæn	عصبانی شدن
animal husbandry, herd-tending	gæledari	گله داری
Ankara 2	ankara	آنکارا
another	digæri (digei)	دیگری (دیگه ای)
answer, reply 3	jævab	جواب
"she/he ANSWERs" 2	(jævab mide)	جواب میده
to ANSWER	jævab dadæn	جواب دادن
"Answer!" 1	jævab bedid	(جواب بدید)
anthropologist	mærdomshenas	مردم‌شناس
anthropology	mærdomshenasi	مردم‌شناسی
anxious, nervous, flustered	dæstpache	دستپاچه
anxious, worried	negæran (negærun)	نگران (نگرون)
any (one); each (one); every (one)	hær kodam (hær kodum)	هر کدام (هر کدوم)
anymore; other; else, more	digær (dige)	دیگر (دیگه)
anywhere, somewhere	jai	جایی
apartment	aparteman	آپارتمان
to APOLOGIZE, excuse oneself 6	mæ:zæræt khastæn	معذرت خواستن
apparent, manifest	zaher	ظاهر
"It seems that... It APPEARS that..." 6	mesl-e inke	مثل اینکه
apple 5	sib	سیب
application, usage, use (n)	kar-bord	کار برد
appreciative, thankful	motæshæk(k)er	متشکر
apprentice, student (through high school),5	shagerd	شاگرد
appropriate	beja	بجا
approximately, about 6	tæqribæn; dær hodud-e	تقریباً، در حدود
April	avril	آوریل
Arab 6	æræb	عرب

G5

English	Transliteration	Persian
Arabic 2	æræbi	عربی
archeologist	bastanshenas	باستانشناس
archeology	bastanshenasi	باستانشناسی
architect	me:mar	معمار
architecture	me:mari	معماری
area, extent	vos'æt	وسعت
area, region, country	særzæmin	سرزمین
arm, bosom	bæqæl	بغل
Armenia 6	ærmænestan	ارمنستان
Armenian 6	ærmani	ارمنی
army	ærtesh	ارتش
around	dowr (dor)	دور ۱
arrange; pick (flowers)	chid/chin	چین/چید
to ARRANGE; to pick (flowers)	chidæn	چیدن
to make ARRANGEMENTS, to agree upon, to set (up)	qærar gozashtæn	قرار گذاشتن
to ARRIVE	residæn	رسیدن
	resid/res	رس/رسید
art	honær	هنر
art history	tarikh-e honær	تاریخ هنر
as, just as, in the same way, likewise	hæmintowr (hæmintor)	همینطور
as it happens, as a matter of fact	etefaqæn	اتفاقاً
aside from	gozæshte æz	گذشته از
to ASK, to question 5	porsidæn; soal kærdæn	پرسیدن؛ سوال کردن
"Ask!" 2	beporsid	بپرسید
asleep, sleeping; lying down	khabide	خوابیده
aspirin	asperin	آسپرین
to ASSIST, help, aid	komæk kærdæn (be)	کمک کردن (به)
astronomer, astrologer	setareshenas	ستاره شناس
at, by, on, at the head of 4	sær-e	سر
at all (with negative verb); originally 7	æslæn	اصلاً
at/in his/her/its place	(sær-e jash)	سر جاش
at last, finally (note irregular spelling)	belækhære	بالاخره
at once, immediately	fowræn (foræn)	فوراً
at once, quickly	bezudi	بزودی
at the same time, during	zemn-e	ضمن
at the same time, meanwhile	dær zemn	در ضمن
at work (class) 4	sær-e kar (kelas)	سر کار (کلاس)
athlete	værzeshkar	ورزشکار

Glossary   *MODERN PERSIAN*   واژه نامه

athletics	værzesh	ورزش
August	ut	اوت
aunt (father's sister)	æmme	عمه
aunt (mother's sister)	khale	خاله
Australia	ostralia	استرالیا
Australian	ostraliai	استرالیایی
automobile, car	mashin	ماشین
autumn, fall	paiz	پاییز
awake, alert	bidar	بیدار
Azerbaijan 6	azærbayjan	آذربایجان
Azerbaijan, Eastern 6	azærbayjan shærqi	آذربایجان شرقی
Azerbaijani 6	azærbayjani	آذربایجانی

B

B.A., B.S.	lisans	لیسانس
back; behind	posht	پشت
lower BACK, waist	kæmær	کمر
bad, wrong	bæd	بد
not bad 1	bæd nist	بد نیست
bad tempered, mean	bæd ækhlaq	بد اخلاق
bag, handbag; briefcase; purse	kif	کیف
baker	nanva	نانوا
bakery (bread only)	nanvai	نانوایی
Bakhtaran, formerly Kermanshah	bakhtæran	کرمانشاه/باختران
ball point pen	khodkar	خودکار
banana	mo(w)z	موز
Bandar Abbas	bændær æbbas	بندر عباس
bank 6	bank	بانک
bath, public bath (Turkish style), bathroom	hæmmam (hæmum)	حمام (حموم)
to bathe, wash 5	hæmmam gereftæn (hæmum)	حمام گرفتن (حموم)
to BE	budæn	بودن
	bud/bash/hæst/(--, æst, -st)	بور/باش/هست
to BE situated	qærar dashtæn	قرار داشتن
beard	rish	ریش
beautiful, lovely	khoshgel	خوشگل
beautiful, pretty 6	qæshæng	قشنگ
a BEAUTY; moon, month	mah	ماه
because, in order to (note pronunciation of /chon/)	bæraye inke; chon	برای اینکه، چون

G7

Glossary — MODERN PERSIAN — واژه نامه

English	Transliteration	Persian
to BECOME, get; happen	shodæn	شدن
	shod/show/(sh)	شد/شو/(ش)
bed	tækht-e khab	تخت خواب
bedroom	otaq-e khab	اطاق خواب
beef	gusht-e gav	گوشت گاو
before (preposition)	qæbl æz	قبل از
before, until; by; counter (used in counting)	ta	تا
to BEGIN, start (to start something)	shoru kærdæn	شروع کردن
to BEGIN start (something starts)	shoru shodæn	شروع شدن
to BEGIN to	shoru be__ kærdæn/shoru kærdæn be__	شروع کردن به /شروع به ــ کردن
beginning	shoru	شروع
behind, back	posht (preposition: posht-e)	پشت
Beirut 2	beyrut	بیروت
belief	bavær	باور
believe	bavær kærdæn	باور کردن
to BELONG to someone	mal-e kæsi budæn	مال کسی بودن
belongings, property	mal	مال
below, underneath	zir	زیر
benefit, use, advantage	estefade	استفاده
Berlin	berlen	برلن
better 3	behtær	بهتر
between	beyn(-e)	بین
bicycle 5	dochærkhe	دوچرخه
bicycling, bike riding	dochærkhe-sævari	دوچرخه سواری
big, large 6	bozorg	بزرگ
bigger; older	bozorgtær	بزرگتر
Bijan	bizhæn	بیژن
bike riding, bicycling	dochærkhe-sævari	دوچرخه سواری
bind, tie, close	bæstæn	بستن
biology 2	biolozhi	بیولوژی (زیست شناسی)
bit, small amount, particle	yek khorde (ye khorde)	یک خرده (یه خرده)
black 6	siah	سیاه
blackboard 6	tækhte siah	تخته سیاه
blouse	boluz (buluz)	بلوز
blue; light blue (from "water")	abi	آبی
dark BLUE	sormei	سرمه ای
body	bædæn	بدن
boiled (egg)	ab pæz	آب پز/آبپز

Glossary — MODERN PERSIAN — واژه نامه

English	Transliteration	Persian
bond(s), tie(s)	rabete/rævabet	رابطه/روابط
book 3	ketab	کتاب
to be BORN	be donya amædæn	به دنیا آمدن
boss, chief, president	ræis	رییس
Boston	boston	بستن
both___and	hæm___hæm	هم ــ هم
both, all three...	hær do, hær se.	هر دو، هر سه...
boundaries, limits	hodud	حدود
box carton	jæ:be	جعبه
"Bravo! Excellent!" 3	afærin!	آفرین
bread 5	nan (nun)	نان (نون)
a long triangle of BREAD, heavily ridged	nan-e bærbæri	نان بربری
an ordinary round, flat loaf of BREAD	nan-e taftun	نان تافتون
paper thin, white, crisp flat BREAD	nan-e lævash	نان لواش
BREAD baked on a mound of small stones	sængæk (nan-e sængæk)	نان سنگک
to BREAK	shekæstæn	شکستن
	shekæst/shekæn	شکست/شکن
breakfast 5	sobhane (sobune)	صبحانه (صبونه)
bridegroom; son-in-law	damad	داماد
briefcase; bag, handbag; purse	kif	کیف
to BRING	(ovordæn) aværdæn	آوردن (اوردن)
	aværd/avær (ovord/ar)	آورد/آور (اورد/اور)
broken, spoiled, ruined, rotten	khærab	خراب
brother 1	bæradær	برادر
my brother 1	bæradæræm	برادرم
your brother 2	bæradæretun	برادرتون
brother-in-law	bæradær shohær	برادر شوهر
brown 7	qæhvei	قهوه ای
to BUILD, make	sakhtæn	ساختن
	sakht/saz	ساخت/ساز
building	sakhteman	ساختمان
bull, ox	gav-e nær	گاو نر
bull; cow	gav	گاو
burden, load; time, occurrence	bar	بار
burner, stove	ojaq	اجاق
bus 5	otobus	اتوبوس
busy	mæshqul	مشغول
to have something to do, to be BUSY 7	kar dashtæn	کار داشتن
but	væli; æmma	ولی، اما

"But..., Well..." (interjection)	akhær (akhe)	آخر (آخه)
butter	kære	کره
to BUY	khæridæn	خریدن
	khærid/khær	خرید/خر
by; before, until	ta	تا
by degrees, slowly	kæm kæm	کم کم
by God! (interjection)	vallah	والله
by mistake	ævæzi	عوضی
by the way; "Really?"	rasti	راستی

C

cabaret	kabare	کاباره
cafe	kafe	کافه
Cairo	qahere	قاهره
cake 5	keyk	کیک
calendar	tæqvim	تقویم
California 2	kalifornia	کالیفرنیا
Californian 6	kaliforniai	کالیفرنیایی
calisthenics, exercise; athletics, sports	tæmrin-e værzesh	تمرین ورزش
to CALL something___	be___chizi goftæn	به ــ چیزی گفتن
camera	durbin(-e ækkasi)	دوربین (عکاسی)
can, to be able	tævanestæn (tunestæn)	توانستن (تونستن)
	tævanest/tævan (tunest/tun)	توانست/توان (تونست/تون)
Canada 2	kanada	کانادا
Canadian 6	kanadai	کانادایی
candy, sweets, pastries	shirini	شیرینی
car, automobile	mashin	ماشین
carpenter	næjjar	نجار
carpentry	næjjari	نجاری
carpet	qali	قالی
to CARRY, take (away)	bordæn	بردن
	bord/bær	برد/بر
carton, box	jæ:be	جعبه
cassette	kaset	کاست
Caspian	dæria-ye mazændæran	دریای مازندران
cat	gorbe	گربه
caviar	khaviar	خاویار
to CELEBRATE (a festival)	jæshn gereftæn	جشن گرفتن

Glossary   *MODERN PERSIAN*   واژه نامه

English	Transliteration	Persian
celebration, festival	jæshn	جشن
celery khoresht	khoresh-e kæræfs	خورش کرفس
chelo with broiled meat	chelo kebab	چلو کباب
center; provincial capital	mærkæz	مرکز
certain, sure 6	motmæen	مطمئن
certainly, definitely, for sure 7	hætmæn	حتماً
chair	sændæli	صندلی
chalk 6	gæch	گچ
chance, opportunity	forsæt	فرصت
to CHANGE (intr.)	ævæz shodæn	عوض شدن
to CHANGE (tr.)	ævæz kærdæn	عوض کردن
character, quality	jæmbe	جنبه
cheap, inexpensive 6	ærzan (ærzun)	ارزان (ارزون)
check	chek	چک
chemist	shimidan (shimidun)	شیمی دان
chemistry 2	shimi	شیمی
chess	shætræng	شطرنج
chest	sine	سینه
chic	shik	شیک
Chicago	shikago	شیکاگو
chief, director	modir	مدیر
child 4	bæche	بچه
child care	bæchedari	بچه داری
childhood	bechegi	بچگی
chin	chane (chune)	چانه (چونه)
China 6	chin	چین
Chinese 3	chini	چینی
chocolate	shokolat (shokulat, shukulat)	شکولات/شوکولات
choice	entekhab	انتخاب
choice, prerogative, disposition	ekhtiar	اختیار
"the CHOICE is yours" (taarof)	ekhtiar darid	اختیار دارید
to CHOOSE	entekhab kærdæn	انتخاب کردن
Christmas	eyd-e kerismæs	عید کریسمس
cigarette 5	sigar	سیگار
citizen, inhabitant 6	æhl	اهل
citrus fruit	moræekkæbat	مرکبات
city, town	shæhr	شهر
city planning, urban planning	shæhrsazi	شهرسازی
class 4	kelas	کلاس

Glossary	MODERN PERSIAN	واژه نامه
in/at CLASS; to CLASS	sær-e kelas	سر کلاس
classic; orginal	æsil	اصیل
to be cleaned, get CLEAN	tæmiz shodæn	تمیز شدن
to CLEAN	tæmiz kærdæn	تمیز کردن
clean	tæmiz	تمیز
clear	vazeh	واضح
climate	ab-o hæva	آب و هوا
clock, hour	sææt	ساعت
close, tie, bind	bæstæn	بستن
	bæst/bænd	بست/بند
"Close!" 3	bebændid	ببندید
closed (store, office)	tæ:til	تعطیل
clothes, clothing	lebas	لباس
cloud	æbr	ابر
cloudy	æbri	ابری
coach, lecturer, trainer	moræbbi	مربی
coast, shore	sahel	ساحل
coast, shore, side	kenar/kenare	کنار/کناره
coffee	qæhve	قهوه
cold (adj.)	særd	سرد
to get COLD	særd shodæn	سرد شدن
to be COLLECTED (intr.), gathered	jæm shodæn	جمع شدن
to COLLECT (tr.), gather together	jæm kærdæn	جمع کردن
colloquial	amiane	عامیانه
colloquial, spoken	goftari	گفتاری
color; paint	ræng	رنگ
"What COLOR is it?"	che rængi æst (che rængi-e)	چه رنگی است (چه رنگیه)
colored	rængi	رنگی
comb, shoulder 5	shane (shune)	شانه (شونه)
to COME 7	amædæn (Tehran umædæn)	آمدن (اومدن)
	amæd/ay (Tehran umæd/a)	آمد/آی (اومد/آ)
come back, return	bær gæshtæn	بر گشتن
	bær gæsht/bær gærd	بر گشت/برگرد
"COMMAND it!" (see 3.3.1)	befærmaid	بفرمایید
to COMMAND	færmudæn	فرمودن
	færmud/færma	فرمود/فرما
command, firman	færman	فرمان
commanded (see 12.8)	færmanbær	فرمانبر

G12

Glossary — MODERN PERSIAN — واژه نامه

English	Transliteration	Persian
commander (see 12.8)	færmande	فرمانده
to COMMEND, praise	tæ:rif kærdæn (æz)	تعریف کردن (از)
company	sherkæt	شرکت
to COMPARE	moqayese kærdæn	مقایسه کردن
compote, stewed fruit 5	kompot	کمپوت
concerning, about	dær bare-ye	در باره
concert	konsert	کنسرت
condition (health)	hal	حال
connected, joined, together 8	sær-e hæm	سر هم
to CONSIST of	ebaræt budæn (æz)	عبارت بودن از
contact, "being in touch (with)"	tæmas (ba)	تماس (با)
to make CONTACT; get in touch with	tæmas gereftæn (ba)	تماس گرفتن (با)
content, happy (with), satisfied, pleased	razi	راضی
to satisfy, make CONTENT	razi kærdæn	راضی کردن
continuation	edame	ادامه
to CONTINUE	edame dadæn	ادامه دادن
conversation	sohbæt (so:bæt)	صحبت
conversation, dialogue 4	mokaleme	مکالمه
cook (person)	ashpæz	آشپز
to COOK, to do cooking (intr.)	ashpæzi kærd/kon	آشپزی کرد/کن
to COOK (tr.)	pokhtæn	پختن
	pokht/pæz	پخت/پز
to COOK (tr.); to prepare, make, fix; correct, repair 5	dorost kærdæn	درست کردن
cooked plain rice	chelo	چلو
cookie	biskuit	بیسکویت
cooking (as in someone's cooking)	dæstpokht	دست پخت
cooking (the act of)	ashpæzi	آشپزی
corner	gushe	گوشه
correct	sæhih (sæhi)	صحیح
correct, right	dorost	درست
"That's correct. It's right." 1	dorost-e	(درسته)
to CORRECT	tæs hi kærdæn (tæsi kærdæn)	تصحیح کردن (تصی کردن)
to CORRECT; to prepare, make, fix; cook, repair 5	dorost kærdæn	درست کردن
to COUNT, number out	shomordæn	شمردن
	shomord/shomar	شمرد/شمار
counter (word used in counting); by;	ta	تا

English	Transliteration	Persian
before, until		
country	keshvær	کشور
countryside (outside the city)	birun-e shæhr	بیرون شهر
course (academic) 5	kurs	کورس
cousin (father's brother's daughter)	dokhtær(-e) æme (see 10.2)	دختر عمه
cousin (father's sister's daughter)	dokhtær(-e) æmu (see 10.2)	دختر عمو
cousin (mother's brother's daughter)	dokhtær(-e) dai (see 10.2)	دختر دایی
cousin (mother's sister's daughter)	dokhtær(-e) khale (see 10.2)	دختر خاله
cow; bull	gav	گاو
cow	gav-made	گاو ماده
co-worker	hæmkar	همکار
crowded, noisy, messy	sholuq (shuluq)	شلوغ
to CRY, weep	gerie kærdæn	گریه کردن
cultivable	qabel-e kesht	قابل کشت
cultivating, tilling, sowing	kesht	کشت
culture; dictionary	færhæng	فرهنگ
cup	fenjan (fenjun)	فنجان (فنجون)
custom, habit	adæt	عادت
customs	adab-o rosum	آداب و رسوم
cycling, bike riding	dochærkhe-sævari	دوچرخه سواری

D

English	Transliteration	Persian
daily	ruzane	روزانه
dance, dancing	ræqs	رقص
to DANCE	ræqsidæn	رقصیدن
	ræqsid/raqs	رقصید/رقص
Dari (Afghan Persian) 5	dæri	دری
date(s) (fruit)	khorma	خرما
date; history	tarikh	تاریخ
daughter, girl	dakhtær	دختر
day 4	ruz	روز
days, during the days, in the daytime 4	ruzha (ruza)	روزها (روزا)
dear	æziz	عزیز
dear, soul, life (see 13.1.3) 7	jan (jun)	جان (جون)
"my DEAR"	æzizæm	عزیزم
December	desambr	دسامبر
to DECIDE	tæsmim gereftæn	تصمیم گرفتن
decision	tæsmim	تصمیم
definitely, certainly, for sure 7	hætmæn	حتماً

G14

Glossary　　　*MODERN PERSIAN*　　　واژه نامه

delicious, tasty	khoshmæze	خوشمزه
dentist	dændansaz (dændunsaz)	دندان ساز (دندون ساز)
dentist	dændanpezeshk (dændunpezeshk)	دندان پزشک (دندون پزشک)
dentistry	dændansazi (dændunsazi)	دندان سازی (دندون سازی)
dentistry	dændanpezeshki (dændunpezeshki)	دندان پزشکی (دندون پزشکی)
depart, to set out	hærækæt kærdæn	حرکت کردن
department (university), part, section	bækhsh	بخش
depend on ___	bæstegi dashtæn be___	بستگی داشتن به ــ
dependence	bæstegi	بستگی
to DESCRIBE	tæ:rif kærdæn	تعریف کردن
description; praise	tæ:rif	تعریف
desert	biaban (biabun)	بیابان (بیابون)
desert (adj.)	biabani (biabuni)	بیابانی (بیابونی)
salt DESERT	kævir	کویر
dessert	deser	دسر
to DESIRE or wish to eat	meyl dashtæn	میل داشتن
desire, wish	meyl	میل
to DEVELOP (film), make manifest	zaher kærdæn	ظاهر کردن
dialect; accent 5	læhje	لهجه
dialogue	goftegu	گفتگو
dialogue, conversation 4	mokaleme	مکالمه
diaper; rag; old, worn out	kohne	کهنه
to DICTATE spelling words 5	dikte kærdæn	دیکته کردن
dictation 5	dikte	دیکته
dictionary, glossary	loqætname	لغت نامه
dictionary; culture	færhæng	فرهنگ
to DIFFER, be different (see 7.2)	færq kærdæn/dashtæn	فرق کردن/داشتن
difference	færq	فرق
"There's a difference." "It depends" 6, 9	færq mikonæd(mikone)	فرق میکند (میکنه)
"There's no difference." 6, 9	(færq nemikone)	(فرق نمیکنه)
"What's the difference?" 9	(che færq mikone)	(چه فرق میکنه)
difficult 2	moshkel (moshgel)	مشکل (مشگل)
difficult, hard 6	sækht	سخت
difficulty	eshkal (eshgal)	اشکال (اشگال)
to DIMINISH, reduce	kæm kærdæn	کم کردن
dining room	otaq-e nahar khori	اطاق ناهار خوری

G15

English	Transliteration	Persian
dinner 6	sham	شام
to serve DINNER	sham keshidæn	شام کشیدن
direction	tæræf	طرف
directly	yekrast	یکراست
director, chief	modir	مدیر
directorship	riasæt	ریاست
dirt, ground, soil, earth	zæmin	زمین
dirty	kæsif	کثیف
discourse, speech, utterance 5	hærf	حرف
discuss	bæhs kærdæn	بحث کردن
discussion	bæhs	بحث
dish	zærf	ظرف
to DISLIKE (see 16.11.2 "Type Three")	bæd-e__amædæn (æz)	بد ــ آمدن (از)
display, show, exhibit, exhibition	næmayesh	نمایش
distant, far 6	dur	دور
division	tæqsim	تقسیم
to be DIVIDED	tæqsim shodæn	تقسیم شدن
to DIVIDE	tæqsim kærdæn	تقسیم کردن
to DO	kar kærdæn	کار کردن
to do what	chekar kærdæn	چکار کردن
What does she/he do? What is she doing?1	chekar mikone	(چکار میکنه)
to have something to DO, to be busy 7	kar dashtæn	کار داشتن
	kar dasht/kar dar	کار داشت/کار دار
doctor 6	doktor	دکتر
doctorate	doktora	دکترا
dog	sæg	سگ
domestic, familial	khanevadegi	خانوادگی
door; in, within	dær	در
dormitory 2	khabgah	خوابگاه
down	pain	پایین
drama, play	næmayeshnæme	نمایشنامه
to DRAW (a load or picture); pull	keshidæn	کشیدن
	keshid/kesh	کشید/کش
drawer	kesho	کشو
to DREAM	khab didæn	خواب دیدن
dressmaking, tailoring	khæyyati	خیاطی
drill, practice, exercise 5	tæmrin/tæmrinat	تمرین/تمرینات
to DRINK, eat 5	khordæn	خوردن
	khord/khor	خورد/خور

G16

Glossary — *MODERN PERSIAN* — واژه نامه

to eat or DRINK (polite)	meyl kærdæn	میل کردن
to DRIVE	ranændegi kærdæn	رانندگی کردن
driver	shofer	شوفر
driver (car, bus)	ranænde	راننده
driving	ranændegi	رانندگی
to DRY (tr.)	khoshk kærdæn	خشک کردن
to DRY out, DRY up	khoshk shodæn	خشک شدن
dry	khoshk	خشک
during (preposition)	dær væqt-e	در وقت
during the afternoon, in the afternoons 5	bæ:d-æz-zo(h)ra	(بعدازظهرا)
during the day, in the daytime	ruzha	روزها (روزا)
during the evening(s), in the evenings 4	shæbha (shæba)	شبها (شبا)
during the morning, in the mornings 5	sob(h)ha (soba)	صبح ها (صبا)
Dutch; Dutchman/woman 6	holændi	هلندی
dynamite	dinamit	دینامیت

E

each	hær	هر
each (one); any (one); every (one)	hæryek (hæryeki)	هریک (هر یکی)
each other	hæmdigær (hæmdige)	هم دیگر (هم دیگه)
each other, one another	yekdigær	یکدیگر
each/every day (night, etc.)	hær ruz, hær shæb	هرروز، هرشب...
each; whoever, whichever	hær kodam (hær kodum)	هر کدام (هر کدوم)
ear	gush	گوش
easily	be asani (be asuni)	به آسانی/بآسانی (به آسونی/بآسونی)
East	khavær	خاور
east	shærq	شرق
east	mæshreq	مشرق
Easter	eyd-e pak	عید پاک
eastern	shærqi	شرقی
easy, simple 2	asan (asun)	آسان (آسون)
to EAT, drink 5	khordæn	خوردن
	khord/khor	خورد/خور
to EAT or drink (polite)	meyl kærdæn	میل کردن
economics; economy	eqtesad	اقتصاد
economist	eqtesad dan	اقتصاد دان
education (as a discipline, see next entry)	tæ:lim-o tærbiæt	تعلیم و تربیت
education (more commonly used synonym	amuzesh-o pærværesh	آموزش و پرورش

G17

Glossary — MODERN PERSIAN — واژه نامه

English	Transliteration	Persian
of above)		
effects, possessions	æsbab	اسباب
egg (chicken)	tokhm-e morq	تخم مرغ
boiled EGG	tokhm-e morq-e ab paz	تخم مرغ آبپز
eggplant khoresht	khoresh-e bademjun	خورش بادمجان (بادمجون)
eight 2	hæsht	هشت
eighty 5	hæshtad	هشتاد
either___or	ya___ya	یا ــــ یا
elections	entekhabat	انتخابات
else, other, more; anymore	digær (dige)	دیگر (دیگه)
embarrassment, shyness; shame 5	khejalæt	خجالت
to be EMBARRASSED, shy 5	khejalæt keshidæn	خجالت کشیدن
embassy	sefaræt	سفارت
emphatic	che___!	چه ــــ؟
to be EMPLOYED	estekhdam shodæn	استخدام شدن
to EMPTY	khali kærdæn	خالی کردن
empty	khali	خالی
encounter, meeting (9.1.4.2)	molaqat	ملاقات
to ENCOURAGE	tæshviq kærdæn	تشویق کردن
end, at, in, to; head	sær	سر
end, last, final	akhær	آخر
in the END, after all	akhæresh	آخرش
energy	enerzhi	انرژی
engagement, obligation	gereftari	گرفتاری
engine (car), motor	motor	موتور
engineer (also used as a title like "Doctor") 6	mohændes/mohændesin	مهندس /مهندسین
engineering	mohændesi	مهندسی
England 6	englestan(inglestan)	انگلستان (اینگلستان)
	englis	انگلیس (اینگلیس)
English 6	englisi (inglisi)	انگلیسی
enough	kafi	کافی
enshallah "If God wills." (see 3.3.4)	enshalla	انشاءالله
entomology	entomolozhi	انتمولوژی/حشره شناسی
equal	mosavi	مساوی
equipment, necessities; means	væsile/væsæl	وسیله/وسائل
to make an ERROR (obscene)	qælæt kærdæn	غلط کردن
error	eshtebah	اشتباه

G18

Glossary   MODERN PERSIAN   واژه نامه

English	Transliteration	Persian
error	qælæt	غلط
Esfahan	(see Isfahan)	اصفهان
Esfahanian	esfæhanian	اصفهانیان
especially	mækhsusæn	مخصوصاً
et cetera, and so on	væ qeyre	و غیره
Europe 6	orupa	اروپا
European 6	orupai	اروپایی
European, western(er) (esp.	færængi	فرنگی
evening, night	shæb	شب
evening, in the evening(s) 4	shæbha (shæba)	شبها (شبا)
this EVENING, tonight	emshæb	امشب/امروز شب
every (one); any(one), each (one)	hær kodam (hær kodum)	هر کدام (هر کدوم)
every, all	hæme	همه
everyone	hæmikæs	همه کس
everywhere	hæmeja	همه جا
exact; tiny, minute	dæqiq	دقیق
examination, test 5	emtehan	امتحان
oral EXAMINATION 7	emtehan-e shæfahi	امتحان شفاهی
written EXAMINATION 7	emtehan-e kætbi	امتحان کتبی
to EXAMINE, test 5	emtehan kærdæn /gereftæn æz	امتحان کردن /امتحان گرفتن از
example	nemune/næmune; mæsæl	نمونه؛ مثل
excellent	ali	عالی
"Excellent! Bravo!"	afærin!	آفرین
excessive, extra, too much	ziadi	زیادی
"EXCUSE me!" 6	mæ:zæræt mikhahæm (mikham)	معذرت میخواهم (معذرت میخوام)
to EXCUSE, forgive	bækhshidæn	بخشیدن
"EXCUSE me!" 3	bebækhshid (bebækhshin)	ببخشید (ببخشین)
exercise, sport, athletics	værzesh	ورزش
exercise, practice, drill 5	tæmrin	تمرین/تمرینات
to engage in sport or EXERCISE	værzeq kærdæn	ورزش کردن
to EXIST (used to indicate location)	vojud dashtæn	وجود داشتن
existence	vojud	وجود
expensive; heavy 6	geran (gerun)	گران (گرون)
to EXPLAIN	towzih dadæn (tozi)	توضیح دادن
explanation	towzih (tozi)	توضیح (توضی، تُضی)
extent, area	vos'æt	وسعت

Glossary	*MODERN PERSIAN*	واژه نامه

English	Transliteration	Persian
to be EXTINGUISHED, turned off	khamush shodæn	خاموش شدن
to EXTINGUISH, turn off	khamush kærdæn	خاموش کردن
extinguished, silent	khamush	خاموش
extra, excessive, too much	ziadi	زیادی
extremely, infinitely	bi-næhayæt	بی نهایت
extremely, very	besiar	بسیار
extremely, very	kheyli	خیلی
eye	cheshm	چشم
eyebrow(s)	æbru	ابرو

F

English	Transliteration	Persian
face	suræt	صورت
face	ru	رو
face to face, across from, opposite	ruberu	روبرو
factory 5	karkhane (karkhune)	کارخانه (کارخونه)
fairy tale, story, tale	qesse	قصّه
fall, autumn	paiz	پائیز
to FALL	oftadæn	افتادن
	oftad/oft	افتاد/افت
to FALL down	zæmin khordæn	زمین خوردن
familial	famili	فامیلی (خانواده)
familial, domestic	khanevadegi	خانوادگی
familiar, acquainted (with) 7	ashna, ashena (ba)	آشنا (با)
family	khanevade	خانواده
family, relative	famil	فامیل
fantasy	fantezi	فانتزی (وهم، نقشه خیالی)
far, distant 6	dur	دور
Faride	færide	فریده
farmer	keshaværz	کشاورز
Fars (province in south central Iran)	fars	فارس
fast, quick	zud	زود
fast; harsh	tond	تند
faster	tondtær	تندتر
fat	chaq	چاق
father 1 (for the use of *baba* see 13.1.3)	pedær, baba	پدر (بابا)
to FEAR, be afraid of	tærsidæn (æz)	ترسیدن (از)
	tærsid/tærs	ترسید/ترس
February	fevrie	فوریه
Fereshte "angel" 3	fereshte	فرشته

Glossary — *MODERN PERSIAN* — واژه نامه

English	Transliteration	Persian
Fereydun	fereydun	فریدون
festival	eyd	عید
festival, celebration	jæshn	جشن
field, discipline; mountain chain	reshte	رشته
fifth, etc.	pænjom/pænjomin	پنجم
fifty 5	pænjah	پنجاه
film ("movie" and "camera")	film	فیلم
final, end, last	akhær	آخر
final, ultimate	akhærin	آخرین (آخر + ین)
finally, at last	belækære	بلاخره (سرانجام)
fine, good 3	khub	خوب
"It's fine." "It's good." 1	khube	(خوبه)
"Is it okay? "Is is good?" 2	khube?	(خوبه؟)
finger	ængosht	انگشت
to FINISH	tæmam kærdæn (tæmum)	تمام کردن (تموم)
to be FINISHED	tæmam shodæn (tæmum)	تمام شدن (تموم)
first	ævval	اول
first	yekom	یکم
first name	esm-e kuchek (esm-e kuchik)	اسم کوچک (اسم کوچیک)
Firuzi, Firouzi	firuzi	فیروزی
fish	mahi	ماهی
fishing	mahigiri	ماهی گیری
five 2	pænj	پنج
to be FIXED, repaired, made okay	dorost shodæn	درست شدن
to FIX; to prepare, make, cook;, repair 5	dorost kærdæn	درست کردن
flaw	eyb	عیب
flock, herd	gælle	گله
flower; rose	gol	گل
flustered, anxious, nervous	dæstpache	دستپاچه
flute	folut	فلوت
folklore	folklor	فلکلور (افسانه های قومی)
to be interested (in), to be FOND of	ælaqe dashtæn (be)	علاقه داشتن (به)
fondness, interest, liking	ælaqe	علاقه
food; meal 5	qæza, khorak	غذا، خوراک
foot	pa	پا
at the FOOT/base of	pa-ye	پای
on FOOT 7	piade	پیاده
for	bæraye	برای

G21

English	Transliteration	Persian
for example 3	mæsælæn	مثلاً
foreign, foreigner	khareji	خارجی
forest	jængæl	جنگل
to FORGET	(æz) yad__ræftæn	از یاد ___ رفتن
to FORGIVE; give away, donate, grant	bækhshidæn	بخشیدن
	bækhshid/bæsksh	بخشید/بخش
"Excuse me!" 3	bebækhshid (bebækhshin)	ببخشید
formal bookish (language)	ketabi	کتابی
formal courtesies 3 (see 3.3)	tæarof	تعارف
fortunately	khoshbækhtane	خوشبختانه
forty 5	chehel (chel)	چهل (چل)
forward, in front of	jelo	جلو
I look FORWARD to seeing you;	be omid-e didar	به امید دیدار
four 2	chæhar (char)	چهار (چار)
free	azad	آزاد
to become FREE, get free	azad shodæn	آزاد شدن
to FREE, set free, let loose	azad kærdæn	آزاد کردن
French (person or adjective) 5	færansævi	فرانسوی
French (language); France 3	færanse	فرانسه
fresh; recent, new; recently	taze	تازه
Friday	jom'e (ruz-e jom'e)	جمعه (روز جمعه، آدینه)
friend 1	dust	دوست
friend, pal	ræfiq/rofæqa	رفیق/رفقا
from, of 3	æz	از
from___to/till___	æz___ta___	از ــ تا ــ
fruit	mive	میوه
stewed FRUIT, compote 5	kompot	کمپوت
full	por	پر
funny, laughable	khændedar	خنده دار

G

English	Transliteration	Persian
game	bazi	بازی
garage	garazh	گاراژ
garden, orchard	baq	باغ
gas (gasoline)	benzin	بنزین
gas station 5	pomp-e benzin	پمپ بنزین
to GATHER together, collect (tr.)	jæm kærdæn	جمع کردن
gendarme	zhandarm	ژاندارم
gentleman; sir	aqayan	آقایان (آقایون)

Glossary   *MODERN PERSIAN*   واژه نامه

geographer	jografi dan	جغرافی دان
geography	joqrafi/ jografia	جغرافی/جغرافیا
German 3	almani	آلمانی
Germany	alman	آلمان
to GET, take, receive	gereftæn	گرفتن
	gereft/gir	گرفت
get up, stand up, rise	bolænd shodæn	بلند شدن
girl, daughter	dokhtær	دختر
to GIVE	dadæn	دادن (به)
	dad/dah (/d)	داد / ده
to GIVE away, grant, bestow; forgive	bækhshidæn	بخشیدن
	bækhshid/bækhsh	بخشید/بخش
glad, pleased, happy 5	khoshvæqt, khosh hal	خوشوقت، خوشحال
"GLADLY; I'll be happy to."	khosh hal mishævæm	خوشحال میشوم/
	(khoshal mishæm)	(خوشال میشم)
glance, look	negah	نگاه
glass (for drinking)	livan	لیوان
glasses, eyeglasses	eynæk	عینک
one who wears GLASSES	eynæki	عینکی
to wear GLASSES	eynæk zædæn	عینک زدن
glossary, dictionary	loqætname	لغت نامه، واژه نامه
to GO 7	ræftæn	رفتن / رو / (ر)
	ræft/ræv (-/r)	
to GO by, pass, pass by	gozæshtæn	گذشتن
	gozæsht/gozær	گذشت / گذر
God; lord 5	khoda	خُدا
good; well	khub	خوب
"it's fine," "It's GOOD." 1	khub-e	(خوبه)
Good for you Wonderful!(What God wills)	mashallah	ماشاءالله
Good going! Wonderful! 6	barikælla	بارک الله
"Good!" "What could be better!"	che behtær!	چه بهتر
(I, you, etc.) had a GOOD time.	(be mæn/be shoma) khosh gozæsht	به من / (به شما) خوش گذشت
"Good-bye." (see 2.3.2)	(khodafez) khoda hafez-e shoma bashæd	خدا حافظ شما [باشد]
"Say good-bye!" 2	(khodafezi konid) khoda hafezi konid	خدا حافظی کنید
government	dowlæt (dolæt)	دولت
grade	nomre (nombre)	نمره

G23

Glossary   *MODERN PERSIAN*   واژه نامه

English	Transliteration	Persian
to get a GRADE	nomre aværdæn	نمره آوردن
graduate	fareq-ot-tæhsil	فارغ التحصیل
to GRADUATE	fareq-o-tæhsil shodæn	فارغ التحصیل شدن
grandmother (mother of either parent)	madærbozorg	مادر بزرگ
grape(s)	ængur	انگور
gray	khakestæri	خاکستری
grazing ground, pasture	chæragah	چراگاه
Greece 6	yunan	یونان
Greek 6	yunani	یونانی
green	sæbz	سبز
green herb khoresht	qorme sæbzi	خورش قرمه سبزی (قورمه سبزی)
profusely green, verdant	særsæbz	سر سبز
greens, vegetables, herbs	sæbzi	سبزی
to GREET	sælam kærdæn (be)	سلام کردن (به)
"Greet!" 1	sælam konid be___	سلام کنید به
ground, soil, earth, dirt	zæmin	زمین
grow up	bozorg shodæn	بزرگ شدن
grow, be raised	be æmæl amædæn	بعمل آمدن
grow, raise; pick up	bær dashtæn	بر داشتن
guest	mehman (mehmun)	مهمان (مهمون)
guitar	gitar	گیتار
gulf	khælij	خلیج

H

English	Transliteration	Persian
habit, custom	adæt	عادت
to be in the HABIT of, accustomed to	adæt dashtæn	عادت داشتن
Hafez (14th c. lyric poet)	hafez	حافظ
hair(s)	mu/muha (mua)	مو/موها (موا)
half	nim	نیم
half an hour	nim sæet	نیم ساعت
halt, stand	istadæn (vaystadæn)	ایستادن (وایستادن)
hand	dæst	دست
handbag, bag; briefcase; purse	kif	کیف
handkerchief	dæstmal	دستمال
handwriting 5	khæt	خط
happen; become, get	shodæn	شدن
What happened?	che shod? (chi shod)	چه شد؟ (چی شد)

Glossary   *MODERN PERSIAN*   واژه نامه

English	Transliteration	Persian
Did it work (out)?	shod?	شد؟
happiness, pleasure	khoshhali	خوشحالی
With greatest HAPPINESS, with pleasure	(ba kæmal-e khoshhali)	با کمال خوشحالی
happy, pleased, glad 5	khoshvæqt, khoshhal	خوشوقت، خوشحال
happy (with), satisfied, content, pleased	razi	راضی
"I'm very HAPPY/ pleased to have MET you." 5	kheli khoshvæqt shodæm	خوشوقت شدم
hard, difficult 6	sækht	سخت
Hasan, Hassan	hæsæn	حسن
hat	kolah	کلاه
to HAVE; to keep 5	dashtæn	داشتن
	dasht/dar	داشت/دار
have access ____	be___rah dashtæn	به ــ راه داشتن
he, she ("it" also in colloquial)	u (un)	او (اون)
head; end, at, in, to	sær	سر
headache (physical)	sær-dærd	سر درد
headache (abstract), nuisance	dærd-e sær	درد سر
to HEAR; smell	shenidæn	شنیدن
	shenid/sheno	شنید/شنو
heart (abstract); stomach	del	دل
heart (in physical sense)	qælb	قلب
to be HEATED up, to be warmed	gærm shodæn	گرم شدن
to HEAT up, warm	gærm kærdæn	گرم کردن
heat, warmth	gærma	گرما
heavens, sky	aseman (asemun)	آسمان (آسمون)
heavy	sængin	سنگین
heavy; expensive 6	geran (gerun)	گران (گرون)
Hebrew 5	ebri	عبری
helicopter	hlikopter (chærkhbal)	هلیکوپتر (چرخ بال)
hello 1	sælam	سلام
"Say hello to ___"	sælam konid be___	سلام کنید به
to HELP, aid, assist	komæk kærdæn be	کمک کردن به ــ
Help him/her (out)!	komækesh konid	کمکش کنید
herbs, greens, vegetables	sæbzi	سلام
herd, flock	gælle	گله
herd-tending, animal husbandry	gælledari	گله داری
here 3	inja	اینجا
high school diploma	diplom	دیپلم
high school student	mohæs(s)el	محصل

Glossary	*MODERN PERSIAN*	واژه نامه
high, tall; loud	bolænd	بلند
higher, louder	balændtær	بلند تر
hiking, walking	piade-rævi	پیاده روی
Hindi; Indian (adj. or person) 5	hendi	هندی
historian	tarikhnevis	تاریخ نویس
historiography	tarikhnevisi	تاریخ نویسی، تاریخ نگاری
history; date	tarikh	تاریخ
to HIT, strike; to play (an instrument)	zædæn	زدن
	zæd/zæn	زد / زن
to HOLD; keep, stop	negah dashtæn (negær)	نگاه داشتن (نگر)
holiday	tæ:tilat	تعطیل
holiday(s), vacation	tæ:tilat	تعطیلات
Holland, Netherlands 6	holænd	هلند
home, house 2	khane (khune)	خانه (خونه)
home, house	mænzel	منزل
home cooking	dæstpokht	دست پخت
to miss, be HOMESICK (for)	delæm bæraye__tæng æst (e)	دل برای ــ تنگ بودن
homesick	deltæng	دلتنگ
homework 5	tæklif-e shæb	تکلیف شب
honestly, really	valla(h)	والله
HONORIFICS		
Mister, Sir	aqa	آقا
sir (polite) (see 6.2.1 & 14.3)	qorban (qorbun)	قربان (قربون)
Ms. (Mrs. or Miss); wife	khanom (khanum)	خانم (خانوم)
(used in addressing women)	særkar	سرکار
I HOPE to see you; look forward to seeing.	be omid-e didar	به امید دیدار
horseback riding	æsp-sævari	اسب سواری
Hoseyn, Hosein, Hossein	hoseyn	حسین
hospital	bimarestan	بیمارستان
burning HOT	daq	داغ
hot, warm	gærm	گرم
hotel 5	hotel	هتل
hour, clock	saæt	ساعت
house, home	mænzel, khane (khune)	منزل: خانه (خونه)
housekeeper (wife)	khanedar (khunedar)	خانه دار (خونه دار)
housekeeping	khanedari (khunedari)	خانه داری (خونه داری)
to do HOUSEKEEPING/HOUSEWORK	khanedari kærdæn	خانه داری کردن

Glossary — MODERN PERSIAN — واژه نامه

English	Transliteration	Persian
how; in what manner 7	chetowr (chetor, chetori)	چطور (چطوری)
"HOW are you?" 2	(hal-e shoma)?	(حالِ شما؟)
"HOW are you? 1	hal-e shoma chetowr æst?	حال شما چطور است؟ (چطوره)
how, how come (literally, from where) 3	æz koja	از کُجا
how about, what about 4	chetor? (2)	چطور؟
How do you say_? ("What does_become?")	_chi mishe?	(چی میشه؟)
how long	chænd væqt	چند وقت
how many; several 5	chænd ta	چند (تا)
how much; so much!	cheqædr (cheqæd)	چقدر (چقد)
how, in what way	chejur (chejuri)	چه جور (چجوری)
to be HUMBLE, self-deprecating, modest	shekæstenæfsi kærdæn	شکسته نفسی کردن
humid, moist	mærtub	مرطوب
humility, modesty, self-deprecation	shekæstenæfsi	شکسته نفسی
hundred 5	sæd	صد
hungry	gorosne (Tehrani: goshne)	گرسنه (گشنه)
"HURRY up!"	zud bash	زود باش
to HURT, pain	dærd kærdæn	درد کردن
husband 3	showhær	شوهر

I

English	Transliteration	Persian
I, me 2	mæn	من
ice	yækh	یخ
idiom, expression	estelah	اصطلاح
idle, unoccupied	bikar	بیکار
if	ægær (æge)	اگر (اگه)
to IGNITE, set alight, turn on	rowshæn shodæn	روشن کردن
ill, sick (slightly more polite than مریض)	nakhash	نا خوش
immediately, at once	fowræn	فوراً
impatient, angry	æsæbani (æsæbuni)	عصبانی (عصبونی)
important	mohem	مهم
in 1	dær; tu-ye (tu)	در؛ توی (تو)
in (my) opinion 6	be næzær-e (mæn)	به نظر (من)
in brief, in short	kholase	خلاصه
in class	sær-e kelas	سر کلاس
in English, in German, ect. 2	be farsi, be almani	به فارسی، به آلمانی
in front of	jelo-e/jelo-ye	جلو / جلوی
in front of, forward	jelo	جلو
in order to, because	bæraye inke	برای اینکه

English	Transliteration	Persian
in short, in brief	kholase	خلاصه
in that case (interjection) 5	pæs	پس
in what way, how	chejur (chejuri)	چه جور (چجوری)
in, end, at, to; head	sær	سر
in/at his/her/its place	(sær-e jash)	(سر جاش)
inappropriate	bija	بیجا
to INCONVENIENCE	zæhmæt dadæn (be)	زحمت دادن (به)
inconvenience, trouble	zæhmæt	زحمت
to INCREASE (intr.)	ziad shodæn	زیاد شدن
to INCREASE (tr.)	ziad kærdæn	زیاد کردن
increase; (gr.) Persian genitive (5.2; 5.11.1)	ezafe	اضافه
India 6	hend/hendustan	هند/هندوستان
Indian 6	hendi	هندی
inexpensive, cheap 6	ærzan (ærzun)	ارزان (ارزون)
infinitely, extremely	bi-næhayæt	بی نهایت
infinitive	mæsdær	مصدر
inhabitant, citizen 6	æhl	اهل
ink 6	jowhær (johær)	جوهر
intelligent	bahush	با هوش
intention; meaning (what people mean)	mænzur	منظور
interest, liking, fondness	ælaqe	علاقه
to be INTERESTED (in), to be fond of	ælaqe dashtæn (be)	علاقه داشتن (به)
interesting 6	jaleb	جالب
international	beynolmælæli	بین المللی (جهانی)
interrogative	soali	سوالی
interval (space)	fasele	فاصله
intonation, melody	ahæng	آهنگ
to INTRODUCE (to)	ash(e)na kærdæn (ba)	آشنا کردن (با)
to INTRODUCE (to)	moær(r)efi kærdæn (be)	معرفی کردن (به)
introduction	moær(r)efi	معرفی
invitation	dæ:væt	دعوت
to be INVITED	dæ:væt dashtæn	دعوت داشتن
to INVITE	dæ:væt kærdæn	دعوت کردن
Iran	iran (irun)	ایران (ایرون)
Iranian	irani (iruni)	ایرانی (ایرونی)
Iranian Studies	iranshenasi	ایرانشناسی
Iranist	iranshenas	ایرانشناس
Ireland, Eire	irlænd	ایرلند
Irish	irlændi	ایرلندی

Glossary — MODERN PERSIAN — واژه نامه

English	Transliteration	Persian
is (see budæn)	æst/-st	است
Isfahan	esfæhan	اصفهان
Isfahani	esfæhani	اصفهانی
Israel	esrail	اسرائیل
Israeli	esraili	اسرائیلی
Istanbul	estambol (eslambol)	استانبول/اسلامبول
Istanbuli	estamboli (eslamboli)	استانبولی/اسلامبولی
"it doesn't matter, no problem"	eshgali nædaræd (nædare)	اشکالی ندارد (اشکالی نداره)
Italian 6	italiai	ایتالیائی
Italy 6	italia	ایتالیا

J

English	Transliteration	Persian
Jafari, Jaafari	jæ:færi	جعفری
Jalal	jælal	جلال
jam (jelly)	moræbba	مربا
Jamshid, mythical Iranian king,, Solomon 1	jæmshid	جمشید
January	zhanvie	ژانویه
Japan 6	zhapon	ژاپن
Japanese 3	zhaponi	ژاپنی
jazz	jaz	جاز
Jeanne d'arc (Joan of Arc)	zhandark	ژاندارک
job, work, occupation 5	kar	کار
jogging, running	do(w)	دو
joined, together, connected 8	sær-e hæm	سر هم
joke	shukhi	شوخی
JOKE, to make a joke 5	shukhi kærdæn	شوخی کردن
journey, trip	mosaferæt	مسافرت
juice, water 5	ab	آب
July	zhuie	ژوئن
June	zhuæn	ژوئیه
just as, as, in the same way, likewise	hæmintor (hæmintowr)	همینطور

K

English	Transliteration	Persian
Kamran (one who achieves his desires) 3	kamran	کامران
kebab, (charcoal-) broiled meat 5	kebab	کباب
to KEEP, hold; stop	negæh dashtæn	نگاه داشتن (نگر)
Kerman (a city and province in south)	kerman	کرمان
kerosene, oil	næft	نفت

Glossary	*MODERN PERSIAN*	واژه نامه
kerosene seller	næfti	نفتی
key	kelid	کلید
khoresht (a stew or thick sauce; see 5.12)	khoresh (khoresht)	خورش (خورشت)
kilometer	kilometr	کیلومتر
kind, affectionate	mehreban (mehrebun)	مهربان
kind, type	no(w)	نوع
that KIND of (see also "way")	antowr (untor) anjur (unjur)	آنطور (اونطور)- آنجور (اونجور)
this KIND of (see also "way")	intowr (intor), injur	اینطور- اینجور
KINDLY, to be kind or courteous	lotf dashtæn/kærdæn	لطف داشتن/کردن
kindness, courtesy	lotf	لطف
kindness, generosity	mærhæmmæt	مهربان (مهربون)
kitchen	ashpæzkhane (ashpæzkhune)	آشپزخانه (آشپزخونه)
knee	zanu	زانو
to KNOCK at the door	dær zædæn	در زدن
to KNOW (see 8.2.1 & drills 10.10.3-6)	danestæn (dunestæn) danest/dan (dunest/dun)	دانستن (دونستن) دانست/دان (دونست/دون)
"she/he knows." 2	(midune)	(میدونه)
"you know." 3	(midunin)	(میدونین)
"I know." 3	(midunæm)	(میدونم)
to KNOW (person) (8.2.1 drills 10.10.3-6)	shenakhtæn shenakht/shenas	شناختن شناخت/شناس
to KNOW how to (8.2.1 & drills 10.10)	bolænd budæn bolænd bud/--	بلد بودن بلد بود
knowledge	danesh	دانش
Koran/Qur'an	qor'an	قرآن
korsi (heater and blanket)	korsi	کرسی
Kurd 6	kord	کرد
Kurdistan	kordestan	کردستان

L

laboratory	azmayeshgah	آزمایشگاه
laboratory (archaic word, occasionally)	laboratuar	لابراتوار
lamb meat	gusht-e gusfænd	گوشت گوسفند
lamp, light	cheraq	چراغ
language; tongue 5	zæban (zæbun)	زبان
large, big 6	bozorg	بزرگ

Glossary — MODERN PERSIAN — واژه نامه

English	Transliteration	Persian
last, final, end	zkhær	آخر
last, past	gozæshte	گذشته
last; ago	pish	پیش
last name	esm-e famil	اسم فامیل (نام خانوادگی)
last night	dishæb	دیشب
late	dir	دیر
to be LATE	dir kærdæn	دیر کردن
to LAUGH	khændidæn	خندیدن
	khændid/khænd	خندید/خند
law (other than Qur'anic)	hoquq	حقوق
lawyer	vækil	وکیل
lazy	tæmbæ1	تنبل
to become LAZY	tæmbæl shodæn	تنبل شدن
to LEARN 3	yad gereftæn	یاد گرفتن
to LEAVE (a) space	fasele gozashtæn	فاصله گذاشتن
Lebanese 6	lobnani	لبنان
Lebanon 6	lobnan	لبنانی
lecturer, trainer, coach	moræbbi	مربی
left	chæp	چپ
lesson 5	dærs	درس
letter 5	name	نامه
letter(s) of the alphabet	hærf/horuf	حرف/حروف
librarian 6	ketabdar1	کتابدار
library 5	ketabkhane (ketabkhune)	کتابخانه (کتابخونه)
library science, librarianship	ketabdari	کتابداری
to LIE	doruq goftæn	دروغ گفتن
lie	doruq	دروغ (دوروغ)
to LIE down; to sleep 5	khabidæn	خوابیدن
life 5	zendegi	زندگی
life, dear, soul (see 13.1.3)	jan (jun)	جان (جون)
light (weight)	sæbok	سبک
like	mesl-e	مثل
to LIKE (see 16.11.2 "Type Three")	khosh___amædæn (æz)	(خوش ــ آمدن (از)
to LIKE, love 6	dust dashtæn	دوست داشتن
likewise, in that same way	hæmintor	همینطور
likewise, in that same way	hæmchonan	همچنان
likewise, the same way, just like that	hæmchonin/hæmchenin/be hæmchenin	همچنین/همچنین
liking, interest, fondness	ælaqe	علاقه

English	Transliteration	Persian
lime	limu	لیمو
lime juice (concentrated)	ab limu	آب لیمو
limits, boundaries	hodud	حدود
linguist	zæbanshenas	زبانشناس
linguistics	zæbanshenasi	زبانشناسی
lip	læb	لب
to LISTEN	gush kærdæn/dadæn	گوش کردن/دادن
"Listen!" 1	gush konid	گوش کنید
lit; luminous	rowshæn (roshan)	روشن
literary	ædæbi	ادبی
literary (vs. colloquial), written	neveshtæri	نوشتاری
literature	ædæbiat	ادبیات
a LITTLE, (very) little; seldom 3	kæm	کم
a LITTLE	yek zærre (ye zære)	یک ذره (یه ذره)
a LITTLE bit	zærre (zære)	ذره
little, small; young 6	kuchek (kuchik)	کوچک (کوچیک)
to LIVE	zendegi kærdæn	زندگی کردن
"she/he lives" 1	zendegi mikone	(زندگی میکنه)
living room	otaq-e pæzirani	اطاق پذیرائی
load, burden; time, occurrence	bar	بار
located, situated	vaqe	واقع
London 2	lændæn	لندن
lonely; alone; only 5	tænha	تنها
look, glance	negah	نگاه
to LOOK (at)	negah kærdæn	نگاه کردن (به)
lord; God	khoda خدا	
Los Angeles 1	los anjeles	لوس آنجلس
LOSE, to lose	gom kærdæn	گم کردن
LOST, to become lost	gom shodæn	گم شدن
lost	gom	گم
a LOT, very, much; too, too much; often 3	ziad	زیاد
loud; high 3	bolænd	بلند
louder; higher 3	bolændtær	بلند تر
in LOVE	asheq عاشق	
to be/fall in LOVE with someone	asheq-e kæsi budæn/shodæn	عاشق کسی بودن/شدن
to LOVE, like 6	dust dashtæn	دوست داشتن
love	eshq	عشق
lovely, beautiful	khoshgel	خوشگل

lower back, waist	kæmær	کمر
luck	shans	شانس
to be LUCKY, fortunate	shans aværdæn/dashtæn	شانس آوردن/داشتن
lump sugar, sugar cubes	qænd	قند
lunch 6	nahar/næhar	ناهار/نهار
lying down, asleep, sleeping	khabide	خوابیده
lyric, poetry, poem, song	she:r	شعر/اشعار

M

M.A., M.S.	fowq-e lisans	فوق لیسانس (کارشناسی ارشد)
magazine 5	mæjælle	مجله
magic marker	mazhik	ماژیک
Mahin	mæhin	مهین
mail 5	post	پست
to MAIL (a letter)	post kærdæn	پست کردن
majority	æksæriæt	اکثریت
to MAKE, build	sakhtæn	ساختن
to MAKE; to prepare correct; cook, repair 5	dorost kærdæn	درست کردن
man 5	mærd	مرد
Manije	mænizhe	منیژه
manliness	mærdi	مردی
many, various	mokhtælef	مختلف
map; plan	næqshe	نقشه
March	mars	مارس
market	bazar	بازار
marriage	ezdevaj	ازدواج
married	motæ'æhhel	متأهل
to MARRY (get a husband)	showhær kærdæn	شوهر کردن
to MARRY (get a wife)	zæn gereftæn	زن گرفتن
to MARRY (to get married) (to)	ezdevaj kærdæn (ba)	ازدواج کردن (با)
match(es) 5	kebrit	کبریت
mathematician	riazidan (riazidun)	ریاضی دان (ریاضی دون)
mathematics	riazi	ریاضی
May	me	مه
"May I... May one..." (see 10.8.3 n.1)	(momken-e...)	(ممکنه)
"May I?, May one?"	ejaze hæst	(اجازه هست؟)
maybe, perhaps	shayæd	شاید
Mazandaran	mazændæran	مازندران
Mazandarani	mazændærani	مازندرانی

Glossary	MODERN PERSIAN	واژه نامه

me, I	mæn	من
"me too", "me neither"	mæn hæm (mæn-æm) hæmintor	من هم همینطور (منم همینطور)
meal; food 5	qæza, khorak	غذا، خوراک
to MEAN, intend	___ra goftæn	را گفتن
"Do you MEAN this?"	(ino migin?)	(اینو میگین؟)
meaning/s	mæ:ni/mæani	معنی/معانی
meaning; intention	mænzur	منظور
it MEANS, that is 1	yæ:ni	یعنی
means; equipment, necessities	væsile/væsæl	وسیله/وسائل
by no MEANS, no way!	be hich væj(h)!	به هیچ وجه!
meanwhile, at the same time	dær zemn	در ضمن
meat	gusht	گوشت
medicine	tebb	طب، پزشکی
to be pleased to MEET someone	khosh væqt shodæn	خوشوقت شدن
to MEET	ash(e)na shodæn (ba)	آشنا شدن (با)
"I'm very happy to have MET you" 5	kosh væqt shodæm	خوشوقت شدم
meeting, encounter (see 9.14.2)	molaqat	ملاقات
Mehri	mehri	مهری
melody; intonation	ahæng	آهنگ
to MEMORIZE, preserve	hefz kærdæn	حفظ کردن
memory	hafeze	حافظه
memory; mind	yad	یاد
mention	zekr	ذکر
to MENTION	zekr kærdæn	ذکر کردن
"You were MENTIONED with approval."	zekr-e kheyr-e shoma bud	ذکر خیر شما بود
Meshed, Mashhad	mæshæd	مشهد
from MESHED, a pilgrim to Meshed	mæshædi (mæshdi)	مشهدی (مشدی)
messy, noisy, crowded, busy	sholuq	شلوغ
to make a MESS, create an uproar	sholuq kærdæn	شلوغ کردن
method	metod	متد، روش، شیوه
Mexico 2	megzik	مکزیک
Mexican 6	megziki	مکزیکی
microfilm	mikrofilm	میکروفیلم
middle	væsæt	وسط
Middle East	khavær-e miane	خاورمیانه
milk	shir	شیر
mimograph 5	polikopi	پلی کپی
to MIMOGRAPH, ditto 5	polikopi kærdæn	پلی کپی کردن

G34

Glossary   *MODERN PERSIAN*   واژه نامه

English	Transliteration	Persian
Mina	mina	مینا
miniskirt	mini zhup	مینی ژوپ
Minnesota	minisota	مینی سوتا
minute	dæqiqe (dæiqe)	دقیقه (دئیقه)
minute, tiny; exact	dæqiq	دقیق
to make a MISTAKE	eshtebah kærdæn	اشتباه کردن
Mister, Sir	aqa	آقا
mode, current fashion	mod	مد
model	model	مدل
moderate, temperate	mo'tædel	معتدل
modern 6	modern	مدرن
to be MODEST, humble, self-deprecating	shekæstenæfsi kærdæn	شکسته نفسی کردن
modesty, humility, self-deprecation	shekæstenæfsi	شکسته نفسی
Mohammadi, Mohammedi	mohæmmædi	محمدی
moist, humid	mærtub	مرطوب
Monday	doshæmbe	دوشنبه
month, moon; a beauty	mah	ماه
more 3	bishtær	بیشتر
to MORE___(the better)	hærche___tær (behtær)	هر چه ـ تر بهتر
more, other; else; anymore	digær (dige)	دیگر
morning 5	sobh (sob)	صبح (صب)
early morning	sobh-e zud	صبح زود
"Good MORNING!"	sob(h)bekheyr	صبح بخیر
this MORNING	emruz sobh	امروز صبح
mornings, in the morning 5	sob(h)ha (soba)	صبح ها (صبا)
Moscow 2	mosku/mosko	مسکو
most (of)	æksær-e	اکثر
most of the time	bishtær-e owqat	بیشتر اوقات
mostly	æksæræn	اکثراً
mother 1	madær	مادر
motion	hærækæt	حرکت
motor, engine (car)	motor	موتور
Moulin Rouge	mulan ruzh	مولن روژ
mountain	kuh	کوه
mountain climbing	kuh-næværdi	کوه نوردی
mountainous	kuhestani	کوهستانی
mountainous region	kuhestan	کوهستان
moustache	sebil (sibil)	سبیل (سیبیل)
mouth	dæhan (dæhæn)	دهان (دهن)

G35

movie producer	filmsaz	فیلمساز
movies, movie theater	sinema	سینما
Ms. (Mrs. or Miss); wife	khanom (khanum)	خانم (خانوم)
multicolored	rængaræng	رنگارنگ
Munich 2	munikh	مونیخ
music	muzik	موزیک
music (more common that above)	musiqi	موسیقی
musician	muzisiæn	موزیسین
musicologist	musiqishenas	موسیقی شناس
musicology	musiqishenasi	موسیقی شناسی
must, obliged	nachar	ناچار
must, should, ought	bayæd	باید

N

name	nam	نام
name; noun	esm	اسم/اسامی
first NAME	esm-e kuchek (esm-e kuchik)	اسم کوچک (نام کوچک)
last NAME	esm-e famili	اسم فامیلی (نام خانوادگی)
Native to what place, of what origin?	kojai; æhl-e	کجائی/کجایی، اهل
natural gas	gaz	گاز
near 6	næzdik	نزدیک
necessary	lazem	لازم
necessities, equipment; means	væsile/væsael	وسیله/وسائل
neck	gærdæn	گردن
necktie, tie 6	keravat	کراوات
to NEED	lazem dashtæn	لازم داشتن
negative	mænfi	منفی
negative (film)	negativ	نگاتیو
neighbor	hæmsaye	همسایه
neighborhood	mæhælle	محله
neither; none	hich kodam (hich kodum)	هیچ کدام (هیچ کدوم)
Nejad, Nezhad	nezhad	نژاد
nerve(s)	æsæb/æ:sab	عصب/اعصاب
"My NERVES are shot."	æ:sabæm khord æst (e)	اعصابم خرد است (ه)
nervous, anxious, flustered	dæstpache	دستپاچه
never 4	hichvæqt	هیچ وقت
"NEVER mind. No problem."	eyb nædaræd (eyb nædare)	عیب ندارد (نداره)
new	no(w)	نو

Glossary   *MODERN PERSIAN*   واژه نامه

English	Transliteration	Persian
new, modern	jædid	جدید
New Jersey	nio jerzi	نیوجرسی
news (both sg. and pl. in Persian)	khæbær/ækhbar	خبر/اخبار
I have no NEWS/information (about)	khæbær nædaræm (æz)	خبر ندارم (از)
newspaper 5	ruzname	روزنامه
next (in time), other; else, more; anymore	digær (dige)	دیگر (دیگه)
next to (person)	bæqæl-e dæst-e	بغل دست
next to (thing)	bæqæl-e	بغل
Niagara Falls	niagara	نیاگارا
night, evening	shæb	شب
"Good NIGHT!"	shæb bekheyr	شب بخیر
last NIGHT	dishæb	دیشب
night before last	pærishæb	پریشب
nights	shæbha (shæba)	شب ها (شبا)
nine 2	noh	نه
ninety 2	nævæd	نود
no 2	næ	نّه
no (adj.); nothing	hich	هیچ
no one	hichkæs	هیچ کس
none; neither	hichkodam (hichkodum)	هیچ کدام (هیچ کدوم)
nothing	hich chiz (hich(ch)i)	هیچ چیز (هیچی)
no (polite) 3	nækheyr (nækher)	نخیر
by NO means, NO way!	be hich væj(h)!	به هیچ وجه
"NO problem, It doesn't matter"	eshgali nædaræd (nædare)	اشکالی ندارد (نداره)
noise, sound; voice	seda	صدا
noisy, crowded, messy	sholuq (shuluq)	شلوغ
nomadism, squatter, transhumance	kuchneshini	کوچ نشینی
noon	zohr (zo(h)r)	ظهر
right at NOON, noon sharp	sær-e zohr	سر ظهر
north	shomal	شمال
northern, northerner	shomali	شمالی
nose	dæmaq	دماغ
not bad 1	bæd nist	بد نیست
note (musical notation) 5	not	نت
notebook; office	dæftær	دفتر
nothing	hich chiz (hich(ch)i)	هیچ چیز
nothing; no (in compounds)	hich	هیچ
noun; name	esm	اسم/اسامی
novel 6	roman	رمان

G37

Glossary	MODERN PERSIAN	واژه نامه
November	novambr	نوامبر
now 3	hala; æl'an	حالا، الآن
now, right now 7	fe:læn	فعلاً
No Ruz (New Year) (see 8.2)	eyd-e now ruz	عید نوروز
nuisance; headache (abstract)	dærd-e sær	درد سر
number	te:dad	تعداد
number; issue (of a magazine)	shomare	شماره
Nurbakhsh	nurbækhsh	نوربخش
Nuri	nuri	نوری

O

obligation, engagement	gereftari	گرفتاری
obliged, must	nachar; mæjbur	ناچار، مجبور
occupation, work, job 5	kar	کار
occurrence, time; burden, load	bar	بار
October	Oktobr	اکتبر
odor, smell, scent	bu	بو
of course	ælbæte	البته
to be turned OFF, extinguished	khamush shodæn	خاموش شدن
to turn OFF, extinguish	khamush kærdæn	خاموش کردن
to OFFER (to)	taarof kærdæn (be)	تعارف کردن (به)
office (gov't, business)	edare	اداره
office; notebook	dæftær	دفتر
official	ræsmi	رسمی
oil, kerosene	næft	نفت
oil company	sherkæt-e næft	شرکت نفت
to be fixed, repaired, made OKAY	dorost kærdæn	درست کردن
okay; all right (see 9.1.1)	bashæd (bashe)	باشد (باشه)
old, ancient; out of date	qædimi	قدیمی، باستانی، کهن
old, worn out; rag	kohne	کهنه
old age	piri	پیری
older, bigger	bozorgtær	بزرگتر
olive	zeytun	زیتون
on, upon 7	ru-ye (ru)	روی
on time	sær-e saæt; sær-e væqt	سر ساعت، سر وقت
one, a 2	yek (ye)	یک (یه)
"ONE," a person	adæm	آدم
one another, each other	yekdigær	یکدیگر
one by one, singly 7	yeki yeki (dune-dune)	یکی یکی (دونه دونه)

Glossary　　　　　*MODERN PERSIAN*　　　　　واژه نامه

English	Transliteration	Persian
only 4	fæqæt	فقط
only; alone; lonely	tænha	تنها
open	baz	باز
open (intr.)	baz shodæn	باز شدن
to OPEN (tr.)	baz kærdæn	باز کردن
opera	opera	اپرا
opinion 6	næzær	نظر
in my OPINION 6	be næzær-e mæn	به نظر من
opportunity, chance	forsæt	فرصت
find the OPPORTUNITY (to), to have a chance (to)	forsæt kærdæn	فرصت کردن
opposite	bær æks	برعکس
opposite, face to face, across from	ruberu	روبرو
or 4	ya	یا
orange 5	portoqal/porteqal	پرتقال
orange (color)	portoqali	پرتقالی
orange (color)	narenji	نارنجی
orchard, garden	baq	باغ
organization; society	sazman	سازمان
of what ORIGIN, native to what place	kojai; æhl-e	کجائی/کجایی، اهل کجا
original; classic	æsil	اصیل
originally; at all (with neg.)	æslæn	اصلاً
other; else, more; anymore, next (in time)	digær (dige)	دیگر (دیگه)
ought, must, should	bayæd	باید
out, outside	birun	بیرون
out of date; old, ancient	qædimi	قدیمی
out-of-sorts; unwell	kesel	کسل
ox, bull	gav-e nær	گاو نر

P

English	Transliteration	Persian
package	bæste	بسته
page; record	sæfhe (sæfe)	صفحه
pain	dærd	درد
to take PAINS, to go through the trouble	zæhmæt keshidæn	زحمت کشیدن
paint; color	ræng	رنگ
to PAINT	næqqashi kærdæn	نقاشی کردن
painter	næqqash	نقاش
painting	næqqashi	نقاشی
Pakistan 6	pakestan	پاکستان

Glossary — MODERN PERSIAN — واژه نامه

English	Transliteration	Persian
Pakistani 6	pakestani	پاکستانی
pants, trousers	shælvar	شلوار
paper 4	kaqæz	کاغذ
part, section, department (university)	bækhsh	بخش
part, section, portion	qesmæt	قسمت
particle, small amount, bit	yek (ye) khorde	یک (یه) خورده
party	mehmani	مهمانی
Parvin, (name; constellation Pleiades)	pærvin	پروین
to PASS, go by, pass by	gozæshtæn	گذشتن
	gozæsht/gozær	گذشت/گذر
past, last	gozæshte	گذشته
pastries, sweets, candy	shirini	شیرینی
patience	sæbr	صبر
patient, a sick person; sick 6	mæriz; bimar	مریض، بیمار
pen	qælæm	قلم
automatic fountain PEN	khodnevis	خودنویس
ball point PEN	khodkar	خودکار
pencil	medad	مداد
people	mærdom	مردم
percentage	dær sæd	درصد
perfection	kæmal	کمال
perhaps, maybe	shayæd	شاید
permission	ejaze	اجازه
"PERMIT me! Allow me!"	ejaze bedin	(اجازه بدین)
to PERMIT	ejaze dadæn	اجازه دادن
Persian Gulf	khælij-e fars	خلیج فارس
Persian 2	farsi	فارسی
person	kæs	کس
person (often used as a numerator)	næfær	نفر
a PERSON, "one"	adæm	آدم
a PERSON, someone	kæsi	کسی
philosophy	fælsæfe	فلسفه
photocopy 5	fotokopi	فتوکپی
to PHOTOCOPY	fotokopi kærdæn	فتوکپی کردن
photograph, picture	æks	عکس
photographer	ækkas	عکاس
photography	ækkasi	عکاسی
to do PHOTOGRAPHY	ækkasi kærdæn	عکاسی کردن
phrase	ebaræt	عبارت

Glossary — MODERN PERSIAN — واژه نامه

English	Transliteration	Persian
physicist	fizikdan (fizikdun)	فیزیک دان
physics 2	fizik	فیزیک
to PICK (flowers); arrange	chidæn	چیدن
	chid/chin	چید/چین
pick up	bær dashtæn	برداشتن
	bær dasht/bær dar	برداشت/بردار
pick up (as a child), embrace	bæqæl kærdæn	بغل کردن
pick up; grow, raise	bær dashtæn	بر داشتن
to take PICTURE(s) (of)	æks gereftæn (æz)	عکس گرفتن (از)
a PILGRIM to Meshed; Meshedi	mæshædi (mæshdi)	مشهدی (مشدی)
pink	suræti	صورتی
Too bad! It's (really) a shame/PITY	heyf!/kheyli heyf æst (heyf-e)	حیف/خیلی حیف است (حیفه)
to PLACE, put; allow	gozashtæn	گذاشتن
	gozasht/gozar (zasht/zar)	گذاشت/گذر
place 8	ja	جا
place 8	mæhæll-e	محل
place of work	mæhæll-e kar	محل کار
plain	dæsht	دشت
plan; map	næqshe	نقشه
plan, program	bærname	برنامه
to PLAN, intend, have in mind	dær nærær dashtæn	در نظر داشتن
The PLAN Organization	sazman-e bærname	سازمان برنامه
to PLANT	kashtæn	کاشتن
	kasht/kar	کاش/کار
play, drama	næmayeshname	نمایشنامه
to PLAY 5	bazi kærdæn	بازی کردن
to PLAY (an instrument); to hik, strike	zædæn	زدن
plaza, square	meydan (meydun)	میدان (میدون)
pleasant, agreeable, nice	khoshækhlaq	خوش اخلاق
"please!" (taarof) (see 3.3)	khahesh mikonæm (khaesh)	خواهش میکنم
"Please!" 1	lotfæn; (lotf konid)	لطفاً (لطف کنید)
pleased, glad, happy 5	khoshvæqt, khoshhal	خوشوقت، خوشحال
pleased, happy (with), satisfied, content	razi	راضی
"I'm happy/PLEASED to have met you" 5	khoshvæqt shodæm	خوشوقت شدم
to be happy, PLEASED	khoshhal shodæn	خوشحال شدن
"With greatest PLEASURE"	(ba kæmal-e meyl)	با کمال میل
"With greatest PLEASURE"	ba kæmal-e khoshhali	با کمال خوشحالی
pleasure, happiness	khoshhali	خوشحالی

G41

plum, tomato (originally only "plum")	go(w)je	گوجه
plural	jæm	جمع
p.m., afternoon	bæ:d æz zo(h)r	بعد از ظهر
pocket	jib	جیب
poem, poetry, song, lyric	she:r	شعر/اشعار
point of view	næzær	نظر
from the POINT of view of...	az næzær-e...	از نظر
polite response to a request	chæshm 2	چشم
political science	olum-e siasi	علوم سیاسی
politics, diplomacy, tact, policy	siasæt	سیاست
pomegranate	ænar	انار
pomegranate and walnut *khoresht*	khoresh-e fesenjun	خورش فسنجون
poor	fæqir	فقیر
population	jæmiæt	جمعیت
port	bændær	بندر
portion, part, section	qesmæt	قسمت
positive, affirmative	mosbæt	مثبت
possessions, effects	æsbab	اسباب
possible 5	momken	ممکن
"It's POSSIBLE." "Is is possible?" 5	mishe	(میشه/ممکنه)
"It's not POSSIBLE."	momken nist	ممکن نیست
potato and dried yellow pea *khoresh*	khoresh-e qiyme	خورش قیمه
practice, exercise, drill 5	tæmrin	تمرین/تمرینات
to PRACTICE	tæmrin kærdæn	تمرین کردن
to PRAISE, commend	tæ:rif kærdæn (æz)	تعریف کردن (از)
praise; description	tæ:rif	تعریف
to PREPARE	tæhie kærdæn	تهیه کردن
to PREPARE, make ready	hazer kærdæn	حاضر کردن
to PREPARE; to correct, make, fix; cook 5	dorost kærdæn	درست کردن
present, ready 6	hazer	حاضر
pretty, beautiful 6	qæshæng	قشنگ
previous, prior	qæbli	قبلی
previous to, ago	qæbl	قبل
previously	qæblæn	قبلاً
price	qeymæt	قیمت
to PRINT	chap kærdæn	چاپ کردن
print, printing	chap	چاپ
to be PRINTED	chap shodæn	چاپ شدن
printing	chap	چاپ

Glossary — MODERN PERSIAN — واژه نامه

English	Transliteration	Persian
"No PROBLEM, it doesn't matter"	eshgali nædaræd (nædare)	اشکالی ندارد (اشکالی نداره)
product (esp. agricultural)	mæhsul.mæsulat	محصول/محصولات
professor	ostad	استاد
associate PROFESSOR	daneshyar	دانشیار
program, plan	bærname	برنامه
to PROMISE	qo(w)l dadæn	قول دادن
reflexive, emphatic PRONOUN, self, 5.11.	khod	خود
to PRONOUNCE	tælæffoz kærdæn (tælæfoz)	تلفظ کردن
"Pronounce!" 1	tælæffoz konid	تلفظ کنید
pronunciation	tælæffoz	تلفظ
property; belongings	mal	مال
province	ostan	استان
provincial capital; center	mærkæz	مرکز
psyche	rævan	روان
psychologist 8	rævanshenas	روانشناس
psychology 8	rævanshenasi	روانشناسی
to PULL, draw	keshidæn	کشیدن
	keshid/kesh	کشید/کش
pullover, sweater 6	pulover	پولور
punctual	væqtshenas	وقت شناسی
pupil, student (through high school); apprentice 5	shagerd	شاگرد
purple, violet	bænæfsh	بنفش
purse; bag, handbag; briefcase	kif	کیف
to PUT, place; allow	gozashtæn	گذاشتن
	gozasht/gozar (zasht/zar)	گذاشت/گذار
to PUT on clothes	lebas pushidæn	لباس پوشیدن

Q

English	Transliteration	Persian
Qashqai (a Turkish tribe from South)	qæshqai	قشقائی
quality, character	jæmbe	جنبه
quarter	rob	ربع
quarter of an hour	rob saæt	ربع ساعت
question 3	soal	سؤال/سؤال، سؤالات
to QUESTION, to ask	porisdæn; soal kærdæn	پرسیدن: سؤال کردن
quick, fast	zud	زود
quickly, soon	bezudi	بزودی
quiet, quietly, softly; slow 3	yævash	یواش، آهسته

Glossary	MODERN PERSIAN	واژه نامه
quiet, silent	saket	ساکت
quieter; slower	yævashtær	یواشتر
quite a few, a number	chændin	چندین

R

radar	radar	رادار
radio	radio	رادیو
rag; old, worn out	kohne	کهنه
rain	baran (barun)	باران (بارون)
rain	baran amædæn (barun)	باران آمدن (باریدن)
raincoat, rainy	barani (baruni)	بارانی (بارونی)
rainy, raincoat	barani (baruni)	بارانی (بارونی)
raise	bozorg kærdæn	بزرگ کردن
raise, grow; pick up	bær dashtæn	برداشتن
be RAISED, grow	be æmæl amædæn	بعمل آمدن
Rasht (capital of the Gilan province)	ræsht	رشت
to READ, study (with object); to sing 4	khandæn	خواندن (خوندن)
	khand/khan (khund/khun)	خواند/خوان (خوند/خون)
readable, legible	khana	خوانا
ready, present 6	hazer	حاضر
to become READY	hazer shodæn	حاضر شدن
to make READY, prepare	hazer kærdæn	حاضر کردن
reality	vaqeiæt	واقعیت
"Really?"; 1	(rast migin?)	(راست میگن؟)
"Really?"; by the way	rasti	راستی
really, honestly 5	valla(h)	والله
really, truly	vaqeæn (vaqæ:n)	واقعاً
really, truly	jeddæn	جداً
to RECALL, remember	yad___amædæn	یاد ـــ آمدن
receipt, receiving	dær yaft	دریافت
to RECEIVE	dær yaft kærdæn	دریافت کردن
to RECEIVE, get, take	gereftæn	گرفتن
	gereft/gir	گرفت/گیر
receiving, receipt	dær yaft	دریافت
recently, a little while ago	chændi pish	چندی پیش
recently, fresh	taze	تازه
to RECORD	zæbt kærdæn	ضبط کردن
record; page	sæfhe (sæfe)	صفحه (صفه)

English	Transliteration	Persian
tape RECORDER	zæbt-e sowt	ضبط صوت
red 7	qermez	قرمز
to REDUCE, diminish	kæm kærdæn	کم کردن
refrigerator	yækhchal	یخچال
region	nahie	ناحیه
region, country	særzæmin	سرزمین
regretful, sorry	motæ'æssef	متأسف
regretfully, unfortunately	motæ'æssefane	متأسفانه
relative (to)	nesbæt (be)	نسبت
relative, family	famil	فامیل، خانواده
relatively 6	nesbætæn	نسبتاً
relevant (to)	mærbut (be)	مربوط (به)
religion	din/ædyan	دین/ادیان
to stay, REMAIN	mandæn	ماندن
	mand/man (mund/mun)	ماند/مان (موند/مون)
to REMEMBER	yad___budæn	یاد ___ بودن
to REMEMBER, recall	yad___amædæn	یاد ___ آمدن
rent	ejare	اجاره
to RENT (from)	ejare kærdæn (æz)	اجاره کردن (از)
to RENT (to)	ejare dadæn (be)	اجاره دادن (به)
to REPAIR; make, fix; correct; cook 5	dorost kærdæn	درست کردن
to REPEAT	tekrar kærdæn	تکرار کردن
"Repeat!" 1	tekrar konid	تکرار کنید
repetition	tekrar	تکرار
reply, answer	jævab	جواب
reporter 6	khæbærnegar	خبرنگار
request	khahesh (khaesh); dær khast	خواهش، درخواست
to REQUEST	dær khast kærdæn	درخواست کردن
to REQUEST (of, from)	khahesh kærdæn (khaesh)	خواهش کردن
to REQUEST, want	khastæn	خواستن
to do RESEARCH	tæhqiq kærdæn	تحقیق کردن
research	tæhqiq/tæhqiqat	تحقیق/تحقیقات
resembling each other, alike	mesl-e hæm	مثل هم
to REST 5	estærahæt kærdæn	استراحت کردن
rest 5	estærahæt	استراحت
restaurant 5	restoran	رستوران
result(s)	nætije/næteyej	نتیجه/نتایج

to RETURN, come back	bær gæshtæn	برگشتن
	bær gæsht/bær gærd	برگشت/برگرد
review 7	do(w)re	دوره
to REVIEW 7	do(w)re kærd/kon	دوره کردن
"Let's REVIEW!" 7	do(w)re konim	دوره کنیم
to REVOLVE, turn	chærkhidæn	چرخیدن
Reza	reza	رضا
rice (uncooked)	berenj	برنج
right (direction); true; straight	rast	راست
right, correct	dorost	درست
"That's correct. It's right." 1	dorost-e	(درسته)
"Is that correct? Is it right?" 2	dorost-e?	(درسته؟)
right at noon, noon sharp	sær-e zohr	سر ظهر
ring (but not just a plain band)	ængoshtær	انگشتر
ripped, torn	pare	پاره
rise, stand up, get up	bolænd shodæn	بلند شدن
river	rud/rudkhane (rudkhune)	رود/رودخانه (رودخونه)
road	rah	راه
road construction	rahsazi	راهسازی
Rome 2	rom	رم
room	otaq	اتاق
bedroom	otaq-e khab	اتاق خواب
dining room	otaq-e nahar khori	اتاق ناهار خوری
living room	otaq-e pazirai	اتاق پذیرایی
roommate	hæmotaq (hæmotaqi)	هم اتاق (هم اتاقی)
rose; flower	gol	گل
Rumi, Jalaleddin, great mystical poet	mowlana jælal-ed-din-e rumi	مولانا جلال الدین رومی
to RUN	dævidæn (/doidæn/)	دویدن
running, jogging	do(w)	دو
Russia 6	rusie	روسیه
Russian (adj., n.) 2	rusi	روسی
Russian (n.) 6	rus	روس

S
Saba	sæba	صبا
sad	qæmgin	غمگین
Sadeqi, Sadeghi	sadeqi	صادقی

Glossary — *MODERN PERSIAN* — واژه نامه

English	Transliteration	Persian
Salaam ("Peace!")	sælam	سلام
salad	salad	سالاد
salesperson	forushænde	فروشنده
in the SAME way, just as, as, likewise	hæmintowr (hæmintor)	همینطور
San Francisco	san feransisko	سان فرانسیسکو
sandwich	sandvich	ساندویچ
santur 7	sæntur	سنتور
satisfied, pleased, content, happy (with)	razi	راضی
satisfied, content	qane	قانع
to become SATISFIED, convinced	qane shodæn	قانع شدن
to SATISFY, make content, convince	qane kærdæn	قانع کردن
to SATISFY, make content	razi kærdæn	راضی کردن
Saturday	shæmbe	شنبه
say	goftæn	گفتن
	goft/gu (-g)	گفت/گو (گ)
to SAY	goftæn	گفتن
to SAY something esp. apt	(gol goftæn)	(گل گفتن)
scent, smell, odor	bu	بو
school 2	mædræse (mædrese)	مدرسه
elementary SCHOOL	dæbestan	دبستان
science	elm/olum	علم/علوم
sea	dærya	دریا
seamstress, tailor	khæyyat	خیاط
season	fæsl	فصل
second	dovvom/dovvomin	دوم/دومین
secretary (not as a title)	monshi	منشی
secretary (not as common as monshi)	sekreter	سکرتر
section, part, department (university)	bækhsh	بخش
section, part, portion	qesmæt	قسمت
to SEE	didæn	دیدن
	did/bin	دید/بین
"It SEEMS that... It appears that..."	mesl-e inke	مثل اینکه
self, reflexive or emphatic (15.11.6)	khod	خود
to be SELF-DEPRECATING, humble	shekæstenæfsi kærdæn	شکسته نفسی کردن
self-deprecation, humility, modesty	shekæstenæfsi	شکسته نفسی
to SEE	forukhtæn	فروختن
	forukht/forush	فروخت/فروش
to SEND	ferestadæn	فرستادن

	ferestad/ferest	فرستاد/فرست
sentence 7	jomle/jomælat	جمله/جملات
separate, separately	joda/joda-joda	جدا/جدا جدا
to SEPARATE	joda kærd/kon	جدا کردن
September	septambr	سپتامبر
to SERVE a meal	qæza keshidæn	غذا کشیدن
to SET OUT, depart	kærækæt kærdæn	حرکت کردن
to SET UP, agree upon, make arrangements	qærar gozashtæn	قرار گذاشتن
seven	hæft	هفت
seventy	hæftad	هفتاد
several; how many	chænd (ta)	چند (تا)
to SEW, work as a tailor, seamstress	khæyyati kærdæn	خیاطی کردن
shadow	saye	سایه
Shahin	shæhin	شهین
Shahla	shæhla	شهلا
Shahnaz	shæhnaz	شهناز
shame; embarrassment, shyness 5	khejalæt	خجالت
Too bad! It's (really) a SHAME/pity.	heyf!/(kheyli) heyf æst (e)	حیف (خیلی حیف است!) حیفه
shampoo	shampu	شامپو
sheep	gusfænd	گوسفند
Shemran (north-Tehran suburb)	shemiran (shemrun)	شمیران (شمرون)
ship	keshti	کشتی
Shiraz	shiraz	شیراز
shoe(s)	kæfsh	کفش
shopping	khærid	خرید
shore, coast	sahel	ساحل
shore, coast, side	kenar/kenare	کنار/کناره
short (length)	kutah	کوتاه
short (stature)	qæd kutah	قد کوتاه
to SHORTEN	kutah kærdæn	کوتاه کردن
should, must, ought	bayæd	باید
shoulder; comb 5	shane (shune)	شانه (شونه)
to SHOW	neshan dadæn (neshun)	نشان دادن (نشون)
show, display, exhibit, exhibition	næmayesh	نمایش
"SHUT up!"	saket sho(w)	ساکت شو
to be SHY, embarrassed 5	khejalæt keshidæn	خجالت کشیدن
shyness, embarrassment; shame	khejalæt	خجالت
sick; a sick person, patient	mæriz; bimar	مریض؛ بیمار

Glossary   *MODERN PERSIAN*   واژه نامه

English	Transliteration	Persian
sick, ill (slightly more polite than مریض)	nakhosh	ناخوش
"On (my) mother's/father's SIDE"	æz tæræf-madær/pedær(æm)	از طرف مادر/پدر(م)
side, coast, shore	kenar/kenare	کنار/کناره
to become SILENT	saket shodæn	ساکت شدن
silent, extinguished	khamush	خاموش
silent, quiet	saket	ساکت
simple	sade	ساده
since	æz inke	از اینکه
"Since when?" (see 7.3)	æz kay ta hala	از کی تا حالا
to SING; to read, study (with object) 4	khandæn	خواندن (خوندن)
single, unmarried	mojærræd (mojæræd)	مجرد
singly, one by one	yeki yeki	یکی یکی
singular	mofræd	مفرد
sir (polite) (see 6.2.1 & 10.3)	qorban (qorbun)	قربان
Sir, Mister	aqa	آقا
sirs, gentlemen	aqayan (aqayun)	آقایان
Sirus, Cyrus	sirus	سیروس
sister 2	khahær	خواهر
sister-in-law	khahær zæn	خواهر زن
to SIT	neshæstæn	نشستن
	neshæst/neshin	نشست/نشین
sitting, seated (French: assis)	neshæste	نشسته
six 2	shesh (shish)	شش
sixty 5	shæst	شصت
skirt	damæn	دامن
to SLEEP; to lie down	khabidæn	خوابیدن
	khabid/khab	خوابید/خواب
sleep; asleep; dream	khab	خواب
sleeping, lying down, asleep	khabide	خوابیده
"I'm SLEEPY"	(khabæm miad)	(خوابم میاد)
to become SLEEPY	khab amædæn (umædæn)	خواب آمدن
to get SLEEPY (see 11.11)	khab amædæn	خواب آمدن
slope (of a mountain)	damæne	داماد
slow, slowly; quiet 2	yævash, ahesteh	یواش
slower; quieter	yævashtær	یواشتر
slowly, by degrees	kæm kæm	کم کم
small, little; young	kuchek (kuchik)	کوچک
small, tiny	khord	خرد
small amount, bit, particle	khorde	خرده

G49

English	Transliteration	Persian
smaller; younger (see 8.8)	kuchektær (kuchiktær)	کوچکتر
smell (tr.)	bu kærdæn	بو کردن
to SMELL (tr.), hear	shenidæn	شنیدن
	shenid/sheno	شنید/شنو
smell, scent, odor	bu	بو
smile	læbkhænd	لبخند
to SMILE	læbkhænd zædæn	لبخند زدن
to SMOKE cigarettes 5	sigar keshidæn	سیگار کشیدن
snow	bærf	برف
to (be) SNOW ing	bærf amædæn	برف آمدن (باریدن)
so much!; how much	cheqædr (cheqæd)	چقدر
soap	sabun	صابون
soccer 5	futbal	فوتبال
social sciences	olum-e ejtemai	علوم اجتماعی
society	jame'e	جامعه
society; organization	sazman	سازمان
sociologist	jame'e shenas	جامعه شناس
sociology	jame'e shenasi	جامعه شناسی
sock(s), stockings	jurab	جوراب
soil, earth, ground	zæmin	زمین
soldier	særbaz	سرباز
some	(bæ:zia)	(بعضیا)
some (of)	bæ:zi (æz)	بعضی (از)
someone, anyone, no one; a person	kæsi	کسی
something, anything, nothing	chizi	چیزی
sometimes	bæ:zi væqt ha (væqta)	بعضی وقتها
sometime	bæ:zi owqat	بعضی اوقات
somewhere, anywhere, nowhere	jai	جایی
song 5	avaz	آواز
song, poetry, poem, lyric	she:r	شعر
son-in-law; bridegroom	damad	داماد
soon, quickly	bezudi	بزودی
sorry, regretful	motæ'æssef	متأسف
to feel SORRY (for)	del sukhtæn (bæraye)	دل سوختن (برای)
soul, dear, life (see 9.3.3)	jan (jun)	جان (جون)
to SOUND; to call	seda kærdæn	صدا کردن
sound; voice, noise	seda	صدا
soup	sup	سوپ، آش
sour plum *khoresht*	khoresh-e alu	خورشت آلو

Glossary *MODERN PERSIAN* واژه نامه

English	Transliteration	Persian
south	jonub (junub)	جنوب
sowing, cultivating, tilling	kesht	کشت
Spain	espania	اسپانیا
Spanish 2	espaniai (espanioli)	اسپانیایی (اسپانیولی)
Spanish (language)	espanioli	اسپانیولی
Spanish (person, adj.)	espaniai	اسپانیایی
to SPEAK, talk	hærf zædæn	حرف زدن
he/she speaks 2	hærf mizæne	حرف میزنه
"Speak!"	hærf bezænid	حرف بزنید
special	mækhsus	مخصوص
specialist 8	motækhæsses	متخصص
specialization 8	tækhæssos	تخصص
speech, discourse, utterance 5	hærf	حرف
spelling	heji	هجی
spelling	emla(')	املا
to SPOIL (intr.)	khærab shodæn	خراب شدن
to SPOIL (tr.)	khærab kærdæn	خراب کردن
spoiled, ruined, rotten, broken	khærab	خراب
sport; exercise	værzesh	ورزش
to engage in SPORT or exercise	værzesh kærdæn	ورزش کردن
sport coat, suit coat	kot	کت
spring	bæhar	بهار
square, plaza	meydan (meydun)	میدان
square(d)	moræbbæ'	مربع
to STAND, halt	istadæn (vaystadæn)	ایستادن
	istad/ist (vaystad/vayst)	ایستاد/ایست
stand up, get up, rise	bolænd shodæn	بلند شدن
standing (French *debout*)	istade (vaystade)	ایستاده
star	setare	ستاره
to START, begin (intr.= something starts)	shoru shodæn	شروع شدن
to START begin (tr.= to start something)	shoru kærdæn	شروع کردن
state (of the U.S., etc.) 6	æyalæt, eyalæt (pl. æyalat, eyalat)	ایالت/ایالات
stature	qæd	قد
to STAY, remain	mandæn	ماندن
	mand/man (mund/mun)	ماند/مان
still, yet 3	hænuz	هنوز
stockings, sock(s)	jurab	جوراب
stomach; belly	shekæm	شکستن

Glossary   *MODERN PERSIAN*   واژه نامه

stone	sæng	سنگ
stony	sængi	سنگی
to STOP; keep, hold	negæh dashtæn (negær)	نگاه داشتن
store 6	mæqaze	مغازه
to STORE	ænbar kærdæn	انبار کردن
storeroom	ænbar (æmbar)	انبار
story	dastan	داستان
story, tale, fairy tale	qesse	قصه
to tell a STORY	qesse goftæn	قصه گفتن
stove, burner	ojaq	اجاق
straight; true; right (direction)	rast	راست
to STRAIGHTEN	rast kærdæn	راست گفتن
strange, weird; wonderful	æjib	عجیب
strange, weird	æjibo qærib	عجیب و غریب
street	khiaban (khiabun)	خیابان
narrow side STREET	kuche	کوچه
strength	zur	زور
to STRIKE, hit; to play (instrument)	zædæn	زدن
strong	qævi	قوی
student (thru school), pupil; apprentice 5	shagerd	شاگرد
student (university) 6	daneshju	دانشجو
fellow STUDENT	hæmdærs (hæmdærsi)	همدرس
to STUDY	dærs khandæn (khundæn)	درس خواندن
to STUDY (in school)	tæhsil kærdæn	تحصیل کردن
to STUDY (with obj.), read; to sing 4	khandæn (khundæn)	خواندن (خوندن)
she/he reads; studies; sings 2	(mikhune)	(میخونه)
to STUDY, examine carefully	motalee kærdæn	مطالعه کردن
study/studies	tæhsil(at)	تحصیل/تحصیلات
subject, topic	mo(w)zu	موضوع
successful	movæf(f)æq	موفق
such as, like, as	hæmchon	همچون
such as, like, as	hæmchonin/hæmchenin	همچونین
	(hæmchin)	(همچین)
sugar	shekær	شکر
sugar cane	neyshekær	نی شکر
suit	kotshælvær	کت شلوار
summer	tabestæn (tabestun)	تابستان
Sunday	yekshæmbe (yeshæmbe)	یکشنبه
supermarket	super	سوپر، عالی

G52

Glossary — MODERN PERSIAN — واژه نامه

English	Transliteration	Persian
sure, certain 6	motmæen	مطمئن
sweater, pullover 6	pulover	پولور
sweet	shirin	شیرین
to SWEETEN	shirin kærdæn	شیرین کردن
to grow SWEETER	shirin shodæn	شیرین سخن
sweets, candy, pastries	shirini	شیرینی
to SWIM	shena kærdæn	شنا کردن
swim suit	mayo	مایو، لباس شنا
swimming	shena (shena/sheno)	شنا (شنا/شنو)
Swiss 6	suisi	سوئیسی
Switzerland 6	suis	سوئیس

T

English	Transliteration	Persian
tæarof (taarof) (see 3.3 II) 5	taarof	تعارف
"command it!" (see 3.3 taarof)	befærmaid	بفرمائید
"May your shadow never deminish."	saye-ye shoma kæm næshævæd (næshe)	سایه شما کم نشود
"Thank you"	qorban-e shoma/qorban-e to	قربان شما
"Thank you!"	mærhæmmæt-e shoma ziad	مرحمت شما زیاد
table	miz	میز
table cloth	rumizi	رومیزی
Tabriz	tæbriz	تبریز
tailor; seamstress	khæyyat	خیاط
to work as a TAILOR, seamstress	khæyyati kærdæn	خیاطی کردن
tailoring, dressmaking	khæyyati	خیاطی
Tajik (the Pesian of Tajikistan)	tajiki	تاجیکی
Tajik (person from Tajikistan) 6	tajiki/tajik	تاجیکی/تاجیک
Tajikistan 6	tajikestan	تاجیکستان
to TAKE (away), carry	bordæn	بردن
	bord/bær	برد/بر
to TAKE, to get, receive	gereftæn	گرفتن
	gereft/gir	گرفت/گیر
tale, story, fairy tale	qesse	قصه
talent	este:dad	استعداد
talented	ba este:dad	با استعداد
to TALK	sohbæt (so:bæt) kærdæn	صحبت کردن
tall	qæd bolænd	قد بلند
tank	tank	تانک
tape	nævar	نوار

English	Transliteration	Persian
to TASTE	mæzze kærdæn	مزه کردن
taste, flavor	mæzze	مزه
tasty, delicious	khoshmæzze	خوشمزه
taxi	taksi	تاکسی
tea 5	chay (chai)	چای (چائی)
TEACH, to teach	dærs dadæn	درس دادن
teacher 4	moællem	معلم
team	tim	تیم، گروه
technology	teknolozhi	تکنولوژی، فن آوری
Tehran	tehran	تهران
Tehrani	tehrani	تهرانی
telephone 5	telefon	تلفن
to TELEPHONE 5	telefon kærdæn	تلفن کردن/زدن
television	televizion	تلویزیون، سیما
temperate, moderate	mo'tædel	معتدل
ten	dæh	ده
tennis	tenis	تنیس
tense (grammar); time	zæman	زمان
past TENSE	zæman-e gozæshte	زمان گذشته
present TENSE	zæman-e hal	زمان حال
test, examination 5	emtehan	امتحان
to take a TEST 5	emtehan dadæn	امتحان دادن
to TEST, examine	emtehan kærdæn (æz)	امتحان کردن
Texan	tegzasi	تگزاسی
Texas	tegzas	تگزاس
text	mætn/motun	متن/متون
to THANK	tæshækkor kærdæn (æz)	تشکر کردن (از)
thank you 1	mersi; motæshækkeræm	مرسی، متشکرم، سپاسگزارم
thankful, appreciative	motæshækker (motshækeræm)	متشکر
thanks (n.)	tæshækkor, sepas	تشکر، سپاس
that, which	ke	که/کی (کی)
that is, it means	yæ:ni	یعنی
that very (emphatic)	hæman (hæmun)	همان
that way	antowr, anjur (unjuri)	آنطور، آنجور
theatre	teatr	تآتر
there 1	anja (unja)	آنجا
there is (are); is	hæst	هست

Glossary   *MODERN PERSIAN*   واژه نامه

they, these people	inha (ina)	اینها
they, those people	anha (una)	آنها
thin	laqær	لاغر
thing	chiz	چیز
to THINK 5	fekr kærdæn	فکر کردن
third	sevvom/sevvomin	سوم/سومین
thirsty	teshne	تشنه
thirty 5	si	سی
this (demonstrative pron. or adj.)	in	این
this one	(in yeki)	(این یکی)
this very (emphatic)	hæmin	همین
this way	intowr, injur (injuri)	ینطور، اینجور
thou	see: "you (sing. familiar)	تو
thought 5	fekr	فکر
three 2	se	سه
throat	gælu	گلو
Thursday	pænjshæmbe	پنج شنبه
ticket 5	belit (bilit)	بلیت
tie(s), bond(s)	rabete/rævabet	رابطه/روابط
tie, bond, close	bæstæn	بستن
tie, necktie 6	keravat	کراوات
tilling, cultivating	kesht	کشت
time	væqt/owqat (oqat)	وقت/اوقات
(I, you, etc.) had a good TIME	(be mæn/be shoma) khosh gozæsht	(به من/به شما) خوش گذشت
a period of TIME	moddæt	مدت
on TIME	sær-e sæat	سر ساعت
time (in sense of repetition), occurrence	bar	بار
time(s) (in sense of repetition)	dæf'e (dæfe/dæ:fe)	دفعه
time, moment	mo(w)qe	موقع
time; tense (grammar)	zæman	زمان
tiny, minute; exact	dæqiq	دقیق
tiny, small	khord	خرد
tired	khæste	خسته
to make TIRED	khæste kærdæn	خسته کردن
to; by; at; in	be	به
to, end, at, in; head	sær	سر
to/at (used for nouns as in تخته and تلفن)	pa-ye	پای
today 5	emruz	امروز

G55

Glossary	MODERN PERSIAN	واژه نامه
toe	ængosht-e pa	انگشت پا
together 1	bahmæn	بهمن
together (as in "seated together")	dowr-e hæm	دور هم
together, joined, connected 8	sær-e hæm	سرهم
tomato	go(w)je (færængi)	گوجه فرنگی
tomorrow 5	færda	فردا
tomorrow morning 7	færda sob	فردا صبح
tomorrow afternoon 7	færda bæ:d-æz-zohr	فردا بعد الظهر
tomorrow night 7	færda shæb	فردا شب
tongue; language 5	zæban	زبان
tonight 5	emshæb	امشب
Too bad! It's (really) a shame/pity.	heyf!/(kheyli) heyf æst (e)!	حیف
too much, a lot 3	ziad	زیاد
too much, extra, excessive	ziadi	زیادی
tooth	dændan (dændun)	دندان (دندون)
topic, subject	mo(w)zu(')	موضوع
torn, ripped	pare	پاره
town, city	shæhr	شهر
traffic	ræft-o amæd/amæd-o ræft	رفت و آمد
train 7	teren/teræn	ترن، قطار
trainer, lecturer, coach	moræbbi	مربی
transhumance, nomadism	kuchneshini	کوچ نشینی
to TRANSLATE	tærjome kærdæn	ترجمه کردن
translate 4	bærd gærdand/bærd gærdan	بر گرداند/بر گردان
translate convert	bærgærdandæn/ bærgærdanidæn	بر گرداندن/گردانیدن
translation 4	tærjome	ترجمه
traveler	mosafer	مسافر
tree	derækht/dærækht	درخت
tribe (sing. form is uncommon)	æshire/æshayer	عشیره/عشایر
to go on a journey, take a TRIP	mosafæræt kærdæn/ræftæn	مسافرت کردن/رفتن
trip, journey	mosaferæt	مسافرت
to go to TROUBLE, to take pains	zæhmæt keshidæn	زحمت کشیدن
trousers, pants	shælvar	شلوار
true; straight; right (direction)	rast	راست
truly, really	jeddæn; vaqeæn	جداً، واقعاً
to tell the TRUTH	rast goftæn	راست گفتن
to TRY, to attempt	sæy kærdæn	سعی کردن
Tuesday	seshæmbe	سه شنبه

Glossary — *MODERN PERSIAN* — واژه نامه

Turk 6	tork	ترک
Turkey 6	torkie	ترکی
Turkish, Azerbaijani (Turkish) 3	torki	ترکی
Turkmenistan, Turkmenia 6	tork(æ)mænestan	ترکمنستان
Turkoman (person) 6	tork(æ)mæn	ترکمن
Turkomani (adj., language) 6	tork(æ)mæn	ترکمن
turn 5	no(w)bæt	نوبت
turn, revolve	chærkhid/chærkh	چرخیدن/چرخ
turn, revolve	gæsht/gærd	گشت/گرد
to TURN, revolve	chærkhidæn	چرخیدن
to TURN AROUND	dowr zædæn	دور زدن
to TURN ON, ignite	rowshæn kærdæn	روشن کردن
by TURNS	no(w)bæti	نوبتی
twenty 5	bist	بیست
twins	doqolu	دوقلو
two 2	do	دو
typing	mashin nevisi	ماشین نویسی
typist	mashin nevis	ماشین نویس

U

ugly	zesht	زشت
uncle (father's brother)	æmu	عمو
uncle (mother's brother)	dai	دایی
under	zir-e	زیر
underneath, below	zir	زیر
to UNDERSTAND 3	fæhmidæn	فهمیدن
	fæhmid/fæhm	فهمید/فهم
understandable	qabel-e fæhm	قابل فهم
"poor," he poor thing, UNFORTUNATE	bichare	بیچاره
unfortunately, regretfully	motæ'æssefane	متأسفانه
unhappy, upset, angry	narahæt	ناراحت
to make upset, UNHAPPY	narakæt kærdæn	ناراحت کردن
uniform	yekjur	یکجور
university 2	daneshga(h)	دانشگاه
unmarried, single	mojærræd (mojæræd)	مجرد
unoccupied, idle	bikar	بیکار
until, before; by; counter (in counting)	ta	تا
up, above	bala	بالا
upon, on	ru-ye (ru)	روی

English	Transliteration	Persian
upset, unhappy, angry	narahæt	ناراحت
to make UPSET, unhappy	narahæt kærdæn	ناراحت کردن
"Don't be UPSET!"	narahæt næsho(w)	ناراحت نشو
urban planning, city planning	shæhrsazi	شهرسازی
Urdu 5	ordu	اردو
usage, use (n.), application	kar bord	کاربرد
to make USE of, have the benefit of	estefae kærdæn (æz)	استفاده کردن (از)
use, advantage, benefit	maziyyat, estefade	مزیت، استفاده
use, employ (as a word)	bekar bordæn	بکار بردن
useful	mofid	مفید
usual	mæ:mul	معمول
usually 7	mæ:mulæn	معمولا
utterance, discourse, speech 5	hærf	حرف
Uzbek 5	ozbæki	ازبکی
Uzbekistan 6	ozbækestan	ازبکستان

V

English	Transliteration	Persian
vacation, holiday(s)	tæ:tilat	تعطیلات
vanilla	vanil	وانیل
various, many	mokhtælef	مختلف
vegetables, greens, herbs	sæbzi	سبزی
verb	fe'l/æf'al	فعل/افعال
very, extremely 3	kheyli, besiar	خیلی، بسیار
Vida	vida	ویدا
village(s)	deh/dehat; rusta	ده/دهات، روستا
villager	rustai	روستایی
visa	viza	ویزا، روادید
vitamin	vitamin	ویتامین
volleyball	valibal	والیبال

W

English	Transliteration	Persian
waist, lower back	kæmær	کمر
to WAIT	sæbr kærdæn	صبر کردن
to WAIT for someone	montæzer-e kæsi budæn	منتظر کسی بودن
waiting, awaiting	montæzer	منتظر
wake up (intr.)	bidar shodæn	بیدار شدن
wake up (tr.)	bidar kærdæn	بیدار کردن
walking, hiking	piade-rævi	پیاده روی
wall	divar	دیوار

G58

Glossary *MODERN PERSIAN* واژه نامه

English	Transliteration	Persian
want	khast/khah (-/kha/)	خواست/خواه
to WANT, request	khastæn	خواستن
to WANT, wish to	mayel budæn	مایل بودن
to heat up, WARM	gærm kærdæn	گرم کردن
warm, hot	gærm	گرم
warmth, heat	gærma	گرما
wash	shost/shuy (shur)	شست و شوی (شور)
to WASH	shostæn	شستن
Washington	vashængton	واشنگتن
watch, to watch (as TV)	tæmasha kærdæn	تماشا کردن
water, juice 5	ab	آب
wax (as for shoes)	vaks	واکس
that WAY	antowr, anjur (unjuri)	آنطور، آنجور
this WAY	intowr, injur (injuri)	اینطور، اینجور
likewise, in that same WAY	hæmchonan	همچنان
likewise, in this same WAY	hæmchonin/hæmchenin/ ve hæmchenin	همچنین و همچنین
no WAY! by no means	be hich væj(h)!	به هیچ وجه
we 4	ma	ما
weak	zæif	ضعیف
to put on/WEAR clothes	lebas pushidæn	لباس پوشیدن
to WEAR/put on a necktie	keravat zædæn	کراوات زدن
to become WEARY, tired	khæste shodæn	خسته شدن
weather; air	hæva	هوس
Wednesday	chæharshæmbe (charshæmbe)	چهارشنبه
week	hæfte	هفته
to WEEP, cry	gerie kærdæn	گریه کردن
weeping	gerie	گریه
well-known, famous	mæ:ruf	معروف
"Well,..., But..." (interjection)	akhær (akhe)	آخر (آخه)
well; good	khub	خوب
west	qærb	غرب
west	mæqreb	مغرب
western	qærbi	غربی
western(er), European (in compounds)	færængi	فرنگی
wet, damp	khis	خیس
what 2	che (chi)	چه (چی)
what (noun)? which (noun)?	ch___i	چــی
what about, how about 4	chetor? (2)	چطور؟

G59

Glossary — MODERN PERSIAN — واژه نامه

English	Transliteration	Persian
what color	chæræng (chærængi)	چه رنگی (چه رنگ)
what number (first, second.); "how many?"	chændom	چندم
whatever	hærche	هرچه
What's up? What's wrong? (see 7.3)	che khæbær æst (e)	چه خبر است (ه)
"WHAT does it/that mean?" 1	yæ:ni che (yæ:ni chi)	یعنی چه (ینی چی)
wheat	gændom	گندم
when	key 2	کی
when, while	væqtike	وقتی که
when, while	mo(w)qeike	موقعی که
whenever	hær væqt	هر وقت
where 1	koja	کجا
wherever	hærja; hærkoja	هرجا، هر کجا
which	kodam (kodum/kudum)	کدام (کدوم)
which (noun)? what (noun)?	che___i	چه ـ ی
which one?	kodam yek (kodum yeki)	کدامیک
which, that	ke 1	که
while, when	mo(w)qeike	موقعی که
while, when	væqtike	وقتی که
white 7	sefid	سفید
to become WHITE, turn white	sefid shodæn	سفید شدن
white-collar worker 6	karmænd	کارمند
to WHITEN	sefid kærdæn	سفید کردن
who 2	ki/ke (ki)	کی/که
whoever	hær kæs	هرکس
why 4	chera	چرا
wife; Ms. (Mrs. or Miss)	khanom (khanum)	خانم (خانوم)
willing	hazer (3)	حاضر
wind	bad	باد
windy	badi	بادی
be WINDY, blow	bad amædæn	باد آمدن
wine	shærab	شراب
winter	zemestan (zemestun)	زمستان
to desire or WISH to eat	meyl dashtæn	میل داشتن
wish, desire	meyl	میل
to want, WISH to	mayel budæn	مایل بودن
with 4	ba	با
with, in the company of	hæmrah	همراه
"WITH the greatest pleasure"	ba kæmal-e khoshhali; meyl	با کمال خوشحالی، میل

Glossary	MODERN PERSIAN	واژه نامه
within, in; door	dær	در
without	bedun-e (bidun-e)	بدون
without, -less	bi	بی
woman 5	zæn	زن
wonderful, great	ali	عالی
wonderful, strange	ajib	عجیب
Wonderful! Good for you! 3	mashallah	ماشاءالله
Wonderful! Good going! 6	barikælla	بارک الله
wood	chub	چوب
word/words	kæleme/kælemat	کلمه/کلمات، واژه ها
word/words	loqæt/loqat	لغت/لغات، واژه ها
work, job, occupation 5	kar	کار
at WORK (with verb of motion)	sær-e kar	سر کار
white-collar WORKER 6	karmænd	کارمند
working hours	saat-e kar	ساعت کار
world	donya	دنیا
worn out, old; rag	kohne	کهنه
worried, anxious	negæran (negærun)	نگران
to WRITE 4	neveshtæn	نوشتن
	nevesht/	نوشت/نویس
in WRITING 7	kætbæn	کتباً
written 7	kætbi	کتبی
written, literary	neveshtari	نوشتاری

X

| to XEROX, photocopy | ziraks kærdæn | زیراکس کردن |

Y

Yazd (capital of Yazd province)	yæzd	یزد
year	sal	سال
last YEAR	parsal	پارسال
this YEAR	emsal	امسال
year before last	pirarsal	پیرارسال
yellow 7	zærd	زرد
yes 2	bæle	بله
yesterday	diruz	دیروز
yesterday afternoon	diruz bæ:d-æz-zohr	دیروز بعد الظهر
yesterday evening	diruz æsr	دیروز عصر

Glossary　　　　　　　　　　*MODERN PERSIAN*　　　　　　　　　　واژه نامه

yesterday morning	diruz sob(h)	دیروز صبح
yesterday noon	diruz zo(h)r	دیروز ظهر
yet, still	hænuz	هنوز
yogurt	mast	ماست
yogurt and water	duq	دوغ
you (2nd person pl.; sing. honorific) 2	shoma	شما
you (2nd person sing., familiar) 3	to	تو
young; a youth	jævan (jævun)	جوان (جوون)
young; little, small 6	kuchek (kuchik)	کوچک (کوچیک)
younger	jævantær (jævuntær)	جوانتر
younger; smaller	kuckektær (kuchiktær)	کوچکتر
youth (a young person/young man); young	jævan (jævun)	جوان

Z

Zabol	zabol	زابل
Zahedan	zahedan	زاهدان
Zhaleh, Jaleh	zhale	ژاله
zipper	zip	زیپ

APPENDIX A: VERBS IN THE FIRST PERSON
The following verbs are arranged alphabetically by spelling of the English infinitive.

English	Persian	Transliteration
I allow; place (see 9.9)	میگذارم (میذارم)	migozaræm (mizaræm)
I arrive	میرسم	miresæm
I ask, I question 5	سوال می کنم	soál mìkonæm
I ask, question	می پرسم	miporsæm
I bathe, take a bath	حمام میکنم	hæmmam mikonæm (hæmum mikonæm)
I become	می شوم (می شم)	mishævæm (mishæm)
I break	میشکنم	mishkenæm
I bring	میاورم (می ارم)	miaværæm (miaræm)
I build	می سازم	misazæm
I am busy, have things to do 7	کار دارم	kár daræm
I buy	میخرم	mikhæræm
I can, am able to	می توانم (می تونم)	mitævanæm (mitunæm)
I carry	می برم	mibæræm
I close (the door), tie (a package)	می بندم	mibændæm
I'm cold	سردم است (سردمه)	særdæm-æst (særdæm-e)
I come	می آیم (می ام)	miayæm (miam)
I cook	می پزم	mipæzæm
I count	می شمرم	mishemoræm
I dance	می رقصم	miræqsæm
I die	می میرم	mimiræm
I drive	می رانم	miranæm
I drop	می اندازم	miændazæm
I draw	می کشم	mikeshæm
I drink 5	می نوشم	minushæm
I eat, drink 5	می خورم	mikhoræm
I exercise, play sports	ورزش می کنم	værzesh mikonæm
I fall	می افتم	mioftæm
I fear	می ترسم	mitærsæm
I fix, prepare	درست می کنم	dorost mikonæm
I get, receive	می گیرم	migiræm
I give	می دهم (می دم)	midehæm (midæm)
I go 7	می روم (می رم)	mirævæm (miræm)

G63

Glossary — MODERN PERSIAN — واژه نامه

English	Persian	Transliteration
I have 5	دارم	daræm
I hear, smell	می شنوم	mish(e)novæm
I hit, strike	می زنم	mizænæm
I'm hungry	گرسنه هستم (گرسنه مه)	gorosne hæstæm (gorosnæm-e)
I ignite, set alight	روشن می کنم	rowshæn mikonæm
I joke, kid around	شوخی می کنم	shukhi mikonæm
I know 3	می دانم (می دونم)	midanæm (midunæm)
I know (how to)	بلدم	bælædæm
I know, am familiar with	می شناسم	mish(e)nasæm
I laugh	می خندم	mikhændæm
I burst out LAUGHING	خنده م گرفت	(khændæm gereft)
I learn 3	یاد می گیرم	yad migiræm
I lie down, sleep 5	می خوابم	mikhabæm
I lift, pick up	بر می دارم (ور می دارم)	bær midaræm (vær midaræm)
I like it	(خوشم می آد)	khoshæm miad
I would LIKE to	مایلم	mayelæm
I live	زندگی می کنم	zendegi mikonæm
I miss, am homesick (for)	دلم برای ـ تنگ است (اه)	delæm bæraye _ tæng æst (tæng-e)
I make a MISTAKE	اشتباه می کنم	eshtebah mikonæm
I need	لازم دارم	lazem daræm
I pass, go by	می گذرم	mig(o)zæræm
I pick up, lift	بر می دارم (ور می دارم)	bær midaræm (vær midaræm)
I place; I allow (see 9.9)	می گذارم (می ذارم)	migozaræm (mizaræm)
I plant	می کارم	mikaræm
I play 5 (games, sports)	بازی می کنم	bazi mikonæm
I play 6 (music)	می زنم	mizænæm
I prepare, fix	درست می کنم	dorost mikonæm
I put, place	می گذارم (می ذارم)	migozaræm (mizaræm)
I put on, wear	می پوشم	mipushæm
I read, study, sing	می خوانم (می خونم)	mikhanæm (mikhunæm)
I remain	می مانم (می مونم)	mimanæm (mimunæm)
I repeat 1	تکرار می کنم	tekrár mikonæm
I'll say it again, will REPEAT it. 1	دوباره می گویم (می گم)	dobare miguyæm (migæm)
I rest 5	استراحت می کنم	esterahæt mikonæm
I return	بر می گردم	bær migærdæm
I run	می دوم	midævæm

Glossary — MODERN PERSIAN — واژه نامه

English	Persian	Transliteration
I say 1	می گویم (می گم)	miguyæm (migæm)
I am scared	می ترسم	mitærsæm
I see 6	می بینم	mibinæm
I sell	می فروشم	miforushæm
I send	می فرستم	miferestæm
I sing; read	می خوانم (می خونم)	mikhanæm (mikhunæm)
I sit, sit down (see 9.9)	می نشینم (می شینم)	mineshinæm (mishinæm)
I sleep, lie down	می خوابم	mikhabæm
I smell, hear	می شنوم	mish(e)novæm
I smoke cigarettes	سیگار می کشم	sigar mikeshæm
I feel SORRY (for).	دلم می سوزد (برای) (می سوزه)	delæm bæraye _misuzæd (misuze)
I speak	حرف می زنم	hærf mizænæm
I stand	می ایستم (وای میستم)	miistæm (vaymistæm)
I stand up	بلند می شوم (پا می شوم، می شم)	pa mishævæm (mishæm)
I stay	می مانم	mimanæm
I strike, hit	می زنم	mizænæm
I study 5	درس میخوانم (میخونم)	dærs mikhanæm (dærs mikhunæm)
I take	می گیرم	migiræm
I take a test 5 (of the student)	امتحان می دهم (می دم)	emtehán midehæm (mìdæm)
I teach (with to) 1	درس می دهم (می دم)	dærs midehæm (midæm)
I telephone/call up	تلفن می کنم، می زنم	telefon mikonæm
I test, examine 5 (said teacher)	امتحان می کنم (+ ا)	emtehán mìkonæm (+ æz)
I test, try out 15	امتحان می کنم (+ را)	emtehán mìkonæm (+ ra)
I think, I think so 5	فکر می کنم	fekr mìkonæm
I'm thirsty	تشنه هستم (تشنه مه)	teshne hæstæm (teshnæm-e)
I tie (as a package), close	می بندم	mibændæm
I get TIRED	خسته می شوم (می شم)	khæste mishævæm (mishæm)
I translate	ترجمه میکنم (برمیگردانم)	tærjome mikonæm
I understand (in general) 3	می فهم	mifæhmæm (mifæ:mæm)
I understand (what you said)	فهمیدم	fæhmidæm
I wake up	بیدار می شوم	bidar mishævæm
I want (to)	می خواهم (می خوام)	mikhahæm (mikham)
I want (to)	دلم می خواهد (می خواد)	delæm mikhahæd (delæm mikhad)

Glossary　　　　　*MODERN PERSIAN*　　　　　واژه نامه

I wash	می شویم (می شورم)	mishuyæm (mishuræm)
I watch	تماشا می کنم	tæmasha mikonæm
I wear, put on	می پوشم	mipushæm
I work 3	کار می کنم	kar mikonæm
I write (see 9.9)	می نویسم	minevisæm

Glossary   MODERN PERSIAN   واژه نامه

Persian to English

Introduction

How to use the glossary
This half of the glossary includes all the Persian words that have appeared in the vocabulary lists of the lessons. It does not include words that appear in phonology drills, word-building sections, the readings that appear in section 12, or each lesson's final text unless those words have also been included in the vocabulary for the lesson. It does include the cultural and classroom expressions given in section 3 of most lessons. For reasons of economy and clarity the entries are limited to the words and phrases that appear in the textbook. Definitions are as brief as possible and have been limited to the meanings that appear there. Where a lengthy explanation is required you are directed to the appropriate lesson and section with the phrase, (see....).

Alphabetization is, of course, by the Persian alphabet and only the written letters are considered. Verbs are alphabetized under the stem forms. Infinitives are listed below the verb stems. Thus آوردن (أوردن) will be found below آورد/آور (أورد/آر). The glossary entries are based on the written form of the word, but the colloquial form is given afterward in parentheses, as in the examples just given. Compound verbs will be listed by all of their principal elements. Thus به دست آوردن will be listed under the preposition به as well as both دست and آوردن (أوردن). In most Persian dictionaries verbs are listed only by the infinitive (*mæsdær*). Only the larger Haïm's dictionaries give compound verbs and there they are listed as they are here, under all the principal elements. Haïm does not list colloquial forms, except very rarely, nor does any other major Persian dictionary.

All verbs used in lessons one through nine are listed together in lesson nine (9.2.1). We have listed the first person singular present tense of all the verbs introduced in an appendix that appears between the two sections of this glossary.

When a verb uses a preposition with an object, the preposition will be listed. If no preposition is given one may assume that the verb uses (را) with objects.

Since virtually any noun or adjective may be used with the verb بودن "to be" it will not be listed with nouns except where we wish to emphasize the verbal aspect of the construct, as with بلد بودن "to know, know how to."

Glossary   *MODERN PERSIAN*   واژه نامه

Nouns are listed by their single form. Where the Arabic plural of a word has also been used in the book, it will be listed with the singular as well (ایالت/ایالات). Broken Arabic plurals will be listed separately where necessary. You will finds "news" under both اخبار and خبر, but علوم will not be listed separately from علم. Colloquial forms of all words will be given in parentheses. Thus آشپزخانه (آشپزخونه) appears under آشپز as well as خانه (خونه). When a single element of a phrase differs in colloquial and written it will be represented separately (as listed under اعصاب, عصب, and خرد.

Glossary   *MODERN PERSIAN*   واژه نامه

	ælef mædde	آ
water	ab	آب
boiled (egg)	ab pæz	آبپز/آب پز
weather	ab-o hæva	آب و هوا
blue	abi	آبی
Abadan	abadan	آبادان
(of or from) Abadan	abadani	آبادانی
apartment	aparteman	آپارتمان
mixed nuts (trail mix); seeds and dired fruit	ajil	آجیل
last, final, end	akhær	آخر
"Well..." "But..." (interjection)	akhær (akhe)	آخر (آخه)ش
final, ultimate	akhærin	آخرین (آخر + ین)
in the end	akhæresh	آخرش
customs	adab-o rosum	آداب و رسوم
address	adres	آدرس
a person, "one"	adæm	آدم
yeah, uh-huh	are	آره
Azerbaijan	azærbayjan	آذربایجان
Eastern Azerbaijan	azærbayjan shærqi	آذربایجان شرقی
Western Azerbaijan	azærbayjan qærbi	آذربایجان غربی
of or from Azerbaijan	azærbayjani	آذربایجانی
free	azad	آزاد
to free, let free	azad kærdæn	آزاد کردن
to become free	azad shodæn	آزاد شدن
laboratory	azmayeshgah	آزمایشگاه
easy, simple	asan (asun)	آسان (آسون)
with ease, easily	be asani (be asuni)	به آسانی (به آسونی)
sky, heavens	aseman (asemun)	آسمان (آسمون)
aspirin	asperin	آسپرین
cook	ashpæz	آشپز
cooking	ashpæzi	آشپزی
to cook	ashpæzi kærd / kon	آشپزی کرد/کن
kitchen	ashpæzkhane (ashpæzkune)	آشپزخانه (آشپزخونه)

G69

Glossary	MODERN PERSIAN	واژه نامه
familiar, acquainted (with)	ashena, ashna (ba)	آشنا (با)
"Get acquainted!"	ash(e)na beshævid	(آشنا بشوید)
		آشنا بشید
to meet	ash(e)na shodæn	آشنا شدن (با)
to introduce	(ash(e)na kardæn (ba)	آشنا کردن (با)
sun	aftab	آفتاب
sunny	aftabi	آفتابی
"Excellent!" "Bravo!"	afærin	آفرین
sir, mister	aqa	آقا
gentlemen	aqayan (aqayun)	آقایان (آقایون)
album	albom	آلبوم
allergy	alerzhi	آلرژی
Germany	alman	آلمان
German	almani	آلمانی
aluminum	aluminiom	آلومینیوم
ready, prepared	amade	آماده
to prepare	amade kærdæn	آماده کردن
to come	amædæn (umædæn)	آمدن (اومدن)
traffic	amæd-o ræft	آمد و رفت
America (United States)	amrika	آمریکا
American	amrikai	آمریکائی
education (as a discipline)	amuzesh-o pærværesh	آموزش و پرورش
that	an (un)	آن (اون)
those / (those people)	anha (una)	آنها (اونا)
there	anja (unja)	آنجا (اونجا)
that kind of	antowr/anjur	آنطور (اونطور)
	(untor/unjur)	آنجور (اونجور)
that way	antowr/anjur	آنطوری (اونطوری)
	(untori/unjuri)	آنجوری (اونجوری)
Ankara	ankara	آنکارا
song	avaz	آواز
to sing	avaz khandæn	آواز خواندن
to bring	aværdæn (ovordæn)	آوردن (اوردن)
	aværd / avær	آور/آورد
	(ovord/ar)	(آر)/اورد
April	avril	آوریل
melody; intonation	ahæng	آهنگ

ælef   ا

Glossary — MODERN PERSIAN — واژه نامه

cloud	æbr	ابر
eyebrow	æbru	ابرو
cloudy	æbri	ابری
opera	opera	اپرا
bus	otobus	اتوبوس
as it happens, as a matter of fact	ettefaqæn	اتفاقاً
rent	ejare	اجاره
to rent (from)	ejare kærdæn (æz)	اجاره کردن (از)
to rent (to)	ejare dadæn (be)	اجاره دادن (به)
permission	ejaze	اجازه
"May I? May one?"	ejaze hæst	اجازه هست
to permit	ejaze dadæn	اجازه دادن
"Permit me! Allow me!"	ejaze bedin	اجازه بدین
stove, burner	ojaq	اجاق
news (both sg. and pl. in Persian)	ækhbar/khæbær	اخبار \ خبر
choice, prerogative, disposition	ekhtiar	اختیار
"the choice is yours" (taarof)	ekhtiar darid	اختیار دارید
office (gov't, business)	edare	اداره
continuation	edame	ادامه
to continue	edame dadæn	ادامه دادن
literary	ædæbi	ادبی
literature	ædæbiat	ادبیات
army	ærtesh	ارتش
Urdu	ordu	اردو
cheap, inexpensive	ærzan (ærzun)	ارزان (ارزون)
Armenia	æmænestan	ارمنستان
Armenian	ærmæni	ارمنی
Europe	orupa	اروپا
European	orupai	اروپایی
from, of	æz	از
from ____ to/till ____	æz ____ ta ____	از ____ تا ____
"Since when?" (9.3)	æz key ta hala	از کی تا حالا
how, whence	æz koja	از کجا
Uzbekistan	ozbækestan	ازبکستان
Uzbek	ozbæki	ازبکی
marriage	ezdevaj	ازدواج
to marry, to get married (to)	ezdevaj kærdæn (ba)	ازدواج کردن (با)
horseback riding	æsb-sævari	اسب سواری

possessions, tools, effects	æsbab	اسباب
Spain	espania	اسپانیا
Spanish (person, adjective)	espaniai	اسپانیائی
Spanish (language)	espanioli	اسپانیولی
is (see budæn)	æst/-st	است
professor, master craftsman	ostad	استاد
province	ostan	استان
Istanbul	estambol (eslambol)	استانبول \ اسلامبول
of or pertaining to Istanbul	estamboli (eslamboli)	استانبولی \ اسلامبولی
to be employed, hired	estekhdam shodæn	استخدام شدن
rest	esterahæt	استراحت
to rest	esterahæt kærdæn	استراحت کردن
Australia	ostralia	استرالیا
Australian	ostraliai	استرالیایی
talent	este:dad	استعداد
talented	ba este:dad	با استعداد
use, advantage, benefit	estefade	استفاده
to make use of, have the benefit of	estefade kærdæn (æz)	استفاده کردن (از)
Israel	esrail	اسرائیل
Israeli	esraili	اسرائیلی
name, noun	esm	اسم/اسامی
first name	esm-e kuchek	اسم کوچک
	(esm-e kuchik)	(اسم کوچیک)
last name	esm-e famili	اسم فامیلی
error	eshtebah	اشتباه
to make a mistake	eshtebah kærdæn	اشتباه کردن
difficulty	eshkal (eshgal)	اشکال (اشگال)
"It doesn't matter, no problem"	(eshkali nædare)	اشکالی ندارد
idiom, expression	estelah	اصطلاح
Isfahan	esfæhan	اصفهان
Isfahani	esfæhani	اصفهانی
P.N. (last name)	esfæhanian	اصفهانیان
original; classic	æsil	اصیل
originally; at all (w. neg.)	æslæn	اصلاً
increase (see Reading Persian 7.1)	ezafe	اضافه
to add to	ezafe kædæn (be)	اضافه کردن (به)
room	otaq	اطاق \ اتاق
living room, parlor	otaq-e pazirai	اطاق پذیرائی
bedroom	otaq-e khab	اطاق خواب

Glossary	MODERN PERSIAN	واژه نامه
dining room	otaq-e nahar khori	اطاق ناهار خوری
nerves (p.)	æ:sab/æsæb	اعصاب \ عصب
"My nerves are shot."	(æ:sabæm khord æst (e))	اعصابم خرد است (ه)
to fall	oftadæn	افتادن
	oftad/oft	افتاد/افت
Afghanistan	æfqanestan	افغانستان
Afghani	æfqani	افغانی
economics; economy	eqtesad	اقتصاد
economist	eqtesad dan	اقتصاد دان
October	oktobr	اکتبر
most (of)	æksær-e	اکثر
mostly, for the most part	æksæræn	اکثراً
majority	æksæriæt	اکثریت
now	æl:an	الآن
of course	ælbæte	البته
but	æmma	اما
test, examination 5	emtehan	امتحان
to take a test	emtehan dadæn	امتحان دادن
to test, examine	emtehan kærdæn (æz)	امتحان کردن (از)
today	emruz	امروز
this morning	emruz sobh	امروز صبح
this afternoon	emruz bæ:dæzzo(h)r	امروز بعد از ظهر
American, U.S.A.	emrika	امریکا
American	emrikai	امریکائی
this year	emsal	امسال
tonight	emshæb	امشب
spelling (see also هجی)	emla(:)	املاء
I look forward to/hope to see you	be omid-e didar	امید: به امید دیدار
pomegranate	ænar	انار
storeroom	æmbar	انبار
to store	æmbar kærdæn	انبار کردن
choice	entekhab	انتخاب
to choose	entekhab kærdæn	انتخاب کردن
elections	entekhabat	انتخابات
entomology	entomolozhi	انتمولوژی
energy	enerzhi	انرژی
finger	ængosht	انگشت

Glossary　　　　　*MODERN PERSIAN*　　　　　واژه نامه

toe	ængosht-e pa	انگشت پا
ring	ængoshtær	انگشتر
England	englestan	انگستان
	(inglestan)	(اینگلیستان)
English	englisi (inglisi)	انگلیسی (اینگیسی)
grape(s)	ængur	انگور
he, she, it	u (un)	او (اون)
August	ut	اوت
first	ævval	اول
Ahwaz	æhvaz	اهواز
state (of the U.S., etc.)	æyalæt, eyalæt	ایالت
	(pl. æyalat, eyalat)	ایالات
Italy	italia	ایتالیا
Italian	italiai	ایتالیائی
Iran	iran (irun)	ایران (ایرون)
Iranist, Persianist	iranshenas	ایرانشناس
Iranian Studies, Iranology	iranshenasi	ایرانشناسی
Iranian	irani (iruni)	ایرانی (ایرونی)
Ireland, Eire	irlænd	ایرلند
Irish	irlændi	ایرلندی
to stand, halt	istadæn (vaystadæn)	ایستادن (وایستادن)
	istad/ist	ایستاد \ ایست
	(vaystad/vayst)	(وا ایستاد \ وایست)
standing (French *debout*)	istade (vaystade)	ایستاده (وایستاده)
this (demonstrative pronoun)	in	این
this one	(in yeki)	این یکی
this kind of	intowr/injur	اینطور- اینجور
this way	intowr/injur	اینطور- اینجور
	(intori/injuri)	(اینطوری \ اینجوری)
here	inja	اینجا
they, these people	inha (ina)	اینها (اینا)

be　　　　　　　　　　　　　　　　　　　　　ب

with	ba	با
talented	ba este:dad	با استعداد
although	ba inke	با اینکه
"with the greatest pleasure"	ba kæmal-e khoshhali	با کمال خوشحالی
"with the greatest pleasure"	ba kæmal-e meyl	با کمال میل

G74

Glossary — MODERN PERSIAN — واژه نامه

together	ba hæm	با هم
intelligent	bahush	با هوش
father, and see 9.3	baba	با با
wind	bad	باد
to be windy, blow	bad amædæn	باد آمدن
windy	badi	بادی
burden, load; time, occurrence	bar	بار
rain	baran (baruni)	باران (بارون)
to rain	baran amædæn (barun amædæn)	باران آمدن (بارون آمدن)
raincoat; rainy	barani (baruni)	بارانی (بارونی)
open	baz	باز
to open (tr.)	baz kærdæn	باز کردن
to open (intr.)	baz shodæn	باز شدن
market	bazar	بازار
game	bazi	بازی
to play	bazi kærdæn	بازی کردن
ancient times, antiquity	bastan	باستان
archeologist	bastanshenas	باستانشناس
archeology	bastanshenasi	باستانشناسی
let it be, so be it, Ok (subjunctive of to be)	bashæd bashe	باشد (باشه)
garden, orchard	baq	باغ
up, above	bala	بالا
finally, at last	belækhære	بالاخره
bank	bank	بانک
belief	bavær	باور
to believe	bavær kærdæn	باور کردن
must, should, ought	bayæd	باید
	see بست/بند	ببندید
	see پرسید/پرس	بپرسید
	see بخشید/بخش	ببخشید (ببخشین)
	see خواند/خوان (خوند/خون)	بخوانید
appropriate	beja	بجا
discussion	bæhs	بحث
child	bæch(ch)e	بچه
childhood	bæch(ch)egi	بچگی
child care	bæch(ch)edari	بچه داری
to discuss	bæhs kærdæn	بحث کردن
part, section, department (univ.)	bækhsh	بخش

G75

English	Transliteration	Persian
to forgive; grant, bestow, donate	bækhshidæn	بخشیدن
	bækhshid/bækhsh	بخشید/بخش
excuse me	bebækhshid	ببخشید
bad, wrong	bæd	بد
to dislike	bæd-e___	بد ـــ
	amædæn (æz)	آمدن (از)
	(bæd-e___	بد ـــ
	umædæn) (æz)	اومدن (از)
bad tempered, mean	bæd ækhlaq	بد اخلاق
body	bædæn	بدن
without	bedun-e (bi)	بدون (بی)
opposite	bær æks	برعکس
brother	bærædær	برادر
for	bæraye	برای
because, in order to	bæraye inke	برای اینکه
to carry, take away	bordæn	بردن
	bord/bær	برد/بر
to use, employ (as a word)	bekar bordæn	بکاربردن
to grow, raise; to pick up	bær dashtæn	بر داشتن
	bær dasht/bær dar	برداشت \ بردار
to return (tr.), to translate; turn over	bær gærdandæn /	بر گرداندن/گردانیدن
	bær gærdanidæn	بر گردانیدن
	bær gærdand/bær gærdan	بر گرداند/بر گردان
to return (intr.), come back	bær gæshtan	بر گشتن
	bær gæsht/bær gærd	برگشت/برگرد
snow	bærf	برف
to snow	bærf amædæn	برف آمدن (باریدن)
plan, program	bærname	برنامه
The Plan Organization	sazman-e bærname	سازمان برنامه
Berlin	berlæn	برلن
rice (uncooked)	berenj	برنج
big, large	bozorg	بزرگ
to raise	bozorg kærdæn	بزرگ کردن
to grow up	bozorg shodæn	بزرگ شدن
bigger; older	bozorgtær	بزرگتر
to tie, bind	bæstæn	بستن
	bæst/bænd	بند/بست
"Close!"	bebændid	ببندید
package	bæste	بسته

Glossary — MODERN PERSIAN — واژه نامه

English	Transliteration	Persian
dependence	bæstegi	بستگی
to depend on ___	bæstegi dashtæn be ___	بستگی داشتن به ـــ
Boston	boston	بستن
very, extremely	besiar	بسیار
after, then	bæ:d	بعد
after (preposition)	bæ:d æz	بعد از
afternoon, p.m.	bæ:d æz zo(h)r	بعد از ظهر
afternoons, in the afternoon	bæ:d æ zo(h)ra	(بعد از ظهرا)
afterwards	bæ:dæn	بعداً
some (of)	bæ:zi (æz)	بعضی (از)
some	(bæ:zia)	(بعضیا)
sometimes	bæ:zi owqat	بعضی اوقات
sometimes	(bæ:zi væqta)	(بعضی وقتها)
arm, bosom	bæqæl	بغل
next to (things)	bæqæl-e	بغل
next to (person)	bæqæ-e dæst-e	بغل دست
to pick up (as a child) embrace	bæqæl kærdæn	بغل کردن
	see فرمود/فرما	بفرمائید
	see گفت/گو	بگید
to know, be familiar with (see 7.2)	bælæd budæn	بلد بودن
high, all; loud	bolænd	بلند
tall	qæd bolænd	قد بلند
to stand up, get up, rise	bolænd shodæn	بلند شدن
higher, louder	bolændtær	بلند تر
blouse	boluz (buluz)	بلوز
yes	bæle	بله
ticket	belit (bilit)	بلیط \ بلیت (بیلیت)
port	bændær	بندر
Bandar Abbas	bændær æbbas	بندر عباس
gasoline	benzin	بنزین
purple, violet	bænæfsh	بنفش
smell, scent, odor	bu	بو
to be	budæn	بودن
(See 6.11.2 for enclitic forms)	bud/bash/hæst (æst, -st)	بود \ باش \ هست
to; by; at; in	be	به
easily	be asani (be asuni)	بآسانی/به آسانی (به آسونی/بآسونی)
appropriate	beja	بجا
to acquire	bedæst aværdæn	به دست آوردن

G77

(to bring)	(ovordæn)	(اوردن)
to have access to ____	be ____ rah dashtæn	به ____ راه داشتن
quickly, at once	bezudi	بزودی
to grow, be raised	be æmæl amædæn	بعمل آمدن
in Persian, in German, etc.	be farsi, be almani	به فارسی، به آلمانی
to use, employ (e.g., word, phrase)	bekar bordæn	بکاربردن
in (my) opinion	be næzær-e (mæn)	به نظر (من)
spring	bæhar	بهار
better	behtær	بهتر
without, -less	bi	بی
extremely, infinitely	bi-næhayæt	بی نهایت
inappropriate	bija	بیجا
unfortunate	bichare	بیچاره
unoccupied, idle	bikar	بیکار
between	beyn(-e)	بین
without limit, extremely	binehayæt	بینهایت
desert	biaban (biabun)	بیابان (بیابون)
desert (adj.)	biabani (biabuni)	بیابانی (بیابونی)
awake, alert	bidar	بیدار
to wake up (intrans.)	bidar shodæn	بیدار شدن
to wake up (trans.)	bidar kærdæn	بیدار کردن
Beirut	beyrut	بیروت
outside	birun	بیرون
countryside (outside of the city)	birun-e shæhr	بیرون شهر
P.N. (man's)	bizhæn	بیژن
cookie	biskuit	بیسکویت
more	bishtær	بیشتر
most of the time	bishtær-e owqat	بیشتر اوقات
	see افتاد/افت	بیفتم
sick, a sick person	bimar	بیمار
hospital	bimarestan	بیمارستان
international	beynolmælæli	بین المللی
biology	biolozhi	بیولوژی (زیست شناسی)

pe   پ

foot	pa	پا
at the foot/base of	pa-ye	پای
to/at (certain nouns as in تخته/تلفن)	pa-ye tækhte	پای تخته

Glossary — MODERN PERSIAN — واژه نامه

English	Transliteration	Persian
at the blackboard		
to get up, stand up	pa shodæn	پا شدن
P.N. (last name)	parsa	پارسا
last year	parsal	پارسال
parking lot	parking	پارکینگ
torn, ripped	pare	پاره
to tear, rip	pare kærdæn	پاره کردن
Paris 1	paris	پاریس
passport	pasport	پاسپورت (گذرنامه)
Pacific	pasifik	پاسیفیک
clean	pak	پاک
to erase (blackboard, tape, etc.)	pak kærdæn	پاک کردن
to be erased	pak shodæn	پاک شدن
envelope; paper bag	pakæt	پاکت
Pakistan	pakestan	پاکستان
Pakistani	pakestani	پاکستانی
overcoat	palto	پالتو
capital (of a nation)	pay(e)tækht	پایتخت
fall, autumn	paiz	پائیز
below; down	pain	پائین
to cook	pokhtæn	پختن
	pokht/pæz	پخت/پز
father	pedær (baba)	پدر (بابا)
grandfather	pedær bozorg	پدر بزرگ
acceptance	pæziresh	پذیرش
full	por	پر
to fill	por kærdæn	پرکردن
to become full	por shodæn	پرشدن
orange; Portugal	portoqal	پرتقال
orange (color)	portoqali	پرتقالی
to ask, question	porsidæn	پرسیدن؛ سوال کردن
	porsid/pors	پرسید / پرس
bird	pærænde	پرنده
P.N. (woman's)	pærvin	پروین
day before yesterday	pæriruz	پریروز
day before yesterday afternoon	pæriruz bæ:dæzzo(h)r	پریروز بعد از ظهر
day before yesterday morning	pæriruz sobh (sob)	پریروز صبح
day before yesterday noon	pæriruz (zo(h)r)	پریروز ظهر
night before last	pærishæb	پریشب

Glossary	MODERN PERSIAN	واژه نامه
airs (lit. "pose")	poz	پز
then (interjection); in that case 5	pæs	پس
to give back	pæs dadæn	پس دادن
to take/receive back	pæs gereftæn	پس گرفتن
the day after tomorrow	pæsfærda	پس فردا
the day after tomorrow afternoon	pæsfarda bæ:dæzzo(h)r	پس فردا بعد از ظهر
the day after tomorrow evening	pæsfarda shæb	پس فردا شب
the day after tomorrow morning	pæsfarda sobh (sob)	پس فردا صبح
the day after tomorrow noon	pæsfarda zo(h)r	پس فردا ظهر
after	pæs æz	پس از
mail 5	post	پست
to send a letter, to mail	post kærdæn	پست کردن
post office	postkhane (postkhune)	پستخانه (پستخونه)
pistachios	peste	پسته
son; boy	pesær	پسر
cousin (mother's sister's son)	pesærkhale (see 10.5)	پسر خاله
cousin (mother's brother's son)	pesærdai (see 10.5)	پسر دائی
cousin (father's sister's son)	pesæræ(m)me (see 10.5)	پسر عمه
cousin (father's brother's son)	pesæræmu (see 10.5)	پسر عمو
back; behind	posht	پشت
pilaf	polo	پلو
stair	pelle	پله
stairway	pelleha	پله ها
stairway	pellekan	پلکان
mimeograph, ditto 5	polikopi	پلی کپی
to mimeograph, ditto 5	polikopi kærdæn	پلی کپی کردن
"I mimeograph"	polikopi mikonæm	پلی کپی میکنم
gas pump, gas station	pomp-e benzin	پمپ بنزین
cotton	pæmbe	پنبه
five	pænj	پنج
window	pænjære/pænjere	پنجره
puncture, flat	pænchær	پنچر
Thursday	pænjshæmbe	پنج شنبه
fifth, etc.	pænjomin	پنجم \ پنجمین
cheese	pænir	پنیر
to wear, put on, dress; to cover	pushidæn	پوشیدن
	pushid/push	پوشید
money	pul	پول
rich, wealthy	puldar	پولدار

G80

Glossary	MODERN PERSIAN	واژه نامه
sweater	pulover	پولور
wide, extensive	pæhnavær	پهناور
on foot 7	piade	پیاده
hiking, walking	piade-rævi	پیاده روی
onion	piaz	پیاز
piano	piano	پیانو
to turn	pichidæn	پیچیدن
	pichid/pich	پیچید \ پیچ
complicated	pichide	پیچیده
apparent	peyda	پیدا
to find	peyda kærdæn	پیدا کردن
to be found, available	peyda shodæn	پیدا شدن
old	pir	پیر
to make old	pir kærdæn	پیر کردن
to become old, age	pir shodæn	پیر شدن
year before last	pirarsal	پیرارسال
shirt; dress	pirahæn	پیراهن
	(pirhæn/piræn)	(پیرهن \ پیرن)
old age	piri	پیری
pajamas	pizhame	پیژامه
last; ago	pish	پیش
near; to, toward; chez	pish-e	پیشِ
before (time; more commonly: قبل از)	pish æz	پیشِ از
recently	chændi pish	چندی پیش
waiter, servant	pishkhedmæt	پیشخدمت
progress	pishræft	پیشرفت
to advance, make progress	pishræft kærdæn	پیشرفت کردن
suggestion	pishnehad	پیشنهاد
to suggest	pishnehad kærdæn	پیشنهاد کردن

te		ت
before, until; by	ta	تا
counter (word used in counting)	ta	تا
summer	tabestan (tabestun)	تابستان (تابستون)
theater	teatr	تآتر
Tajikistan	tajikestan	تاجیکستان
Tajik (the Persian of Tajikistan)	tajiki	تاجیکی

G81

Glossary	MODERN PERSIAN	واژه نامه
history; date	tarikh	تاریخ
historian	tarikhnevis	تاریخ نویس
historiography	tarikhnevisi	تاریخ نویسی
art history	tarikh- honær	تاریخ هنر
fresh; recently	taze	تازه
taxi	taksi	تاکسی
tank	tank	تانک
Tabriz	tæbriz	تبریز
advertisement; propaganda	tæbliqat (pl. as sg.)	تبلیغات (تبلیغ + ات)
study/studies	tæhsil (at)	تحصیل/تحصیلات
to study	tæhsil kærdæn	تحصیل کردن
research	tæhqiq (tæ:qiq)	تحقیق/تحقیقات
to do research	tæhqiq kærdæn	تحقیق کردن
bed	tækht-e khab	تخت خواب
blackboard	tækhte siah	تخته سیاه
specialization	tækhæssos	تخصص
egg (chicken)	tokhm-e morq	تخم مرغ
boiled egg	tokhm-e morq-e ab paz	تخم مرغ آبپز
translation	tærjome	ترجمه
to translate	tærjome kærdæn	ترجمه کردن
"I translate"	tærjome mikonæm	ترجمه میکنم
to fear	tærsidæn (æz)	ترسیدن (از)
	tærsid/tærs	ترسید/ترس
Turk	tork	ترک
Turkish, Azerbaijani (Turkish)	torki	ترکی
Turkoman (person)	tork(æ)mæn	ترکمن
Turkmenistan, Turkmenia	tork(æ)mænstan	ترکمنستان
Turkoman (adjective, language)	tork(æ)mæn	ترکمنی
Turkey	torkie, qætar	ترکیه
train	træn	ترن، قطار
thanks	tæshækkor (tæshækor)	تشکر
to thank	tæshækkor kærdæn (æz)	تشکر کردن (از)
thirsty	teshne	تشنه
to encourage	tæshviq kærdæn	تشویق کردن
to correct	tæshih kærdæn	تصحیح کردن
	(tæsi kærdæn)	(تصی کردن)
decision	tæsmim	تصمیم
to decide	tæsmim gereftæn	تصمیم گرفتن
formal courtesies	tæarof (taarof)	تعارف

Glossary — MODERN PERSIAN — واژه نامه

English	Transliteration	Persian
to offer (to)	tæarof kærdæn (be)	تعارف کردن (به)
number	te:dad	تعداد
description, definition; praise	tæ:rif	تعریف
to praise, commend, describe, define	tæ:rif kærdæn (æz)	تعریف کردن (از)
holiday, day off; closed (store, office)	tæ:til	تعطیل
holiday(s), vacation	tæ:tilat	تعطیلات
education (as a discipline)	tæ:lim-o tærbiæt	تعلیم و تربیت
approximately	tæqribæn	تقریباً
division	tæqsim	تقسیم
to divide	tæqsim kærdæn	تقسیم کردن
to be divided	tæqsim shodæn	تقسیم شدن
calendar	tæqvim	تقویم
repetition	tekrar	تکرار
to repeat	tekrar kærdæn	تکرار کردن
homework	tæklif-e shæb	تکلیف شب
technology	teknolozhi	تکنولوژی
Texas	tegzas	تگزاس
pronunciation	tælæffoz (tælæfoz)	تلفظ
to pronounce	tælæffoz kærdæn (tælæfoz)	تلفظ کردن
telephone	telefon	تلفن
to telephone (to)	telefon kærdæn (be)	تلفن کردن (به)
"I telephone/call up"	telefon mikonæm	تلفن میکنم
television	televizion	تلویزیون
contact, "being in touch (with)"	tæmas (ba)	تماس (با)
to make contact/get in touch with	tæmas gereftæn (ba)	تماس گرفتن (با)
to watch (as TV)	tæmasha kærdæn	تماشا کردن
all	tæmam (tæmum)	تمام (تموم)
all of	tæmam-e (tæmum-e)	تمام (تموم)
to finish	tæmam kærdæn (tæmum)	تمام کردن (تموم)
to be finished	tæmam shodæn (tæmum)	تمام شدن (تموم)
practice, drill, exercise	tæmrin	تمرین/تمرینات
to practice	tæmrin kærdæn	تمرین کردن
"I practice"	tæmrin mikonæm	تمرین میکنم
clean	tæmiz	تمیز
to clean	tæmiz kærdæn	تمیز کردن
to be cleaned, get clean	tæmiz shodæn	تمیز شدن
lazy	tæmbæl	تنبل
fast; harsh	tond	تند
faster	tondtær	تندتر

G83

Glossary	MODERN PERSIAN	واژه نامه

alone, only	tænha	تنها
tennis	tenis	تنیس
you (singular, familiar), thou	to	تو
in	tu-ye (tu)	توی (تو)
to be able, can	tævanestæn (tunestæn)	توانستن (تونستن)
	tævanest/tævan (tunest/tun)	توانست/توان (تونست/تون)
explanation	towzih (tozi)	توضیح (توضی، تُضی)
to explain	towzih dadæn (tozi)	توضیح دادن
Tehran	tehran (te:run)	تهران (تهرون)
to prepare; provide	tæhie kærdæn	تهیه کردن
team	tim	تیم

jim ج

place	ja	جا
somewhere, anywhere, nowhere	jai	جایی
there	anja (unja)	آنجا
here	inja	اینجا
jazz	jaz	جاز
interesting	jaleb	جالب
society	jame:e	جامعه
sociologist	jame:e shenas	جامعه شناس
sociology	jame:e shenasi	جامعه شناسی
dear, soul, life (see 9.3.3)	jan (jun)	جان (جون)
separate, separately	joda/joda-joda	جدا/جدا جدا
to separate	joda kærd/kon	جدا کرد \ کن
really, truly	jeddæn	جداً
new, modern	jædid	جدید
festival, celebration	jæshn	جشن
to celebrate (a festival)	jæshn gereftæn	جشن گرفتن
box, carton	jæ:be	جعبه
P.N. (last name)	jæ:færi	جعفری
geography	jaqrafi/ jografia	جغرافی/جغرافیا
geographer	jografi dan	جغرافی دان
P.N. (man's)	jælal	جلال
in front of, forward	jelo	جلو
in front of	jelo-e/jelo-ye	جلو / جلوی
P.N. (man's)	jæmshid	جمشید

Glossary — *MODERN PERSIAN* — واژه نامه

English	Transliteration	Persian
plural	jæm:	جمع
to gather together, collect (tr.)	jæm: kærdæn	جمع کردن
to be gathered, assemble (intr.)	jæm shodæn	جمع شدن
population	jæmiæt	جمعیت
Friday (see Reading Persian 12.6)	jom'e/ruz-e jom:e (jome)	جمعه (روز جمعه)
sentence	jomle/jomælat	جمله/جملات
quality, character	jæmbe	جنبه
forest	jængæl	جنگل
south	jonub (junub)	جنوب
answer, reply	jævab	جواب
to answer	jævab dadæn	جواب دادن
"answer!"	(jævab bedid)	جواب میده (جواب بدید)
"s/he answers"	jævab midæhid (jævab mide)	جواب میدهید (جواب میده)
young; a youth	jævan (jævun)	جوان (جوون)
younger	jævantær (jævuntær)	جوانتر
socks(s), stockings	jurab	جوراب
ink	jowhær (johær)	جوهر
pocket	jib	جیب

che — چ

English	Transliteration	Persian
print, printing	chap	چاپ
to print	chap kærdæn	چاپ کردن
to be printed	chap shodæn	چاپ شدن
	see چهار	چار
fat	chaq	چاق
chin	chane (chune)	چانه (چونه)
tea	chay (chai)	چای (چائی)
left	chæp	چپ
how, in what way	chejur (chejuri)	چه جور (چه جوری)
why	chera	چرا
lamp	cheraq	چراغ
pasture, grazing ground	chæragah	چراگاه
to turn, revolve	chærkhidæn	چرخیدن
	chærkhid/chærkh	چرخید/چرخ
what color	chæræng (chærængi)	چه رنگ (چه رنگی)
eye	cheshm1	چشم
polite response to a request	chæshm2	چشم

G85

Glossary — MODERN PERSIAN — واژه نامه

English	Transliteration	Persian
how (chetor=description, chetori=manner)	chetowr (chetor, chetori)	چطور (چطوری)
how much; so much!	cheqædr (cheqæd)	چقدر (چقد)
check	chek	چک
see next entry	chekar	چکار
to do what	chekar kærdæn	چکار کردن
cooked plain rice	chelo	چلو
celo with broiled meat	chelo kebab	چلو کباب
such a, such, so	chonan	چنان
how many; several	chænd (ta)	چند (تا)
what number (first, second, etc.)	chændom	چندم
how long	chændvæqt	چند وقت
a number, quite a few	chændin	چندین
recently	chændi pish	چندی پیش
wood	chub	چوب
such a, such, so	chenin/chonin	چنین
because	chun	چون (چن)
what	che (chi)	چه (چی)
(emphatic)	che ____	چه ـــ؟
how good, "what could be better!"	che behtær	چه بهتر
what (noun)? which (noun)?	che ____ i	چه ـ ی
What's up? What's wrong? (7.3)	che khæbær æst/(che khæbær-e)	چه خبر است؟ چه خبره؟
"What's the difference?"	(che færq mikone)	چه فرق میکنه؟
to arrange; to pick (flowers, fruit)	chidæn	چیدن
	chid/chin	چید/چین
thing	chiz	چیز
something, anything, nothing	chizi	چیزی
China	chin	چین
Chinese	chini	چینی

he — ح

English	Transliteration	Persian
ready, present, willing	hazer	حاضر
to make ready, prepare	hazer kærdæn	حاضر کردن
to become ready	hazer shodæn	حاضر شدن
14th century lyric poet	hafez	حافظ
memory	hafeze	حافظه
condition	hal	حال
"How are you?"	(hal-e soma)	(حال شما؟)

G86

Glossary   MODERN PERSIAN   واژه نامه

English	Transliteration	Persian
"How are you?"	hal-e shoma cetowr æst? (cetore?)	حالِ شما چطور است؟ (چطوره)
now	hala	حالا
definitely, certainly, for sure	hætmæn	حتماً
limits, boundaries	hodud	حدود
about, approximately	dær hodud-e	در حدود
letter of the alphabet	hærf/horuf1	حرف/حروف
speech, discourse	hærf2	حرف
to speak, talk	hærf zædæn	حرف زدن
"I speak"	hærf mizænæm	حرف میزنم
motion	hærækæt	حرکت
to set out, depart	hærækæt kærdæn	حرکت کردن
P.N. (man's)	hæsæn	حسن
P.N. (man's)	hoseyn	حسین
memory	hefz	حفظ
to memorize	hefz kærdæn	حفظ کردن
bathroom, bathhouse	hæmmam (hæmum)	حمام (حموم)
to wash, bathe	hæmmam kærdæn (hæmum)	حمام کردن (حموم)
I bathe, take a bath	hæmmam mikonæm	حمام میکنم

khe   خ

English	Transliteration	Persian
foreign, foreigner	khareji	خارجی
gray	khakestæri	خاکستری
mother's sister	khale	خاله
empty	khali	خالی
to empty	khali kærdæn	خالی کردن
extinguished, silent	khamush	خاموش
to turn off, extinguish	khamush kærdæn	خاموش کردن
to be turned off, extinguished	khamus shodæn	خاموش شدن
legible, readable	khana	خوانا
wife; Ms. (Ms. or Miss)	khanom (khanum)	خانم (خانوم)
house, home	khane (khune)	خانه (خونه)
housekeeper (wife)	khanedar (khunedar)	خانه دار (خونه دار)
housekeeping	khanedari (khunedari)	خانه داری (خونه داری)
to take care of the house	khanedari kærdæn (khune dari)	خانه داری کردن (خونه داری)
family	khanevade	خانواده
familial, domestic	khanevadegi	خانوادگی

East	khavær	خاور
Middle East	khavær-e miane	خاورمیانه
caviar	khaviar	خاویار
news (both sg. and pl. in Persian)	khæbær/ækhbar	خبر/اخبار
I have no news/information (about)	khæbær nædaræm (æz)	خبر ندارم (از)
What's up? What's wrong? (7.3)	che khæbær æst /	چه خبر است؟
	(che khæbær-e)	چه خبره؟
reporter	khæbærnegar	خبرنگار
embarrassment, shyness; shame	khejalæt	خجالت
to be embarrassed, to be shy	khejalæt keshidæn	خجالت کشیدن
God; lord	khoda	خُدا
good-bye	khoda hafez (khodafez)	خدا حافظ
May God be your preserver	khoda hafez-e soma bashæd	خدا حافظ شما (باشد)
spoiled, ruined, rotten, broken	khærab	خراب
to spoil (tr.)	khærab kærdæn	خراب کردن
to spoil (intr.)	khærab shodæn	خراب شدن
small, tiny	khord	خرد
"My nerves are shot"	(æ:sabæm khord æst (e))	اعصابم خرد است (ه)
a small amount, bit, particle	yek khorde	یک خرده
	(yekhorde)	(یه خرده)
date(s)	khorma	خرما
to buy	khæridæn	خریدن
	khærid/khær	خرید/خر
shopping	khærid	خرید
tired	khæste	خسته
to make tired	khæste kærdæn	خسته کردن
to become weary, tired	khæste shodæn	خسته شدن
"I get tired"	khæste mishævæm	خسته میشوم
	(misæm)	(میشم)
dry	khosk	خشک
to dry (tr.)	khosk kærdæn	خشک کردن
to dry out, dry up	khosk shodæn	خشک شدن
handwriting	khætt	خط
in brief, in short	kholase	خلاصه
gulf	khælij	خلیج
Persian Gulf	khælij-e fars	خلیج فارس
to laugh	khændidæn	خندیدن
	khændid/khænd	خندید/خند
funny	khændedar	خنده دار

Glossary MODERN PERSIAN واژه نامه

"I burst out laughing"	(khændæm gereft)	خنده م گرفت
smile	labkhænd	لبخند
to smile	labkhænd zædæn	لبخند زدن
to sleep; to lie down 5	khabidæn	خوابیدن
	khabid/khab	خوابید/خواب
sleep; asleep; dream	khab	خواب
to get sleepy (see 11.11)	khab amædæn	خواب آمدن
"I'm sleepy"	(khabæm miad)	(خوابم میاد)
to dream	khab didæn	خواب دیدن
dormitory	khabgah	خوابگاه
asleep, sleeping; lying down	khabide	خوابیده
food	khorak	خوراک
to request, want	khastæn	خواستن
	khast/khah (-/kha/)	خواست/خواه (خوا)
to read, study; to sing	khandæn	خواندن (خوندن)
	khand/khan	خواند/خوان
	(khun/khun)	(خوند/خون)
"I read, study."	mikhanæm (mikhunæm)	میخوانم (میخونم)
sister	khahær	خواهر
sister-in-law (wife's sister)	khahær zæn	خواهر زن
sister-in-law (husband's sister)	khahær showhær	خواهر شوهر
request	khahesh (khaesh)	خواهش
to request (of, from)	khahesh kærdæn (khaesh)	خواهش کردن
"Please!" (ta:rof)	khahesh mikonæm (khaesh)	خواهش میکنم
good, well	khub	خوب
"It's fine, good."	khube	(خوبه)
"well" (interjection)	(khob)	(خب)
reflexive or emphatic pronoun	khod	خود
ball point pen	khodkar	خودکار
automatic fountain pen	khodnevis	خود نویس
to eat; to encounter	khordæn	خوردن
	khord/khor	خورد/خور
to fall down	zæmin khordæn	زمین خوردن
a stew or thick sauce	khoresh (khoresht)	خورش (خورشت)
eggplant khoresh	khoresh-e bademjan (bademjun)	خورش بادمجان (بادمجون)
pomegranate and walnut khoresh	khoresh-e fesenjun	خورش فسنجون
green herb khoresh	qorme sæbzi	قرمه سبزی
sour plum khoresh	khoresh-e alu	خورشت آلو

G89

potato and dried yellow pea khoresh	khoresh-e qeyme	خورش قیمه
celery khoresh	khoresh-e kæræfs	خورش کرفس
to like	khosh amædæn	خوش آمدن (از)
"I like (it)."	khoshæm miad	خوشم میاد
to have a good time	khosh gozæshtæn	خوش گذشتن
(I, you, etc.) had a good time."	(be man/be shoma)	(به من \ به شما)
	khosh gozæsht	خوش گذشت
pleasant, agreeable, nice	khoshækhlaq	خوش اخلاق
fortunately	khoshbækhtane	خوشبختانه
happy, pleased	khoshhal	خوشحال
to be happy, pleased	khoshhal shodæn	خوشحال شدن
"Gladly; I'll be happy to"	khoshhal mishævæm	خوشحال میشوم/
	(khosh(h)al mishæm)	(خوشال میشم)
happiness, pleasure	khoshhali	خوشحالی
"With greatest happiness"	(ba kæmal-e khoshhali)	با کمال خوشحالی
lovely, beautiful	khoshgel	خوشگل
tasty, savory	khoshmæze	خوشمزه
happy, fortunate	khoshvæqt	خوشوقت
to be pleased to meet someone	khosh væqt shodæn	خوشوقت شدن
"I'm pleased to have met you"	khosh væqt shodæm	خوشوقت شدم
street, road, highway	khiaban (khiabun)	خیابان (خیابون)
tailor; seamstress	khæyyat	خیاط
tailoring, dressmaking	khæyyati	خیاطی
to work as tailor, seamstress	khæyyati kærdæn	خیاطی کردن
wet, damp	khis	خیس
very, extremely	kheyli	خیلی

dal   د

to give	dadæn	دادن (به)
	dad/deh (/d)	داد / ده
"I give"	midahæm (midæm)	میدهم (میدم)
to teach	dærs dadæn	درس دادن
"I teach"	dærs midahæm (midæm)	درس میدهم (میدم)
story	dastan	داستان
to have; to keep	dashtæn	داشتن
	dasht/dar	داشت/دار
to be interested (in), to be fond of	ælaqe dashtæn (be)	علاقه داشتن (به)
burning hot	daq	داغ

Glossary	MODERN PERSIAN	واژه نامه

son-in-law; bridegroom	damad	داماد
skirt	damæn	دامن
slope (of a mountain)	damæne	دامنه
to know (facts, etc., not people)	danestan (dunestæn)	دانستن (دونستن)
	danest/dan (dunest/dun)	دانست/دان
		(دونست/دون)
"I know"	midanæm (midunæm)	میدانم (میدونم)
knowledge	danesh	دانش
university student	daneshju	دانشجو
university	daneshga(h)	دانشگاه (دانشگا)
associate professor	daneshyar	دانشیار
mother's brother	dai	دائی
elementary school	dæbestan	دبستان
daughter, girl	dokhtær	دختر
cousin (mother's sister's daughter)	dokhtær(-e) khale (see 10.5)	دختر خاله
cousin (mohter's brother's daughter)	dokhtær(-e) dai (see 10.5)	دختر دائی
cousin (father's sister's daughter)	dokhtær(-e) æmu (see 10.5)	دختر عمو
cousin (father's brother's daughter)	dokhtær(-e) æmme (see 10.5)	دختر عمه
in, within; door	dær	در
to knock at the door	dær zædæn	در زدن
about, concerning	dær bare-ye	در باره
about, approximately	dær hodud-e	در حدود
request	dær khast	درخواست
to request	dærkhast kærdæn	درخواست کردن
percentage	dær sæd	در صد
meanwhile, at the same time	dær zemn	در ضمن
to have in mind, intend, plan	dær næzær dashtæn	در نظر داشتن
during (preposition)	dær væqt-e	در وقت
tree	derækht/dærækht	درخت
pain	dærd	درد
headache (physical)	sær-dærd	سر درد
headache (abstract), nuisance	dærd-e sær	درد سر
to hurt, pain	dærd kærdæn	درد کردن
lesson	dærs	درس
to study	dærs khandæn (khundæn)	درس خواندن (خوندن)
to teach	dærs dadæn	درس دادن
right, correct	dorost	درست
to fix; to prepare	dorost kærdæn	درست کردن
"I fix, prepare"	dorost mikonæm	درست میکنم

G91

Glossary — MODERN PERSIAN — واژه نامه

to be fixed, repaired, made okay	dorost shodæn	درست شدن
lie	doruq	دروغ (دوروغ)
to lie	doruq goftæn	دروغ گفتن
Dari (Afghan Persian)	dæri	دری
sea	dæria	دریا
Caspian	dæria-ye mazændæran	دریای مازندران
receiving, receipt	dæryaft	دریافت
to receive	dæraft kærdæn	دریافت کردن
December	desambr	دسامبر
hand	dæst	دست
to acquire	bedæst aværdæn (ovordæn)	به دست آوردن (اوردن)
nervous, anxious, flustered	dæstpache	دستپاچه
home cooking	dæstpokht	دست پخت
handkerchief	dæstmal	دستمال
dessert	deser	دسر
plain	dæsht	دشت
invitation	dæ:væt	دعوت
to be invited	dæ:væt dashtæn	دعوت داشتن
to invite	dæ:væt kærdæn	دعوت کردن
notebook; office	dæftær	دفتر
exact; tiny, minute	dæqiq	دقیق
minute	dæqiq (dæiqe)	دقیقه (دئیقه)
doctor	doktor	دکتر
doctorate	doktora	دکترا
heart	del	دل
homesick	deltæng	دلتنگ
"I miss, am homesick (for)"	delæm bæraye __ tæng æst(e)	دلم برای __ تنگ است
to want (to do)	del__khastæn	دل __ خواستن
"I want (to)"	delæm mikhahæd (mikhad)	دلم میخواهد (میخواد)
to feel sorry for	del sukhtæn	دل __ سوختن (برای)
"I feel sorry (for)"	delæm bæraye__misuzæd (misuze)	دلم میسوزد (برای) (میسوزه)
nose	dæmaq	دماغ
tooth	dændan (dændun)	دندان (دندون)
dentist	dændansaz (dædunsaz)	دندان ساز (دندون ساز)
dentistry	dændansazi (dædunsazi)	دندان سازی (دندون سازی)

English	Transliteration	Persian
dentist	dendanpezeshk (dædunspezeshk)	دندان پزشک (دندون پزشک)
dentistry	dændanpezeshki (dædunspezeshki)	دندان پزشکی (دندون پزشکی)
world	donya	دنیا
to be born	be donya amædæn	به دنیا آمدن
two	do	دو
running, jogging	do(w)	دو
again	dobare	دوباره
bicycle	docærkhe	دوچرخه
bike riding, (bi)cycling	docærkhe-sævari	دوچرخه سواری
Monday	doshæmbe	دوشنبه
around	dowr (dor)1	دور
to turn around	dowr zædæn	دور زدن
together (as in "seated together")	dowr-e hæm	دور هم
distant, far	dur2	دور
camera	durbin(-e ækkasi)	دوربین (عکاسی)
friend	dust	دوست
to like, love	dust dashtæn	دوست داشتن
yogurt and water	duq	دوغ
twins	doqolu	دوقلو
government	dowlæt (dolæt)	دولت
second	dovvom/dovvomin	دوم/دومین
to run	dævidæn (/doidæn/)	دویدن
ten	dæh	ده
village	deh/dehat	ده/دهات
mouth	dæhan (dæhæn)	دهان (دهن)
high school diploma	diplom	دیپلم
to see	didæn	دیدن
	did/bin	دید/بین
late	dir	دیر
to be late	dir kærdæn	دیر کردن
yesterday	diruz	دیروز
yesterday afternoon	diruz bæ:dæzzo(h)r	دیروز بعد از ظهر
yesterday everning	diruz æsr	دیروز عصر
yesterday morning	diruz sob(h)	دیروز صبح
yesterday noon	diruz zo(h)r	دیروز ظهر
last night	dishæb	دیشب
dictation	dikte	دیکته

Glossary   *MODERN PERSIAN*   واژه نامه

other; else, more; anymore; next (in time)	digær (dige)	دیگر (دیگه)
another	digæri (digei)	دیگری (دیگه ای)
religion	din/ædyan	دین/ادیان
dynamite	dinamit	دینامیت
wall	divar	دیوار

zal   ذ

a little bit	zærre (zære)	ذره
a little	yek zærre (ye zære)	یک ذره (یه ذره)
mention	zekr	ذکر
to mention	zekr kærdæn	ذکر کردن
"People spoke well of you"	zekr-e kheyr-e shoma bud	ذکر خیر شما بود

re   ر

tie(s), bond(s)	rabete/rævabet	رابطه/روابط
about, regarding	raje be	راجع به
radar	radar	رادار
radio	radio	رادیو
true; straight; right (direction)	rast	راست
to tell the truth	rast goftæn	راست گفتن
"Really?"	(rast migid?)	راست میگید؟
to straighten	rast kærdæn	راست کردن
by the way; "Really?"	rasti	راستی
satisfied	razi	راضی
to satisfy, make content, please	razi kærdæn	راضی کردن
driver (car, bus)	ranænde	راننده
drivingr	ranændegi	رانندگی
to drive	rænændegi kærdæn	رانندگی کردن
road	rah	راه
to have access to __	be __ rah dastæn	به ــ راه داشتن
road construction	rahsazi	راهسازی \ راه سازی
quarter	rob	ربع
P.N. (man's)	reza	رضا
restaurant	restoran	رستوران
official	ræsmi	رسمی
to arrive	residæn	رسیدن
	resid/res	رسید/رس

Glossary — MODERN PERSIAN — واژه نامه

English	Transliteration	Persian
the capital of Gilan province	ræsht	رشت
field, dicipline; noodles	reshte	رشته
to go	ræftæn	رفتن
	ræft/ræv (-/r/)	رفت / رو / (ر)
traffic	ræft-o amæd	رفت و آمد
	(also amæd-o ræft)	(آمد و رفت)
friend	ræfiq/rofæqa	رفیق/رفقا
to dance	ræqsidæn	رقصیدن
	ræqsid/ræqs	رقصید/رقص
dancing	ræqs	رقص
Rome 1	rom	رم
novel	roman	رمان
color; paint	ræng	رنگ
multicolored	rængeræng	رنگارنگ
colored	rængi	رنگی
"What color is it?"	che rængi-e	چه رنگیه \ چه رنگیه
face	ru	رو
face to face (opposite)	ruberu	رو برو
on, upon	ru-ye (ru)	روی (رو)
tie(s), bond(s)	rævabet/rabete	روابط \ رابطه
table cloth	rumizi	رومیزی
psyche	rævan	روان
psychologist	rævanshenas	روانشناس
psychology	rævanshenasi	روانشناسی
river	rud/rudkhane	رود/رودخانه
	rudkhune)	(رودخونه)
day	ruz	روز
during the day	ruzha (ruza)	روزها (روزا)
daily	ruzane	روزانه
newspaper	ruzname	روزنامه
village	rusta	روستا
villager	rustai	روستائی
Russian (n.)	rus	روس
Russian (adj.)	rusi	روسی
Russia	rusie	روسیه
lit; illuminated	rowshæn (roshæn)	روشن
to turn on, ignite	rowshæn kærdæn	روشن کردن
to be ignited	rowshæn shodæn	روشن شدن
directorship	riasæt	ریاست

mathematics	riazi	ریاضی
mathematician	riazidan	ریاضی دان
	(riazidun)	(ریاضی دون)
boss, chief, president	ræis	رئیس
beard	rish	ریش

ze ز

Zabol	zabol	زابل
knee	zanu	زانو
Zahedan	zahedan	زاهدان
language	zæban (zæbun)	زبان (زبون)
linguist	zæbanshenas	زبانشناس
linguistics	zæbanshenasi	زبانشناسی
inconvenience, trouble	zæhmæt	زحمت
to inconvenience	zæhmæt dadæn (be)	زحمت دادن (به)
to take pains (for someone else)	zæhmæt keshidæn (bæraye)	زحمت کشیدن
to hit, strike; to play (an instrument)	zædæn	زدن
	zæd/zæn	زد / زن
yellow	zærd	زرد
time; tense (grammer)	zæman	زمان
present tense	zæman-e hal	زمان حال
past tense	zæman-e gozæshte	زمان گذشته
winter	zemestan (zemestun)	زمستان (زمستون)
soil, earth, ground	zæmin	زمین
to fall down	zæmin khordæn	زمین خوردن
region, country	særzæmin	سر زمین
woman	zæn	زن
to marry (take a wife)	zæn gereftæn	زن گرفتن
life	zendegi	زندگی
to live	zendegi kærdæn	زندگی کردن
"s/he lives"	zendegi mikonæd	زندگی میکند
fast, quick	zud	زود
"Hurry up!"	zud bash	زود باش
soon, quickly	bezudi	بزودی
strength	zur	زور
a lot, too much	ziad	زیاد
too much, extra, excessive	ziadi	زیادی
to increase (tr.)	ziad kærdæn	زیاد کردن

Glossary	MODERN PERSIAN	واژه نامه
to increase (intr.)	ziad shodæn	زیاد شدن
zipper	zip	زیپ
olive	zeytun	زیتون
below, underneath	zir	زیر
under	zir-e	زیر
to photoduplicate, to "xerox"	ziraks kærdæn	زیراکس کردن

zhe ژ

January	zhanvie	ژانویه
Japan	zhapon	ژاپن
Japanese	zhaponi	ژاپنی
P.N. (woman's)	zhale	ژاله
Jeanne d'arc	zhandark	ژاندارک
gendarme	zhandarm	ژاندارم
June	zhuæn	ژوئن
July	zhuie	ژوئیه

sin س

coast, shore	sahel	ساحل
to build, make	sakhtæn	ساختن
	sakht/saz	ساخت/ساز
building	sakhteman	ساختمان
simple	sade	ساده
organization, society	sazman	سازمان
hour, clock	saæt	ساعت
quarter of an hour	rob saæt	ربع ساعت
half an hour	nim saæt	نیم ساعت
right on the hour	sær-e saæt	سر ساعت
working hours	saat-e kar	ساعت کار
silent, quiet	saket	ساکت
to become silent	saket shodæn	ساکت شدن
"Shut up!"	saket sho(w)	ساکت شو
year	sal	سال
last year	parsal	پارسال
salad	salad	سالاد
sandwich 5	sandvic	ساندویچ
San Francisco	san feransisko	سان فرانسیسکو

G97

Glossary	*MODERN PERSIAN*	واژه نامه
shadow	saye	سایه
"May your shadow never diminish"	saye-ye shome kæm næsævæd	سایه شما کم نشود
green	sæbz	سبز
vegetables, greens, herbs	sæbzi	سبزی
light, easy	sæbok	سبک
style	sæbk	سبک
moustache	sebil (sibil)	سبیل (سیبیل)
September	septambr	سپتامبر
star	setare	ستاره
astronomer, astrologer	setareshenas	ستاره شناس
difficult	sækht	سخت
head; end, at, in, to	sær	سر
at, by, on, at the head of	sær-e	سر
at or in his/her/its place	(sær-e jash)	سر جاش
right on the hour	sær-e saæt	سر ساعت
right at noon, noon sharp	sær-e zohr	سر ظهر
to/in class	sær-e kelas	سر کلاس
to/at work	sær-e kar	سر کار
joined, together, connected	sær-e hæm	سر هم
on time	sær-e væqt	سر وقت
(an intensifier)	sær	سر
profusely green, verdant	særsæbz	سر سبز
soldier	særbaz	سر باز
cold (adj.)	særd	سرد
to get cold	særd shodæn	سرد شدن
to be or become cold	særd ___ budæn shodæn	سرد ___ بودن \ شدن
area, region, country	særzæmin	سر زمین
(honorific used in addressing women)	særkar	سرکار
dark blue	sormei	سرمه ای
to try, to attempt	sæy kærdæn	سعی کردن
embassy	sefaræt	سفارت
white	sefid	سفید
to whiten	sefid kærdæn	سفید کردن
to become white, turn white	sefid shodæn	سفید شدن
secretary (not as a title)	sekreter	سکرتر
dog	sæg	سگ
a greeting "peace"	sælam	سلام

Glossary   *MODERN PERSIAN*   واژه نامه

English	Transliteration	Persian
to greet	sælam kærdæn (be)	سلام کردن (به)
"Say hello to ___"	sælam konid be ___	سلام کنید به ___
santur	sæntur	سنتور
stone	sæng	سنگ
bread baked on small stones	sængæk (nan-e sængæk)	سنگک (نان سنگک)
stony	sængi	سنگی
heavy	sængin	سنگین
soup	sup	سوپ
super market	super	سوپر
third	sevvom/sevvomin	سوم/سومین
Switzerland	suis	سوئیس
Swiss	suisi	سوئیسی
three	se	سه
Tuesday	seshæmbe	سه شنبه
politics, diplomacy, tact, policy	siasæt	سیاست
black	siah	سیاه
apple	sib	سیب
P.N. (man's)	sirus	سیروس
cigarette	sigar	سیگار
to smoke cigarette	sigar keshidæn	سیگار کشیدن
I smoke, am smoking a cigarette	sigar mikeshæm	سیگار میکشم
movies, movie theatre	sinema	سینما
chest	sine	سینه
question	soal / soalat (plural)	سؤال \ سئوال / سؤالات \ سئوالات
interrogative	soali	سئوالی
to ask a question	soal kærdæn	سئوال کردن

shin   ش

English	Transliteration	Persian
student (through high school); apprentice	shagerd	شاگرد
dinner	sham	شام
to serve dinner	sham keshidæn	شام کشیدن
shampoo	shampu	شامپو
luck	shans	شانس
to be lucky, fortunate	shans aværdæn/dashtæn	شانس آوردن/داشتن
comb, shoulder	shane (shune)	شانه (شونه)
perhaps, maybe	shayæd	شاید

Glossary — MODERN PERSIAN — واژه نامه

English	Transliteration	Persian
night	shæb	شب
nights	shæbha (shæba)	شب ها (شبا)
"Good night!"	shæbbekheyr (shæbekher)	شب به خیر
night before last	pærishæb	پریشب
last night	dishæb	دیشب
to become, get; happen	shodæn	شدن
	shod/show/(sh)	شد/شو/(ش)
wine	shærab	شراب
east	shærq	شرق
eastern	shærqi	شرقی
company	sherkæt	شرکت
beginning, start	shoru	شروع
to begin, start (tr.)	shoru kærdæn	شروع کردن
to begin, start (intr.)	shoru shodæn	شروع شدن
to begin to	shoru be __ kærdæn	شروع به ـ کردن
to wash	shostæn	شستن
	shost/shuy (shur)	شست \ شوی (شور)
six	shesh (shish)	شش (شیش)
chess	shætrænj	شطرنج
poetry, poem, song, lyric	she:r	شعر/اشعار
sugar	shekær	شکر
to break	shekæstæn	شکستن
	shekæst/sekæn	شکست/شکن
self-deprecation	shekæstenæfsi	شکسته نفسی
to humble, modest, self-deprecating	shekæstenæfsi kærdæn	شکسته نفسی کردن
stomach; belly	shekæm	شکم
chocolate	shokolat (shokulat, shukulat)	شکولات/شوکولات
trousers, pants	shælvar	شلوار
suit	kotshælvar	کت شلوار
noisy, crowded, messy	sholuq (suluq)	شلوق\شلوغ (شولوق)
to make a mess, create a uproar	sholuq kærdæn	شلوق کردن
you (2nd. pl., 2nd sg. honorific)	shoma	شما
number; issue (of manganzine)	shomare	شماره
north	shomal	شمال
northern, northerner	shomali	شمالی
to count, number out	shomordæn	شمردن
	shomord/shomar	شمرد/شمار
Shemran (a north-Tehran suburb)	shemiran (shemrun)	شمیران (شمرون)
swimming	shena (shena/shenow)	شنا (شنا/شنو)

Glossary	MODERN PERSIAN	واژه نامه
to swim	shena kærdæn	شنا کردن
to know, be familiar with	shenakhtæn	شناختن
(see 7.2.1 and 8.6.9-12)	shenakht/shenas	شناخت/شناس
Saturday	shæmbe	شنبه
Sunday	yekshæmbe	یک شنبه
Monday	doshæmbe	دو شنبه
Tuesday	seshæmbe	سه شنبه
Wednesday	chæharshæmbe	چهار شنبه
	(charshæmbe)	(چارشنبه)
Thursday	pænjshæmbe	پنج شنبه
to hear; to smell (with *bu*)	shenidæn	شنیدن
	shenid/sheno	شنید/شنو
joke	shukhi	شوخی
to make a joke	shukhi kærdæn	شوخی کردن
driver	shofer	شوفر
husband	showhær (shohær)	شوهر
to marry (said of a woman)	showhær kærdæn	شوهر کردن
city, town	shæhr	شهر
city planning, urban planning	shæhrsazi	شهرسازی
P.N. (woman's)	shæhin	شهین
P.N. (woman's)	shæhla	شهلا
P.N. (woman's)	shæhnaz	شهناز
milk	shir	شیر
Shiraz	shiraz	شیراز
sweet	shirin	شیرین
to sweeten	shirin kærdæn	شیرین کردن
to grow sweeter	shirin shodæn	شیرین شدن
sweets, candy, pastries	shirini	شیرینی
chic	shik	شیک
Chicago	shikago	شیکاگو
chemistry	shimi	شیمی
chemist	shimidan	شیمی دان
	(shimidun)	(شیمی دون)

sad ص

soap	sabun	صابون
P.N. (last name)	sadeqi	صادقی
morning	sobh (sob)	صبح

Glossary *MODERN PERSIAN* واژه نامه

English	Transliteration	Persian
mornings, in the morning	sob(h)ha (soba)	صبح ها (صبا)
"Good mornings!"	sob(h) bekheyr	صبح به خیر
breakfast	sobhane (sobune)	صبحانه (صبونه)
early morning	sobh-e zud	صبح زود
P.N. (last name)	sæba	صبا
patience	sæbr	صبر
to wait	sæbr kærdæn	صبر کردن
conversation	sohbæt (so:bæt)	صحبت
to talk	sohbæt kærdæn (so:bæt kærdæn)	صحبت کردن
correct	sæhid (sæhi)	صحیح
sound; voice	seda	صدا
to sound; to call	seda kærdæn	صدا کردن
record; page	sæfhe (sæfe)	صفحه (صفه)
chair	sændæli	صندلی
face	suræt	صورت
pink	suræri	صورتی

zad ض

English	Transliteration	Persian
to record	zæbt kærdæn	ضبط کردن
tape recorder	zæbt-e sowt	ضبط صوت
weak	zæif	ضعیف
at the same time, during	zemn-e	ضمن

ta ط

English	Transliteration	Persian
medicine	tebb (pezeshki)	طب (پزشکی)
direction	tæræf	طرف
"On (my) mother's/father's side"	æz tæræf-e madær(æm)/ pedar(æm)	از طرف مادر(م) / پدر(م)

za ظ

English	Transliteration	Persian
apparent, manifest	zaher	ظاهر
to develop (film), make manifest	zaher kærdæn	ظاهر کردن
dish	zærf	ظرف
noon	zo(h)r	ظهر
afternoon, p.m.	bæ:dæzzo(h)r	بعد از ظهر

Glossary	MODERN PERSIAN	واژه نامه
a.m.	pishæzzo(h)r	پیش از ظهر
eyn		**ع**
habit, custom	adæt	عادت
to be accustomed to	adæt dashtæn	عادت داشتن
excellent, wonderful	ali	عالی
colloquial	amiane (amiune)	عامیانه (عامیونه)
in love	asheq	عاشق
to be in love with someone	asheq-e kæsi budæn	عاشق کسی بودن
to fall in love with someone	asheq-e kæsi shodæn	عاشق کسی شدن
phrase	ebaræt	عبارت
to consist of	ebaræt budæn æz	عبارت بودن از
Hebrew	ebri	عبری
strange, wonderful	æjib	عجیب
Arab	æræb	عرب
Arabic	græbi	عربی
dear	æziz	عزیز
"my dear"	ælzizæm	عزیزم
love	eshq	عشق
tribe	æshire/æshayer	عشیره/عشایر
nerve/(s)	æsab/æ:sab	عصب/اعصاب
"My nerves are shot."	æ:sabæm khord æst /(khurd-e)	اعصابم خرد است (خورده)
angry; impatient	æsæbani	عصبانی (عصبونی)
photographer	ækkas	عکاس
photography	ækkasi	عکاسی
to do photography	ækkasi kærdæn	عکاسی کردن
photograph; picture	æks	عکس
to take picture(s) of	æks gereftæn (æz)	عکس گرفتن (از)
interest, liking, fondness	ælaqe	علاقه
to be interested (in), to like	ælaqe dashtæn (be)	علاقه داشتن (به)
science	elm/olum	علم/علوم
social science	olum-e ejtemai	علوم اجتماعی
political science	olum-e siasi	علوم سیاسی
P.N. (man's)	æli	علی
P.N. (last name)	ælizade	علیزاده
Amman	æmman	عمان
uncle (father's brother)	æmu	عمو

G103

Glossary	MODERN PERSIAN	واژه نامه

aunt (father's sister)	æmme	عمه
to change (tr.)	ævæz kærdæn	عوض کردن
to change (intr.)	ævæz shodæn	عوض شدن
by mistake	ævæzi	عوضی
flaw	eyb	عیب
"Never mind. No problem"	eyb nædaræd (eyb nædare)	عیب ندارد (عیب نداره)
festival	eyd	عید
Now Ruz (New Year)	eyd-e now ruz	عید نوروز
Christmas	eyd-e kerismæs	عید کریسمس
Easter	eyd-e pak	عید پاک
eyeglasses	eynæk	عینک
to wear eyeglasses	eynæk zædæn	عینک زدن
one who wears eyeglasses	eynæki	عینکی

qeyn غ

absent	qayeb	غایب
food	qæza	غذا
to serve a meal	qæza keshidæn	غذا کشیدن
west	qærb	غرب
western	qærbi	غربی
P.N. (man's)	qolamhoseyn	غلامحسین
error (noun); wrong (adj.)	qælæt	غلط
sad	qæmgin	غمگین

fe ف

A province in south central Iran	fars	فارس
Persian	farsi	فارسی
graduate	fareq-ot-tæhsil	فارغ التحصیل
to graduate	fareq-ot-tæhsil shodæn	فارغ التحصیل شدن
interval (space)	fasele	فاصله
to leave (a) space	fasele gozashtæn	فاصله گذاشتن
fantasy	fantezi	فانتزی
family, relative	famil	فامیل
familial	famili	فامیلی
photocopy	fotokopi	فتوکپی
to photocopy	fotokopi kærdæn	فتوکپی کردن
French (adj)	færansævi	فرانسوی

G104

Glossary   *MODERN PERSIAN*   واژه نامه

English	Transliteration	Persian
French (noun); France	færanse	فرانسه
tomorrow	færda	فردا
to send	ferestadæn	فرستادن
	ferestad/ferest	فرستاد/فرست
P.N. "angel"	fereshte	فرشته
opportunity, chance	forsæt	فرصت
to have a chance, find the opportunity (to)	forsæt kærdæn	فرصت کردن
difference	færq	فرق
to differ, be different (see 7.2)	færq kærdæn/dashtæn	فرق کردن/ داشتن
"It makes a difference"	færq mikonæd (mikone)	فرق میکند (میکنه)
"What's the difference?"	(che færq mikone)	چه فرق میکنه؟
to command	færmudæn	فرمودن
	færmud/færma	فرمود/فرما
please ("Command it!" (see 8.3))	befærmaid	بفرمائید
command, firman	færman	فرمان
commanded (see 9.8)	færmanbær	فرمانبر
commander (see 9.8)	færmande	فرمانده
European (used on compounds)	færængi	فرنگی
culture, dictionary	færhæng	فرهنگ
to sell	forukhtæn	فروختن
	forukht/forush	فروخت/فروش
store	forushgah	فروشگاه
salesperson, seller	forushænde	فروشنده
airport	forudgah	فرودگاه
P.N. (man's)	fereydun	فریدون
P.N. (woman's)	færide	فریده
walnut and pomegranate *khoresh*	fesenjan (fesenjun)	فسنجان (فسنجون)
season	fæsl	فصل
now, for now	fe:læn	فعلاً
only	fæqæt	فقط
poor	fæqir	فقیر
thought	fekr	فکر
to think	fekr kærdæn	فکر کردن
philosophy	fælsæfe	فلسفه
folklorist	folklorist	فلکلوریست
season	fæsl	فصل
flute	folut (fulut)	فلوت
cup	fenjan (fenjun)	فنجان (فنجون)
soccer	futbal	فوتبال

at once, immediately	fowræn (foræn)	فوراً
February	fevrie	فوریه
M.A./M.S.	fowq-e lisans (kar shenasi)	فوق لیسانس (کارشناسی ارشد)
to understand	fæhmidæn fæhmid/fæhm	فهمیدن فهمید/فهم
"I understand" (in general)	mifæhmæm (mifæ:mæm)	میفهمم
"I understand" (what you said)	fæhmidæm	فهمیدم
P.N. (last name)	firuzi	فیروزی
physics	fizik	فیزیک
physicist	fizikdan (fizikdun)	فیزیک دان
film (both "movie" and "camera")	film	فیلم
movie producer	filmsaz	فیلمساز

qaf ق

"-able " in combinations	qabel-e	قابل
understandable	qabel-e fæhm	قابل فهم
cultivable	qabel-e kesht	قابل کشت
carpet	qali	قالی
satisfied, content	qane	قانع
to satisfy, make content	qane kærdæn	قانع کردن
to become satisfied	qane shodæn	قانع شدن
Cairo	qahere	قاهره
ago, previous to	qæbl	قبل
previously	qæblæn	قبلاً
previouis, prior	qæbli	قبلی
before (conjunction)	qæbl æz	قبل از
to accept	qæbul kærdæn	قبول کردن
to be accepted	qæbul shodæn	قبول
stature	qæd	قد
tall	qæd bolænd	قد بلند
short	qæd kutah	قد کوتاه
old, ancient, former; out of date	qædimi	قدیمی
to be situated	qærar dashtæn	قرار داشتن
to agree upon, to make arrangements	qærar gozashtæn	قرار گذاشتن
sir (polite) (see 6.2.1 & 10.3)	qorban (qorbun)	قربان (قربون)
"Thank you"	qorban-e shoma/qorban-e to	قربان شما \ قربان تو
red	qermez	قرمز

Glossary — *MODERN PERSIAN* — واژه نامه

English	Transliteration	Persian
part, section, portion	qesmæt	قسمت
a Turkish tribe from Southern Iran	qæshqai	قشقائی
pretty, beautiful	qæshæng	قشنگ
story, tale, fairy tale	qesse	قصّه
to tell a story	qesse goftæn	قصهَ گفتن
heart (in physical sense)	qælb	قلب
pen	qælæm	قلم
lump sugar	qænd	قند
to promise	qo(w)l dadæn	قول دادن
strong	qævi	قوی
coffee	qæhve	قهوه
brown	qæhvei	قهوه ای
price	qeymæt	قیمت

kaf — ک

English	Transliteration	Persian
cabaret	kabare	کاباره
work, job, occupation	kar	کار
to do	kar kærdæn	کار کردن
to have something to do	kar dashtæn	کار داشتن
usage, use (n), application	kar-bord	کار برد
factory	karkhane (karkhune)	کارخانه (کارخونه)
white-collar worker 6	karmænd	کارمند
cassette	kaset	کاست
to plant	kashtæn	کاشتن
	kasht/kar	کاشت\کار
paper	kaqæz	کاغذ
cafe	kafe	کافه
enough	kafi	کافی
California	kalifornia	کالیفرنیا
Californian	kaliforniai	کالیفرنیائی
Canada	kanada	کانادا
Canadian	kanadai	کانادائی
match(es)	kebrit	کبریت
sport coat, suit coat	kot	کت
suit	kotshælvar	کت شلوار
book	ketab	کتاب
formal, bookish (language)	ketabi	کتبی
librarian	ketabdar	کتابدار

G107

Glossary	*MODERN PERSIAN*	واژه نامه

library science, librarianship	ketabdari	کتابداری
library	ketabkhane (ketabkhune)	کتابخانه (کتابخونه)
dirty	kæsif	کثیف
where	koja	کجا
"Of what origin/place?"	kojai	کجائی
which	kodam (kodum/kudum)	کدام (کدوم)
any(one); each(one); every(one)	hær kodam	هرکدام (یک)
necktie	keravat	کراوات
to wear/put on a necktie	keravat zædæn	کراوات زدن
stool, (heater)	korsi	کرسی
Kerman	kerman	کرمان
Kermanshah, now Bakhtaran	kermanshah/bakhtæran	کرمانشان \ باختران
butter	kære	کره
person	kæs	کس
no one	hich kæs	هیچ کس
a person, someone	kæsi	کسی
out-of-sorts; unwell	kesel	کسل
farmer	keshaværz	کشاورز
agriculture	keshaværzi	کشاورزی
cultivating, tilling, sowing	kesht	کشت
ship	keshti	کشتی
drawer	kesho	کشو
country	keshvær	کشور
to draw (a load or a picture)	keshidæn	کشیدن
	keshid/kesh	کشید/کش
to serve a meal	qæza keshidæn	غذا کشیدن
shoe(s)	kæfsh	کفش
class	kelas	کلاس
hat	kolah	کلاه
word/words	kæleme/kælemat	کلمه/کلمات
key	kelid	کلید
a small amount	kæm	کم
lower BACK, waist	kæmær	کمر
a little	kæmi	کمی
slowly, by degrees	kæm kæm	کم کم
to reduce, diminish; turn down (radio, etc.)	kæm kærdæn	کم کردن
perfection	kæmal	کمال
"With greatest pleasure"	(ba kæmal-e meyl)	با کمال میل

Glossary — MODERN PERSIAN — واژه نامه

English	Transliteration	Persian
"With greatest happiness"	(ba kæmal-e khoshhali)	با کمال خوشحالی
stewed fruit, compote	kompot	کمپوت
to help, aid, assist	komæk kærdæn (be)	کمک کردن (به)
coast, shore, side	kenar/kenare	کنار/کناره
concert	konsert	کنسرت
short (length)	kutah	کوتاه
short (stature)	qæd kutah	قد کوتاه
to shorten	kutah kærdæn	کوتاه کردن
little, small; young	kuchek (kuchik)	کوچک (کوچیک)
smaller, younger (see 8.8)	kuchektær (kuchiktær)	کوچکتر (کوچیکتر)
transhumance, nomadism	kuchneshini	کوچ نشینی
narrow side street	kuche	کوچه
course (academic)	kurs	کورس
mountain	kuh	کوه
mountain climbing	kuh-næværdi	کوه نوردی
mountainous region	kuhestan	کوهستان
mountainous	kuhestani	کوهستانی
salt desert	kævir	کویر
rag; diaper; old, worn out	kohne	کهنه
that, which (relative conjunctive)	ke	که
who	ke/ki (ki)	که \ کی (کی)
when	key	کی
cake	keyk	کیک
(hand)bag; briefcase; purse	kif	کیف
kilometer	kilometr	کیلومتر

gaf — گ

English	Transliteration	Persian
garage	garazh	گاراژ
bull; cow	gav	گاو
cow	gav-e made	گاوماده
bull, ox	gav-e nær	گاو نر
natural gas	gaz	گاز
chalk 6	gæch	گچ
to put, place, allow	gozashtæn gozasht/gozar (zasht/zar)	گذاشتن گذاشت/گذار (-ذاشت/-ذار)
to pass, pass by, go by	gozæshtæn	گذشتن

G109

	gozæsht/gozær	گذشت / گذر
past, last	gozæshte	گذشته
past tense	zæman-e gozæshte	زمان گذشته
aside from	gozæshte æz	گذشته از
expensive; heavy	geran (gerun)	گران (گرون)
cat	gorbe	گربه
hungry	gorosne	(گشنه)
	(goshne)	(گشنه)
to get, take, seize	gereftæn	گرفتن
	gereft/gir	گرفت/گیر
to learn	yad gereftæn	یاد گرفت
engagement, obligation	gereftari	گرفتاری
warm, hot	gærm	گرم
to heat up, warm	gærm kærdæn	گرم کردن
to be heated up, grow warm, get hot	gærm shodæn	گرم شدن
warmth, heat	gærma	گرما
weeping	gerie	گریه
to cry, weep	gerie kærdæn	گریستن
to cry, weep	gerie kærdæn	گریه کردن
to return	bær gæshtæn	بر گشتن
	gæsht/gærd	گشت/گرد
to say	goftæn	گفتن
	goft/gu (-/g)	گفت/گو (گ)
colloquial, spoken	goftari	گفتاری
dialog	goftegu	گفتگو
to mean, intend ―	―ra goftæn	― را گفتن
"Do you mean this?"	(ino migin?)	(اینو میگین؟)
to call something ―	be chizi ― goftæn	به چیزی ― گفتن
flower; rose	gol	گل
to say something especially apt	(gol goftæn)	(گل گفتن)
throat	gælu	گلو
herd, flock	gælle	گله
herd-tending, animal husbandry	gælledari	گله داری
lost	gom	گم
to lose	gom kærdæn	گم کردن
to become lost (not for directions)	gom sodæn	گم شدن
wheat	gændom	گندم
plum, tomato (originally only "plum")	go(w)je	گوجه
tomato	go(w)je færængi	گوجه فرنگی

Glossary — MODERN PERSIAN — واژه نامه

English	Transliteration	Persian
sheep	gusfænd	گوسفند
ear	gush	گوش
to listen	gush kærdæn/dadæn	گوش کردن/دادن
"Listen!"	gush konid	گوش کنید
meat	gusht	گوشت
beef	gusht-e gav	گوشت گاو
lamb	gusht-e gusfænd	گوشت گوسفند
corner	gushe	گوشه
guitar	gitar	گیتار

lam — ل

English	Transliteration	Persian
laboratory	laboratuar	لابراتوار
necessary	lazem	لازم
to need	lazem dashtæn	لازم داشتن
Los Angeles	los anjeles	لوس آنجلس
thin	laqær	لاغر
lip	læb	لب
clothes, clothing	lebas	لباس
to put on or wear clothes	lebas pushidæn	لباس پوشیدن
smile	læbkhænd	لبخند
to smile	læbkhænd zædæn	لبخند زدن
Lebanon	lobnan	لبنان
Lebanese	lobnani	لبنانی
kindness, courtesy	lotf	لطف
"please"	loftæn	لطفاً
"please"	(loft konid)	(لطف کنید = لطفاً)
to be kind or courteous	lotf dashtæn/kærdæn	لطف داشتن/کردن
word/words	loqæt/loqat	لغت/لغات
glossary, dictionary	loqætname	لغت نامه
London	lændæn	لندن
accent; dialect	læhje (læ:je)	لهجه
B.A., B.S.	lisans	لیسانس
M.A., M.S.	fowq-e lisans	فوق لیسانس
lime	limu	لیمو
concentrated lime juice	ab limu	آب لیمو
glass (for drinking)	livan	لیوان

mim — م

Glossary — MODERN PERSIAN — واژه نامه

English	Transliteration	Persian
we	ma	ما
mother	madær	مادر
grandmother	madærbozorg	مادر بزرگ
March	mars	مارس
Mazandaran	mazændæran	مازندران
Mazandarani	mazændærani	مازندرانی
magic marker	mazhik	ماژیک
yogurt	mast	ماست
Good for you!; Wonderful!	mashallah	ماشاءالله
car; automobile	mashin	ماشین
typist	mashin nevis	ماشین نویس
typing	mashin nevisi	ماشین نویسی
property; belongings	mal	مال
to belong to someone	mal-e kæsi budæn	مال کسی بودن
to stay, remain	mandæn	ماندن
	mand/man (mund/mun)	ماند/مان (موند/مون)
moon, month; a beauty	mah	ماه
fish	mahi	ماهی
fishing	mahigiri	ماهی گیری
to be inclined to, wish to	mayel budæn	مایل بودن
swim suit	mayo	مایو
married	motæ æhhel	متأهل
regretful, sorry	motæ æssef	متأسف
regretfully, unfortunately	motæ æssefane	متأسفانه
specialist	motækhæsses	متخصص
method	metod	متد
engine (car), motor	motor	موتور
thankful, appreciative	motæshæk(k)er	متشکر
text	mætn/motun	متن/متون
affirmative, positive	mosbæt	مثبت
infinitive	mæsdær	مصدر
like	mesl-e	مثل
"It seems that... It appears that..."	mesl-e inke	مثل اینکه
resembling each other, alike	mesl-e hæm	مثل هم
example	mæsæl	مثل
for example	mæsælæn	مثلاً
obliged	mæjbur	مجبور
single, unmarried	mojærræd	مجرد

G112

Glossary *MODERN PERSIAN* واژه نامه

English	Transliteration	Persian
magazine	mæjælle	مجله
high school student	mohæs(s)el	محصل
product (esp. agricultural)	mæhsul/mæhsulat	محصول/محصولات
place, locale	mæhæll	محل
place of work	mæhæll-e kar	محل کار
neighborhood	mæhælle	محله
P.N. (last name)	mohæmmædi	محمدی
various; many	mokhtælef	مختلف
special	mækhsus	مخصوص
especially	mækhsusæn	مخصوصاً
mode, current fashion	mod	مد
pencil	medad	مداد
a period of time	moddæt	مدت
school	mædræse (mædrese)	مدرسه
model	model	مدل
director, chief	modir	مدیر
administrative division	modiriyæt	مدیریت
jam	moræbba	مربا
square(d)	moræbbæ	مربع
lecturer, trainer, coach	moræbbi	مربی
relevant (to)	mærbut (be)	مربوط (به)
kindness, generosity	mærhæmmæt	مرحمت
"Thank you!" (ta:rof)	mærhæmmæt-e shoma ziad	مرحمت شما زیاد
man	mærd	مرد
manliness	mærdi	مردی
people	mærdom	مردم
anthropologist	mærdomshenas	مردمشناس
anthropology	mærdomshenasi	مردمشناسی
thank you	mersi	مرسی
moist, humid	mærtub	مرطوب
citrus fruit	morækkæbat (morækæbat)	مرکبات
center; provincial capital	mærkæz	مرکز
sick; a sick person, patient	mæriz	مریض
taste, flavor	mæzze	مزه
to taste	mæzze kærdæn	مزه کردن
traveler	mosafer	مسافر
journey, trip	mosaferæt	مسافرت
to go on a journey, take a trip	mosaferæt kærdæn/ræftæn	مسافرت کردن/رفتن
equal	mosavi	مساوی

G113

Glossary	MODERN PERSIAN	واژه نامه

Moscow	mosku/mosko	مسکو
east	mæshreq	مشرق
busy	mæshqul	مشغول
difficult 2	moshkel (mosgel)	مشکل (مشگل)
Meshed	mæshhæd	مشهد
from Meshed, a pilgrim to Meshed	mæshhædi (mæsdi)	مشهدی (مشدی)
study	motale'e/motaleat	مطالعه \ مطالعات
to study	matatlee kærdæn	مطالعه کردن
certain, sure	motmæen	مطمئن
moderate, temperate	mo:tædel	معتدل
to apologize, excuse oneself	mæ:zæræt/mæ:zeræt khastæn	معذرت خواستن
"Excuse me!"	mæ:zæræt mikhahæm /	معذرت میخواهم
	mæ:zeræt (mikham)	(معذرت میخوام)
introduction	moær(r)efi	معرفی
to introduce (to)	moær(r)efi kærdæn (be)	معرفی کردن (به)
well-known, famous	mæ:ruf	معروف
teacher	moællem	معلم
architect	me:mar	معمار
architecture	me:mari	معماری
usual	mæ:mul	معمول
usually	mæ:mulæn	معمولا
meaning	mæ:ni/mæani	معنی/معانی
singular	mofræd	مفرد
store	mæqaze	مغازه
west	mæqreb	مغرب
useful	mofid	مفید
to compare	moqayese kærdæn	مقایسه کردن
conversation, dialog	mokaleme	مکالمه
interrogative interjection	mægær (mæge)	مگر (مگه)
Mexico	mekzik	مکزیک
Mexican	megziki	مکزیکی
meeting, encounter (see 9.1.4)	molaqat	ملاقات
possible	momken	ممکن
"May I... May one..." (see 8.8.3 n.1)	(momken-e...)	(ممکنه)
I, me	mæn	من
"me, too", "me neither"	mæn hæm hæmintor	من هم همینطور
	(mæn-æm hæmintor)	(منم همینطور)
waiting, awaiting	montæzer	منتظر
to wait for someone	montæzer-e kæsi budæn	منتظر کسی بودن

G114

Glossary — MODERN PERSIAN — واژه نامه

English	Transliteration	Persian
house, home	mænzel	منزل
secretary (not as a title)	monshi	منشی
meaning (what people mean) intention	mænzur	منظور
negative	mænfi	منفی
P.N. (woman's)	mænizhe	منیژه
hair(s)	mu/muha (mua)	مو/موها (موا)
in agreement, in accord, concurring	movafeq	موافق
banana	mo(w)z	موز
music	muzik	موزیک
musician	muziciæn	موزیسین
music	musiqi	موسیقی
musicologist	musiqishenas	موسیقی شناس
musicology	musiqishenasi	موسیقی شناسی
subject, topic	mo(w)zu	موضوع
successful	movæf(f)æq	موفق
time, moment	mo(w)qe	موقع
while, when	mo(w)qeike	موقعی که
Moulin Rouge	mulan ruz	مولن روژ
Rumi, the great mystical poet	mowlana jælal-ed-din-e rumi	مولانا جلال الدین رومی
Munich	munikh	مونیخ
May	me	مه
kind, affectionate	mehreban (mehrebun)	مهربان (مهربون)
P.N. (woman's)	mehri	مهری
important	mohem(m)	مهم
guest	mehman (mehmun)	مهمان (مهمون)
party	mehmani	مهمانی
engineer	mohændes/mohændesin	مهندس/مهندسین
engineering	mohændesi	مهندسی
P.N. (woman's)	mæhin	مهین
verbal prefix in present and past continuous/habitual	mi-	می
"I fall"	mioftæm	میافتم
"I bring"	miaværæm (miaræm)	میاورم (میارم)
"I stand"	miistæm (vaymistæm)	میاستم (وای میستم)
"I come"	miayæm (miam)	میایم (میام)

G115

Glossary   *MODERN PERSIAN*   واژه نامه

English	Transliteration	Persian
square, plaza	meydan (meydun)	میدان (میدون)
"I carry"	mibæræm	میبرم
"I lift, pick up"	bær midaræm	بر میدارم
	(vær midaræm)	(ور می دارم)
"I return"	bær migærdæm	برمیگردم
"I close, tie (as a package)"	mibændæm	میبندم
"I see"	mibinæm	میبینم
"I ask, question"	miporsæm	میپرسم
"I cook"	mipæzæm	میپزم
"I wear, put on"	mipushæm	میپوشم
"I fear"	mitærsæm	میترسم
"I can, am able to"	mitævanæm	میتوانم
	mitunæm	(میتونم)
"I buy"	mikhæræm	میخرم
"I sleep, lie down"	mikhabæm	میخوابم
"I read, sing	mikhanæm	میخوانم
	(mikhunæm)	(میخونم)
"I want"	mikhahæm	میخواهم
	(mikham)	(میخوام)
"I eat, drink"	mikhoræm	میخورم
"I know"	midanæm	میدانم
	(midunæm)	(مید ونم)
"I give"	midehæm	مید هم
	(midæm)	(میدم)
"I arrive"	miresæm	میرسم
"I go"	mirævæm	میروم
	(miræm)	(میرم)
"I stike, hit"	mizænæm	میزنم
"I build"	misazæm	میسازم
"I break"	mishkenæm	میشکنم
"I know, am familiar with" (see 9.9)	mish(e)næsæm	میشناسم
"I hear, smell"	mish(e)novæm	میشنوم
"I become"	mishævæm	میشوم
	(mishæm)	(میشم)
"I wash"	mishuyæm	میشویم
	(misuræm)	(میشورم)
"I send"	miferestæm	میفرستم
"I sell"	miforushæm	میفروشم
"I understand"	mifæhmæm (mifæ:mæm)	میفهمم

Glossary	MODERN PERSIAN	واژه نامه
"I plant"	mikaræm	میکارم
(verbalizer)	mikonæm	میکنم
"I say"	miguyæm (migæm)	میگویم (میگم)
"I place; I allow" (see 9.9)	migozaræm (mizaræm)	میگذارم (میذارم)
"I pass, go by"	mig(o)zæræm	میگذرم (میگذرم)
"I remain"	mimanæm (mimunæm)	میمانم (میمونم)
"I sit, sit down" (see 9.9)	mineshinæm (mishinæm)	مینشینم (میشینم)
"I write" (see 9,9)	minevisæm	مینویسم (مینویسم)
table	miz	میز
"It's possible", "Is it possible?"	mishe	(میشه)
microfilm	mikrofilm	میکروفیلم
P.N. (woman's)	mina	مینا
miniskirt	mini zhup	مینی ژوپ
Minnesota	minisota	مینی سوتا
desire, wish	meyl	میل
"with the greatest pleasure"	ba kæmal-e khoshhali	با کمال خوشحالی
to desire or wish to eat	meyl dashtæn	میل داشتن
to eat or drink (polite)	meyl kærdæn	میل کردن
fruit	mive	میوه

nun ن

obliged, "must"	nachar	ناچار
sick, ill (more polite than مریض)	nakhosh	نا خوش
region	nahie	ناحیه
unhappy, upset, angry	narahæt	ناراحت
"Don't be upset!"	narahæt næsho(w)	ناراحت نشو
to make upset, unhappy	narahæt kærdæn	ناراحت کردن
orange	narenji	نارنجی
name	nam	نام
letter	name	نامه
bread	nan (nun)	نان (نون)
long triangle, heavily ridged	nan-e bærbæri	نان بربری

English	Transliteration	Persian
ordinary round loaf	nan-e taftun	نان تافتون
baked on a mound of small stones	nan-e sængæk	نان سنگک
paper thin, white, crisp	nan-e lævash	نان لواش
baker	nanva	نانوا
bakery (bread only)	nanvai	نانوائی
lunch	nahar/næhar	ناهار، نهار
note (musical notation)	not	نُت
result(s)	nætije/nætayej	نتیجه/نتایج
carpenter	næjjar	نجار
carpentry	næjjari	نجاری
no (polite)	nækheyr (nækher)	نخیر
near	næzdik	نزدیک
P.N. (last name)	nezhad	نژاد
relative to	nesbæt (be)	نسبت (به)
relatively	nesbætæn	نسبتاً
to show	neshan dadæn (neshu n)	نشان دادن (نشون)
address	neshani (neshuni)	نشانی (نشونی)
to sit	neshæstæn	نشستن
	neshæst/neshin	نشست/نشین
sitting, seated (French: assis)	neshæste	نشسته
half	nesf	نصف
opinion	næzær	نظر
in my opinion	be næzær-e mæn	به نظر من
from the point of view of...	æz næzær-e...	از نظر
oil, kerosene	næft	نفت
the oil company	sherkæt-e næft	شرکت نفت
kerosene seller	næfti	نفتی
person (sometimes used as a counter)	næfær	نفر
painter	næqqash	نقاش
painting	næqqashi	نقاشی
to paint	næqqashi kærdæn	نقاشی کردن
plan; map	næqshe	نقشه
negative (film)	negativ	نگاتیو
look, glance	negah	نگاه
to look (at)	negah kærdæn (be)	نگاه کردن (به)
to keep, hold; stop	negæh dashtæn (negær)	نگاه داشتن (نگر)
worried, anxious	negæran (negærun)	نگران (نگرون)
display, show	næmayesh	نمایش
play, drama	næmayeshname	نمایشنامه

Glossary	MODERN PERSIAN	واژه نامه
grade	nomre (nombre)	نمره (نمبره)
to get a grade	nomre aværdæn	نمره آوردن
example	nemune/næmune	نمونه
new	no(w)	نو
No Ruz (see 8.12)	now ruz	نو روز
tape	nævar	نوار
November	novambr	نوامبر
turn	no(w)bæt	نوبت
to be done by turns	no(w)bæti	نوبتی
P.N. (last name)	nurbækhsh	نوربخش
P.N. (last name)	nuri	نوری
to write	neveshtæn	نوشتن
	nevesht/nevis	نوشت/نویس
written, literary	neveshtari	نوشتاری
kind, type	no(w)	نوع
no	næ	نه
no (polite)	nækheyr (nækher)	نه خیر (نخیر)
nine	noh	نُه
sugar cane	neyshekær	نیشکر
Niagara Falls	niagara	نیاگارا
also (literary)	niz	نیز
is not	nist	نیست
half	nim	نیم
half an hour	nim saæt	نیم ساعت
New Jersey	nio jerzi	نیوجرسی
New York	nio york	نیو یورک
New Yorker, New Yorkers	nio yorki	نیو یورکی

vav و

and	væ (o, vo)	و
and so on, et cetera	væ qeyre	و غیره
Washington	vashængton	واشنگتن
clear	vazeh	واضح
situated, located	vaqe	واقع
"truly, really!"	vaqeæn (vaqæ:n)	واقعاً
"That's really interesting!"	(vaqæ:n jalebe)	(واقعاً جالبه)
reality	vaqeiæt	واقعیت
wax (as for shoes)	vaks	واکس

G119

Glossary — MODERN PERSIAN — واژه نامه

English	Transliteration	Persian
by God! (interjection)	vallah	والله
volleyball	valibal	والیبال
vanilla	vanil	وانیل
existence	vojud	وجود
to exist (used to indicate location)	vojud dashtæn	وجود داشتن
sport; exercise	værzesh	ورزش
to engage in sport or exercise	værzesh kærdæn	ورزش کردن
"I exercise, play sports"	værzesh mikonæm	ورزش میکنم
calisthenics, exercise	tæmrin-e værzesh	تمرین ورزش
athlete	værzeshkar	ورزشکار
middle	væsæt	وسط
area, extent	vos:æt	وسعت
means; equipment, necessities	væsile/væsael	وسیله/وسائل
time	væqt/owqat (oqat)	وقت/اوقات
to find time (to do)	væqt kærdæn	وقت کردن
punctual	væqtshenas	وقت شناس
when, while	væqttike	وقتی که
lawyer	vækil	وکیل
but	væli	ولی
vitamin	vitamin	ویتامین
P.N. (woman's)	vida	ویدا
visa	viza	ویزا

he — ه

English	Transliteration	Persian
plural morpheme	-ha (-a/ha)	ها
spelling (see also املا)	heji	هجی
each	hær	هر
wherever	hærja	هر جا
whatever, anything that	hærche	هر چه
the more___(the better)	hærche___tær (behtær)	هر چه ــ تر بهتر
both, all three...	hær do, hær se...	هر دو، هر سه...
each/every day (night, etc.)	hær ruz, hær shæb	هرروز، هرشب
each; whoever, whichever	hær kodam	هر کدام (هر کدوم)
whoever	hær kæs	هرکس
whenever	hær væqt	هر وقت
there is (are); is	hæst	هست
eight	hæsht	هشت
seven	hæft	هفت

Glossary — MODERN PERSIAN — واژه نامه

English	Transliteration	Persian
week	hæfte	هفته
Holland, Netherlands	holænd	هلند
Dutch; Dutchman/Dutchwoman	holændi	هلندی
helicopter	helikopter	هلیکوپتر (چرخ بال)
also; same (in compounds)	hæm (æm/hæm)	هم
both ___ and	hæm ___ hæm	هم ـ ـ هم
roommate	hæmotaq (hæmotaqi)	هم اتاق (هم اتاقی)
fellow student	hæmdærs (hæmdærsi)	هم درس (هم درسی)
each other	hæmdigær (hæmdige)	هم دیگر (هم دیگه)
that very (emphatic)	hæman (hæmun)	همان (همون)
likewise, in this same way	hæmchonan	همچنان
such as, like, as	hæmchon	همچون
such as, like, as	hæmchonin / hæmchenin (hæmchin)	همچنین (همچین)
likewise, in this same way	hæmchonin/hæmchenin/ be hæmchenin	همچنین/ به همچنین
Hamadan	hæmædan	همدان
with, in the company of	hæmrah	همراه
neighbor	hæmsaye	همسایه
co-worker	hæmkar	همکار
together	bahæm	با هم
all, every	hæme	همه
all of it	hæmeæs (hæmæs)	همه اش
everywhere	hæmeja	همه جا
everyone	hæmekæs	همه کس
always	hæmishe	همیشه
this very (emphatic)	hæmin	همین
just as, as, in the same way, likewise	hæmintowr (hæmintor)	همینطور
India	hend/hendustan	هند/هندوستان
Indian, Hindi	hendi	هندی
art	honær	هنر
still, yet	hænuz	هنوز
weather; air	hæva	هوا
climate	ab-o hæva	آب و هوا
airplane	hævapeyma	هواپیما
nothing; no (in compounds)	hich	هیچ
nothing	hich chiz (hich(ch)i)	هیچ چیز (هیچی)
neither; none	hich kodam (hich kodum)	هیچ کدام (هیچ کدوم)

Glossary	MODERN PERSIAN	واژه نامه
no one	hich kæs	هیچ کس
never	hich væqt	هیچ وقت

ye ى

or	ya	یا
either ___ or	ya ___ ya	یا ___ یا
memory	yad	یاد
to learn	yad gereftæn	یاد گرفتن
to recall, remember	yad ___ amædæn	یاد ___ آمدن
remember	yad ___ budæn	یاد ___ بودن
to forget	(æz) yad ___ ræftæn	از یاد ___ رفتن
ice	yækh	یخ
refrigerator	yækhchal	یخچال
Yazd (capital of Yazd province)	yæzd	یزد
it means, "that is"	yæ:ni	یعنی
"What does it/that mean?"	yæ:ni che (yæ:ni chi)	یعنی چه (ینی چی)
a, one	yek (ye)	یک (یه)
uniform	yekjur	یک جور
a little	yek khorde (ye khorde)	یک خورده یه خرده
directly	yekrast	یکراست
Sunday	yeksæmbe (yesæmbe)	یکشنبه
first	yekom	یکم
one by one, singly	yeki yeki	یکی یکی
each other, one another	yekdigær	یکدیگر
slow; quiet	yævash	یواش
slower; quieter	yævastær	یواشتر
Greece	yunan	یونان
Greek	yunani	یونانی